MOCKE

The Life and Stories of Eben Mocke

Trooper of the British South Africa Police

ALAN STOCK JOHN BERRY

First published in 2007 by the United Kingdom Branch of the British South Africa Police Regimental Association. Second edition published 2008, current edition published 2023.

ISBN: 978-1-915660-59-6

Copyright, unless otherwise stated, belongs to the United Kingdom Branch of the British South Africa Police Regimental Association.

All rights reserved. No part of this publication may be reproduced, stored in a retrieval system or transmitted in any form by any means; electronic, mechanical, photocopying, recording or otherwise, except brief extracts for the purpose of review, without written permission of the publisher and copyright owners.

Acknowledgement and thanks go to:
National Archives of Zimbabwe.
The Outpost Magazine of the British South Africa Police.
Les Burrow (9591) Designer of the 'Books of the B.S.A.P.' Crest.
The History Section Committee, UK Branch Regimental Association.

Apology is made for standard of some photographs. This is caused by scanning from old magazines with poor paper quality

Researched and edited by Alan Stock (6063), Editor of *The Outpost* from 1966 to 1984.
Designed and typeset by John Berry (5584).

In reprinting this text, no changes have been made to the language used as it historically reflects the time. It is recognised that some terminology is deemed inappropriate today and it is hoped that readers will accept the text for the historical document it is and that offense is not intended.

CONTENTS

Introduction	5
Early Life	7
The Biographical Submission	11
Fifty Years On	29
Obituary	37

The Stories:

The Taking of Pretoria	41
Tommy Pals	43
President Kruger's Buried Gold	51
Scotty Smith	56
The Biltong Hunters	67
Kalahari Patrol	74
Gwaai Incidents	182
Lost on the Gwaai	189
Elephant Graveyard	196
The Twins	200
South African Rebellion	208
The Gamblers & Sequel	239
"Mongoose" and the Gutu Patrol	249
Makaha	256
The Devil's Cataract	306
Zambesi Duck Hunt	317
Commentary	328
Map of Southern Rhodesia	4
Photograph of Eben Mocke	36

Note; For page numbers of maps and photographs relating to Kalahari Patrol, Makaha, South African Rebellion and Devil's Cataract, see these stories' respective Contents.

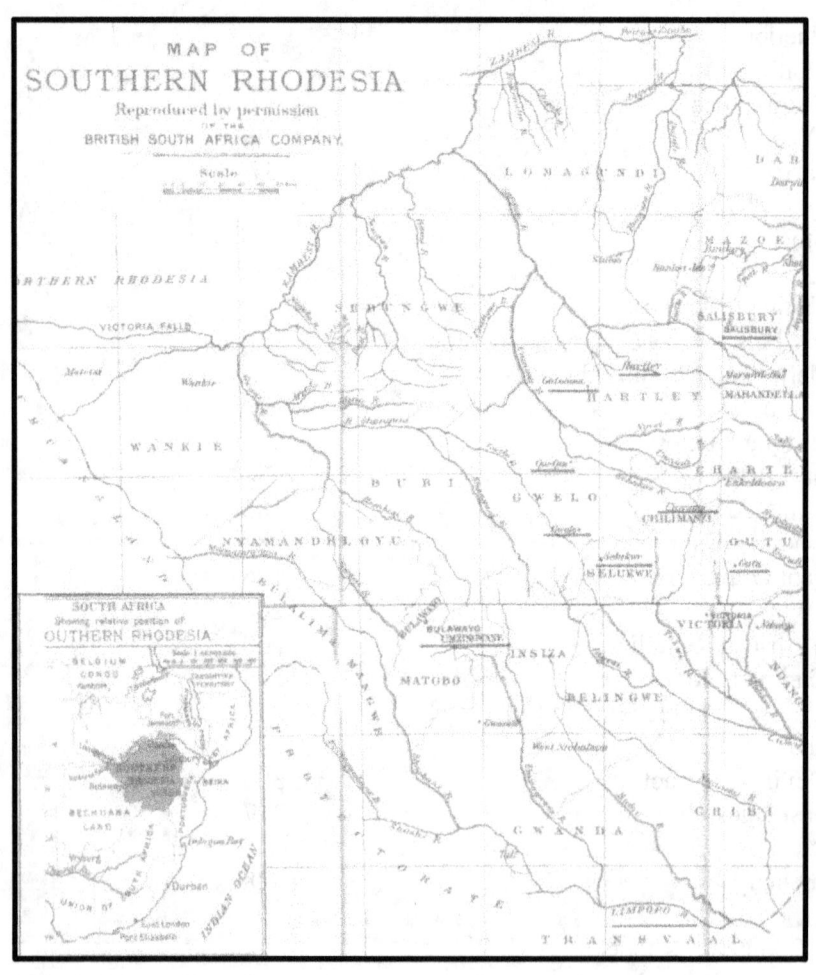

INTRODUCTION

In the late 1960s, staff of the National Archives of Rhodesia interviewed Pioneers and those they considered "late pioneers" and tape-recorded their memories of early Rhodesia. Archives also asked many of them to write brief life-histories in a question-and-answer format and so provide valuable and in many cases intimate records both of themselves and people they knew. How much of this material now remains accessible by historians in the 21st century is debateable but among the "late pioneers" was one of the most prolific contributors to the B.S.A. Police magazine, *The Outpost*, Eben Mocke, (Trooper 1437).

He gave to the magazine's editor a written copy of his response to the archivists but the precise questions can only be guessed at. This lengthy document, a background in every sense, offers some commentary for most but not all of Eben's memories. A few of his tales, especially those in which there is little or no personal involvement, murmur against a rigid timeslot in his chronicle but they offer another face of history – or legend, where facts are a bit scarce – and their inclusion in Eben Mocke's legacy is justified. Some of his stories had no direct connection with police work, did not appear in *The Outpost* and are in print here for the first time. The following picture of the first thirty years of Eben's life is based on the National Archives Submission and other research.

Alan Stock
Eastbourne
November 2007

EARLY LIFE

JOHAN GODFRIED MOCKE arrived in South Africa in 1763 from Thann as an employee of the East India Company. He married Rebecca Plagman on 20th January, 1771 and such was the beginning of a family which was to become well-known in many parts of the country in the following centuries. David Stephen Mocke, one of Johan's descendants, married Elizabeth Minaar and she gave birth to Ebenezer Mocke at Boshoff in the Orange Free State on 13th July, 1888. There were nine children in all – six sons and three daughters.

David Mocke was patriotic and a staunch Republican who, when he died, had still to forgive Britain for the Boer War. Four of Eben's brothers fought against the British in that war and their father, a horse breeder, supplied numerous mounts for the Burghers. The "blue-black" currency, issued by the Government and with which the horses were purchased, became worthless at the end of hostilities. It ruined David who, with some justification, blamed the British for his downfall. Cecil Rhodes was mud in David's eyes, especially after the Jameson Raid. His attitude changed somewhat after the war when an old friend, Bernie Melville, who had changed his allegiance after eight years in the Transvaal to become a Burgher and fight against the British, introduced a number of "foreigners" to David and Elizabeth who were invited to the Mocke house in Pretoria to share Musical Evenings!

Further illustration of thawing relations was that all three of Eben's sisters married rooineks, perhaps not entirely the consequence of those musical evenings! The eldest, Dolly, married Charlie Preston from Rhodesia who was responsible for arousing his young brother-in-law's interest in the north. Petronella (Babs) married Lt. Col. V.C. Leckie, DSO. He was a veterinary surgeon attached to the Hussars under Lord Methuen and survived both World Wars to write a book: *A Centaur Looks Back*. Col Leckie retired to Hampshire where he died, his wife surviving him for only three years. They had three daughters, the eldest of whom, Joan, married a Lt. Col. Thomas and gave birth to three sons who were strongly pro-Rhodes and with whom Eben was corresponding up to the time of his death. Eben's third sister, Irene, married a Jock Craig, lived in Durban and was still alive in the late 1960s.

In kindergarten school in Boshoff, a Mrs Brummer taught Eben and his brothers and sisters. When the family moved to Pretoria, eighteen months before the Jameson Raid in 1896, all the schools had been closed but neighbours and close friends of the Mocke parents were the Botha family who employed a Miss

Meatly as governess to teach their children, Helen, Louis, Francis and Manie Botha. It was arranged that Babs, Godfrey, Irene and Eben should also benefit from Miss Meatley's teaching.

The arrangement worked well for a couple of years until the authorities decided – for reasons best known to themselves – that the chaste English teacher was persona non grata and should be expelled. She was duly escorted to the Natal border en route to Durban and an elderly grey-haired Hollander, who could speak not a word of English, became the tutor. High Dutch replaced English as the teaching medium, much to the disappointment of the children – although the home language of them all was Afrikaans.

Mrs Mocke, aware of the importance of English in her children's education despite the ongoing conflict, was most concerned. The solution came when the Ludorf family, refugees from Bloemfontein, arrived in Pretoria. The daughter, Louise Ludorf and her step-sister, Mary von Epron, were qualified English teachers. They were persuaded to open a school and from them the younger Mocke children received excellent tuition until long after peace was declared at Vereeninging in 1902.

Twelve years after the hollow victory that resulted in the British troops straggling into Pretoria on the afternoon of 5th June 1900, Eben was to recall the event with a sadness that bridged his adolescence. Having joined the B.S.A. Police on 9th May 1911, he wrote about those traumatic days back at the turn of the century in Pretoria for the July 1912, issue of *The Police Review*. "K" Troop colleagues of Trooper Mocke had established the journal in Bulawayo in March of the previous year. This magazine was incorporated in *The Rhodesia Defence Force Journal* in November 1914, after the outbreak of World War One and then became *The Outpost* in July 1923. Fifty years later, Eben recalled with some poetic licence another childhood experience with his Tommy Pals, a story that remained unpublished until now.

In 1904, the Eendracht School was built and opened by the Dutch Reformed Church. The headmaster was a Dr Hoogenhout, an excellent teacher of English and Dutch in his own right and whom a charming middle-aged woman, Miss Frames, also well-qualified in English, assisted. Eben proved himself a good student and passed Standard Six before the family's finances saw him enrolled as an Articled Clerk with the Pretoria solicitors; Findlay, McRobert and Niemeyer. The position carried the princely wage of fifty shillings per month.

Formal education did continue at night school. John Stuart, a Scots teacher in one of the new Government Schools, taught English and History; C. de Villiers, a deposed DRC parson, unveiled the mysteries of Algebra and Euclid (geometry). The evening lessons were under threat, however. Fifty shillings a month demanded for tuition fees left little for a contribution to the family's household expenses.

Mr F.F. Pienaar, Secretary at the newly opened Land Settlement Department which had been set up to assist indigent farmers get back on their feet, offered the young Mocke a vacant position on the Land Board. The salary of sixteen pounds per month was a great improvement on the earnings of a solicitor's clerk. Night school, where Gideon Louw, the Commandant's son, joined Eben, continued and the pair burnt the midnight oil cramming for Matriculation. They both failed.

Despondent at his examination failure and unhappy with the job itself where he felt senior civil servants favoured the careers of young Australians and Englishmen, Mocke voiced his dissatisfaction to the Assistant Surveyor General, Bernie Melville, his father's friend and a regular participant in the Mocke family's musical evenings.

"If I was your age," advised his senior, "I would go to Rhodesia. It is a young and promising country with plenty of opportunities for young men prepared to work hard." Charlie Preston, the Rhodesian who had married Dolly Mocke, Eben's sister, was even more persuasive. "If it were not for the malaria fever, I would be back there tomorrow. It doesn't matter what nationality you are, all are welcome in building the new Rhodesia."

Mr and Mrs Mocke were not in favour and it was against their wishes that their son sent for application forms to join the B.S.A. Police. Bernie Melville came up with two important letters of introduction – one to Atherstone, the Salisbury Surveyor General. Preston's encouragement took the form of a fifty pound donation towards travel expenses.

Mocke records the excitement of the journey north and the immediate appeal of the wide-open spaces. He entered Rhodesia on 11th April 1910 and quickly discovered that there was a variety of employment opportunities available.

In Salisbury's Manica Road, Mocke bumped into an old friend from Pretoria who had been transferred to the National Bank. Lampard, offering a salary of £16-13-4d per month plus a tropical allowance of another £5, begged the new arrival to join him in the Bank. Pen pushing was not an occupation Mocke wished to resume. Atherstone, to whom Bernie Melville had addressed one introductory letter, also came up with the offer of immediate employment with the Surveyor General – at exactly the same monthly wage as the bank plus some cash compensation for an unkind climate. Again, the offer was declined. But Burns-Begg, to whom Melville had also conveyed his sponsorship of Eben, was all for the police career. "It is an excellent corps where you will meet up with a fine bunch of gentlemen, see the country and, in your first three year contract, decide where you like it best and decide to settle."

On 9th May 1911, Eben Mocke joined the B.S.A. Police...and records his surprise at finding several other Afrikaans-speaking South Africans among his colleagues.

The two-month Recruits Course held few fears for the new-comer. As the son of a successful horse breeder, he was an excellent horseman. Nor was he a stranger to firearms, having shot with muzzle-loaders before graduating to his father's Martini-Henry when hunting springbok around Boshoff. These skills and his bilingualism, to which could be added some knowledge of Zulu, meant that only the drills and discipline of Depot represented new challenges.

Trooper Mocke's service record, measured against the travels detailed in his adventures, was typically unrevealing. From Depot, he was posted to Bulawayo, then to Nyamandhlovu, Inyati, Gwaai – where he built the original police station – then back to Salisbury for briefing on special duties in connection with the threatened South African Rebellion. There was then a spell as Immigration Officer in Bulawayo...followed by his unauthorised emigration to India! Fetched back by Lieutenant Morris after some extradition wrangles, a Special Board of Officers consisting of Lieutenants Masterman, Spain and Thornton awarded him six months detention in the Depot Guardroom, five months of which were actually spent in Salisbury Hospital. On recovery, he was sent to Makaha for nearly two years and then came a short spell in Salisbury District HQ before completing his service on 13th October 1918.

From the viewpoint of rounding out his biography, it is useful to position Eben's available stories alongside his travels and so gain the natural sequence of his eventful life. In "The Taking of Pretoria" which was published in *The Police Review* in July 1912, Trooper Mocke, with barely a year's service, showed that he had heeded the plea of Trooper Bussy, the founder-editor of the equally new *Police* magazine, by contributing his boyhood memories of the British occupation of Pretoria in June 1900. Half-a-century later, Moore-Ritchie, who succeeded Bussy as *Police Review* editor, remembered the "Matabeleland" Mocke. But many years must have passed before he wrote what can only be described as a rather contrived mixture of fact and fiction with "Tommy Pals". Regardless of when the story was actually set down, what it does reveal is Eben's early struggle for identity, faced with the conflict of his Afrikaans and English upbringing.

The narrative is now taken up by Eben in the transcript of a copy of the National Archives of Rhodesia (N.A.R.) submission which was handed by him to Allan Stock in 1968. Some of the facts recorded have already been included in this summary, but the transcript is important for its historical value and as a source.

MOCKE's BIOGRAPHICAL SUBMISSION to N.A.R.

One

Born: Boshoff, Orange Free State, 13th July 1888.
Father's Name: David Stephen Mocke.
Mother's Name: Elizabeth (born Minnaar).
Other children: Six brothers including myself. Three sisters.
Education: At Boshoff Kindergarten. Teacher; Mrs Brummer.

Moved from Boshoff to Pretoria, eighteen months before the Jameson Raid, which took place in 1896.
  Employed by the Land Settlement Board in Pretoria before coming to Rhodesia.
  Entered Rhodesia on 11th of April, 1910.
  Served in Salisbury on Recruit's course. After two months transferred to Bulawayo. Then to Nyamandhlovu, Inyati, Gwaai. Back to Salisbury from where I was sent on special duty in connection with South African Rebellion. Immigration Officer for Rhodesia at Bulawayo.
  Deserted from Bulawayo and went to India. Brought back under escort of Lt. Morris. Special Board of Officers: Masterman, Spain and Thornton. Six months in Camp Gaol, five months of which was spent in Salisbury Hospital.
  After discharge from Hospital, transferred to Makaha, 1916. Beginning of 1918, a dose of blackwater fever, through which I was nursed by Dr Gurney, an American Missionary Doctor. I was re-transferred to Salisbury to recoup my health. Worked in the District Police Office.
  Just before peace was declared in 1918, I got my discharge.
  The tossing of a coin decided me to go to Durban. Here I joined the firm of North & Son, Implement Dealers and Importers. Sold their implements in the Eastern Transvaal: until I started my own business in Heidelberg, as a wool and grain buyer and farm implement dealer.
  1921. I proceeded to the Cape. Acquired Onrust, a piece of ground next to Hermanus and cut the ground into a township.
  1922. John Austin, a well-known General Dealer, came to the Cape for a holiday, from Que Que. He bought ground on Onrust and became my agent to sell the ground in Rhodesia. He sold most of it! I came to Rhodesia in 1922 to

square accounts with John Austin. Remained in Rhodesia and married my second wife. Apart from holidays, I have not been back to South Africa.

My first wife I married in Machadodorp, in the Eastern Transvaal towards the end of 1914. She went with me to India and later joined me at Makaha. Early in 1921 her father died in England, leaving her a considerable sum of money. She left for Britain and wanted me to join her. I was not prepared to do this and sued for divorce. We remained friends until she remarried. I believe she died in Singapore. (There were no children).

My second wife, Mrs Rosina James (born Lombard) I married in 1922 in Bulawayo. There were no children. She died on the 12th June 1967.

Two

I do not profess to be a scribe! Only recently, since I have retired and, on the request of the Editor of *Outpost*, did I write my adventures in the Kalahari. These appeared in *The Outpost*, in serial form, for about one year – some 40,000 words. Other short stories have also appeared: "The Gamblers", "Gwaai Incidents", "Lost on the Gwaai", "A Duck Shoot on the Zambesi", "Scotty Smith", "Elephant Graveyard", "Occupation of Pretoria" (was published in 1911 when the present *Outpost* was known as the *Police Review*). The Editor was: E. Moore-Ritchie, now 82 years of age, living in Cornwall and with whom I correspond!), "The Devil's Cataract", and several others whose titles I have forgotten.

Three

Cannot remember having read books on Rhodesian history! Recently read: *The Rhodesia that was my life*, by Sir Robert Tredgold. Some of Selous' books, *Gibbs* and several on UDI. *Pre-Pioneers of Rhodesia* by Servaas le Roux (my brother-in-law). I have, however, had the privilege of having long talks on Rhodesian History with Col. Frank Johnston, who, on occasion, came to my farm in the Gwelo area to shoot duck. Cornelius Van Rooyen was another who gave me much information on Rhodesia before and after the Occupation. I spent many days with this man in the hunting veld.

Four

The forefather of the Mocke family was: Johan Godfried, who came from Thann in the year 1763 in the employ of the East India Company. He married on the 20th January 1771, Rebecca Plagman. All the Mockes in South Africa, and there are many, suffer for their sins today!

My father was patriotic and a strong Republican. Up to the time of his death, he never forgave Britain for the Boer War. Four of his sons fought against the British in that war. He was a horse breeder and supplied many horses to the Burgers in that war. The "blue-black" notes, issued by the Government, were of no value after the war, it broke him and he blamed the British. Rhodes was "mud" in his eyes. Especially after the Jameson Raid.

His attitude changed considerably after the war, especially when Britishers, introduced by Bernie Melville, an old friend (who was a sworn Burger after 8 years in the Transvaal and who fought against the British) came to the house and had "Musical Evenings".

All three sisters married Britishers! Dollie, the eldest, to Charlie Preston, who came from Rhodesia and whose tales of Rhodesia excited my interest to a large extent. Babs (Petronella) married Lt. Col. V.C. Leckie, D.S.O. He was a Veterinary Surgeon attached to the Hussars under Lord Methuen. He went through both World Wars, wrote a book *A Centaur Looks Back*, after he retired to a home they bought in Hants. After his death, my sister lived for three years and also died. They left three daughters. Joan, the eldest (Mrs Lt. Col. Thomas) has three sons, all three of whom are strongly pro-Rhodesian. We correspond. Irene, the third sister, married Jock Craik. He died in Durban. Irene is still alive and lives in Durban.

Note; I mention these mixed Afrikaans-British marriages to show that the hatred between Brit and Boer has vanished, or has melded, all for the good of South Africa and Rhodesia.

Our home language was Afrikaans (taal).

Five

Education; did not run smooth! There were no schools in Pretoria during the Boer War. Fortunately, my family was very friendly with the Botha family, we lived close together. In their home, they had a governess, Miss Meatly, who gave schooling to Helen, Louis, Francis and Manie and mother arranged with Mrs Botha that Babs, Godfrey, myself and Irene could join the tuition.

This arrangement went well for two years, when the authorities decided, for reasons best known to themselves, that Miss Meatly, a pure English girl, had to be expelled from the country. After she was escorted to the Natal Border on her way to Durban, an elderly grey-haired Hollander was appointed to carry on the tuition. The medium of English was now changed, to our disappointment, to High Dutch. Our teacher could not speak a word of English, although highly qualified in High Dutch!

My mother was worried. She was of opinion English was essential. Just at that time, the Ludorf family arrived in Pretoria from Bloemfontein as refugees. The two daughters: Louis Ludorf and Mary von Epron (step-sisters) were qualified English teachers. Mother persuaded them to open a school. From them we had excellent tuition, until long after peace was declared at Vereeniging.

The Dutch Reformed Church built and opened the "Eendracht School" in 1904. Dr Hoogenhout, a highly qualified teacher in English and Dutch, was Headmaster. Miss Frames was the English teacher, a charming, middle-aged woman, who was highly qualified in the English language. I made good progress and passed Standard Six. Unfortunately, I had to leave as my parents could not afford to pay the tuition fees.

I joined Findlay MacRobert and Niemeyer, Solicitors, with the intention of becoming a solicitor. As an Articled Clerk I was paid £2.10.0 per month. To further my education I attended Night Schools: John Stuart, a Scotsman and teacher in one of the newly opened Government schools, taught me English and History and C. de Villiers (a deposed Dutch Reformed Parson) taught me Algebra and Euclid. My salary of £2.10.0 could not cover the fees they required and at the same time to give a donation to the house for food.

F.F. Pienaar, Secretary to Land Settlements, a new Department opened by the Government to help indigent farmers on to their feet, offered me a vacant position in the Land Board. I took it at £16 per month.

Gideon, a son of Commandant Louw, joined me at night classes and we crammed, at all hours of the night, to pass our Matric. We both failed.

Despondent and not happy with my job, as I felt the heads of Civil Servants Departments were biased against the Boer clerks and pushing Australians and English to the fore, I lamented and moaned my opinions to Bernie Melville, who was then Assistant Surveyor General.

"If I was a young man," he advised, "I would go to Rhodesia. It is a young and coming country, where one could not miss to be successful, if one tried."

Charley Preston, my brother-in-law, said, "If it was not for the malaria fever, I would go back there tomorrow. It does not matter what nationality you are, you would be welcome to help build the new Rhodesia."

My parents were not happy with the idea. Against their wishes I wrote to Salisbury for application forms to join the B.S.A. Police. Before the forms arrived, Melville gave me two letters of introduction: One to Atherstone, the Surveyor General in Salisbury, and another to Burns-Begg. Charley Preston gave me £50, and I entrained for Salisbury. My journey up was marvellous. The vast open spaces were most appealing.

In Manica Road, I met Lampard, a friend of mine from Pretoria who had been transferred to the National Bank. He insisted I join him in the Bank, offering me £16.13.4 per month, plus £5 Tropical Allowance! I remonstrated – pen pushing in an office – and gracefully refused his kind offer. Atherstone, the Surveyor General, offered me immediate employment at £16.13.4 per month and £5 Tropical Allowance! (obviously a standard wage at the time in Salisbury). Burns-Begg suggested joining the Police, pointing out: "It is an excellent corps, where you will meet up with fine gentlemen, see the country and, during the three years for which you sign on, decide where you like it best and decide to settle." I joined the Police and, to my surprise, met several South Africans (Boers) who had joined the corps!

Six

Work after school. See Five.

My father being a horse-breeder, we lived on horses and consequently we were excellent horsemen. At a very young age I fired muzzle-loaders and later shot several springbok in the Boshoff area with my father's Martini-Henri! Thus, being conversant with firearms, a good horseman, bi-lingual and a meagre knowledge of Zulu, I did not find the Recruits course difficult. The drilling and discipline was a bit tough.

Seven

See Five. Preston's advice and explanation of conditions in Rhodesia helped to make me realise what to expect. I was not disappointed or surprised.

Eight

All the years I have been in Rhodesia, I only met two Englishmen who made derogatory remarks against me as a Boer. At a party Kay-Robinson remarked: "We have shot you and the likes of you without £5 licences before today." Unfortunately for Kay-Robinson, he was not aware that I was quite a boxer in my day, having been taught the noble art by one Cameron, a physical instructor for the Eendracht school. I punished him quite severely and knocked him out. Another one, Holden, a Cambridge educated man, at Nyamandhovu remarked: "Why you, you cannot even speak the King's English." I replied: "Listen to the Cockney and his accent. No mistaking you were born within the sounds of the Bow-Bells."

He invited me outside! He was not my size, so I gave him a clout with the flat of my right hand and left him on the ground! He subsequently came and apologised, the same as Robinson did. In fact, we, Kay-Robinson and I, became very good friends. He later called on my people in Pretoria. These were the only two occasions, over 68 years!

Nine

Recruits course was, as far as I was concerned, a wonderful exercise to get physically fit. Some of the recruits from overseas had difficulty in getting used to horses and found it difficult to retain their balance. On the whole, however, they soon got used to the training and the Instructors, competent men, were there to help them along. Fifty per cent of the men joined for the sole purpose of making the Police their career. Others, like myself, to see the country and find other outlets to make a living. Many, the better educated types, seconded to the Civil Service, especially the Native Department.

Ten

In my story of the "Biltong Hunters", I give a full description where Trooper Hughes-Halls and one Reggie Brown accompanied me to arrest a number of Dutch hunters who had shot game for biltong, and Royal Game at that. I applied for assistance to arrest these men as I was convinced one of them had attempted to shoot me. I could not, however, prove that they were guilty of the attempt.

Eleven

The Gwaai Police Station I opened for the purpose of preventing game being slaughtered. Previous to my presence in the area, game was destroyed in their hundreds, the meat being cut into biltong and the hides into whips and reims. Seventy-five per cent of the product was sent to South African markets. It was much later laws were promulgated to prevent the traffic in dry meat and hides.
   The camp consisted of "pole and dagga" huts and was situated some distance from the Railway Station, on the banks of the Gwaai River, from where one had a good view of the Bridge over the Gwaai. My biggest problem was the vast area to be patrolled. It was very seldom I remained in the camp for very long. The hunters gave me a wide berth and, when they realised I was on their tracks, they moved, and moved fast, to other areas like the Sebungwe and Wankie. I was only inspected once during the time I was on the Gwaai, and it was not

really an inspection! Captain Murray, from Bulawayo (my headquarters), vacated the train to "find out how I was getting along." He continued his journey, to Wankie and the Falls, on the next goods train!

After charging several hunters and having them convicted, the parties left that area. They moved further north to the Hartley and Gokwe districts. It was proposed that I should transfer and follow them, when the report came through about cattle movements on the Bechuanaland border and I went on the "Kalahari Patrol."

Twelve

My stories in the *Outpost*: "Kalahari Patrol" is based on true facts. A great grand-child of van Rooyen recently wrote and asked me to supply her with all the information I had of van Rooyen. I did, copying the articles in *Outpost* and adding several more. It covered 37 pages, a copy of which I enclose herewith.

Thirteen

My relationship with my superiors were of the very best. I respected them and, I think, they had a great deal of respect for me. I had the advantage, however, of being very remote on the out-lying stations of which I was in charge. It might have been different had I been in daily contact with them, but I do not think so. I always received the very best of help and advice from them.

Favouritism! No, not to my knowledge. It was mentioned to me on several occasions: "If you are related to one of the Directors of the Chartered Company, your Commission is forthcoming at an early date after you join." These facts never came to my notice. Personally I never looked for or expected promotion. I was very happy in the bundu and, like the "trek boers", always inquisitive to see new forests and game. I NEVER shot game for the fun of killing. When, and only when, I was in need for meat for myself and followers.

Fourteen

The African constables in my charge, and other Africans, I treated as children! They obeyed me implicitly and with respect. On lonely patrols one cannot help but become friends and helpful to one another. I could speak the Matabele language reasonably well – but where and when an interpreter is available, I made use of him. In the Kalahari I had Kleeinbooi who could speak Africaans fluently and did most of the interpretation. This was, to an extent, a mistake. He had his likes and dislikes. It is best to do one's own talking and explaining. I feel strongly that every policeman who has to deal with Africans, should speak their language. There is not the slightest doubt the white and black man should be able to speak one another's language. So many misunderstandings could be ironed out for the benefit of both.

Fifteen

When I returned from my third trip to the Kalahari in 1914, Col. Tomlinson, i/c of Bulawayo, advised that General Edwards wanted to see me in Salisbury. When I interviewed the General, he explained the necessity of having someone on the Limpopo Border to ascertain if some of the Rebels from South Africa had any intention of coming into Rhodesia; that this precaution was necessary in case rebels entered Rhodesia, joined up with other Nationals and started making trouble in this country. I was appointed Intelligence Officer.

My first job was to report on a meeting of Dutch subjects, from different parts of Rhodesia, who were gathering to discuss the South African rebellion.

One, Martain, from Chipinga, was in the chair. The Hall was packed with Dutchmen from: Chipinga, Plumtree, Enkeldoorn, Hartley, Sinoia and many other districts in Rhodesia.

One thing was quite certain, from the discussions that night, that there was no intention of giving the rebel movement down south any sympathy. BUT, they were angry that the Government had deprived them of their weapons! Especially the men on the borders, who claimed they had no means of defending themselves against the natives. They were of opinion, since the world was at war, the natives may rise at any time.

I reported fully to the Government and suggested, with insistence, that the Dutchmen be given back their rifles. Eight years later, Mr Huggins (Lord Malvern) was having a sundowner with a tall grey haired man in the Salisbury Club. When I came in, Huggins invited me to join them (he had that day performed an operation on my wife) and introduced me to Martain who shook my hand warmly and said: "I owe you an apology and also a great 'thank you'." He went on to explain: "The Dutchmen in Rhodesia must thank you for being instrumental in getting back their rifles, at the time of the Rebellion. I also apologise for thinking you were a spy for the Government." It was only then I recognised Martain as the Chairman of the meeting.

On the Limpopo, I reported to the Officer Commanding troops on the border. We arranged that my reports were to be left under a stone under an enormous figtree on the banks of the river. And, that it might not be advisable to shew myself.

I continued my journey to Messina and booked in at the hotel. One Sacks was the Manager/Owner of the hotel. Apparently he had difficulty in having some bulls castrated and complained the Veterinary Surgeon of Louis Trichardt charged 10/- per head. This was a general conversation over beers in the bar.

"I will do it for half the price," I stated in a joke.

"I will be glad if you will do the job. It will save £25," he stated with eager anticipation of saving money.

The next day I castrated 100 young calves and earned £25, within the first 24 hours I was in Messina!

My first report, placed under the pre-arranged stone, was delivered with difficulty. The Limpopo was in flood! However, I entered the water some distance above the drift (where the Bridge is now), and drifted for nearly two miles before I got out on to the other side bank.

My return journey was even worse. The flood waters had increased and I had to walk for three miles before landing in a submerged mimosa tree, the thorns of which scratched blood over my body. I was completely exhausted by the time I arrived at the spot where I had left my clothes. I was stiff for days after the exercise.

In Messina, there was no evidence, not even a rumour, that Nationals had any intention of crossing into Rhodesia. I boarded the train and continued on to Louis Trichardt. Here I met one Botha Kritzinger, an old friend of mine, who practised as a Solicitor. He informed me General Moller, a Nationalist leader, was preparing to invade and take over Louis Trichardt. On this information, the Government had prepared Louis Trichardt gaol as a fort for the defence of the town. Kritzinger was a strong Nationalist himself. Word had come to him a gathering of Nationalists at Mara would decide when the approach to Louis Trichardt would take place. He attended the meeting but nothing definite had been decided. According to him a cache of rifles and ammunition was hidden in the sands of the Sandriver and it was proposed, when the time was ripe, to gather at this point, issue weapons to the Nationalists and move on to Louis Trichardt.

I was arrested by a detective and taken to the Magistrate. Stops (the Magistrate) wanted to know what I was doing in the area of Louis Trichardt. I asked him to send the guards out of his office and I would tell him. He did and I told him. In the absence of identification papers, I had to report to him daily until confirmation came from Salisbury. When word came through confirming my mission, I informed Stops of the hidden armaments in the Sandriver. They made a successful raid.

I went on to Pietersburg and later to Pretoria. At Pretoria, Godfrey, my brother, advanced an opinion on the death of General de la Rey. An opinion with which I did not agree.

According to Godfrey, he was having dinner with the Bothas the night de la Rey was shot. The General was in his study and it was known by the family that the General was having an interview with de la Rey. (This interview took place 48 hours before the Rebellion was declared.) Suddenly, the family heard the front door slam and seconds later, Botha popped his head into the dining room and said: "Don't wait dinner for me, I am going down town," and vanished.

They heard his car roaring out of the gates. Mrs Botha stood silent for a moment in a pensive mood and said: "More trouble, I suppose. I am sorry about General de la Rey, he has great influence amongst our people. Come along, let us eat." It was a silent dinner and Godfrey left soon after. Next morning, news came through that General de la Rey had been shot.

Apparently a guard had tried to stop the General's car and, it refusing to do so, the guard fired at the car. The bullet went through the back of the car and entered de la Rey's kidney. Godfrey was of opinion that General Botha had dashed down to the Police station in Pretoria, given the alarm, and instructions to shoot de la Rey.

Against this opinion, there was conclusive proof that all roads leading into Johannesburg were guarded by the Police, with strict instructions to stop all cars, with the intention of arresting the Foster Gang. A gang who had played havoc in and around Johannesburg, robbing and shooting people. The gang eventually took refuge in a mine tunnel, where the Police had them cornered, and where, in the tunnel, they shot themselves.

The guards who shot de la Rey stated, under oath, that they had no idea General de la Rey was in the car, they only carried out their strict instructions when the car refused to stop. There is no doubt, the death of General de la Rey prevented many Nationalists joining up with the rebels.

The Nationalists were sure Germany was going to win the war and they took full advantage of the conditions prevailing, to avenge themselves against the many wrongs Britain had committed against South Africa.

The shooting of Joppie Fourie (who is a far relation of mine) aggravated the conditions. Johannes Fourie, the youngest brother of Joppie, who was also captured and given the death sentence, was later reprieved and sentenced to five years. He only did a few months and was discharged. Visiting their farm, Blouwildebeestoek (where I spent many happy holidays), I asked Johannes "what it felt like to be sentenced to death," and he replied: "Every hole in your body opens wide and refuses to close!"

No, I have not written any articles on the Rebellion.

Sixteen

Two reasons for my desertion made me take the step.
1) I was time expired and, had it not been that I was in the Kalahari, knowing nothing of the war, until November, 1914, I would have taken my discharge in April of that year, when my 3 years had expired.
2) I wanted to get married and realised that my salary would not cover the expenses of keeping a wife.
At the time of my desertion, I was Immigration Officer and did not like the work one bit. The only reason members deserted at the time was to go to the war. I have no knowledge of unrest in the corps, other than this one reason.

Seventeen

In Bombay, I reported to the Staff Officer under Brig. Gen. Knight and explained who I was. I offered my services in the remount section. They were very short of help in this department, but could not accept my services. They were not sure what action the Rhodesian authorities might take. On their recommendation, I approached Baldock's, who imported horses from Australia and was accepted immediately.
At this time, horseflesh was scarce. The Army under Smuts in East Africa, was losing thousands of animals in actions and horse-sickness, especially the latter. And in France many horses were killed daily. The Government had made a contract with Baldock's to pay them 400 rupees (one shilling and fourpence at that time) for all horses imported to India that may be suitable for army work.
Baldock himself was in Australia buying horses and Robinson managed the stables in Bombay, which was situated in Byculla. It was a huge concern where thousands of horses could be accommodated under roof. Cover was essential against the monsoon season when from 100-200 inches of rain fell in the season. Major Hunt, on behalf of the Government, had first pick of any boat-load of horses that arrived from Australia. The sorting out of the animals, discarding any with blemishes, was quite an exercise. On behalf of the Government, I was put in charge of several boat-loads that were transported to Mombasa for Smuts, in East Africa. No facilities were available for off-loading, all animals had to be slung by derricks into lighters.

Eighteen

All deserters who were brought back were given six months in the Guard Room.

I was no exception. One can understand, the Government had to make examples. The Police were the FIRST line of defence and severe action had to be taken to prevent mass desertion. Especially as the majority of Police wanted to be in the war. Had the Authorities discharged all time expired men, very few would have been left to defend Rhodesia, in case of a native rebellion.

Nineteen

Loyalty of Dutch Rhodesians, is more fully explained under Fifteen.

Twenty

My discharge from the Police came after a fight in which I knocked out the teeth of my opponent, and the Salisbury *Herald* echoed the incident in large front page letters: "A POLICEMAN'S CRIME." This was too much for General Edwards and I got my discharge! With grateful thanks to Herring, the victim, for being responsible for my discharge, I paid for a new set of dentals, which cost me £45.

Twenty One

1923 Referendum. I was so certain that Rhodesia would join the South, that I made a bet with Hacker Matthews, Manager of the Que Que Hotel, for a £100. I paid the bet with despondent disgust. After a struggle in which I travelled miles to convince people that Smuts had made a generous offer. Although I met with stiff opposition, especially from those who feared Afrikander domination and could still remember the Boer War and the 1914 Rebellion, I was convinced the majority would vote for Smuts. I was very disappointed on the results. Matthews was very bitter against the Afrikander. He had reason to be! During the Boer War he was captured, his boots removed and had to fend for himself, on bare feet, over miles of burned stubble! Matthews was an ex B.S.A. Policeman.

Twenty Two

Que Que in 1923 was one of the biggest mining camps in the Midlands. Apart from John Austin's General Dealer's Store, Que Que Stores, and the usual tin shanty stores run by Asiatics, the buildings in Que Que were few and far between. The Globe and Phoenix Mine had substantial buildings and the homesteads, for their married employees, were good buildings. The streets and roads were gravel and dusty. The community consisted, mostly, of mine employees and miners from the nearby mines known as small workers. Being on the main road, travellers could always be found in the Que Que Hotel, which at that time was owned by Tom Meikle.

The biggest and richest small mine was the Moss, which belonged to my wife and Dr Worthington. The mine was managed by Hubert Mitchell. Dr Worthington and I inspected the mine once a month and signed cheques in payment of the monthly accounts and wages. The Moss mine was situated three miles from Que Que, just off the main road to Salisbury going north, on the Rennie Taylor Concessions. The property was tributed from the then management of the Goldfields and, later, by Lonrho. The tribute conditions were pretty stiff: Any out-puts of gold over the sum of £2,200 per month, we had to pay 15% interest. Anything less than £2,200 per month, 11%. Consequently we kept the out-puts less than £2 200, with the result that considerable amounts of amalgam were accumulated in the safe! At times, when the gold lenses were rich underground, we could have declared up to £5 – £6,000 per month! When the reef on the sixth level petered out, we closed the mine.

After closing the Moss, I erected an 8 stamp battery on the "Mary's Dream" mine, on the outskirts of Que Que town. I did considerable work on this property but found it unpayable and closed it after losing a considerable amount of money. Then I removed my machinery to the "Golden Spider" mine, 20 miles from Que Que. This also proved unpayable. Moving the machinery to the "Denbigh", 8 miles from Umvuma and 60 miles from the "Golden Spider", was a costly business.

The "Denbigh" also proved a failure, and I moved to the "Best Give", 16 miles from Selukwe. Here I did a terrific amount of work on the reef, found it unpayable, closed the concern and moved to the "Guinea Fowl", 10 miles from Gwelo on the main road to Selukwe. This was an old company mine which had an incline shaft to the 600' level. The dewatering of this old mine cost a lot of cash. However, I revealed the reef and drove on the shoot, struck a payable lens, which contained much gelena (lead). The ore was not free milling and I installed shaking tables and four decantation tanks of 20 000 gallons each, with the necessary cyanide plant. The recovery of gold hardly paid expenses, let alone making a profit. I closed up and sold the machinery.

While I worked on these different mining ventures, on the farm "Riverdale", where my wife stayed, we continued to breed Short-horn and Aberdeen Angus cattle. Some of the bulls had been imported from Scotland and England. But, cattle did not pay! The ruling price for well-bred steers was only £3 – £4.

Harry Cumming (a partner of Tom Meikle in the Gwelo business) suggested, on information I had given him, that we try to find an outlet for our beef via the Congo and Lobito, to the west coast, where the Africans are meat eaters and in very short supply of beef. In 1928, the Congo staged an Exhibition at Elizabethville and, furnished with a letter of introduction to the Governor of the Congo and the Governor of Angola, I left Gwelo by car and proceeded to Elizabethville.

Both the Congo and Angola were enthusiastic that beef, in cold cars, be sent to their respective countries, and promised their help in every respect. Unfortunately, the railway line from Lobito to Elizabethville, was a different gauge than the one from Gwelo to Elizabethville. The idea was to send the beef in refrigeration cars from Gwelo. The difference in the railway gauges prevented us from going ahead with the suggestion. The market was there and unfailing.

The RHODESIA TOWN PLANNING ACT came about after my case against the Minister of the Interior, Leggate.

I cut up and divided the farm Raylands into a Township, three miles from Gwelo. The permission of the local authority had to be obtained, in this case the Minister of the Interior. Blue Prints were presented and Jacobson, the Mayor of Gwelo, Dr Maitland, the Medical Officer of Health, were instructed to make a report. They did, and in due course the necessary permission was granted by Leggate. Within three months the ground was sold and, finding the business good, I divided the balance of Raylands into residential sites. Blue Prints were presented to Leggate for his approval.

Several weeks passed and I heard nothing from the Minister. Max Danziger, who was then Minister of Finance and my Solicitor, was asked his opinion as to whether I could continue selling, considering I had a traveller in Northern Rhodesia who was selling the land. Danziger thought there would be no difficulty, especially as the two previous advisers, Jacobson and Maitland, had passed the second blue prints. I continued to sell and had almost sold all the sites when Leggate decided not to pass the new suggestions!

Legally, he need not give his reasons for turning the scheme down. I sued the Minister to shew his reasons.

The case came before Sir Murray Bisset, the Chief Justice. Hudson, the Attorney General was for the Crown and Lewis (later Judge and father of the present Judge) was instructed (briefed) to represent me. Arguments lasted three days. At the end, Sir Murray Bisset said: "The case was of such importance to the country, that he feels he should have another Judge to help him come to a decision." Later, Judge MacElwaine joined the Chief Justice on the bench and the whole case was re-argued for another three days.

Finally, judgement was given against me. Gilchrist, brother-in-law to Leggate, advised me strongly not to appeal to Bloemfontein and so did many other friends who were in the know. Fortunately, my Deed of Sale was a very well drawn document by Dempers Moore and van Ryneveld, of Cape Town. One clause stipulated, "unless an instalment is paid on due date, the sale becomes null and void, and all payments made are confiscated."

The news in the Rhodesian papers frightened the buyers and instalments ceased, especially those buyers in Northern Rhodesia who could not, or would not, understand that those on Raylands "A" were safe, but not those who had bought on Raylands "B". At great expense and cursing Leggate, I proceeded to Northern Rhodesia and interviewed every buyer, from Livingstone to Nchanga in the far north, who had bought on "B", and transferred their names on to "A" where building sites had been cancelled for the non-payment of their instalments. This manoeuvre of mine came to the ears of Leggate who, I was told, was considerably upset, as he took no further action. When Leggate lost his seat in Parliament, I wrote him a letter, a letter which must have made his ears burn! Some of the wording of which will not be found in the dictionary.

Harry Cumming, the owner of Christmas Gift Farm, adjoining the Gwelo Township, invited me to cut up and divide ground on the Gwelo River into 10 acre plots. According to the new Planning Act (for which the above case was responsible) authority was not necessary when ground exceeded 10 or more acres. The selling of these plots was a great success. Cumming was happy with the success and we decided to establish Gwelo North.

Gwelo North was a new township with one acre building sites. The survey complied to all the conditions laid down by the Planning Act. Eighty foot roads, lanes, parks, etc., etc., cost a considerable sum of money. Before the ground was ready for inspection, Harry Cumming died and his Trustees refused to carry on with the scheme. There was no contract between Cumming and myself – nothing in black and white, with the result that the Master of the High Court refused to recognise my account for my share of the expenses.

The Falcon Sand Dump at Umvuma shews an assay value of one and a half million in pounds, shillings and pence. Unfortunately, the dump is cuprous and very acid. However, B.C. Michell, a metallurgist and assayer for Barclay's Bank in Gwelo, was a friend of mine and we decided to have samples of the sand tested in his laboratory. I took 83 samples with a sand auger, some coming from as deep as 84 feet. After weeks and weeks of testing we eventually found an extraction of the gold could be made with a weak solution of sulphuric acid, applied to a tank of sand and then discharging the sand into another tank and washing it with 4 applications of clean water, thereby getting rid of all acids.

This procedure neutralised the substance, allowing the cyanide to dissolve the gold in the sand.

Six cement tanks – 40' x 20' x 3'6" – were built in pairs and the sand was treated as mentioned above. The extraction was fair, but I did not get more than half a penny weight. Water was bought from the local Village Management Board at £80 per month. As time went on, the extraction improved, especially when we got into a section of the dump which was rich. When the second W.W. was declared, all sulphuric acid was commandeered by the Government for the making of munitions, and I had to close up the work on the Falcon Dump.

The Gutu Patrol took place in 1913. Hughes Halls and I were both on this patrol. When we arrived by train at Umvuma, at that time the rail head, construction work was then going on at the Falcon Mine. Little did I dream that in years to come I would be treating the residue of that mine.

Whilst treating the sands at Umvuma, I bought the farm Elandsvlei, some four miles from Umvuma. There was a good home-stead on the property where my wife joined me. Peter How was manager and we went in for the growing of wheat in a big way. When the Italian prisoners of war were established at Umvuma, we grew vegetables on a large scale for the Government, which was issued to the detainees.

The Chrome Mines at Selukwe offered and I accepted, a contract to supply the Company with mining timbers. Chrome was in big demand during the second war. I bought three 3 ton Chev. lorries and one 4 ton. Obtained permission from Central Estates to cut timber on their 360 000 acre ranch at Umvuma and hired 4 Italian mechanics to look after the lorries at 1/- per day plus their food! They were competent men and very, very first class mechanics. At one time during the contract, one truck load of timber was dispatched each day. A load of timber was worth from £75 to £100 per truck, depending on the length and thickness of the timber. None had to be less than 7 inches at the thin end and 8 feet in length.

Twenty Four

Anecdotes in Police days and amusing incidents were numerous.

On my arrival at the guard room, after having been sentenced to six months, one Tiger Smith, a member of the CID in Bulawayo, had been sentenced to 6 weeks for insubordination. Tiger was a tough guy and had a wonderful sense of humour. Our daily guard outside the guardroom was one Trooper Butler. He was an American and insisted on dressing like a cowboy with high heeled top boots and wearing a "five gallon" hat. Our gaoler was one Sgt. Bob Patten, very fond of a tot of dop.

One morning, Bob put us on to pruning the lemon trees surrounding the square. Tiger made himself comfortable in one tree and I in another, whilst our guard, who was deaf, explained how unsuitable the B.S.A. Police uniform was and compared it to the comfortable garb he was wearing, saying: "In America, we study comfort …"

"But you are not in America now, you know," thundered a harsh, gravelly voice at his back and Jimmy Blatherwick appeared on the scene.

How and from where, the Camp Commandant appeared, is anyone's guess. But there he was, with his iron grey moustache bristling. He continued, "You look like a Christmas tree in that high stetson hat and high heeled boots. Put your prisoners in the guard room and go to the barracks and get yourself properly dressed. I do not want to see you again looking like a fighting cock."

Four days before Tiger Smith was due for his discharge from the camp guard room, he suggested going down town that evening.

"How can we get down town, you seem to forget we are in gaol?" I replied.

"Come here and I will show you how," and he led me into the toilet. Pointing to the removable seat in the P.K., he explained, "By removing the seat and shoving the tarred bucket to one side, what is to prevent us from crawling through the aperture from where the night soil service remove the bucket?"

The idea appealed to me and we made arrangements to leave at 9 o'clock, the hour when the Flying Sentry struck the bell outside the guard room and locked the door leading into the cells. Trooper Jarvis was on duty that particular Saturday night. He had no sooner struck the bell and locked the door, when we made our escape.

It was easier said than done! We were both big men and the struggle we had to squeeze through that small hole was a major exercise. However, we managed the squeeze, our woolly grey back shirts and khaki slacks covered in streaks of tar! I was well supplied with golden sovereigns, which were kept on the brick window sill, high from the ground, in the main cell. (This money was handed to me by Matt Scallan after I was sentenced. The cash was mine, which was handed to him for safe keeping). Handing £3 to Tiger and retaining £5 for myself, the two bandits walked down the main road looking for a rickshaw!

Eventually we found one, boarded the vehicle and directed him to the Imperial Hotel. This hotel was managed by Jack Lefevre and was situated where Kingston's are established today.

Whiskys and sodas were gulped with relish to the tune of dance music on a piano in the lounge. The drinks soon promoted dutch courage and we joined in the fun. Dancing with Mrs Lefevre, she asked: "Where have you boys come from? You smell of tar."

"From the bundu, in a damned scotch cart, which has mucked us up properly," I replied.

The fun continued and so did the whisky, which in those days cost 1/- per tot. Long after closing hours, Tiger and I left, climbed into a rickshaw and returned to camp.

On our journey to the camp in the rickshaw, it was agreed that the return through the P.K. aperture was too much of an exercise and Tiger was sure he could "bamboozle the Flying Sentry." As bold as brass we entered the guard room: "In God's name, where the hell have you fellows come from?" demanded Jarvis.

"Look here, laddie, for your own sake keep our movements under your hat. You were fast asleep when we passed out and went for a walk," bluffed Tiger.

"To hell with that explanation," remonstrated Jarvis, "the door is locked, you could not have come this way."

"Be that as it may, we came this way, found you fast asleep, popped out and went for a walk. In any case, that is our story, so, to save your own skin, open the door, we want to go to bed."

"Christ, you will get me hung for this," spluttered Jarvis, as he took the keys off the board and proceeded to open the door.

The following night, Sunday, immediately after the hour of ten was struck on the bell, the main door rattled and in walked the Camp Commandant, Jimmy Blatherwick.

"Ah, so you are here tonight," when he saw us tucked under blankets. "Make sure you are here every night. Remember you are on active service and, if it happens again, you may get shot."

That was the final word we ever heard on the incident of our mad escapade.

He, Jimmy Blatherwick, was a lovable character. He played the role of a patient father to all members of the B.S.A. Police. No wonder the magnificent Memorial, established in the camp, was erected to one of the finest men I ever met.

FIFTY YEARS ON

Editor's Note. This article by Eben Mocke is placed in this part of the book instead of in his Stories section as it seems more fitting as a part of his life story.
 Author's Note: I make no apologies if I have digressed and spent a few words on what might seem to be rather trite recollections in this account of my wonderful visit to Bulawayo. Many of my contemporaries would fail to appreciate the changes since our days together and I feel that they will be as interested as I was in the developments. To this end I have wandered...

It was 8.30 a.m. on May Day when I met the Editor, his wife and his parents who were visiting Rhodesia from England, for the trip to Bulawayo. Thirty minutes later, we were out of the Salisbury traffic and speeding towards our destination in the utilitarian, though speedy, Peugeot.
 Many years have passed since I last travelled this road – younger readers might not realise how age and the relative isolation of retirement on the farm encroach upon one's travels – and we were through Norton and past the cairn commemorating the recent World Ploughing Championships before I had finished my first cigarette. Fields of cotton, in the process of being picked, flashed by and then we were through Hartley. Twenty miles on came Gatooma and both this town and Hartley seemed to have changed out of all recognition since my exploits at the Cam and Motor Mine in 1914. Gatooma is now the hub of the cotton industry and, with Gwelo and Que Que, the future wealth of the Midlands is vividly indicated in the development of the three towns. We crossed the Sebakwe and then another store of memories was unleashed as we passed the turn-off to the Moss Gold Mine where a partner and I had extracted over half a million pounds worth of the precious metal. Then we were in Que Que and pausing to stretch our legs and saviour the delicious coffee served in the charming little restaurant of the Que Que Hotel.
 Once more on the road, we passed through Manyami – memories again of the days when I used to transport beef from my ranch to the South African markets. Christmas Gift Homestead was the next landmark, the property of the late Harry Cumming with whom I had laid out and established the suburb of Gwelo North.
 We coasted into Gwelo, the metropolis and boom town of the Midlands where more cattle are bought and sold than at any other point north of the Limpopo. The Midlands Hotel, erected by that wonderful pioneer Tom Meikle, reminded

me of the opening in 1927. Drinks had been "on the house" and the citizens of Gwelo had experienced a very lively occasion. I always consider Gwelo to be my "home town" for I spent many enjoyable years there and in the surrounding district. Through Gwelo, we raced on past Willoughby which in 1914 boasted the only diamond mine in Rhodesia. The Somabula Flats in their vastness reminded me of 1911 when I had been delivering two grey ponies, the property of Lieut. Gus Myburgh, to Gwelo, following the officer's transfer from Bulawayo.

On the Flats I had met an ostrich hen with a clutch of chicks and accompanied by the proud father of the brood. The latter did not like the look of us, spread his wings and charged the horses. The led pony was frightened out of his wits at the galloping, winged monster, jerked the lead riem from my hand and fled madly across the country leaving me to follow as best I could. Some miles further on, I managed to catch and subdue the frightened animal.

We reached the Shangani and the memorial. Several white people, including a fair-haired little girl had been brutally murdered there during the 1896 Rebellion. The aftermath had been seen by a commando in charge of Cornelius van Rooyen and he told me how the gruesome sight had killed all thoughts of mercy for the perpetrators.

We stopped for a few minutes to refuel at Insiza and were on the move again for the last few miles of the journey. We sighed to a halt in front of Bulawayo's Palace Hotel.

Lunch in the Palm Court of the Palace was a reminder of the time when Jack Everett, the saddler, appeared outside the bar on horseback. Several of us inside the bar challenged him to ride in for a drink. He did, to the utter consternation of the screaming barmaid.

Having paused again at the Plaza Hotel to drop off the Editor's family, he took me on to Hillside Police Station. There I was introduced to Inspector Day, the Member in Charge, and to Section Officers Mason and Kennedy. The Mess Caterer, Patrol Officer Lynn, then showed me to my accommodation on the station. And what a surprise that accommodation was! I was given the run of a compact little flat – bedroom, lounge, bathroom with hot and cold water, all over-looking the green lawns. Compared with pre-World War 1 standards, this was luxury indeed.

After a welcome siesta and bath, I was shown the rest of the quarters. The main mess was the size of the barracks of my day which had housed 44 men. It doubled as dining room and lounge and was even equipped with a corner bar, bar stools, tables and comfortable easy chairs. The single bedrooms of Hillside's policemen were up to good hotel standards. Things have come a long way in 55 years when we lived, slept and relaxed in our communal barracks furnished almost entirely with telescopic iron beds, each with three coir "biscuits", adjoining cement baths and cold showers which in the winter months turned one's skin a mottled blue and promoted pimples like the pin feathers of a dead duck. There was just no comparison between the old and the new and if today's policemen have "jam on it", they deserve it.

By sundown the bar was open and some of the station staff were gathered around with cold beers in their fists. It was the beginning of a long evening and I mention the names of my companions, Inspector Day, Section Officer Kennedy, Patrol Officers Pritchard, Lynn, Macintyre and Golightly, not in any "name-dropping" sense, but in very real appreciation of their wonderful hospitality. Dinner, prepared by a cook who certainly knew his job (and here again, the Hillside kitchen would have gladdened the heart of any proud housewife) was a feast and I ate heartily. The rest of the evening was spent in the delightful company of the Hillside complement and I sincerely hope I didn't bore them with my tales. If I did, it's their own fault for being such a wonderful audience.

At nine the following morning, the Editor collected me and took me to the Trade Fair. At the B.S.A.P. Pavilion, I was introduced to Superintendent Short and Inspector Jones, the officers responsible for the exhibit. I was given a guided tour and was very impressed. As I subsequently gathered, I followed the general trend of later spectators in my deep interest of the captured weapons exhibit. The almost frightening range of Russian-designed and Chinese-made arms and equipment were displayed with an art which would have done credit to a professional window-dresser. The Pavilion, in its magnificence, disclosed the weeks of planning, painting and hard work that had gone into it. My verdict is that it was well worthwhile.

The mounted details on their sleek and well-groomed horses drew considerable attention. I saw one little girl petting the nose of one of the horses. She then produced a handkerchief and wiped the horse's nostrils! Neither horse nor rider winked an eye. They stood there like a grand granite statue.

His Excellency, the Officer Administering the Government, was scheduled to visit the Pavilion at 3 p.m. and it had been arranged that just prior to his arrival, I would meet, after over fifty years, the old Bushman, C'wai. As the time drew nearer, I was beginning to feel apprehensive. Would we recognise each other after over half a century? Would the faithful old tracker remember those very distant days?

At 2.30 p.m. I was trying to relax in the lounge of the Pavilion. A few minutes later, the Editor called me and took me to the balcony overlooking the foyer.

And there, coming through the main entrance, clad in a ragged boiler suit, was C'wai. I hurried down the stairs, greeted him with "koga, kaga milata ce tasha," and shook his hand. He jerked as if someone has stuck a needle into him. It was a moment I shall never forget.

"You, Gwana Mpisa!" and a grin gradually developed and extended from ear to ear on the lined and scarred old dry apricot face. After 55 years he had recognised me.

It was fortunate that at that moment the Police Band heralded the arrival of His Excellency for we were both considerably moved. C'wai, I think, could scarcely understand the events of the last few days leading up to this confrontation and, for myself, I was almost overwhelmed by the reunion. We stood together in front of *The Outpost* exhibit and were introduced to His Excellency by Superintendent Short. The latter mentioned my relationship to C'wai in the context of Kalahari Patrol. To my surprise, Mr Dupont cut short the introduction.

"Yes, I have read the story with interest. And now the two of you meet again after all these years."

After a brief, informal chat with His Excellency, Mr Dupont continued his inspection. C'wai and I mounted the stairs, made ourselves comfortable in the lounge and began our reminiscences interrupted by flashing cameras and enquiring newspaper reporters.

My emotions were considerably stirred as I gazed into the wizened old face with its straggling grey hairs. The scars, C'wai told me, were the result of an argument with a leopard. The cat had nearly killed him before he got the better of the brute. His face crinkled like parched brown paper at the memory. Though years of hard living had taken their toll, the very presence of the honest and faithful old man was testimony to the hardiness of his race.

C'wai must be older than my eighty years but his memory was equal to mine. In the old days, I had been forced to rely on the services of an interpreter when talking with him, but in the years since he had picked up a very adequate understanding of Ndebele. He told me that his immediate family were all dead apart from one daughter (not the little girl I had known as "Plover") who was living in Francistown. Many of the other Bushmen who had attached themselves to me on the Gwaai had intermarried with the Makaranga and Matabele. Some of them had returned to Bechuanaland (Botswana). We talked on for the best part of an hour before it was time for us to leave. I was feeling quite exhausted by the excitement and welcomed the opportunity for peace and quiet.

By evening, I had recovered, fortunately. The Hillside policemen had again excelled themselves and for my benefit had arranged a braaivleis. Inspector Day, Section Officers Mason and Vincent, Patrol Officers Wheatley, Campbell, Finn, Freeman and Hope joined my friends of the night before and, together with wives and girlfriends we embarked on another round of merry-making. It was a second late night in succession! Friday dawned, but the hue and cry was not over. It had been arranged that C'wai and I should be interviewed by the RBC. I again met C'wai at the Trade Fair and was grateful for the person who managed to scrounge for him a decent pair of trousers and a rather large but respectable jacket. At 11 a.m. we chatted with Keith Kennedy –a former policeman who was perhaps more able to understand the depth of the reunion than an ordinary layman. C'wai, oblivious to the gadgetry of the recording studio, seemed quite at ease throughout the interview, but I suspect that he was in a state nearing that of suspended animation during his entire visit to Bulawayo. He asked me constantly what it was all about but no explanation I could offer would get across to him what all the commotion signified.

I wish that I could have been with C'wai a few days later when the broadcast came over the air. It was most peculiar to listen to one's own voice and what the effect would have been on the old Bushman, I cannot guess.

After the interview, I had the pleasure of meeting Section Officer Chris Pollard who had been responsible for tracing C'wai and for initiating the arrangements to bring him to the Trade Fair. He is yet another of today's policemen, together with the staff at Tjolotjo, to whom I shall be eternally grateful.

After the busy morning at the Fair, I was quite happy to get back to Hillside. But again, I was given little opportunity to relax (although I would not have missed the subsequent visit for the world) and was taken to see Mrs Geise, the widow of Albert Geise, who had discovered the Wankie coal deposits. Mrs Geise is now 88 but still makes an annual pilgrimage to her husband's grave on the farm which was granted to him by Cecil Rhodes. Although I had not known her in 1912, Mrs Geise was very interested to hear of my connection with her late husband in those days. She lives by herself in her cottage at Hillside which is named Wankie Geise.

After this lunch and a quick siesta, I was travelling again, this time escorted by Inspector Day. The intention was to visit some of my old haunts but I was disappointed to find that most of them had vanished beneath the skyscrapers and huge office blocks of today's Bulawayo. The old police camp which I had known was gone completely and an institution of comparative luxury stands in its place. I met the Mess Caterer and was shown the kitchen with its huge anthracite ovens, cold rooms and storerooms, and the dining rooms, one for patrol officers, one for section officers and inspectors and a third which was used by anyone of any rank who wishes to entertain guests (even girlfriends) with a meal. Both single and married quarters were beyond description to anyone thinking in terms of the tin shacks of my younger days. Trimmed hedges, green lawns and beautiful flower gardens completed the picture. I felt like rejoining – something I have not considered since 1918!

That evening, C'wai and I were to have our final ordeal in the limelight at the Bulawayo Television Studios. After a short interview with the presenter, Ken Jackson, C'wai, the Editor and I entered the studio to be met with a barrage of lights which gave a temperature in excess of the Kalahari noon, and a barrage of sound coming from a rhythm group which occupied a quarter of the available space.

I hope I am breaking no confidences, but the sight of the group's drummer, hammering away in a sports coat thrown over police uniform, was a measure of comfort in the intimidating surroundings. The interview went very well, despite my butterflies – an indication of Mr Jackson's skill at putting his guests at ease. C'wai sat in his chair as if a television appearance was part of his daily routine. The only time I saw him sit up was when the cameras zoomed in for a close-up. The interview lasted six minutes, quite long enough in the steaming heat and glaring lights.

I am left in no doubt as to the power of television. Immediately after the programme, I received no less than five telephone calls from acquaintances of long ago, people thought to be dead.

I eventually got away from the telephone and went with Inspector Jones and C'wai to the Mzilikaze Camp where the old Bushman was staying. At the clinic, I escorted C'wai, who was clutching a bottle of beer, to his bed and said my farewells. I don't think he has ever been as rich as he was then. Everybody seemed to ladle out ten shilling notes in his direction and they were all tied into a grubby handkerchief. I only hope that after his experience he landed safely at home with his money intact and that the comparative wealth will bring the wonderful old man a few small comforts in his darkening years. He deserves every penny of the money.

Having said goodbye with a heavy heart, Inspector Jones took me to the Blue Lamp, the main Bulawayo canteen, where yet another host of welcomes awaited. Introductions came thick and fast and so did the drinks. Our few minutes of television appeared to have gone down well. Questions and answers followed and, with a glass which never seemed to empty itself, I hope that I entertained as much as I was entertained. It was a wonderful evening.

Very late that night, Inspector Jones took me back to my flat. I must thank him again for his hospitality. The whole of that evening I seemed to be swimming through waves and waves of froth. Each wave, as it broke, revealed yet another smiling face asking me to "have another."

At five in the morning I was awakened by the patrol officer on night shift who brought with him a jug of scalding coffee. It was time to start the journey homeward after three hectic days and three very hectic nights. I shall never forget those days in Bulawayo or the people who made the visit possible and so enjoyable.

Thank you, everyone.

TWO WHO SAVED EACH OTHER 55 YEARS AGO

Chronicle Reporter

TWO men who, 55 years ago, each saved the other's life, met again yesterday, with tears in his eyes, Mr. Ebenezer Mocke flung his arms around N'cwai, a Bushman he had found dying of thirst with a large ostrich in his foot in the Kalahari Desert.

Mr. Mocke, a trooper with the BSAP at the time, was trekking down on safari routine. He nursed N'cwai back to health — and the African never forgot.

Soon afterwards, Mr. Mocke was charged by an elephant. He was knocked against a tree and his kneecap was shattered. N'cwai made a skin bandage and poultice from animal guts.

Then, as Mr. Mocke was recovering, a wilderness came at him out of the brush. He could not move out of the way. But N'cwai killed it with a hunting axe.

Eventually N'cwai got Mr. Mocke to hospital. As doctors were marvelling at the way in which his time had responded to the primitive treatment, N'cwai was heading back to his kraal — his debt paid. He later moved to Tjolotjo.

Yesterday they were reunited at the BSAP pavilion at the Trade Fair. They clasped hands and tears filled their eyes.

Mr. Mocke (80) is now retired on his great-nephew's farm near Salisbury.

He said: "I just can't believe it — had it not been for N'cwai I would not be here today. He is a very wonderful man — I just don't know what to say."

N'cwai, who is over 75, just sat and grinned as they talked of the old times and the adventures they had together. They will now return to their homes — with memories of the old days much fresher in their minds.

The two old warriors, Mr. Mocke and N'cwai, meet after 55 years.

Cutting from Bulawayo Chronicle, May 1968

OBITUARY

THE REGIMENTAL NUMBER 1437 has been seen for the last time among the credits to stories in this magazine. Eben Mocke died in the Salisbury General Hospital on February 16 after several years of poor health. Born in the Orange Free State in 1891, he grew up in Pretoria during the time of the Boer War, and shared with General Louis Botha's children the services of an English governess. Later he attended night school with a job as a solicitor's clerk during the day. Finally, in 1911, he came to Rhodesia and on May 9 joined the B.S.A. Police.

Mr. Mocke's career in the Force has been adequately chronicled over the years within these pages. His patrols in 1912 and 1913 were the foundations for the story "Kalahari Patrol" and the more recent and unfortunately incomplete "South African Rebellion" told of his activities as an intelligence officer in the Transvaal. In 1915 with his initial contract with the Force expired, but being unable to secure his release because of World War I, Mr. Mocke went to India – without official permission – with the intention of joining the British Army there. After a court battle over his "extradition", he was eventually escorted back to Rhodesia by Lieutenant (later Commissioner) J.S. Morris. After serving a short sentence in the Depot Guardroom, he was sent to Makaha on the Eastern Border and his experiences there were again described in *Outpost*. Having contracted a severe dose of blackwater fever, he was sent back to Salisbury and left the Force on October 13, 1918.

Eben then went back to South Africa but in 1922 returned to Rhodesia where he engaged in mining activities and various land deals. He was largely responsible for the sub-division of farms in the immediate vicinity of Gwelo and the development of these areas as suburbs of the town. Later he returned to mining and then farmed for many years at Elandsvei near Umvuma. Finally he came to live on his nephew's farm on the outskirts of Salisbury. To condense the life of Eben Mocke into a few lines is almost impossible; to summarise the character of someone who really deserves the title of latter-day pioneer is impossible. A small indication of the esteem in which he was held was when he visited the Bulawayo Trade Fair in 1968 and stayed in the Police Mess at Hillside. The young patrol officers at the station kept Eben from his bed until the small hours, urging him to tell more of his stories of the early days. Although a fund of his writings have been published, there was so much more which could have been written.

The cremation service took place at Warren Hills on February 18. Trumpeters of the B.S.A. Police sounded the "Last Post" and Superintendent F.A.

Punter, Superintendent D.F. Jones (who had hosted Eben during his Bulawayo visit), *Outpost's* editor and several old comrades were among the mourners.

To Eben's sisters in South Africa and his niece and her husband, Mr and Mrs J.D. McClymount, we offer the deepest condolences on the loss of a great friend.

Alan Stock
Salisbury
March 1972

THE STORIES OF EBEN MOCKE

"1437"

Editor's Note.

Before advancing too far from the Boer War, Mocke interpreted a couple of legends of the time with the formerly unpublished commentary on President Kruger's "hidden bullion" and the even more romantic adventures of South Africa's Robin Hood of the late 19th century, Scotty Smith. These early stories also included "The Taking of Pretoria" and "Tommy Pals".

THE TAKING OF PRETORIA

An Englishman's Account

"We have pleasure to publish the following interesting footnote to history." Editor: *Police Review*

The night and day previous to the taking of the capital of the late South African Republic are indelibly stamped on my mind.

Fighting had been going on all this day. If you happened to ask a citizen the meaning of this continual firing (which could be plainly heard in town), he would reply: "It is the artillery practising to get into form when the 'rooies' (red-necks) should chance to march on Pretoria."

This and numerous other conjectures were heard on all sides up to midday, but at this time a balloon, obviously belonging to Lord Roberts' column, was seen to pass over the town, whereupon the "practising" assumed more serious proportions.

The news spread like wildfire that the British troops were outside the town. A panic among the womenfolk immediately followed; they rushed all the shops and helped themselves to anything they fancied. I happened to be passing a produce store on this fatal day and, on hearing a great commotion in the place, directed my steps thereto. To my amazement, I saw no less than 25 women trying to get at various items such as mealies, salt, flour, coffee, corn, etc. This place was absolutely blocked with these different commodities. It was a common sight to see women sling bags of mealies over their shoulders and march out of the store with them, arguing as to the owner of this and that bag – fighting, pulling hair, biting and even kicking one another in argument. One woman, never realising the danger of the act, pulled some bags out of the middle of a stack and the whole lot collapsed on top of her. She died of suffocation before she was released.

The real owners of these different stores became desperate. They took to arms, killing and wounding several people during the course of the day.

About seven o'clock in the evening, the Dutch were driven from the south-eastern fort and rushed pell-mell through the streets of Pretoria, eventually getting into the open country beyond. After the Dutch garrison had all left the town, things became quiet and remained so throughout the succeeding night.

The sun, on rising next morning, showed the British in possession of Pretoria. Martial law was immediately proclaimed.

One of the earliest noticeable signs of the British occupation was the remarkable change in the demeanour of the natives resident in the town. They crowded onto the pavements and jostled the white inhabitants in a manner hitherto undreamed of. In ensuing scuffles, several natives got injured and died of the effects.

At 10 a.m., the British prisoners confined in the Boer camp were released and marched back to their own lines. Great was their rejoicing. The British troops presented rather a doleful spectacle on entering the city. They were unwashed and unkempt – nearly choked with dust – suffering greatly from the pangs of hunger and thirst. Demands for bread and water were heard on all sides.

As is known, the taking of Pretoria practically marked the conclusion of the Boer War.

"Spectator"

TOMMY PALS

Lord Roberts had occupied Pretoria and British soldiers were stationed throughout the city acting as policemen.

It was mid-afternoon and my twelfth birthday was still a month away as I peered through the gap in the cypress hedge around our house, the gap which my younger brother, Godfrey, and I regarded as our escape route into the new and unknown world of our invaded city. My eyes widened and a shiver went down my back. There were two Tommies just a few yards down the road, apparently guarding the junction of Boom and Market Streets. These were the intruders my parents and grown-up brothers had whispered about when they thought Godfrey and I and our sisters were not listening.

Carefully I withdrew from my vantage point and ran as fast as my bare feet would carry me to where Godfrey was playing with our clay horses under the apple trees in the back yard.

"Godfrey, Godfrey," I stammered breathlessly. "The Tommies are right outside in the street."

"Where? Show me." His excitement did nothing to calm my nervousness.

"On the corner…and they have rifles and long knives hanging from their belts. But we must tie Nero in his kennel before he gets wind of them and starts barking. They are sure to shoot him," I gulped.

Our pet Newfoundland dog was duly tethered before we made our way to the gap in the hedge.

"Don't make a noise and don't let them see you," I whispered.

Cautiously I poked my head through the thick cypress in the direction of the intersection with Godfrey impatiently nudging me in order to get a clearer view. But now there was only one soldier standing there, partially obscured by a tree. We leaned out further for a clearer view.

"Hello there, Sonny," came a hoarse croaking voice from the road behind us. Two heads turned as one and then froze. Our fright must have been very apparent.

"Don't be afraid, boys."

The second soldier had obviously walked up the road past our hole in the hedge. There was no escape. I stumbled onto the road with Godfrey clinging to my waist and nervously extended my right hand.

"Dag, Oomie," I mumbled.

The soldier smiled at my discomfort but gently shook my hand. For the first time I noticed how soiled his uniform was. His unshaven face was dirt-streaked, the white furrows telling their own story of sweat and strain. He was certainly a sorry sight and his next words underlined his discomfort.

"Reckon you could find us something to eat and drink?" he asked.

By this time the Tommy had been joined by his companion who was in a similar distressed and dishevelled state. My agitation had turned to sympathy.

"I will try, Oomie. Wait here."

Grabbing Godfrey's hand, I dragged him after me through the hedge, down the garden path, into the kitchen and the passage beyond.

"Mama, Mama, where are you?"

"Here, what on earth is the matter?" Mother came out of her bedroom.

"Mama, there are two Tommies dying on the road. They need water and something to eat."

"Take them some water if you must. But I have nothing for them to eat. Let Lord Roberts feed his troops, that's his job. We have barely enough for ourselves."

Despite the reduced circumstances that had accompanied our move from the farm into Pretoria, Mother had continued to work miracles in the kitchen. Godfrey and I protested:

"No, no, Mama. You must help them. They will die unless we give them some proper food. Please, Mama?"

Still muttering her protests, mother led us to the pantry and handed us a loaf of potato bread (flour had not been seen for months), a chunk of butter, a jug of milk and an enamel cup. Clutching the provisions we hurried back to the hole in the hedge.

"God bless you both," said "Our Tommies" who by sharing our food had been formally adopted by my brother and me. We watched as the bread was washed down with great gulps of milk, interrupted only by further expressions of gratitude. Eventually the milk jug and the enamel jug were returned to me and, with what I thought was a bit more spring in their steps and another chorus of thanks and farewell, the two soldiers shuffled off back to the intersection where I had first spotted them. Godfrey and I watched them for a while and then we went back into the house. I do not know when their duties ended and I expected never to see them again.

At sunset, I was sent on my second chore of charity of the day. Mother told me to take a jug of milk to an elderly neighbour just down the road.

"Please tell Mrs. Pentz that this is all I can spare today – thanks to you and your soldier friends." Mother had discovered the old lady living alone – her two sons off fighting somewhere – and had taken pity on her.

As I neared the Pentz homestead, I was surprised to hear loud, angry and abusive words punctuating the silence of the night. With the typical inquisitiveness of a twelve-year-old, I shamelessly crept in through the kitchen door, on into the passage which ran from the front to the back of the Pentz house and peeped through a crack in the curtain that divided the dining room from the corridor.

Mrs Pentz was sitting in her usual chair in great despair, heaving great sobs of anguish into her handkerchief. Standing in front of her and on either side were two young men whom I much later identified as her sons, Koen and Michael Pentz. The unshaven Koen, dressed in ragged clothing and battered leggings, was in stark contrast to the younger, slightly slimmer soldier in his neat khaki uniform complete with puttees and strong polished boots. Koen was in a fearsome rage, the cords in his neck standing out beneath a red perspiring face. The torrent of abuse, totally unfit for the ears of a young eavesdropper but of no doubt as to meaning, was directed at his brother. The reason for Koen's anger was that Michael had just enlisted in the British Army.

"You bloody turncoat! I can't forgive you for joining the filthy British! I'll kill you if I get you in my sights after this night."

"That's enough, Koen. God will never forgive you for threatening to kill your brother," pleaded Mrs Pentz before relapsing into another fit of sobs and groans. But there was no stopping Koen.

"With the greatest respect to God and to you, Mother, Michael has decided to join our sworn enemies, those who murdered our father, our relatives and our many friends in this unjust war of their making. How my own brother could become a verdomde hands-upper, a traitor, I cannot understand. I no longer recognise him as my kin and I challenge his choice of joining those who go on killing those who I am proud to call my brothers."

Michael stood there just shaking his head. As Koen paused for breath, he answered the charges in – to start with, at least – a more reasoned tone.

"How did you expect Mother and me to live while you were roaming the country being a nationalist hero? Our supplies of food ran out months ago so how could I return to the Kommando and leave Mama alone here in Pretoria to starve?"

One question was met with another.

"How in hell's name did all the others manage to survive without joining the bloody British?" demanded Koen.

I think the argument would have gone back and forth for ever if Mrs Pentz had not exhibited another dramatic outburst, her clenched fists beating in frustration on the arms of her chair in time with her sobbing while the tears continued to pour down her cheeks, all interspersed with pleas that the brothers forgive each other. But Koen was unmoved by his mother's distress. Again he yelled his accusations of treachery at his brother before taking his departure.

"I will not stay for another minute under the same roof as this damned 'hands-upper'. It matters not that the whole British Army has surrounded Pretoria. I am getting out and joining General de la Rey at the Swartruggens. This war is far from over and our sacrifices will ensure our victory…" A last insult flung at his brother "unlike traitors such as my cowardly former brother here whose cold feet have sped them into the ranks of the enemy."

As Koen embraced his mother in farewell, I looked for somewhere to hide and pressed myself behind coats hanging at the side of a cupboard in the passage. Koen raged past me and, as I waited for him to get clear, I heard Michael trying to comfort Mrs Pentz. I left the milk jug on the kitchen table and ran home as fast as I could, half expecting to hear shots as my "Tommy Pals" encountered the distraught Koen Pentz as he made his escape.

Two years later Peace had been declared at Vereeniging but there was still enough tension in Pretoria to warrant issuing a Proclamation providing for a dawn-to-dusk curfew. However, the removal of the threat posed by the remaining Transvaal bittereinders was sufficient to prompt my father into thoughts of the future. After supper and prayers one evening, my father said to me:

"Sonny, do you think you can get to the farm on Buller, see what has happened there and return before sunset the same day?"

I had been allowed to bring Buller, my pony named in happier times after General Sir Redvers Buller, to Pretoria, a concession which, in respect of what it cost to keep the pony fed, must have had a crippling effect on my mother's housekeeping resources. Here was a chance to justify Buller's upkeep, in addition to the excitement the journey offered me.

"Of course, Papa," I replied excitedly. "Buller is very fit and I could be back here long before sunset." But another voice had to be heard…

"No, no, David," Mama pleaded with my father. "It is still far too dangerous. You cannot let the child go that far by himself. Anything might happen and we would never forgive ourselves."

"But, Lizzie," argued my father, "there might be livestock surviving at the farm and requiring urgent attention. It is time we thought of the future."

"And Mama," I joined in, "Buller is so fast that nothing can catch us. I promise I will be very careful."

The arguments for and against the venture went back and forth but eventually Papa won the day – but with my mother extracting all sorts of cautionary promises from me.

I left just before dawn the next day…after once again swearing to heed Mama's injunctions while at the same time gambling that there would be no troops trying to enforce the curfew in the initial stages of the journey. Buller relished his release as we cantered through Pretoria; past Berea Park, past Jesse's Cottage of Rider Haggard fame, through the vista of weeping willow trees leading down to the old wooden bridge spanning the bubbling current downstream of The Fountains, Pretoria's main water supply. By this time dawn was breaking fast with the twittering of the birds swelling into a chorus to welcome the new day; the rising sun painting the unruffled leaves with a delicate pink. But there was still something unsettling about the morning, not least the grotesque shadows creeping out from under the trees surrounding us. I was almost beginning to think that Mama was right in her caution as Buller cantered into this spooky environment. Before reaching the bridge, I reined in and walked Buller right into the water. A large notice warned "Brug Gevaarlik", but there was no difficulty in fording the river and rejoining the road on the far side of the bridge. It was time for Buller to draw breath and perhaps take a drink.

The pony shuffled sideways in the stream, nuzzling for refreshment at a different point. Suddenly Buller snorted, pricked his ears forward and strained his head in the direction of the riverbank ahead of me. I followed his gaze and went cold as I made out a man's figure outstretched and motionless on the far riverbank. I turned Buller and edged closer.

Never before had I seen a corpse but there was no doubt that this figure in the khaki uniform was very dead. I took in the glazed eyes staring unseeingly heavenwards. Even more shocking was the hideous red line framed in the blood-soaked loosened neck of the tunic. Around the open mouth, from which I imagined a last desperate cry for help was forever frozen, the thin stubble of the soldier's beard looked like the pin feathers of a plucked chicken.

My stomach heaved. I dug my heels into Bller's flanks, guided him around the horror on the riverbank and gave the pony his head. He seemed to share my near panic and we raced up the road at a barely-controlled gallop. Why hadn't I listened to my mother's advice?

The road was straight for some distance before one rounded a slight bend and the blockhouse beside the gate across the road was revealed. I reined Buller back from his madcap gallop as we reached the gate but his snorting was enough to bring the uniformed sentry from his refuge with many complaints.

"Where d'you think you are going at this time of day, young man? The sun is still asleep and you should still be safe in bed. I can only let you through…" His tone changed suddenly. "Good God!" he exclaimed, "It's good Samaritan. Sam, Sam, bring the keys and come and welcome a little friend of ours."

Only then did I recognise the first of the two Tommies that Godfrey and I had adopted outside our house those many months ago. His colleague, pulling on his tunic, strode from the blockhouse. In the meantime, the first Tommy must have realised from my ashen face that I was close to panic. As soon as the gate had been unlocked, I was helped from the saddle while Sam's companion, Bill, held my sweating pony's reins.

"What brings you here in such a state, first thing in the morning, Sonny?" asked Sam gently with a calming hand on my shoulder.

"Oomie, Oomie," I stuttered. "I have just seen a dead man, a dead soldier, back there by the river." In my broken English, I tried to communicate the full horror of the scene I had encountered beside the bridge. I got more and more frustrated as the two Tommies appeared to take my all too recent experience only half-seriously.

"Calm down, Sonny. Come and have a cup of tea and tell us all about it in your own good time." With his hand still on my shoulder, Sam steered me towards the door of the blockhouse. Bill relocked the gate and led Buller in our wake.

Inside the blockhouse were another half-dozen or so soldiers, a few of them still sleeping while others prepared themselves for the day. After Sam had introduced me – the way he spoke, you would think Godfrey and I had laid on a feast for Bill and himself that morning in Pretoria – a mug of sugar-laced tea was pressed into my hand, instructions were given to off- saddle Buller, rub him down, water and feed him a loaf of bread. I was given a large piece of chocolate before the subject of the dead man by the river was mentioned.

"Now then, Sonny, what's this about the dead man you say you've just seen?" asked Bill. The other soldiers stopped what they were doing to hang on to my answer.

"Ja, Oomie, down by the old footbridge. Under the willows. He looked like a soldier and…I think his throat's been cut!" Although I was still in a state of shock, I didn't miss the looks that passed between some of my audience – here was a teenager with too much imagination. Bill was more sympathetic. He turned to Sam.

"We had better take a look after the corporal has made his rounds, Sam. Perhaps the lad has seen something. So what are you up to so early in the morning and so soon after curfew?"

I explained how Papa had asked me to ride down to the farm that we had left at the height of the troubles. I told him that I was supposed to find out what was left of our livestock and the state of the buildings. That led to questions about the exact location of the farm, what we had been doing before taking refuge in Pretoria, how we had managed to survive in the city and many other enquiries.

My tales of hardship, told against a background of kitchen noises and the delicious smell of bacon frying, fortuitously ended in an invitation to share the Tommies' breakfast. During the meal, my programme for the day was mapped out for me.

"There has been no trouble around here for many weeks," said Sam. "You will be safe on the road to the farm and you should get there just after midday without difficulty. Take your time looking around and try to get back here before five o'clock and we'll see you back to Pretoria safely before sunset. Meanwhile, we'll look into your story of the man with his throat cut."

My pony had been looked after almost as generously as its owner and with the good wishes of the Tommies ringing in our ears, we were soon on the way to the farm again.

Sam's estimate was good and we reached the farm just before noon. But I was horrified at the complete devastation of the home I had grown up in. Only the stone walls of the house and the large stables had been left standing. Even the big orchard and the gum plantation had been set on fire, leaving gaunt, black-ended stumps where once Godfrey and I had climbed so happily. There was no trace of wildlife other than a few red, long-legged plovers that screeched their annoyance at my intrusion.

The desolation was such that all I wanted to do was to return to Pretoria as soon as possible. The journey back was uneventful and it was only mid-afternoon when we reached the blockhouse. Although there seemed to be a much greater sense of purpose among the Tommies than I had sensed – despite my shocked state – at sun-up, I was given a warm reception, more tea and food and subjected to a barrage of questions about what I had found at the farm. Years later, I came to the conclusion that the soldiers' concern at my findings on the farm and their earlier interest on how we had managed to exist as a family amid Pretoria's hardships, had something to do with a collective sense of guilt at the scorched earth tactics of the hostilities.

It was Sam who eventually ended the discussions, reminding me that I still had a few miles to cover to get home before sunset. As I tightened Buller's girth, a knapsack swollen with an assortment of groceries was secured behind the saddle. Sam said something about this being no more than the thanks my family deserved for our generosity when the troops had marched into Pretoria.

Their hospitality was so overwhelming that it was only when I was in the saddle that it struck me that the old bridge and its horror lay ahead. "Did you find the dead man at the bridge, Oomie?" I enquired.

"Yes, Sonny, we did. I didn't want to mention it earlier and remind you of your frightening experience. The man was a Joiner, who was supposed to help us here as an interpreter. Despite all the troubles, we can't understand why he should have been killed so brutally.

He lived close to you in Pretoria.

His name was Michael Pentz."

PRESIDENT KRUGER'S BURIED GOLD

Rumours of buried gold are almost impossible to erase from the minds of the greedy and the credulous. The Anglo-Boer War sowed more than a few such seeds but the most widespread gossip of the time, and for many years thereafter, was over the bullion that the former President, Paul Kruger, was supposed to have buried somewhere in the Transvaal. Those who undoubtedly and exclusively reaped the benefits of such tales were the swindlers who set up syndicates to finance expeditions in search of the legendary, if fictitious, hoard.

Among the latter was Count von Veltheim who artfully promoted the Kruger Gold story to the extent of floating not one but two successive syndicates which attracted considerable sums of money from contributors. A large part of the investment found its way into the Count's pocket and the failure of his first attempt to find the buried treasure apparently did nothing to deter a second group of backers from falling prey to his persistence and sponsoring another search.

Unsurprisingly, the Count's title lacked no more substance than his proclaimed objective and he was exposed as no more than a German soldier of fortune. Although he had bamboozled his way into government circles, he was banished from the country. Von Veltheim wriggled his way back into South Africa via Rhodesia and Portuguese East Africa some years later but was quickly discovered and expelled for the second time.

The Count was by no means the only one to claim knowledge of the whereabouts of the Kruger Gold. The legend was a magnet not only for wealthy investors but also for the financially deprived – but ambitious…such as myself.

I had just started work in my first job at the Land Settlement Board in Pretoria. One of my young colleagues there was President Kruger's grandson – not that this relationship had any direct bearing on the invitation that followed. He came to me one day and asked if I wanted money and lots of it. I replied predictably.

"Old Man Immelman knows where my grandfather's gold is buried but wants some help digging for it. Immelman's 14-year-old son, Isaac, has been told by the spirit of his dead mother where the fortune is to be found. If you promise to keep the location secret and help us with the digging, the fortune will be equally divided among those who do the work."

O credulous youth! I may have had my doubts but I was all for the venture and it was arranged that we should meet Immelman and his son at the drift in the

Aapies River after work the next afternoon. The father produced a chart and pointed out the direction we should follow. About a mile from the drift and some distance from the road to Eloffsdal, the son stopped, looked round for a couple of minutes and nodded. "It should be hereabouts, Papa," said Isaac, indicating several small bushes in the vicinity.

We hacked at the ground and shovelled dirt after work for three weeks. We discovered perspiration, blisters and aching muscles but not a speck of gold – let alone a cache of gold bars.

Back in 1895 there had been turmoil on the Johannesburg Stock Market and many had been badly bitten. Some of the latter went to "Oom Paul" for sympathy and with the request for strict laws to regulate dealings on the Exchange. The wise old President is reputed to have replied:

"You people remind me of the monkey I once had. I was standing at the fire one night in the bushveld when the monkey came and sat between my legs, began fidgeting and finally ended up with his tail in the fire. Whereupon he bit me on my leg. So it is with you people. You go in for reckless speculation and blame me for the con-sequences."

And so it was with me! I felt like biting young Isaac and telling him to stay awake at night instead of dreaming of gold bars.

Half a century later, the rumour surfaced that the Kruger gold was buried in the Zoutpansberg in the far north. The basis for this was that in 1890 it was half-expected that the President would lead his men in a last stand near what is now Louis Trichardt and that the gold had been sent ahead to finance the battle.

While Paul Kruger's grandson had taken me on a merry chase when I was still wet behind the ears, by the time the Zoutpansberg rumours reached ears which were starting to fade I had discovered strong evidence that Kruger's gold was no more than a fable, evidence from none other than my own brother!

The last gold in the Pretoria State Mint, together with coin from the Standard Bank, all worth an estimated half-million pounds, had been packed, loaded and transported to Pretoria's railway station escorted by a troop of the State Artillery commanded by FS Mocke only a few hours before Roberts marched into the city. Still under escort, the gold had been railed to Delagoa Bay in Mozambique and shipped to Holland. Keeping it in the family, among the Zoutpansberg enthusiasts years later were some cousins of mine.

It appears to have mattered little that before his death my brother had written to the Johannesburg *Sunday Times*, warning members of yet another embryo Kruger gold syndicate that they were wasting their time and money. The syndicate took no notice – such is the deafness accompanying greed – and went ahead with their search, this time mostly in the North Eastern Transvaal around

Alkmaar where a train had tumbled off a bridge. It had been suggested that this was the train that had been carrying the gold.

President Kruger's wealth, buried or not, has been the subject of controversy for decades. One of Cecil Rhodes' biographers, "Vindex" claimed that a characteristic of Rhodes was his admiration for the stout old Boer President who "without a penny in his treasury and no immediate prospects of meeting his obligations, yet set so high and set to work so promptly and vigorously to translate his purpose into action."

Another commentator writes: "At the time of the President's departure, his enemies set on foot the silly rumour to the effect that he was 'running away' and deserting his country. His whole life is the refutation of this canard."

Another piece of gossip, which ultimately grew into a legend, was that Paul Kruger was possessed of millions in gold and that, as he had no time to take this treasure with him, most of it was buried somewhere in the eastern Transvaal, possibly even on the Rand.

"In later years, treasure-hunting expeditions were set on foot to search for the Kruger gold. These originated either from stupidity or a desire to make successful dupes. There was no Kruger gold. Official statements were issued denying its existence. It was shown that the Transvaal Government possessed only £60 000 in cash when war was declared and that the President had given £40 000 to £50 000 of his own private money – he was a creditor of the country when he left Komati Poort in September 1900.

Just before Pretoria was occupied, the President told an American journalist that the war thus far had cost £4 000 000 and, with the help of God Almighty, they would carry it on indefinitely as they were getting £1 000 000 a month from the mines. It was shewn that the monies belonging to the miners – amounting to £280 000 of which £80 000 was invested on mortgage – was in the hands of the Treasurer-General; the deposits in the Post Office Bank were £300 000, also placed on mortgage. At the beginning of 1900 there was a run on the Savings Bank and the Government then authorised the Treasurer-General to pay over to the Paymaster-General £250 000 to meet the calls on the Savings Bank whose mortgages were to serve as security. However, in 1903 it was rumoured that the President and Dr Leyds still retained £1 000 000 as a 'war chest' – but no evidence was forthcoming. The 'Kruger Gold' was a myth!"

                        Acknowledgement to Manfred Nathan

Much has been said of Oom Paul's personal fortune over the years. During a session of the Volksraad in 1892, a provocative member proposed that the annual salary of the President should be reduced from £8 000 to £5 000. The proposal was undoubtedly a personal attack and the President ought to have absented himself from the ensuing debate but he was unwise enough to remain in the Raad. He intervened in the discussion to say that if his salary was to be reduced then the salaries of all officials should be reduced in like proportions. The proposal was rejected.

During the next session (1893), the President himself proposed that his salary be reduced from £8 000 to £7 000 while the salaries of the Commandant-General, General Joubert, and the Vice-President, General Smit, were to be increased. This was accepted and was regarded as a generous gesture on the President's part, seeing that the salaries of all permanent officials had recently been increased. In addition to his salary, the President received an annual allowance of £300 for "coffee money", his customary form of hospitality being the dispensing of innumerable cups of coffee to all and sundry who came calling.

In his book, *Paul Kruger*, Manfred Nathan writes:

"The prattling Wilson tells us that the President insisted that his monthly salary be brought to him in gold – after which it was paid into the bank. According to the same authority, Leyds had invested £700,000 for Kruger in Java and £400,000 in Berlin, while the cash value of his possessions was £2,500,000. He goes on to suggest that the President was of a miserly turn of mind and never spent anything besides his coffee money nor contributed anything to charity.

On the other hand he recalls a personal donation of £500 to a relief fund and a contribution of £100 to a synagogue while after the Dynamite Explosion of 1896 the Executive immediately gave a donation of £25,000 for relief."

In fact, Kruger helped many people with money although his name does not appear on subscription lists.

Despite his ownership of many farms, Kruger was not always possessed of ready cash. It was only in the 1890 session of the Volksraad that the president's salary was fixed at £8 000 having been increased to this figure from the original £3 000. During the same session the Volksraad granted him a loan of £7 000 at two-and-a-half per cent. The reason given was that he was short of ready money and did not want to borrow from financial institutions that might have involved a conflict of interest.

Kruger had numerous relatives who were always coming to see him, seeking assistance. But by the time of the Anglo-Boer War, he had accumulated a good deal and was able to lend the State £40 000 for necessities from his private funds. This loan was never repaid.

Information from S H du Plessis, Master of the Supreme Court, Pretoria, reveals that President Kruger left £35 381-15-1 in cash, and personal effects to the value of only £100. Debts and administrative costs amounted to £6 791-7-1, leaving a balance of £28 690-8-0 for distribution among the heirs. A claim for the repayment by the Government of the £40 000 plus interest was abandoned by the Executors.

Paul Kruger had sixteen children and there were 120 grand-children. This was one reason why the President, notwithstanding his salary of £8 000 per year, died comparatively poor! There was always some importunate member of the clan needing assistance, in addition to which Oom Paul often made loans to needy burghers for which he asked no security nor sought interest. In many instances, it is doubtful if any record of such benevolence was kept.

Riches did not seem to matter to Kruger although his enemies labelled him a moneymaker. He freely contributed to the State's finances and he never expected repayment of his £40 000 loan, made to buy weapons and feed and clothe his field forces as they fought for their existence.

The abiding vision of Paul Kruger is that of a rough, rugged, resolute, daring and dominant figure, an Ajax defying the lightning. He may be compared to a giant crag with its base rooted in the ancient rock, its sides scarred and weathered by many a storm, yet still rearing its head to the skies through the ages to come.

And, may I conclude, completely without the stigma of concealing precious gold beneath the ground while his burghers in the field fought great odds and deprivation to retain their precious independence.

SCOTTY SMITH

Illustration at the head of the story in *The Outpost* of September 1968

Venom dripped from every bitten-off word as the tall fair customer threatened the bank manager in an unmistakable Australian twang.

"I deposited £7 000 in your bank when, on your advice, I bought 7 000 one pound shares in the diamond company that went into liquidation less than a week after I got the script." He pointed his right forefinger at the manager before jabbing him in the chest with it to emphasise each word: "I swear I'll get back my hard-earned money from you, in any way I can!"

Scotty Smith turned and strode out of the office, leaving the manager trembling in fear. The latter had every reason to be frightened...

The next morning, soon after arriving at his bank, he called the police to tell them the bank had been entered during the night, the safe blown, and £6 000 had been stolen. The bank manager signed an affidavit on which Scotty Smith was, with much publicity, arrested. He was duly arraigned before the Kimberley Magistrate and charged with the robbery, but was discharged after producing a watertight alibi.

Johan Beyers drove his Cape-cart through the partially grass-grown street of Boshoff, a small settlement in the Orange Free State around which the neighbouring farms revolved, and brought the fast-moving team of frisky horses to an abrupt halt in front of the bank. He handed the reins over to the Hottentot groom beside him, stepped down and hurried into the building.

"Good morning, Mr Berry," he greeted the bank manager. "I got your urgent message last night and came as soon as I could."

"Good morning, Mr Beyers. I am reluctant to ask you to do this, but could you make another trip for me to Kimberley? I'm very worried about safety and I'd like you to go as soon as you can," Berry continued.

Beyers laughed, showing his white teeth between black moustache and spade beard, but his hazel eyes stared steadily at the manager, who was fluttering his plump hands with worry.

"Of course I'll go. What's the rush? Has Old Man Strydom at last deposited that small fortune he must have got for his diamond mine?"

"No, the old miser hasn't been near the bank, but I've got some other large deposits and I want you to take the money to the bank in Kimberley where it'll be a good deal safer than it would be here."

"Okay, sort out the shekels, seal the bags and I'll sign the receipts and be on the road right away. But what's the rush to get the money to Kimberley?" said Beyers, following Berry through to another room.

While sorting the money into bags and sealing them, Berry, a man in his forties with deceptively piercing blue eyes, asked: "You must have heard of that outlaw, Scotty Smith?" Beyers only nodded as the bank manager continued: "I heard the other day that the authorities on the Diamond fields have been making things hot for him and that he's left there looking for pastures new. Well, I gather he's working over this way and I don't intend being caught unawares with a lot of money in the safe."

Beyers reassured the manager, reminding him of his hard-earned reputation as both a reliable courier and an excellent marksman, helped the banker seal the last of the moneybags, and signed the receipts. He told Berry he would start immediately on the road to Kimberley, spend the night at his farm, which was some way from Boshoff, and continue the long trek at dawn the following day. With the help of two bank officials, the bags of money and a wallet containing other papers were locked in a cubby-hole built for the purpose in the wagon's dashboard and the courier left town. Beyers drove straight to his farm, Merriesfontein, and stepped down from the cart, slapping the dust out of his hat as his wife, Elizabeth, rushed out onto the stoep and threw her arms around him. She watched in silence as he transferred the moneybags from the cart to the house. As he dropped the last bag, she clutched at his arm and spoke quietly, her voice shaking with some urgency.

"Johan, I'm scared at the thought of you going away at this time. Oupa and Ouma Smit called in for coffee while you were in town and told me this bandit Scotty Smith raped a woman near Kimberley and robbed her of all her valuables. Not only that, but he half-killed an old man in the same area for a pitiful ten shillings." She gestured with disgust. "According to Oupa, the authorities have offered a reward for the capture of this ruffian and have published a description of him. You'd better keep an eye out for him: he's six feet tall, slim, fair, clean-shaven and riding a chestnut stallion sixteen hands high with a white blaze and four white socks."

Beyers held his wife to him and reassured her, telling her in so many words that she should not try to apply her respectable standards to the rough crowd of miners, hangers-on and outright criminals who were trying to scrabble a fortune out of the Kimberley diamond fields. To them, he told her, anything that got in the way of them making their fortunes or slowing the path to riches had to be disposed of by fair means or foul and shoved aside with no thought as to the consequences.

"He who worries most has usually the least to worry about. Oupa Smit fits that bill but don't fret about me, my dear. I can handle myself and we're so far from

Kimberley that I very much doubt if Smith will show up to cause trouble here. But, just in case, I'll arrange for the boys to keep an eye out for you and the horses." Not wishing to alarm his wife further, he said nothing to his wife about the bank manager's worries.

At dawn the following morning, Beyers hitched the four eager horses to the Cape-cart, stowed the money in the dashboard and placed his loaded rifle and spare ammunition on the seat beside him where they would be within easy reach.

He then called over the two stable hands and gave them their instructions. They were to stay in or near the stables all the time until he returned and throughout the hours of darkness one of them was to remain awake and on guard because, as he told them, there was possibly a horse thief in the area. The farm had a reputation for the quality of its livestock while Scotty Smith was known to have a very discerning eye for horseflesh and the habit of replacing his mounts at the expense of farmers in the area in which he was operating.

Beyers kissed his wife, told her not to worry once again and turned his spirited team towards the Kimberley road. He held them at a steady trot while maintaining an alert gaze over the veld. After several hours of uneventful travel, the team reached a spruit of clear running water. This was a regular stop on the courier's frequent trips to Kimberley where he could water the horses and let them roll before the final haul into the town. With the exception of several large ant hills, there was no cover from where an ambush on the spruit could be staged. For several minutes, Beyers and his groom Klaas, scanned the veld all around them, but saw not a single living creature.

"Come Klaas, unhitch the horses quickly," Beyers ordered as he jumped down. "We must be on the move again as soon as possible." They outspanned the team and each led two beasts down to the water. While the horses drank, rolled and nibbled at the green grass growing by the stream's edge, Beyers rolled himself a cigarette and Klaas sat watching. Thirty minutes later, they led the rested beasts back up to the road and the cart. As Beyers, in the lead, reached level ground he stopped dead, his eyes opening wide with shock.

Standing next to the cart and nonchalantly swinging a revolver in his right hand, was a stranger. He was wearing the blue shirt, corduroy trousers and laced top boots that, with a jacket, was not unusual wear for the people of those parts. What was not typical was the red handkerchief across his face with two slits cut in it for the eyes. A wide-brimmed hat was pulled low across his forehead.

"Who the devil?" cried Beyers, glancing at his rifle, still lying on the seat of the Cape-cart. He cursed himself for his carelessness. "Don't try any tricks,

Beyers," warned the stranger. His voice had a hard metallic ring, muffled and distorted by the mask. "I'm Scotty Smith." He paused for a moment, as if to let that knowledge sink in. "I've unloaded your rifle and helped myself to no more than one bag of sovereigns. I regret I can't take more, especially as it belongs to those bloodsuckers at the bank. You hitch up and move on. "Beyers exploded with indignation. "If you think you can get away with this, you'd better think again. I'll..."

"Calm down, Beyers, I should hate to break one of your arms or legs with a bullet to make you see sense. You work for the bank by making these deliveries, and now you will share the responsibility for the bank robbing me. I reckon I'm more than entitled to this money. The only difference between what I do and what the bank does is that they steal with an appearance of legality. Come on, in-span and shove off...I've a long way to go."

"Okay. Come on. Klaas, we do as he says." To the grinning gunman: "You'll never get away with this, Smith." Beyer's face was suffused with anger and shame; This would never have happened if he had taken his rifle to the spruit with him. When the horses were hitched, he climbed up onto the seat and grasped the reins. Then the thought struck him: "I'll shoot him as soon as I'm out of range of his revolver."

He said to Smith: "Where did you hide? I can't see your horse and the Hottentot and I had a good look round before we out-spanned."

Smith chuckled into his mask. It was an eerie, expressionless sound. "My horse is hidden further up the spruit where the water has washed away a deep gap in the bank. I hid behind that big ant hill there." He pointed to an outcrop a hundred yards away. "It was easy to help myself to what I wanted when you went down to the spruit. By the way, when you do these hush-hush deliveries for the bank, you'd better be more careful. I found out exactly when you were leaving, how much money you were carrying, and even that you always stop at this spruit on the way into Kimberley."

Smith chuckled again as if reading Beyer's mind: "On your way back tomorrow, you'll find the cartridges for your rifle right here where I'm standing."

Beyers flushed again. Scotty Smith had made a complete fool of him. He started the team onto the road. No longer was he the alert and self-possessed man he had been on leaving his farm that morning.

As the cart disappeared into the distance, heading for the town, Smith checked the contents of the bag. He found £1 500, neatly made up of brown paper rolls with £50 in each. He scrambled down the bank to his horse, threw the bag over the saddle, mounted and turned the horse onto the road, going the opposite direction to Beyers. Smith followed the tracks Beyer's cart had made going the other way, and the sun was setting when a turn-off from the main track showed the wheel tracks plainly leading to a home-stead in the distance. Miles away, Johan Beyers brooded over his downfall. His hatred for Smith, who had destroyed his courier's reputation in a few minutes, boiled up in him until he could taste it. Close to Kimberley, he met his old friend, Pieter Gouws. He outspanned and the two men lit up cigarettes while Beyers related how the notorious Scotty Smith had robbed him at gunpoint on the track to Kimberley.

"That's damned funny," said Gouws. "Last week the police arrested a half-caste Griqua who had been masquerading as Smith. The native admitted to charges of rape, robbery and the theft of two horses. Public opinion against Smith has moderated quite sharply. Perhaps he's not as black as he's been painted."

Meanwhile, Elizabeth Beyers, the courier's wife, a tall comely brunette with large brown eyes and a perfect complexion, was preparing the evening meal for herself and her four children. Her cheeks were flushed a healthy red from the stove where she was on the point of turning a pancake. Frederick, her eldest son, dashed excitedly into the kitchen, shouting to his mother:

"Mama, Mama, there's a man on a horse at the front door who wants to talk to you. 'Wachter' and the other dogs won't let him dismount. Come quickly."

Swiftly, Elizabeth Beyers moved the pans off the hot stove, wiped her hands on her apron, and hurried to the front door of the farmhouse, stopping on the way to pat her hair. She stepped out on the stoep, and her welcoming smile instantly changed to one of concern. Her hands flew to her throat to stop the scream that caught at her.

"Allemagte!" she exclaimed. The man aiming his revolver at her snarling watchdogs was tall, fair and slim. The boerbulls were snapping at the hooves of his chestnut stallion, threatening to unseat him. There was no mistaking the white blaze and the four white socks of the horse. Her husband's warning and the visitor's identity crashed into her realisation. She shouted to the frantic dogs to quieten them and after the animals had reluctantly obeyed and the stranger had holstered his pistol, timidly invited him to dismount before enquiring about his business. Before she could stop herself, she told him in her nervousness that her husband was away and that she was alone apart from the four children. She said it almost as though begging for mercy!

The stranger appeared to recognise her discomfort, smiled kindly and told her he wanted no more than to rest overnight as both he and his horse were tired after their long journey. Mrs Beyers was reassured by the man's friendly attitude...despite the revolver, he sounded and, on closer inspection, looked like a gentleman. Could he really be the rapist Oupa Smit and David had warned her about. Customary bushveld hospitality came to the fore as she invited the visitor into the house.

"Thank you very much, I'll get my blanket roll and saddle-bags into the house, if one of your boys will look after the horse. By the way, my name is Forrester."

Mrs Beyers showed him to an empty room where he dropped his roll on the bed. With much uncertainty still in her mind, she ran back to her own room. She took a rifle from a cupboard, loaded it and hid the gun behind the lace curtains in the dining room. Then she called to Forrester:

"I'll send the girl in with a jug of water in a minute. When you're ready come through to the dining room and I will have supper on the table for you."

Then she ran through the back door to the stables to warn the boys that the robber and horse-thief for whom they were on guard had arrived. Nervously glancing over her shoulder at the main house, she told them that any attempt to steal one of her husband's prize horses must be forestalled, and that they must come to assist her with whatever weapons they might find if she were to call for help. The loyal Hottentots nodded gravely.

Forrester came out of his room just as Elizabeth called to the children that supper was ready. Supper was eaten quietly. Mrs Beyers spoke to the children to distract them from the tense atmosphere, but they were not fooled. Over coffee, Forrester said to Elizabeth: "You have a very nice place here. May I ask who is your husband and where he is?"

"I am sorry," she said. "My husband is Johan Beyers and he has gone on a trip for two days."

Forrester's stare hardened as he sat silently for some seconds, then; "That must

have been him I saw about 20 miles from here driving a Cape-cart on the road to Kimberley." She nodded, fear rising again in her.

Forrester relaxed, smiled and asked: "Aren't you afraid to stay here on your own? You look very nervous."

Elizabeth stiffened, and defiance surged through the fear: "Yes, I am afraid to stay here alone, especially as that robber Scotty Smith is coming to this area. I don't understand why the authorities don't do something about his murders, rapes, robberies and horse-thefts. He should be shot on sight...after all, we shoot rabid dogs and hyenas, and they are less harmful than this swine."

Forrester laughed out loud, rocking back in his chair: "Tell me, Mrs Beyers, where did you hear of this man's obviously heinous crimes? He seems to be a thoroughly bad man."

The fear almost gone for the moment, since the name "Scotty Smith" had been mentioned, she was reassured: "Oh, everyone that passes through here has news of another of his foul deeds." She told him of the beating of the old man and the rape of the woman near Kimberley. "My husband mentioned before he left that we must get rid of our four prize saddle-horses before Smith gets a chance to steal them. If they aren't stolen we should get a good price for them. In Kimberley we can get £15 each, and even around here people will pay £12.10s for one of our horses."

Forrester was interested: "Are you allowed to sell these horses while your husband is away?" Elizabeth said she was, as long as she got the price stipulated by her husband for each horse. Fear again overcame the defiance as it dawned on her that the stranger was ferreting out the details on the horses so he would be able to steal the best one in the morning.

Forrester rose from the table: "Righto – I'll inspect the horses in the morning and if one takes my fancy I'll buy it. If you'll excuse me, I'll turn in now." And he walked down to his room, stopping at the door. "Get a good night's sleep, Mrs Beyers, and don't worry about Scotty Smith. I'll keep an eye out for him." As he closed the door behind him, Elizabeth gave a sigh of relief. She took her rifle from behind the curtains and walked with dragging steps to her bedroom. She lay on the bed fully dressed, determined to stay awake throughout the night, determined to forestall anything "Forrester" might try during the night. But the hands of the clock on her dressing table pointed to two o'clock when she fell into an exhausted sleep.

At dawn she was awakened by the cold and sat up on the side of her bed with a start, rubbing the sleep out of her eyes. Suddenly she stiffened and held her breath...she was reminded of the stranger in the house by the sound of furtive footsteps in the passage outside her door. Mrs Beyers sat, her hand to her mouth and her brain numbed with fright, until the footsteps receded onto the back stoep, and the back door closed quietly.

Before dawn, the Hottentot girl Anna brought Forrester a cup of tea and he got up, washed, tiptoed down the passage and out through the back door to the stables. He stalked round the corner of the stable and stumbled on to Jantjie, the groom, taking his first draw of dagga for the day from a clay pipe buried in the ground. The old Hottentot spluttered and coughed his surprise as he creaked to his feet.

"Morning, Jantjie. How's my horse? Have you fed him?" said Forrester when the stable boy had recovered.

"Ja, Baas. I've fed all the horses, including yours, and groomed them also. Yours is still a bit tired, but he'll be alright if you are going to use him today."

Forrester asked old Jantjie to show him the horses his master wished to sell. The Hottentot lost all his fear of what the stranger might do with the horses when the latter complimented him by saying that he would be able to advise him on which was the best mount. Jantjie led the way into the stable with pride in his voice. He stopped at a stall in which stood a large powerful bay.

"This one, my Baas, is the best of all. He has a fast comfortable 'pas', an armchair 'triple', and is a smart horse as well as good-looking." Jantjie boasted of the horse's fine points while the stranger carefully examined the beast, frequently asking the beaming stable-boy for his opinion.

"On your recommendation, Jantjie, I will buy it," said Forrester, and gave the old man a gleaming half-sovereign. Jantjie was delighted and completely disarmed. Back in the house, Forrester tip-toed to his room, unbuckled his blanket roll and brought out a sealed canvas bag which clinked musically. He broke the seals and disclosed a large sum of money.

Forrester counted out £500 into a handkerchief and tied the points of the handkerchief together, forming a small bundle. After replacing the bag in his bedroll, Forrester went on to the back stoep and after searching around, found a sheep-skin mat rolled up in a corner. Placing the handkerchief containing the £500 in the corner against the wall he carefully covered the small bundle with the mat. Then he went into the lounge, where he sat drinking another cup of coffee, supplied by Anna.

The second time Elizabeth heard the sinister footsteps in the corridor, she was near fainting from terror. The rifle was forgotten. The horses were forgotten.

Then she heard voices from the dining room. She called forth all her courage and went to investigate. The stranger looked surprised at her red-rimmed eyes, crumpled and disarranged dress, dishevelled hair and unusually pale face.

"Good morning, Mrs Beyers," he said concernedly. "Is anything wrong? Did something upset you during the night? You should have called me." He put out his hand in a gesture of sympathy, but she winced and backed away. "No, it's alright, I think...I'm fine now. Please don't worry. Anna, bring me coffee."

When she had gathered herself together, Forrester said he had been inspecting her horses, with the aid of old Jantje.

"I wish to buy the big bay with the blaze. Will you accept my chestnut, a beautiful animal, as a present to you, and £25 for the bay? If you accept my offer you will make me very happy. I will have given you a small token in return for your wonderful hospitality."

"No, no, I cannot accept that," she said agitatedly. "Besides..." Forrester held up his hand to interrupt.

"There is nothing else to say, Mrs Beyers. There is only one more thing I want from you, and I'll consider the deal finished – and that is a good breakfast."

Mrs Beyers, silenced by astonishment, left the room slowly, going into the kitchen to start breakfast. Her mind was churning over the stranger's extraordinary offer, trying desperately to find the catch in it. As she did so, Forrester went to the window and called out to Jantje to saddle his new horse.

They ate a lavish breakfast. Mrs Beyers slowly rejected all her suspicions about the stranger, and smiled timidly at him during the meal. She was sure now he could not possibly be an outlaw after all. She felt a fool for the night of needless terror she had just spent.

After breakfast they went out on to the stoep and stood by the bay, which was saddled and tied to the hitching rail. Forrester took a small leather bag out of his pocket and gave it to Elizabeth.

"There's £25 in here, and the chestnut is in this horse's old stall. By the way, what's his name," said Forrester and was informed that the bay answered to *Traveller*.

"I can't accept all this money. Please take half back. Your horse is worth nearly as much as this one," said a completely changed Elizabeth.

"No more protests, please. I'm paying for a comfortable bed, excellent cooking and your company, as well as for the horse. I shall feel insulted if you don't take it." He shook her hand warmly. When he was comfortably settled in the saddle, Forrester leaned forward towards Elizabeth.

"When I've gone, look under that sheepskin mat in that corner, and give what you find there to your husband with my compliments. And, Mrs Beyers, let me tell you something else. Everything you have heard about Scotty Smith is a pack of gross lies. He has never committed a murder, or molested a woman, and would not dream of stealing from the poor.

"He robbed the bank, but he had his reasons for that. I am telling you the truth, and I know what I am talking about, for I am Scotty Smith."

Elizabeth reeled back from him in horror, both hands to her mouth. Scotty Smith, alias Forrester, saluted her gravely, then turned his horse and cantered out of the yard. Elizabeth sat down until she had recovered from this last shock.

Then, remembering the mat, she looked underneath and found the handkerchief containing the money. She sat in the chair again, took her head in both hands and started sobbing uncontrollably.

She did not know what made her cry.

THE BILTONG HUNTERS

It was just on fifty-four years ago that I was called in by Captain Murray, Officer Commanding "K" Troop of the B.S.A. Police, Bulawayo (afterwards Colonel R.E. Murray, DSO, DCM, commander of the well-known Murray's Column in the First World War). He told me that biltong hunters were becoming very active in the vicinity of the Gwaai, Lupani, Gwampa, Shangani and Bubi Rivers. They were slaughtering game wholesale and destroying the countryside by lighting fires to flush the game. He wanted me to patrol the area incognito in an endeavour to stop the destruction and if possible, charge the guilty persons.

Troop Sergeant-Major G.S. Hough was instructed to give such assistance as I might need for the venture (the last time I was to see Hough was in the private bar of the Grand Hotel, Cape Town, in 1921; he was then quite blind but recognised me by my voice).

In due course I left Bulawayo on a nondescript horse with a pigskin saddle made for me by that craftsman among saddlers, Jack Everett. I had with me four pack donkeys, four constables in mufti and my batman.

My trek to the Gwaai, following tracks, game paths and old roads, took six days. I camped on the Gwaai River for two days and while there sent out the constables in different directions to contact the local tribesmen and get information concerning the whereabouts of any white hunters in the district. From them I learnt that hunters were on the Bembesi near its confluence with the Gwaai, so the following day I moved over to the Bembesi. The river was dry and I continued down its north bank until I came to a large pool of clear, clean water. Here I pitched camp and made kraals for the animals, collecting much dry wood for fires during the night.

It was not a restful night. Lions disturbed the quiet with their muffled growling, hyenas enlivened the stillness with their mournful howlings and crocodiles were grunting in the pools below me. The horse would snort with alarm at every sound, while the donkeys broke wind with alarming frequency. Altogether it was a weird and frightening night, yet at the same time a spellbinding and fascinating experience.

On the following day the constables fanned out in different directions with instructions to pinpoint the hunters. All were back by sundown reporting that there were no human beings whatever anywhere in the area. One of them was in a shocking state of nerves and exhaustion; he had come across a herd of elephant and had been winded by a cow with a small calf, who had come after him with ears extended and trunk in the air. He had had to run for it and did not seem to have stopped running until he reached camp.

I then decided to move over to the Gwampa River, arriving at the junction with the Bubi about five o'clock. That evening, as I was camped at this spot and after it was quite dusk, I heard a single rifle shot.

It was too late to investigate it then, but at daybreak I was in the saddle and following the Gwampa downstream to where the shot had seemed to come from. Only a mile from my camp and close to a pool in the river I came across a white man and several Africans skinning a magnificent eland bull. The shocked surprise on the white man's face proved he was frightened beyond measure at being caught literally red-handed in the act of skinning a royal game carcass.

Remembering my instructions, however, I dismounted, shook hands with the man and congratulated him on getting such a fine specimen. "It was getting dark," he told me. "I thought it was a reedbuck."

Marais (all names have been changed to avoid embarrassment to the families of the men mentioned) invited me to join him in a grill-up of fresh liver and kidneys, followed by a cup of scalding black coffee. As we ate we talked and, quite innocently, he gave me all the information I needed concerning other parties of hunters in the area – where they were camped and how and where they operated. Marais himself was in partnership with his stepfather and was camped further down the Bubi River.

I watched with interest as Marais and his servants prepared the meat. Working at a speed which indicated considerable experience, Marais himself cut the meat away from the bone while the Africans cut it into strips about two inches thick. The prepared strips were then placed on the inside of the eland hide, salted, turned over several times and covered by taking the four corners of the hide and bringing them to the centre. A trestle-work scaffold was then built and after the strips had lain in brine for three hours they were hung to dry. Marais told me that it was important not to over-salt the meat or the biltong would become unpalatable and cause severe thirst after eating.

When all the meat was hung (there was no waste), the whole of the trestle-work was lightly covered with green branches in such a way as to allow a good circulation of air. Marais told me that the strips of biltong would be left in situ for some five to eight days and then transported to the main camp in grain bags on donkeys. The best biltong, he told me, was always treated this way on the very spot where it was slaughtered, and any attempt to remove the freshly killed carcass or freshly butchered meat always resulted in a loss of quality in the biltong.

Two Africans were left to mount guard over the meat. I was surprised that they were willing to undertake these duties with the numbers of carnivorous animals roaming the area, but Marais told me that Africans would follow a good hunter anywhere and do anything for him for the sake of always having satisfied bellies. They certainly looked fit and well fed, these men, and I was assured that they took the precaution of building themselves large fires at night.

It was mid-day when I left Marais and I now thought I would investigate the party of Strydom brothers Marais had told me of. I instructed two of my constables to approach the Strydom camp and seek employment there in order to obtain evidence of their activities.

These two returned after four days to tell me that the white men had proved very suspicious of them and they had been unable to obtain employment. However, they brought with them a local Ndebele who had been present when the Strydoms had shot an elephant near the Unsungamala Valley a few weeks previously. With this witness and the two constables I visited the spot and found a piece of elephant hide in a tree and bones distributed over a wide area. The scaffolding on which the meat had been dried was still in evidence.

Suitable exhibits were collected and taken back to camp. According to Marais, there were other hunters on the Shangani River. With one constable I rode over to the Shangani the following day. Following an elephant path and no more than four miles from my camp I was startled when a rifle cracked nearby and a shot struck a tree a couple of feet to my left and level with my head. For the best part of half an hour the constable and I remained motionless in an effort to detect some movement in the bush. There was none. Throughout the afternoon we endeavoured to pick up the tracks of whoever had fired at me, but without any success whatsoever.

It was too late by then to continue to the Shangani and we returned to camp. Shortly after my arrival, the constables brought in two Africans for questioning. One was Ndebele and the other a Sesutu by the name of Kleinbooi. The latter was sophisticated and spoke fluent Afrikaans. I questioned him closely and from him learnt a great deal about the Strydom brothers. He, incidentally, had been present at the killing of the elephant. I now felt I had my hands full. I told the two Africans they would have to accompany me to Bulawayo and next morning rode over and arrested Marais for killing the eland.

We all then trekked back to Bulawayo. I had been away six weeks.

When making my report to Captain Murray I asked for assistance to go back to the Bubi and arrest the Strydom brothers. He told me that Corporal Hughes Halls and Reggie Brown would be detailed to accompany me. I also recall that I wanted to report sick with a deaf ear. Sergeant Major Hough instructed me to treat it with oil that evening and go along the following morning to the Memorial Hospital to have it syringed. Hughes Halls, who was in the office, said he had some sweet oil in his room which I could use if I came along later.

That evening, however, the deaf ear was forgotten at first. With a party consisting of Corporal Hughes Halls, Trooper W. Bussy (the first editor of this magazine), Trooper "Hacker" Matthews (the camp cook) and Jack Everett (the camp saddler), I went on a night out at the Empire. This was the rendezvous of the troops whenever cash was available and it was here that the barmaids always seemed prettier than in any other pub in Bulawayo. By the time we left the Empire near midnight, I.I. (*sic*) whisky had warmed us considerably. Noting our condition, the ricksha boys gave us a wide berth and we were compelled to walk back to camp. Passing the Bulawayo Club (of which, I need hardly say, we were not members) one of the party suggested dropping in for a drink. In we went and I ordered I.I. whisky and soda from the Indian steward. He looked suspicious but nevertheless produced the drinks. I tried to pay with a gold sovereign, but he wanted coupons. I was out of coupons, I told him offhandedly, so he put the sovereign in the till and gave me my change in coupons. These would not have been of much value to me and the only way to dispose of them was to drink more I.I. This we did, leaving the Club at last in a highly intoxicated state.

I just managed to remember that I was going to have my ear syringed next morning and, back in camp, stumbled over to Hughes Hall's room for the oil. In flickering candlelight H.H. pointed out the bottle of oil and wadding and I poured some into my ear and plugged it.

Next morning at the hospital, Dr Eaton examined my ear and expressed surprise at what he saw there.

"We must get the Sister to syringe this," he said. The Sister was even more surprised at what came out and suggested I take another look at Hughes Hall's bottle. Later H.H. and I did this together and found that I had used cough mixture instead of sweet oil. Hughes Halls found this vastly amusing.

Later I appeared in Court against Marais (he was fined £25 for hunting royal game) and in due course Corporal Hughes Halls, Reggie Brown and I left Bulawayo together for the Gwaai to effect the arrest of the Strydom brothers.

Following my early route, we travelled in easy stages to spare our horses. We knew that however much we hurried Marais would be there before us to warn them of our approach, and we might have to pursue them a long way before we came up with them.

On the fifth day, approaching my old camp on the Bembesi, we passed a copse of mopani trees and saw fresh rhinocerous tracks The horses became uneasy as we approached another clump of trees and suddenly there were grunts and whistles and two rhinos burst from the mopanis. For a few moments they stood with their ears erect, grunting and snorting and peering shortsightedly in our direction. They were so close we could see the enormous folds in their skin. Then, with a final snort, they clumsily trotted off towards the river and the long grass.

The horses, by this time, could not be controlled and we were compelled to gallop off in the opposite direction. The mule, with pack-saddles flapping like the wings of a giant vulture, followed – only to give the horses their second scare when they saw this strange apparition approaching.

It took us some time to calm the animals and we did not reach my old camp much before sunset. With little time left, we had to work hard to get the animals kraaled and everything safe for the night. I had warned my companions that we might have a restless night here, and no sooner had we settled down after our bully beef and onion stew than we heard the first grunt of a lion. Lions were in close proximity all night. Loathsome hyenas hung about just beyond the range of our firelight, emitting their dismal howlings. The horses and the mule were our greatest concern, and we had to take it in turn to stay with the animals, talking to them and petting them. No wonder their nerves were on edge – ours weren't too good either. I remember Reggie Brown in his gravelly voice calling down curses on all biltong hunters – and Hughes Halls reckoned he had never been in such a zoo.

We wasted no time in getting away from that spot in the morning, and made directly for where I thought the Strydoms might be camped at the junction of the Gwaai and Bubi Rivers.

Emerging from a wooded belt we came into open country. To our right a herd of sable was grazing; to our left a lone bull followed slowly in the wake of the herd, and this beast appeared to be carrying a burden on its head. This was puzzling and we decided to find out what it was. Dismounting, H.H. and I managed to get close enough to drop the beast, and another shot killed it.

Imagine our surprise when we came close and found that the sable bull had been carrying a full-grown leopard carcass impaled on its horns. The horns were magnificent, making almost a complete circle. How the leopard had stuck is anyone's guess, but it seemed obvious that the horns had penetrated its body simultaneously, one through the ribs and one through the stomach. Presumably, continual head-shaking by the sable in an attempt to rid itself of its unwanted burden had caused the dead leopard to slip gradually down the horns until it became jambed in the narrow space not far above the head. We found wagon tracks at the Strydoms' old camp at the junction of the Bubi and the Gwaai indicating that they had moved on some time previously. We used their old kraals for our animals that night and slept more peacefully than the night before. It was easy to follow the wagon tracks next day and after a ride of some twenty miles we came to their new camp. There were three wagons, a number of donkeys and one horse. The last belonged to the father, who was present. He told me his sons were out hunting, but that they were expecting us and would be back by sunset.

We pitched camp nearby and awaited the return of the hunters. One by one they came back and when all three were home, they strolled over together to greet us.

Corporal Hughes Halls explained that he had a warrant for their arrest on a charge of shooting an elephant and other game. They admitted shooting the elephant in self-defence when they were charged by it – and claimed that any other game they killed was in terms of their £5 licences. If we thought we had evidence to the contrary they would meet the charges in court in Bulawayo, with an attorney to defend them.

With the air thus cleared they extended to us, with the generosity of their kind, the full hospitality of their encampment. We accepted an invitation to dinner that evening, and there was no doubt the wives of these men knew how to cook. The meal was plain but delectable – stewed marrow bones, stamped mealies, pumpkin, rusks and black coffee. We were not backward in asking for second helpings and did full justice to the excellent cooking of the Strydom wives.

The brothers produced for us from one of the wagons the tusks of the elephant they had shot. The pair together weighed 74 lb. Conversation veered to the place of men and animals in God's world.

With simple biblical faith they pointed out that God had put animals in the world for the benefit of men. Why then should the government impose restrictions on the hunting of game? Friendly argument on these lines continued far into the night but the Strydoms were unshakeable in their convictions. Suddenly I asked which one it was who had tried to shoot me near the Shangani.

There was silence for several seconds, and I saw the glances that passed between them. It was one of these men, I am still convinced, who fired at me – but this was never proved. I also believe that the shot was intended as a warning, or I would not be telling this story today, for the skill of these men with their rifles was almost unbelievable. They asked permission to shoot some fresh meat to leave with their wives before coming back with us to Bulawayo. This was granted, provided I accompany them. I have never, repeat never, seen shooting like these fellows could. If a reed-buck jumped up, it was down and dead within seconds. Of the four reedbuck shot before nine o'clock in the morning, there was not one that was not cleanly killed with the first shot. On our way back to the wagons, a steinbuck jumped up, ran for some distance and vanished near a small tree. The brothers told me that if it jumped up again the three of them would fire and I would find three bullet holes in the carcass. Sure enough, when the little animal made his appearance, three .303 rifles cracked and the little buck turned over. There were six holes in its body when I examined it – three where the bullets had entered and three exits.

I had expressed admiration of their shooting, and the brothers enjoyed displaying their skill. A kingfisher, in flight, hovered momentarily in preparation for its dive to the waters of a stream, and was brought down with a single shot. Imagine – with a .303!

Next morning we started our long trek back to Bulawayo. The Strydoms were mounted on donkeys, so progress was slow. When the donkeys became tired the Strydoms would walk for long distances on foot to rest them. These men were certainly fit. The journey was uneventful. The Strydoms gave us no trouble; they were helpful and full of humour.

The brothers appeared in court before Magistrate Carey. Sergeant Skillon was prosecuting, with H.J. Sonnenberg for the defence. The latter put all his skill into their case but without success. They were heavily fined – so heavily that one told me afterwards that they would have to sell a wagon to meet the cost.

An interesting point arose in the course of the case.

I had mentioned to Captain Vernon New (in command of the town police, Bulawayo) that I was determined to "get" the hunters, especially as (as I had thought then) one of them had tried to kill me. Over a drink at the Grand Hotel Captain New had mentioned my determination to Sonnenberg. The latter brought this up during the trial in an attempt to prove prejudice on my part against the Strydoms. In cross-examination he asked me whether I had in fact made this remark to Captain New. The Magistrate turned to me and said, "You need not answer that question. Your conversation with your superior officer in the course of duty is privileged and need not be divulged."

KALAHARI PATROL – CONTENTS

The Outpost
   Map
   Chapter 1: The Briefing   77
   Chapter 2: Cornelius J. Van Rooyen   79
   Chapter 3: The Trials of a Giraffe   83
   Chapter 4: Blind Eye Provisioning   88
   Chapter 5: Tails of Giraffe   91
   Chapter 6: The King's Beer   95
   Chapter 7: Into the Unknown   98
   Chapter 8: The Thirst Trek   102
   Chapter 9: Bank Holiday   105
   Chapter 10: Saved Again   109
   Chapter 11: More New Arrivals   112
   Chapter 12: On to Tamaseta   116
   Chapter 13: Lions   120
   Chapter 14: A Lion Hunt   125
   Chapter 15: Rogue Elephant   129
   Chapter 16: Ivory Cache   131
   Chapter 17: More Lions   133
   Chapter 18: The Second Herd   135
   Chapter 19: Snake in the Grass   137
   Chapter 20: Hendrik's Pan   140
   Chapter 21: Geise   142
   Chapter 22: Narrow Escape   145
   Chapter 23: Trouble with Father   148
   Chapter 24: Life in Eden   151
   Chapter 25: Thorny Problems   155
   Chapter 26: Attempted Murder   157
   Chapter 27: Rhino Rumpus   159
   Chapter 28: Elephants   163
   Chapter 29: More Elephants – Much Trouble   165
   Chapter 30: First Aid Bushman Style   167
   Chapter 31: The Orphan   169
   Chapter 32: On to Shekwankwi   170
   Chapter 33: Death and Near Death   172
   Chapter 34: The Last Lap   175
   Chapter 35: Shopping Spree   177
   Chapter 36: The Aftermath   179

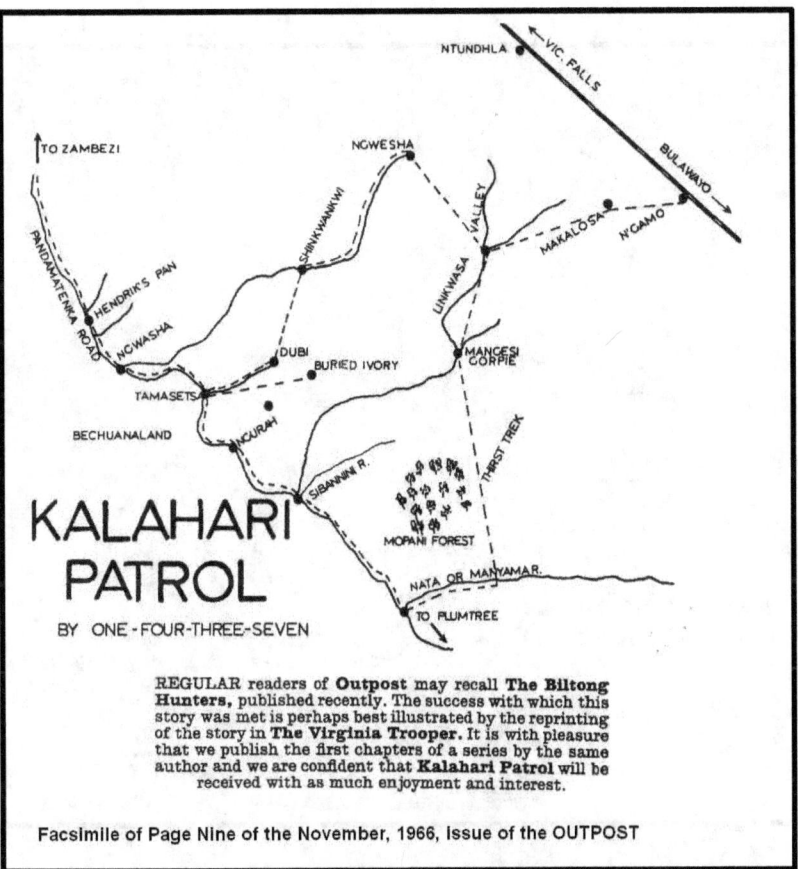

KALAHARI PATROL
BY ONE-FOUR-THREE-SEVEN

REGULAR readers of **Outpost** may recall **The Biltong Hunters**, published recently. The success with which this story was met is perhaps best illustrated by the reprinting of the story in **The Virginia Trooper**. It is with pleasure that we publish the first chapters of a series by the same author and we are confident that **Kalahari Patrol** will be received with as much enjoyment and interest.

Facsimile of Page Nine of the November, 1966, Issue of the OUTPOST

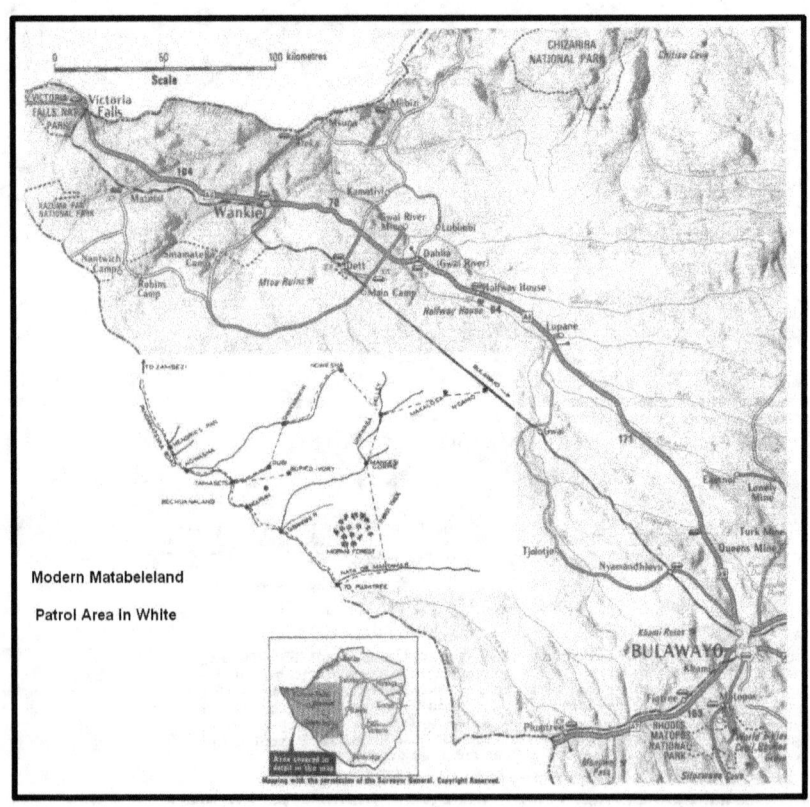

Modern Matabeleland

Patrol Area in White

KALAHARI PATROL

Chapter One – The Briefing

During 1912, Bulawayo Headquarters of the B.S.A. Police decided that it was necessary to establish a Police Camp on the Gwaai River and I was detailed to build the pole and dagga huts and take charge of the area. The country around was wild and uninhabited with the exception of one farmer on the Gwaai, some 25 miles from the Station. To the north and north-west of the Railway Line, the country was occupied by a few roving Bushmen who were never visible and who could only be detected by their tracks.

The main object of the Camp, which was erected close to the Railway Station, not far from the bridge which spans the river, was to keep check on the Biltong Hunters, who invaded that part of Matabeleland during the winter months and slaughtered game in large quantities, in the process burning the veld and thereby destroying the lush vegetation. I was happy with my new command, patrolling the terrain in all directions for a distance of 50 miles or so. It was interesting work and gave me a wonderful opportunity of studying wild life.

One day, my peaceful existence was shattered by a telegram from Bulawayo which read "Report in Bulawayo immediately". The usual addendum "with all kit and equipment" was deleted. I was puzzled and wondered what it was all about, but I boarded the first goods train that evening and the following morning reported to Sergeant Major Hough in Bulawayo.

In due course I was escorted into the presence of Captain Murray, who greeted me with, "Oh, you have arrived. It did not take you long to get here. How is the new Camp?" After the pleasantries, Captain Murray broached the subject of my urgent recall to Bulawayo.

"I want you to investigate a report we have received to the effect that cattle are being smuggled into Southern Rhodesia from Northern Rhodesia. According to the report, the cattle are driven across the Zambesi at, or near, Kasangula. They are then driven along the border of Bechuanaland via Pandamatenka, Hendrik's Pan, Tamasetsa, N'Gurua, the Nata River and on to a siding in Bechuanaland, from where they are trucked for the Johannesburg market. We have been advised that some of the cattle do not reach their destination, and are of the opinion that large numbers are deviated from the route and turned into Southern Rhodesia at a point unknown. We have no information as to who is receiving the cattle. I need not remind you that there are several contagious cattle diseases uncontrolled in Northern Rhodesia and it is therefore strictly forbidden to introduce any of these cattle into this territory. It is extremely important that we stop this traffic before any infectious disease is introduced here, causing the whole of the country to be placed in quarantine.

"We also have information that Bushmen are slaughtering game in the same area on an organised basis. These nomads are being supplied with muzzle-loading guns, Martini Henri rifles and old Schneiders by the Barotse on the other side of the Zambesi. The Bushmen are allowed to retain the meat, but all skins, ivory and rhino horns are handed to the owners of the guns in payment for the use of the weapons. If you can arrest some of these poachers, it may frighten off the others as they are doing great harm in the country in the process of their hunting.

We have no data or maps on the terrain between the Gwaai River and the Bechuanaland Border, so it will be informative if you make a map of the area you cover and enlighten us on the country generally."

Captain Murray continued: "I have no idea if there is a track or tracks leading from the Gwaai, N'Gamo or Ntunla to the border. I have endeavoured to obtain this information but without success. If you go by way of Plumtree and follow the Border, the investigation may be frustrated. If cattle are being brought into the territory, they are surely being driven over the unpopulated country to avoid any suspicion of illegal dealings. I suggest that you proceed directly across country from the Gwaai as you may perhaps come across the tracks on your way to the Border.

I can give you no time limit on this investigation as I have no idea where the search is going to lead you. I leave it in your hands entirely. I wish you the best of luck."

So there it was. I realised that this was to be a major patrol and consequently would require very careful planning. I was allocated one horse, one mule and four donkeys. I was to be accompanied by two African constables, Kleinbooi and Dubani and I knew both of them well as they had been on patrol with me previously. I was especially pleased to have Kleinbooi as he was good in the bush and a smart tracker. My groceries consisted of tea, coffee, salt, sugar and a 100 pound pocket of rice. As a substitute for flour, rice is a wonderful carbohydrate and is a nutrient that is easily cooked rather than involving the chore of baking bread with baking powder and spoiling fifty per cent of the attempts and carrying all the extra cooking pots. I was also given six large, canvas water bags.

Chapter Two – Cornelius J. van Rooyen

A week after my briefing from Captain Murray, I was on my way to N'Gamo Siding, 22 miles from the Gwaai Station where I had returned from Bulawayo by train while the constables brought up the animals. The pack animals were very overloaded and, in consequence, I had to give them frequent rests. On arrival at N'Gamo, I met a Bushman called Bankamakuni. Actually he was not a genuine Bushman but a cross between Bushman and Makaranga. He told me that he was employed by "Nellus" and that the latter was camped at Makalola, eight miles from N'Gamo, where he was capturing giraffe.

"Nellus" was C.J. van Rooyen who was well known in the area and who was very well acquainted with Western Matabeleland. I was extremely anxious to meet him as I was sure that he would advise me and provide me with much information of use to me on my way to the Border. We set out for Makalola and arrived there late in the afternoon.

Cornelius J. van Rooyen was a man in his fifties, about five feet ten inches in height, a full-bodied powerful man and quite extraordinarily handsome. The flesh that covered his bones, though thick-textured and perhaps even on the heavy side, was certainly no hindrance to his speed and suppleness of movement. Thick, tangled hair, somewhere in shade between auburn and iron grey, curled over his heavy forehead and continued in a goatee beard and square moustache. He wore soft riding breeches, high-laced top-boots, khaki shirt and a soft khaki coat. I never saw him in other clothes – I don't think he knew what slacks or shorts looked like.

As I dismounted, he jumped from the camp chair in which he had been seated and approached me with open hand. "How do you do?" he said. "Glad to see you. My name is van Rooyen – better known as 'Nellus'."

I was about to introduce myself, but he went on: "I know, you are the only other white man in this vicinity. The natives always refer to you as Shiwhanga." He called for assistance to off-load and unsaddle my animals and then invited me to make myself comfortable and join him in a cup of coffee. "Nellus" had quite a camp. There were two covered wagons; eight horses; numerous oxen; twelve cows; about twenty donkeys; chickens; dogs; plus a variety of live game – six tame giraffe; three eland; two sable and last, but not least, a small, tame and very naughty warthog. The latter was a really nosey little character, whose antics produced much amusement in the camp. He appeared to delight in bumping his head against the legs of anyone not looking. He would skip to one side, and then run with his tail straight up in the air, emitting short grunts of satisfaction. He was an amusing animal and a great pet.

The giraffe, on the other hand, would at times come close to where we were sitting under an enormous acacia tree and browse quietly among the upper branches. They had remarkable heads which moved with grace from branch to branch. The heads were slender and tapering with flat features, dappled here and there with the colour of pale leather. Their ears were neat little triangles, set sharply erect and they had long thick eye lashes, black and silky as though they had been painted with mascara. The enormously long neck, peculiarly sloped, short body and amusing gait fascinated me for hours at such close quarters. Giraffe are generally reckoned to be one of the most shy and easily frightened species. Yet here, they habitually wandered right up to the wagons on which we were seated and stared curiously, with wonderment in their eyes, at these strange things called humans.

Van Rooyen came to Rhodesia in 1873. He was a man who had figured significantly in the early days among the Natives. He had originally met Lobengula and obtained permission from him to hunt in Matabeleland and Mashonaland. He had been an emissary on Lobengula's behalf and had interviewed President Kruger three times in this capacity. His influence with these two historical characters was considerable. Van Rooyen had introduced F.C. Selous to Lobengula and had persuaded the latter to forgive the former when Selous shot a hippo which was strictly "King's Game" and thereby prohibited. He had assisted Selous to obtain game specimens for Roland Ward, the eminent London taxidermists. He had shot more than a hundred giraffe for Lobengula who wanted the tails as currency for the wives he obtained from the King of Swaziland. The hides of the same giraffe, van Rooyen cut into whips and reims and flooded the market in Pretoria with them! The Charter Company hired him to take the Duke of Westminster on a hunting trip in Northern Rhodesia and the details of this expedition will be well worth recording at a later date. He accompanied Wilson on the Shangani venture but was recalled to command another patrol, a change of plan which saved his life.

Late into the night I listened with undivided attention to this distinguished man raking up the past in his deep clear voice. We eventually went to bed at 2 am.

At dawn the following morning, I joined "Nellus" at the camp fire drinking coffee. Just after I arrived, two of his riders appeared and asked for instructions from their employer. After they had gone, van Rooyen explained to me that the purpose of his camp was to obtain, live, six heifer giraffe and one bull calf. The bull giraffe was required by the Pretoria Zoo where their bull giraffe had died recently. It seemed that the animal had collected strips and bits of wire from the fence at the Zoo, the wire had contaminated the cud and had been found in a post mortem. The heifers were to be sent to London, Germany and Austria. For the past six weeks, he had been trying to capture a bull calf and although many had been located, none of them were young enough to capture. The means of determining the age of the calf was, in itself, quite interesting. If the front hoof of a giraffe measures eight inches or less, then the animal is less than nine months old. Over eight inches and the animal can be a year old.

"The age," "Nellus" explained, "is very important. Over nine months the animals are too old to be captured. They are very difficult to tame and instead of settling down within fourteen days, it may take months and the animal suffers in consequence."

He then asked me the purpose of my patrol, so I told him that I had been sent to verify information that the border demarcation pegs had been destroyed.

"I am not sure that you will get through at this time of the year. You would have a very tough trek in front of you. In fact, I would strongly advise you to go by way of Plumtree. From now onwards, all the pans that may be carrying water are drying up rapidly, and if you get no water you will be in serious trouble – you may lose some of your animals and even die of thirst yourself. I haven't been through here to the west for many years. My last hunt was a long time ago when Selous and I hunted elephant in the Linkwasa Valley. I will send for Bankamakuni who met you at N'Gamo. He knows that area more recently than I do."

Bankamakuni was summoned and he and van Rooyen went into a deep conversation. After a considerable interval, van Rooyen turned to me and said:

"He is much more optimistic than I am. He seems to think that there is always water to be found in the Linkwasa Valley if you are prepared to dig for it. The Mangesi Gorri Pan, he claims, will still have water – it does not dry up until late in the season. If it happens that there is water at Mangesi Gorri there should be water in the Shewanki. If you are unfortunate in that Mangesi Gorri is dry, he suggests that you go south to the Nata River where there is always water. In this event you will have a long trek through very dry country, but not as long as you would if you forked the other way."

After a further conversation with the Bushman, he continued: "To be on the safe side, I will send Bankamakuni with you and I will also give you four extra pack donkeys, an extra horse and one of my lion dogs, Pistol." To say the least of it, his offer of assistance overwhelmed me. I was loud in my thanks, even more so when he added: "I do not hold you responsible if anything should happen to the animals. I do, however, expect you to take care of them."

Subsequent events proved that van Rooyen's wonderful generosity saved my life in more ways than one.

Chapter Three – The Trials of a Giraffe

Whilst we were weighing the chances and debating the success of my trek, we saw the two horsemen to whom van Rooyen had spoken earlier, ride into the camp, off-saddle their horses and come straight towards us, their faces beaming with obvious joy. They handed their employer a length of grass and said in Matabele: "It is a beautiful young bull." The grass was seven and a half inches long and the riders' joy was repeated in van Rooyen's face. With great excitement, he said: "With any luck we will capture him tomorrow and I will be back on my farm in Plumtree within three weeks." He was absolutely delighted.

Around the camp fire that night, he gave me some instruction on the difficult task of catching giraffe and handling them after capture.

"It is essential that the giraffe be caught within the distance of one mile. Further than this and they can run themselves to death. Apart from this, a pony, however well conditioned and trained, cannot keep up the pace for more than a mile while a giraffe, with his peculiar but deceptively fast gait, can keep going for miles.

Cow's milk seems to go down well with giraffe. After the first few days of this diet, his coat changes and an obvious sheen and condition appears."

He asked me if I would assist them on the hunt: "I want you to come with us tomorrow. I will give you a sturdy pony, well-trained to the work, and should the calf come in your direction the pony will take you right up to him. All you have to do is to put the loop over his head…and hang on."

The instructions seemed simple enough, but I was not so sure if I liked the idea of hanging on to a wild, untamed giraffe. I was living in the hopes that the giraffe would not come in my direction.

Early the next morning we were on our way to capture the bull calf giraffe. The pony on which I was mounted was sturdy, big-boned and full of life. It was obvious that van Rooyen looked after his horses for they were in excellent condition. The two horsemen who had reported the location of the giraffe the previous day, accompanied van Rooyen and myself. They too, were well-mounted and I observed with appreciation that the two Africans had excellent seats in the saddle. The men could ride, had been well-trained and were fully conversant with their task. I had no idea which way they were leading us, and for that matter, I did not care. I was happy in the knowledge that they knew the country, were excellent trackers and in due course would lead me back to the camp.

We rode on through secluded patches of veld, the horses jogging along at a fast triple walk, through narrow clearings with thick jungle all around, past clumps of gigantic trees, hemmed in by the forest.

Eventually, some four miles from Makalola, the leaders enered the "guso" forest. The moment they entered the woodland, they parted, one going to the left and the other to the right. Van Rooyen followed the right-hand man and I followed the other. Van Rooyen had given us instructions to always remain in each other's sight. We had penetrated the timberland for about half a mile when "Nellus" waved his arm in our direction, calling to us. Riding up to him, we saw the fresh tracks of a herd of giraffe, and among the tracks, the spoor of the calf was pointed out. One of the riders said that the herd had passed by only an hour before. How, and by what means, he could specify at what hour the giraffe had browsed at this spot was beyond my conception. We moved on, the two trackers following the spoor of the herd, van Rooyen remaining in the centre and instructing me to hold the left hand flank and "get the reim in readiness, in case he comes your way."

I had no sooner loosened the reim from around my body, when I heard a piercing whistle on my right. Seconds after the whistle, I had a glimpse of horses moving at a fast gallop diagonally in front of me. Within a minute, I spotted the giraffe galloping with that slow motion action which is so peculiar and fascinating. The two African riders pushed their horses close to the herd and separated the calf. Then they turned him in my direction! It was only then that I spotted "Nellus" out of the corner of my eye. He was some 150 yards to my extreme right. I was the nearest rider to the calf. The pony made no mistake in letting me know that the capture was up to us. It was the maddest gallop that I have ever experienced on horse back and to make things worse, it was through thickly wooded forest. It was a break-neck run – twisting round trees, plunging through thick undergrowth, jumping over fallen tree trunks, over obstacles only to be confronted by another too high to clear, twisting around, but always getting nearer to the calf. The pony budged not an inch, bouncing from one tree to another and weaving through at a speed that threatened my kneecaps and my life into the bargain. He acted like a dog on a blood spoor and seemed to enjoy the exercise to the limit. A small opening in the thickly wooded forest gave him the opportunity of increasing his speed. The extra acceleration brought us close to the giraffe and standing in the stirrup irons, I flung the loop over the animal's head and hung on. Then the unexpected happened – something that I had not been told. The giraffe reared and, in the process, with my hands firmly on the reim, I was pulled clear out of the saddle to make contact with mother earth with a resounding thud. Still, I hung on. Before I had recovered, several things happened in very quick succession. Van Rooyen took off his khaki jacket and placed it over a long forked stick which had been cut on the spot by one of the riders. Hoisting the coat to the height of the giraffe's head, he awaited an opportune moment and then flung the coat over the head, effectively blindfolding the animal. The bull stood quite still with wide-apart front legs, its sides heaving with laboured breathing. Blood was dripping from its off-side shoulder and van Rooyen, having examined the wound, said, "It is quite a long scar, but it has not penetrated beyond the skin and there is nothing to worry about."

Other than the heavy breathing of horses, humans, and the captured bull, there was complete silence.

Minutes later, when we had rested and recovered somewhat, van Rooyen turned to me and said: "Any bones broken? You had quite a fall – I hope you're not hurt."

"As far as I can tell, I didn't break any bones," I replied, "But every muscle in my body is aching. What does surprise me is that any of us are still alive – these horses of yours don't seem to care what happens to the one in the saddle as long as they do the job in bringing you close to the game!"

One of the riders was sent post-haste to Makalola, with instructions to bring the milking cows and some eats for ourselves.

"Nellus" turned to me and said: "This calf is about eight months old. He will want milk as soon as he has settled down. He is a fine specimen and I want to take great care of him – I have waited a long time to get him."

Close to the scene of the capture was a straight-stemmed mukwa tree (known to the Matabele as the "Avagasa"). It had a black rough bark, and when cut, it "bled" a bright red juice. The bark was thoroughly cleaned off for about ten feet, leaving the smooth, white stem without protruding knots. It was to this tree that the captive was to be tethered.

Van Rooyen and the remaining rider approached the giraffe with a smooth round reim, on the one end of which was a two inch ring. The rider went to the other side of the bull and cast the reim over the withers of the animal to van Rooyen who caught the end and passed it back under the belly. Three times the reim was put around the body and then it was tied, forming a surcingle. On to this surcingle was fastened a breastplate made of rawhide reim and from the breastplate in turn, a loop around the tree would form the last link of the chain in a way that it was free to move up and down the tree. Apart from switching his long tail from side to side, the giraffe made no movement, standing there with his front legs straddled and still blindfolded.

(Author's note: Perhaps I should have explained more fully why it was so necessary to secure the giraffe with such a complicated attachment as the surcingle and breastplate. It was important that nothing should be hitched to the animal's neck or head as this could quite easily result in a broken cervix. This happened on several captures in the past. In fact, van Rooyen had a giraffe in the camp with a pronounced "kink" in its neck, which had been caused when the animal had struggled with a hitch to the neck and had broken the cervical column, fortunately leaving the marrow intact. Strangely, this animal refused to leave the camp and when van Rooyen eventually vacated the camp, the giraffe was left there. The following year, 1913, van Rooyen returned to Makalola and to his surprise, the "V" necked giraffe came to visit the camp.)

In due course, the cows arrived from Makalola together with two Bushmen drivers and other assistants who were carrying more reims and a large dish. Quickly trees were felled and a kraal constructed for the cows. Once inside the kraal, the cows were milked and the enamel dish filled. One of the riders then stood on a hastily-erected platform and lifted the dish containing the milk close to the mouth of the calf. He spilled some of the milk on to the lips and nose in an attempt to induce the animal to drink. With great patience, the rider continued his efforts for some two hours and finally succeeded. Bunching his lips into a sort of knot, the giraffe sipped a little and having got the flavour finally, emptied the dish with a gurgling sound.

The giraffe remained blindfolded by the coat until sunset, when it was removed. The additional reims were attached to the surcingle with another through the loop in the breastplate. With a man on either side and one in front, an attempt was made to move the bull towards the tree. With extreme patience and no force, he moved inch by inch in the desired direction. It took time to get him to a position in which the loop of the breastplate could be secured to the tree, but eventually the tie was completed and he was secured for the night. A night shift was detailed to keep the fires going until morning and van Rooyen and I mounted and returned to the camp for dinner and a well-earned night's rest.

The next morning I was stiff. Taking off my pyjama coat in order to wash, I was shocked to find one side of my body a purple-green colour. All my joints felt as if they were breaking. Still, after a hearty breakfast I was feeling better and by the time we had returned to the scene of the capture, I was quite mobile. It was now necessary to gain the confidence of the calf before he could be moved to the main camp. With insistent perseverance and the utmost patience, the Africans tried to feed the calf without the blindfold. Many times he made vicious chops with his front hooves at the man presenting the dish of milk but finally he accepted the dish without the blindfold. In fact, he soon became most impatient when he saw the dish coming in his direction – making grunting noises and stamping his front feet on the ground. Even his eyes took on an interest – formerly they had been unwinking, a dead stare as though he had been mesmerised.

On the third day after the capture, an attempt was made to move him in the direction of Makalola. The cows and horses went in front of the calf with one man on the lead reim and one on either side, holding a reim attached to the surcingle. It was a slow and patient move. Whenever the calf stopped he was offered the dish of milk. Sometimes it worked and he followed the "carrot", but more often than not, he just stopped, turned his head to the flank and just stared in the one direction. It was fascinating to look into those glamorous, unwinking, "mascara'd" eyes. The five mile move was completed in fifteen hours. We all sighed with relief, Africans and Europeans alike.

It was astonishing how quickly the animal became domesticated and completely subdued, particularly after he had made the acquaintance of the other captured giraffe in the camp. Van Rooyen assured me that within fourteen days, our bull would be browsing with the others and have the freedom of the camp.

Before I left van Rooyen's camp, one of his servants was involved in an extraordinary accident, a mishap which was fatal.

The horses were hitched under the big shady trees. One pony, a dun with black mane, tail and points, had only one eye. The other eye had been destroyed the previous year when the animal had run into a dry branch. The dun pony was asleep on three legs, resting one, eyes closed and the head slightly lowered as horses do when they are asleep. The poor unfortunate African passed the hind quarters of the pony and in doing so, patted the animal with the flat of his hand on the rump. Before he realised what was happening, the horse lashed out with both legs in a mighty kick, landing with "both barrels" square on the African's chest and knocking him sprawling. We rushed to his assistance, but he died soon after.

It was a most unfortunate accident. Nevertheless, it taught me a lesson which I have never forgotten and one which readers may do well to remember. It is dangerous to approach any horse without giving him notice of your presence.

After staying with van Rooyen for five days, I began making my arrangements to make my move into the unknown.

Chapter Four – Blind Eye Provisioning

My packing had been completed and I was all set to continue my patrol to the Linkwasa Valley on the following day. During the afternoon, I was having a cup of tea with van Rooyen, when he said:

"I wonder if you will do me a favour and shoot some fresh meat before you leave? I have a £5 licence and have the necessary permission to catch game including Royal Game, but I have no licence to shoot Royal Game. As you may have noticed, there is at present no game in this vicinity that I can kill with my licence. The waters have dried up and most of the game, with the exception of giraffe, have moved on to where there is water."

"Certainly," I replied. "Apart from assisting you, it will mean that I shall have fresh meat to take with me tomorrow on my way to Linkwasa."

The same two riders who had accompanied me on the hunt for the giraffe were instructed to go with me and we were soon saddled, mounted and away. No more than a mile and a half from Makalola, we came across a herd of nine giraffe. They were browsing in the semi-open country and appeared quite tame as they allowed us within a few hundred yards. Suddenly they became restless and started to move. The pony under me – the same one that had given me a death-defying ride in the previous hunt – also became restless. He pawed at the ground, ears erect, pointing at the giraffe and straining at the reins. I gave him his head and he made a run straight for the herd. Before the giraffe knew what was happening and before they were in full flight, I was galloping on the near side of a young cow. It took only a moment to point the muzzle of the .400 Express within three feet of her shoulder and pull the trigger. The cow stumbled, righted herself, stumbled again and pitched forward to come down with a mighty crash in a cloud of dust – in the process, smashing several trees.

No time was to be lost if all the meat was to reach camp that night. I left the riders at the carcass to begin skinning and started the pony at a fast amble along an old elephant track leading back to the camp, to obtain transport and more hands to assist in the skinning. I knew that I had transgressed the Game Laws in shooting the giraffe but, as I debated the matter in my mind, I thought that when the circumstances had been explained, the matter would be overlooked. The moment that van Rooyen had asked me to shoot "some fresh meat" I had understood that it had to be giraffe. There was no other game in the vicinity and it was probably to save my embarrassment that van Rooyen had not come with me on the hunt. I had no doubt that, in the past he had killed giraffe and I daresay that had I looked for evidence in that direction it would have been forthcoming with no trouble. But who in authority – including myself – was going to lay a charge, especially when the person concerned had helped me with an extra horse, four donkeys and last, but not least, a hunting lion dog.

It was whilst I was returning to the camp at a smart pace and calming my conscience on the way that I barely noticed an ant-heap next to the path we were following. Big trees grew on the ant-heap and thick undergrowth covered the ground. As my horse came abreast of the ant-heap, he gave a frightened snort and reared suddenly. At the same time, I felt a distinct hit against my legging and saw a long black snake moving fast into the undergrowth. The incident was so unexpected that, for the moment, I had no clear conception of what had happened – apart from the fact that I had nearly been flung from the saddle. Getting the pony under control again, I returned to the elephant path and continued my fast amble to Makalola.

Back at the camp I reported my kill to van Rooyen and within a very short time, twelve donkeys and eight Africans left to assist at the kill. I was going to accompany them, but van Rooyen urged me to rest and have some coffee, assuring me that the Africans were easily capable of following my tracks and finding the shot giraffe.

Whilst we were having coffee, I told him about the hunt and casually related my experience with the snake. I thought the man was going berserk! He exploded with loud oaths, rushed over to where I was sitting, grabbed my right leg and had the gaiter off before I could fully gather what was going on. With the legging in his hands, he walked from under the shade of the trees into the rays of the setting sun and studied the gaiter with great care, moving his fingers gingerly up and down the inside of the legging. With a sigh of relief, he flung the legging on the runners of the wagon and said: "You were lucky! From your description of the snake, it was a Mamba and if his fangs had penetrated the leather, you would have been quite dead. From what you have told me, it seems that the horse undoubtedly saved your life. Snorting and rearing away from the snake, he took you away from the full impact of the fangs.

A friend of mine had a similar experience some years ago in Mashonaland. He lost his life. In his case the fangs of the snake broke off inside the legging, leaving two points protruding inside the gaiter. These points came into contact with the skin, festering sores developed and the poison eventually worked into the blood stream and caused his death. But this was not the end of the tragic accident. A friend of the dead man became the owner of the leggings and in due course his leg became inflamed with festering sores. Fortunately he obtained medical help and his life was saved. It was only then that the gaiters were thoroughly examined and the cause of the inflammation was detected.

Needless to say, van Rooyen's story shook me and I wasted no time in putting my leg in hot water, scrubbing it thoroughly and examining it with great care.

Chapter Five – Tails of Giraffe

Whilst we were awaiting the arrival of the meat, I asked van Rooyen to tell me more about Lobengula and the giraffe tails which he had mentioned earlier.

"During 1885," he said, "in this part of Matabeleland, especially here at N'Gamo and on the N'tundhla Flats, giraffe were to be found in their hundreds. I am not exaggerating when I say 'hundreds' – numerous herds with from 25 to 150 in each, roamed this area unmolested. They died in their hundreds in 1896 with that devastating disease, rinderpest. It was a terrible year and apart from the game being almost completely wiped out, we had to face the rebellion of the Matabele as well.

"Anyway, in 1885 I was on the Bembesi when I received a message from Lobengula that I should go and see him urgently. When I arrived in his presence, he greeted me with a smile and said: 'Nellus, I am in great trouble and I want you to get me out of trouble. I have bought wives from the Swazi King and he wants giraffe tails in payment for the women. You will go and kill the giraffe, bring me the tails, give the meat to the young bucks I will send with you and keep the hides for reims, whips and sjamboks.'

"I was delighted with the suggestion since the King would provide the labour to handle the hides and the product would warrant a trip to Pretoria where I had not been for some time – a trip that would also pay handsomely. I immediately agreed to Lobengula's suggestion and asked him how many tails he would require."

"Nellus," he replied, "I want many."

"It is a tradition, a practice which has been handed down – for a reason with which I am not familiar – that the Swazi women will give anything for the tail of a giraffe. They make bangles of the long hair, to be worn around their ankles, above the elbows, even around their necks.

"I have seen Swazi women literally loaded with these ornaments to the extent that they interfere with their natural movements. The Zulu and Matabele women also wear these bangles, but nothing like the extent of the Swazi females. Accompanied by some 300 Matabele with Chiefs in charge of them, I set off for the N'tundhla Flats. When we arrived, the essential scaffolding for the meat was set up and large heavy blocks of timber were cut for the braying of the reims and whips."

(Note: "Braying" is the term applied to the process of initially curing the hides.

In this instance, the hides were cut into long strips and then suspended with the heavy weights attached. Further stretching was caused by turning the blocks and "winding-up" the strips of leather and then releasing them to be turned in the opposite direction.)

"I then proceeded to shoot as many giraffe as could be handled in one day. Twenty-five braying blocks were in full commission. The fat was rendered down for the softening of the whips and reims and the meat was cut into strips and hung on the scaffolding for drying. It was quite a 'factory', but the work was made light with so many hands at my disposal.

"In fourteen days I had shot eighty giraffe and four weeks after my arrival at N'tundhla, I was on my way back to Lobengula's kraal. Imagine my surprise when Lobengula, after examining and counting the trophies said: 'Nellus! If I had sent an impi of young men to go and kill giraffe, they would have returned with many more tails. Do you think the Swazi King will send me virgins for a mere 80 tails? No. He will send me only old women. You must return and collect more'."

"But Inkoos," I replied, "you did not tell me how many tails you wanted. You said 'many' and I thought that 80 tails were 'many' and more than enough. How many more do you want?"

The King thought for a moment and then said: 'I do not know how many are needed. Go and kill many, many more."

I was compelled to return to N'tundhla with a feeling of frustration. I had accumulated many whips, reims and sjamboks on the last hunt and added to those that I had already, I would flood the market in Pretoria. To me, it all seemed a complete waste. However, I did not dare to fall out of favour with Lobengula. He was a good friend, allowing me extraordinary privileges and a free hand to hunt in Mashonaland and Matabeleland. Other hunters envied my friendship with the King.

Thus, a week later I was back at the old camp. In our absence, I think that every hyena, jackal, lion, vulture and wild cat had congregated at N'tundhla. The smell from the remains of the slaughtered giraffe had provided the attraction and the nights were alive with the mournful howls of hyenas and jackals and the grunts and roars of lions. The hyenas, with their skulking bravado, came close to the wagons at night, keeping the livestock on their legs throughout the hours of darkness.

I shot another sixty giraffe and having done this, made up my mind that Lobengula would have to be content with the total of 140 tails. The masses of whips and reims presented a problem of transport if I was ever to get them to Pretoria.

"On this second trip, one of the Bushmen was killed by a giraffe. I had wounded a young, full-grown giraffe bull and was following the blood spoor with two trackers. We spotted the giraffe walking unsteadily and staggering towards some shady trees. The animal was obviously badly wounded and on the point of death. To save ammunition, which was getting scarce, I was loathe to fire again. Entering the shade of the trees, the giraffe stopped and looked in our direction. I waited, hoping the animal would lie down and so enable the Bushmen to cut its throat. Whatever possessed one of the Bushmen to go near the giraffe was beyond me, but as he moved within range, the giraffe made a chop with its off front leg which connected with the unfortunate Bushman's head and smashed his skull like an egg to expose the brain. He died instantly and I shot the giraffe on the spot.

"On our return to the King's kraal, I immediately reported to him and handed him the tails. Again his reception of the tails took me by surprise. He congratulated me on a very successful hunt, saying: 'Nellus' you are indeed a mighty hunter. How long it would have taken me to collect so many tails. I am very thankful and pleased.'

"But, King,' I replied, 'You told me that your hunters could have killed more when I brought you the first lot.'

"Lobengula roared with laughter, his fat belly shaking: 'Oh, so I hurt your feelings, did I? Well I did it in order to awaken your prowess against the agility of my young hunters. It had the desired effect and in the bargain, I have more tails.'"

As van Rooyen was about to launch out on another fascinating tale of his relationship with Lobengula, the first donkeys arrived from the kill with the meat. We got up and went to the scaffolding where the meat was being unloaded.

Observing giraffe at a distance, one has no conception of the weight in the short body. The long neck and legs make the body appear smaller than it really is. The giraffe which I had shot was only medium sized, but at a rough guess, 2,500 lbs of meat were off-loaded from the donkeys – plus shins, head and the huge innards. Giraffe meat compares favourably with beef when the animal is young. The older the giraffe, the coarser the meat and it takes on a peculiar "wild" taste. As biltong, the meat is not too bad, especially if it is thoroughly dried out and crushed, saturated with marrow and then heated. Some of the marrow bones were cooked in the coals of the camp fire, the cook placing the knuckle ends in the embers and reversing the ends at short intervals to thoroughly cook the marrow inside the shin bones. When done, the bone was cracked and the marrow shaken into a preheated dish. The marrow, spread on grid-iron, unleavened scones, with pepper and salt, makes a meal to be remembered. I found it remarkable that one could eat and dispose of such huge quantities of giraffe marrow without being nauseated. Still, if one is fit, healthy and hungry, all food is good, no matter its origin. I have seen my Bushman followers throw their rawhide sandals into the embers of the fire and chew the charcoal residue with relish! I have never tried the sandal, preferring to pull in my belt.

Chapter Six – The King's Beer

After supper, I reminded van Rooyen of the story that he had been about to tell me before the meat arrived.

"Oh, yes," he said. "I was on my way to the King's Kraal one morning in order to pay my respects to Lobengula as I was returning to the lower Bembesi. En route, I met three Matabele warriors coming from the direction of the kraal. One of them was M'hlaba, one of Lobengula's headmen and a leader of an Impi. He was a fine specimen of a man – six feet tall, built in proportion, muscular, straight as an arrow and with a lightish copper-coloured skin. He was wearing wild cat skins with the tails around his loins and the mane of a lion provided his headress. All three had obviously been drinking in the King's enclosure and were laughing, joking and generally full of fun.

As I entered the gate of the stockade, I saw Lobengula in his chair addressing some twenty assembled headmen. Seeing me, he stopped talking, greeted me and invited me to sit down and drink some beer with him. I was no sooner seated and handed a mug of beer when twelve strapping young Matabele girls entered the enclosure, each one carrying a calabash of beer on her head. Each one placed her calabash on the ground in front of the King, knelt before him and clapped her hands in greeting to Lobengula. One of the girls carried no calabash and Lobengula demanded an immediate explanation.

"The girl explained: 'On my way here we met M'hlaba and his two companions and he asked me to let him drink from my calabash. I refused and told him that the beer was the King's. He was insistent and struggled for the beer, making me drop and break the calabash.'

"There was complete silence. Lobengula's face filled with a diabolical rage. Words failed him and the silence was prolonged. Finally he gave instructions for M'hlaba to be brought to him and got up and went into his enormous living hut.

"During the King's absence, one of the headmen explained to me that the King's beer was sacred and that it was a grievous offence to touch it, let alone drink it except at the Royal invitation. There were 14 headmen appointed in the vicinity to brew the King's beer and in turn, each headman delivered 12 four-gallon calabashes every day. In the same way, seven headmen were delegated to provide a young ox every second day for the benefit of the King's kraal. Only two men were in charge of the actual slaughter and if anything was wrong with the meat the lives of those two were in jeopardy."

"Lobengula reappeared from the hut, took his seat and brooded in silence. Not a word was spoken and the audience waited with suppressed excitement. I remained with them, sipping the beer which I had been given. It was the best kaffir beer I have ever tasted – made from kaffir corn, with a reddish tinge, it sparkled like cider and was as cold as ice. The beer was stored in a dark tunnel, open at both ends so that a breeze blew constantly over the calabashes. It was beautifully refreshing but very potent.

"A commotion outside the stockade drew the attention of the gathering and within seconds, M'hlaba was standing to attention before his King with two of Lobengula's bodyguards on either side of him.

"M'hlaba raised his right hand high and greeted the King. The girl who had made the complaint against him was commanded to repeat her story and was then dismissed to rejoin the other eleven girls who were standing awaiting Lobengula's pleasure. M'hlaba made no denial of the charge, but stood there without moving a muscle or flickering an eye.

"The King eyed him with a steady glare for the best part of five minutes during which time not a sound was to be heard. He eventually spoke and demanded a knife, whereupon a knife was hastily sharpened and brought to be laid on the ground before him. Another period of absolute silence passed with Lobengula continuing to fix M'hlaba with that menacing stare. Eventually the King shouted to his bodyguard: 'Cut off his ear close by the skull and let it hang by the lobe.'

"The order was carried out immediately. M'hlaba did not move once. He remained there immobile and as steady as a rock as the operation was performed. Blood poured from the mutilated ear, covering the side of his body and dripping into the skins he was wearing.

"The performance reduced me to that unpleasant state in which one is not ill, but wishes, on the whole, that one might be. I am certain that if M'hlaba had begged for mercy, there would have been an end to the torture, but he showed no such signs. In fact, his posture had taken on an air of defiance and I think that this attitude served only to annoy the King still further. Lobengula commanded that a like treatment be performed on the other ear.

"Even this second assault had no apparent effect on the warrior. His control was amazing. He just stood there and after several minutes of dead silence, the King shouted: 'Now you can go and since your ears have been opened, remember that the beer brewed for your King, belongs to your King and only your King has the privilege of giving it away!'

"M'hlaba saluted Lobengula and swung around in a dancing motion, his ears flapping loose from his head and his body covered in blood. Before anyone had realised what was happening, he seized a stabbing spear from a guard and wheeling to again face the King, he cried: 'My King. You do not realise what a brave General you had. I will show you how brave.'

"And with these words he placed the point of the stabbing spear between his collar bone and neck and pulled downwards on the shaft. He staggered back and forth, all the time pulling the spear deeper into his body with all his strength. His knees buckled with the superhuman will-power, he pulled himself erect, struggling to force the spear still deeper into his chest. He fell on one knee and strove to regain his feet but his strength was fast fading. With a final effort, he strove to regain the upright position but fell forward on his face. His body gave several final quivers, stretched and then became motionless, blood gushing from the nose and mouth.

"I managed to get outside where I was violently ill. The body was removed from the enclosure and sand was strewn over the disgusting red puddles on which the bluebottle flies were already swarming. Beer was ordered and before long, everyone present was swallowing gallons of the stuff – including myself."

Chapter Seven – Into the Unknown

It was with reluctance that we left Makalola and the friendly and fascinating company of Cornelius van Rooyen. The five days spent in his camp had been instructive and full of interest and his generosity in loaning me the second horse, the four additional pack donkeys, Pistol the lion dog and last, but by no means least, the services of Bankamakuni, the Bushman, was something which I was to value beyond measure within a very short time. As we moved from Makalola, the party now consisted of two horses, eight donkeys, a mule, four dogs, the two constables, Kleinbooi and Dubani, Bankamakuni and myself.

We were moving into unknown country and I experienced no small amount of anticipation and apprehension as we followed the tracks from Makalola towards the Linkwasa Valley. The tracks were old elephant foot-paths which had been made in the rainy season. We were forced to change from one track to another to keep on course for our destination. The country through which we were travelling was well timbered.

For long distances we passed through dense forests of giant trees. Emerging from one of these forests late in the afternoon, we abruptly found ourselves travelling downhill into the Linkwasa Valley. The Valley was wide and extended to the West as far as the eye could see. At the bottom of the valley we found water – a green slushy mud. From the tracks it was apparent that warthog and rhino had recently rolled in the puddle and among the tracks of all species of game, the pads of two lions were very obvious.

Bankamakuni was detailed to deepen and clean the depression. The rest of us pitched camp close to the water in the midst of a cluster of mangwe trees. Bankamakuni had been at his task for only a few minutes when, to my surprise, clean water oozed from the fine sand and before sundown, we were drinking fresh clean filtered water.

We passed a restful night, punctuated only by the occasional weird howl from hyenas, until the false dawn of the morning. Then suddenly the animals became restless. Their ears pricked forward in the direction of the water and the dogs started barking. The fires were re-kindled and we sat expectantly for the break of day.

As visibility improved, we were treated to the sight of a wonderful assortment of game. In the valley were giraffe, sable, zebra and six gemsbok. The latter were the first that I had seen in Rhodesia – what handsome animals! With their long straight horns, their fawn grey colour with the distinct black-brown band along the lower sides of the body, the long black tuft of hair on the lower part of the neck and the long tail reaching below the hocks – they were indeed a magnificent specimen of antelope. I was puzzled how, with these long straight sharp horns, the animal defended itself, but I was later to witness two bulls fighting at Tamaseta and the action was amazing.

Shortly before sunrise, we heard a lion roar in the distance. At the water, the pug marks of lion were again seen. Obviously, it had been the nearness of the cats which had caused the excitement amongst our animals before dawn.

There was no time to be lost if we were to continue our journey to Mangesi Gorri. Trekking with donkeys is a very slow business, especially if there is no defined road or path available, and one has to constantly check direction by sun and stars. I doubt if we covered more than two miles an hour – if that! As the sun set we had not reached our objective and we made camp in a thickly wooded area. This in itself was quite a job. Trees had to be felled for our protection and that of the animals, dry wood had to be collected for the fires. During the night, we were considerably disturbed by roaring lions and the incessant wailing of hyenas and jackals.

We set out early the next morning and arrived at the pan at about 10 a.m. The water in the pan was not too good. Unlike Linkwasa, Mangesi Gorri had only surface water which was green and lukewarm. Game had puddled the outer edges of the pan and the centre had received the attentions of a herd of bathing elephants the previous day.

Whilst I was inspecting the pan and the Africans were making camp, I found fresh, barefoot, human prints in the mud. They appeared to be of a child and of a slightly larger person. I called to Bankamakuni and showed him the tracks. We followed them and found a small footpath leading into the forest. We hurried on and heard the yelp of a dog. A few minutes later, we stumbled on some rough shelters, one of which contained a Bushman.

The man was no more than five feet in height, had high-boned cheeks and slanted wide eyes of deep brown, clear and penetrating. His ears were no bigger than a shilling piece and his round head was covered with "pepper-corn" hair. His nose was broad and flat, his lips full and the teeth even and pure white. His colour was a dirt-stained apricot yellow.

One of the poor fellow's legs was swollen from ankle to knee and his body emaciated by illness and starvation. He was in agony and obviously suffering from excruciating pain. His eyes were alive and fierce and he was patently upset at our presence. Had he been capable of moving, I had no doubt that we would never have found him. I asked Bankamakuni to speak to him to convince him that we meant no harm and to allow me to doctor his leg. Leaving the two of them, I returned to the camp for my "medical bag" and instructed Kleinbooi to return with me with a big piece of giraffe meat and an empty paraffin tin. Whilst water was being heated, I examined the Bushman's foot and discovered that a thorn had penetrated the skin and caused the festering. Amongst my medical instruments I had a very useful lancet and with this I made a deep incision into the swelling. Pus burst from the incision, bringing almost immediate relief.

The man's name was C'wai and he was given some grilled meat which he devoured with relish. He called the name of someone and, as from nowhere, a tiny woman and a small girl made their appearance, followed by a smokey-patched pariah bitch – thin, just skin and bone. The woman was carrying an old muzzle loader and a red flat tin, which I later found to contain black powder. A small satchel contained two dozen caps. I pretended that I had not seen them as they approached the fire hesitantly, gazing at me with wonder and fright in their eyes. I offered them each a piece of the grilled meat. They were reluctant to accept it until C'wai, the husband and father, persuaded them to take it. They took the meat with a bashful embarrassment. This small family belonged to the original – or perhaps aboriginal – Bushman type. I felt extremely sorry for them in their plight and was determined to assist them if they would accept such help as I was able to offer. Spending their lives in the wastelands, little better than their animal co-occupants, I had a great respect for their venturesome living.

The encounter with the family placed me in something of a quandary; I could not leave them at Mangesi Gorri as the water was fast drying up. On the other hand, C'wai, with his diseased leg would be unable to move. Left at the spot, they would not survive long, whether lack of water or carnivorous animals brought their end. Whilst I was thinking this over, C'wai was relating to Bankamakuni how his child had nearly been carried away by a hyena only a few nights previously. The child had been saved by her mother who had thrown a burning log at the beast. C'wai also complained of a bold leopard, which, with hoarse grunting and coughing, had closed on their rough shelters the past nights.

Putting aside the larger problem for the moment, I decided to despatch the leopard that same night. It presented a very real threat to both camps. Having made sure that both camps were safe for the coming darkness, Bankamakuni, Kleinbooi and I tracked the leopard's spoor to an elephant path which seemed to be the cat's route to the water. I had borrowed the muzzle loader from C'wai and we secured this to a tree on the path with a large lump of meat securely tied around the muzzle, hoping that if and when the leopard took the meat and pulled, the charge would go off right into its mouth.

At red dawn, the following morning, the trap was discharged. As soon as it was light enough, we approached the spot with all the dogs. To our disappointment, we found no dead leopard! Pistol, with the other dogs in hot pursuit, set off into the bush and within seconds, they all gave tongue. Tracing the yapping, I found "Spots" up a tree, blood dripping from a wound on its cheek and with an evil, malevolent eye and twitching tail, he watched my approach with threatening maliciousness. Before he could try anything, I brought him out of the tree with a charge of slugs from the shotgun. He was dead as he landed on the ground. There is no better weapon at close quarters than a shotgun and apart from this, the gun can keep the pot boiling merrily with feathered and small game. C'wai had told me via Bankamakuni that there were cattle on the Nata River and this information decided me to go on to the Nata to check whether these were the reason for patrol – illegally imported from over the border. Before starting out, however, it was necessary to get the Bushman's leg in better shape and to replenish the larder. The meat supply was getting very low and what was left was pretty "high". I now had seven mouths to feed, including myself, plus the four dogs.

In the afternoon we hunted for fresh meat. We encountered three old sable bulls. They were quite tame and let us within 200 yards. I dropped the leader with a broken back. Unfortunately, I only had fifty rounds for the .400 Westley Richards Express and I was reluctant to expend another shell to kill the bull. Kleinbooi and Bankamakuni tried to get near the animal to finish him off with their small battle axes, but they had no hope of getting within those vicious sweeping horns. With his massive arched neck, the heavy black mane, the pointed ears on the alert and the large eyes showing much white, the sable looked noble and distinguished. This heroism justified the second bullet and the old bull died instantly.

On the fourth day after my arrival at Mangesi Gorri, I decided to make a move. The water in the pan was evaporating quickly and was getting beyond fitness for human consumption. Although our camp fires were close to the water and the dogs barked all night, this did not prevent a rhino from rolling in and literally mucking up our precious water supply. We had to move.

The packs were re-arranged and adjusted in order to leave room for C'wai with his injured leg on one donkey and his little daughter on a second donkey. All available receptacles were filled with water and off we set for the Nata, Bankamakuni leading one horse ahead and the balance of humans and animals behind. It is as well that one cannot see into the future. Had I known what was facing me, I would have returned and taken the Plumtree route.

Chapter Eight – The Thirst Trek

The desert which confronted us stretched out in every direction. By 8 a.m., the sun and the distant mirage against the blue scrub was dazzling and blinding to the eye. Scattered bunches of grass and the occasional clump of green trees gave a very false impression – there was no water. The dry heat was so intense and the direct rays of the sun so hot by 9 a.m., that we were compelled to camp under a cluster of Msasa trees which provided an abundance of shade.

The indigenous Msasa tree, of which there are nine different species, is well distributed throughout Rhodesia. From August, one can see the wonderful bronze or reddish-brown leaves coming to life and eventually turning green. I often wondered how nature provided for this extraordinary phenomenon well before the Spring rains set in. The secret was revealed to me a few years ago. The tap root of the Msasa penetrates to a depth of twenty feet or more and obtains for the tree sufficient water to make it bud before the rains. The leaves are so coloured to protect them from the heat of the sun at this time of the year. If the leaf budded green, it would quickly be scorched.

At about 5 p.m., it was possible to move again and the trek continued. As darkness overtook us, the pace slackened as we had natural obstacles to surmount. Thick tangles of thorny scrub were our greatest difficulty and zig-zagging and twisting through the heavy growth reduced our speed to no more than about one and a half miles per hour. Deep into the night we plodded on until it was evident that the animals had had enough and we were compelled to pitch camp.

At dawn we were on the move again, staggering on until the flaming sun burnt like a branding iron and again we were forced to seek shade and rest. Late in the afternoon the march was continued – but not for long. The horses, pack animals and the dogs – especially the dogs – suffered and were badly in need of water. To make matters worse, we were unable to eat; our tongues had become dry and woolly – there was no saliva to help the food down one's throat. Not a moan came from the Bushmen. C'wai with his wounded leg must have suffered agonies but no word of complaint came from his lips. The little Bushman girl and her mother likewise suffered in silence, their eyes widening hourly and the whites becoming more and more pronounced.

We were in serious trouble and all was lost if we did not reach water soon.

Sleep was out of the question. One's brain becomes diseased and is flooded with false visions of water, ice, rain, snow, running crystal clear streams. Even the sea appeared in one's delirium.

Towards midnight, it became quite chilly and as the burden of suffering was lightened, the brain became clearer. Addressing the constables with Bankamakuni interpreting to the Bushmen, I suggested that Bankamakuni and I should push on ahead and if and when we found water, we would retrace our tracks with filled waterbags. Meanwhile, all the packs on the donkeys should be stacked so that if we failed to return quickly, the rest of the party could follow us as best they were able on the donkeys.

We set off, Bankamakuni leading one of the horses whilst I was mounted on the other. The pack mule followed with my personal belongings. Bankamakuni's powers of perseverance were astonishing. He was like a machine, silent and inscrutable, as we threaded our way through the scrub in a south south-westerly direction.

Shortly after sunrise we came to a depression which showed considerable green growth. The animals tried to increase their pace but without success. We reached the pan to find that it was dry although it must have contained water until quite recently. Now it was dry, the mud in the bottom cracked and curled like dry fish scales.

We were bitterly disappointed and plodded on.

As the sun climbed higher, the discomfort to us and especially to the animals increased. The ground over which we were passing acted as a reflector and flung back the heat. Progress was painfully slow. Battered by the relentless sun and parched with thirst, I felt completely dehydrated and my mouth was filled with an enlarged tongue.

At about ten in the morning, the dogs suddenly started a wobbling trot and the topography of the country changed to mopane. Even the horses attempted a faster pace. Bankamakuni, without looking round, lifted his arm and pointed forward. The ground had become firmer and no longer were the horses ploughing to their fetlocks in the everlasting sand. The dogs had vanished in front of us and now the mule passed us, stumbling and struggling to go faster. We entered a forest of huge mopane trees, straight as candles and reaching upwards some forty or fifty feet.

Within half an hour we had reached the banks of the Nata River and were in sight of a fair-sized pool of clear water.

There was no time or inclination to off-saddle. We staggered to the water, fell down and drank and drank and drank more of the lukewarm, clean water. Suddenly my stomach heaved and I was violently ill. So was Bankamakuni.

After the first spasms had passed, we crawled to the animals and as I struggled with the saddle and bridle of the horse, Bankamakuni removed the pack saddle from the mule. We crawled back to the water where we remained, drinking, vomiting, washing and immersing our heads in the pool.

Chapter Nine – Bank Holiday

It was only after the third attempt that any water remained in my body and I began to feel some relief from our ordeal. With difficulty I managed to get to a shady tree and sat down with my back resting against the trunk. Directly opposite me on the other side of the river was a herd of blue wildebeeste. I had seen them as we approached the river, but at that time, other things had been in my mind! There must have been a couple of hundred of them in the herd – perhaps they had been disturbed from drinking when our dogs had reached the water. They just stood there on the other bank like sentinels, heads erect, their long tails twitching, and making coughing noises as they surveyed the intruders.

Bankamakuni slid on his buttocks to my rifle, retrieved the weapon and handed it to me, at the same time pointing to the herd. Up to that moment, my mind had been fully occupied with water – never a thought for food. His action in handing me the rifle brought me back to earth and I realised that we had nothing to eat. Aiming at one of the bigger animals, I tried to correct the wanderings of the muzzle of the gun and eventually pulled the trigger. A young bull dropped in his tracks – more luck than judgement in view of my condition.

Had the whole situation not been so tragic, it would have been laughable to witness poor Bankamakuni struggling towards the dead animal. He tried to run and promptly fell down. Eventually, scrambling along on hands and knees, he reached the carcass. It was some time before he returned with the pluck, heart, liver and some of the intestines of the wildebeeste. He kindled a fire and started grilling the liver. I still had not the slightest inclination for food, despite the fact that we had not eaten for days. It was only when the sweet smell of the grilling liver assailed my nostrils that my appetite returned with a rush and I had a tremendous craving for food. Before the liver was properly cooked, I started devouring huge chunks of meat. I should have learnt my lesson from the water. I was suddenly and violently ill. I rested for a while, washed and returned to the grill with caution. In a more civilised manner I had my second attempt at the liver and was rewarded when the food remained in my stomach. Bankamakuni was not affected in the same way. He gorged himself to his heart's content with no apparent ill-effects.

No sooner was hunger and thirst gratified and thoroughly appeased when the reaction set in. I became drowsy and was unable to keep my eyes open. Far in my subconscious was the nagging concern that I must return with water to the stragglers but sleep overwhelmed me and before I knew what was happening, I was lifted on to a feather bed, surrounded by soft, enfolding clouds and sleep, glorious sleep, wrapped me in unconsciousness.

I did not awake until the following morning at dawn, feeling cold, sore, worried and guilty. My first thoughts were for the animals. I need not have worried about them – they were all there, feeding on the green reeds in the river. They seemed none the worse for the gruelling punishment they had received during the past four days. They were full and showed considerably more signs of life than I was able to muster.

Bankamakuni, "the machine", was skinning and quartering the wildebeeste accompanied by all the dogs. I shouted to him to leave the meat and to come at once and help me get ready for the return journey. He did so reluctantly.

I had my head under the flap of the saddle whilst I was tightening the girth when I heard a noise. The horse raised his head and following the direction of his gaze, I saw one of the donkeys with Kleinbooi on its back, coming through the mopanes and struggling towards the water. We rushed to him, lifted him from the donkey and laid him on his back under the tree beneath which I had slept. Bankamakuni ran for water and we splashed it on his face and on his body but Kleinbooi was deep in coma. With difficulty we managed to get water into his mouth and he swallowed a few drops. Persisting in our attempts, we managed to get more liquid into him and continued bathing his body, head and wrists. His pulse was very weak and irregular. After about thirty minutes he opened his eyes and stared upwards, unblinkingly, lifelessly. Worried, I kept on with the treatment and finally, with a moan, he made a grab for the tin of water. That grab was the start of his return from the dead and within a few minutes some life was restored to his eyes and his arms went out for more water which we gave to him in small quantities.

Fully an hour after the arrival of Kleinbooi and whilst we were still ministering to his needs, a commotion at our backs made us turn to witness the remainder of our pitiful caravan staggering towards the water. It is impossible to describe the distressing state of the donkeys and the remnant of humans on their backs. Those pathetic long-eared little animals, swaying from side to side, as they stumbled to the banks of the river brought a lump to my throat and I would have broken down there and then had I not busied myself to aid the distressed with the assistance of Bankamakuni. We helped them from their mounts and laid them beside Kleinbooi who was still moaning.

The wonderful little donkeys wobbled to the pool, entered the water and lay down.

At this juncture, I had the most unexpected bit of luck. As from nowhere, three Bushmen and one woman appeared in the camp. They had ostrich egg shells in which they carried their water – our utensils were still back in the desert – and I instructed Banakmakuni to order them to help us. They brought water, water and more water with which we bathed our patients and forced it into their mouths. By degrees and after much patience, our efforts were rewarded and by sunset, we were feeding them small pieces of meat. As they regained their appetites and ate their fill, sleep overtook them as it had submerged me. They slept the sleep of the dead until the following day.

The donkeys received my heartfelt appreciation. Those lowly, patient, long-suffering animals awakened in me a respect which I would never have thought I possessed. To this day, this respect has not been forgotten. When they appeared laden with the lives they had undoubtedly saved, my thanks to them and to God were deep with emotion. Had it not been for them, this patrol, long and arduous as it had been already, would have foundered in calamity.

The next day, C'wai's leg was almost normal and this hardy little Bushman and his daughter were the first to be on their feet. The other African constable, Dubani, was the only real problem now. He had suffered more than the others, only for the reason, I think, that he was fat and tall and had made up his mind that he was going to die!

The strange Bushmen who had walked into the camp behaved without fear or reproach. The others, perhaps Bankamakuni, must have told them where we were going and that I wanted "followers". They attached themselves to the party and using tolerance, patience and consideration, my motto with these wild people, they were of tremendous help with my problems.

There were now eleven mouths to feed and considering there was nothing but meat, it was amazing how quickly a wildebeeste vanished with these half-starved Bushmen. In the afternoon I shot two roan antelope.

The next day, having seen Bankamakuni off with his three new companions, on the retrieving mission, I took the shot gun and on "Shanks's pony" followed the river to investigate the whereabouts of the cattle reported by C'wai. Some eight miles up the river I came to cattle kraals which were in daily use. Two native women told me that there were three hundred cattle grazing in the vicinity, the property of one Fath, a farmer in the Plumtree area. He had permission to run cattle in this area and came to inspect them monthly. They knew of no other cattle and no other animals had joined the herd from other directions. I was unable to shake their statements and ended by being convinced that these were not the cattle in which I was interested. I returned to the camp and shot three guinea fowl on the way.

Bankamakuni was back with the pack mule before noon on the following day with our property. The leopard skin was intact but the sable skin had been destroyed by hyenas.

We remained on the Nata for a week before going on to Tamasetsa.

Chapter Ten – Saved Again

The exhausting thirst trek which had so nearly ended in tragedy, forced us to take a long rest on the banks of the Nata River. The punishment had been severe and it took time for us all, especially Dubani, to recover from our ordeal and get back on our feet. The experience taught me an astonishing thing which I am convinced is more than a mere psychological phenomenon. As we returned to normal by degrees, I felt charged with excessive energy and a general feeling of extreme well-being. To this day, whenever I feel sluggish, I fast – and I mean a diet of nothing – no food, no cigarettes, only water. It is surprising how well one feels after this self-discipline.

The animals remained in and around the water grazing and obviously enjoying the green reeds. Grain for the animals was finished and to keep them in condition they had to have long periods of grazing. I experimented by cutting the reeds into quarter inch lengths to provide fodder during the night. It was a great success. The animals not only regained their condition, but looked better than when they had been fed on their normal diet.

According to the Bushmen, game was scarce further to the north, apart from elephant, giraffe and eland, and they suggested that whilst we were among the mopanes, we kill some of the numerous blue wildebeeste to provide a supply of biltong for the journey to Sibannini. Accompanied by Bankamakuni and C'wai – whose leg had completely healed and who insisted on being present – I shot four of the animals and came near to a nasty accident in the process.

Having fired at a large bull on the outside of the herd, the solid, hard-nosed .400 Express bullet went through the vitals of the first animal and struck another high up in the shoulder, paralysing it. When the herd moved we were surprised to find two wildebeeste on the ground. The wounded animal watched our hurried approach with red, frightened, enlarged eyes and its head, ears and mane erect. It looked dangerous and full of fight. When I was quite close, it made a scrambling movement, gained its legs and charged! Before I could get out of the way, I was flung to the ground. The huge beast was about to swipe me with its sharp vicious horns when C'wai, with a lightning action, buried his small hunting axe deep into the animal's skull. This all happened with such speed that I did not realise the extreme danger until it was all over. C'wai had undoubtedly saved my life – a fact of which he was to remind me on several occasions, especially when he became entangled with a boa-constrictor.

When I returned to the camp, I was perturbed to find that six more Bushmen and two women had quietly joined us. The "bush telegraph" had spread the news that food was available at my camp.

Bushmen can eat many pounds of meat in one day besides drinking many gallons of rendered down fat and marrow! With thirteen mouths to feed, I foresaw difficulties in maintaining supplies for both humans and animals, but I raised no objections to the new arrivals, who were quite happy to join the "hunting expedition."

A week after our dramatic arrival at the Nata River, I led the swelling caravan northwards to Sibannini Pan.

(NOTE: It was here, to Sibannini, that Sekuma Khama was banished by the authorities after a quarrel with his son, the present Sir Seretse Khama. The Pan proved so unhealthy and Sekuma lost so many of his followers, horses and cattle that he was later sent with his people to Nekati, some 40 miles from Sibannini. Later I was to meet Sekuma at Tamasetse where he came to hunt for elephant and eland. The Bechuanaland Government had given him a permit to shoot two of each and some smaller game. Sekuma was a strikingly handsome man, over six foot tall, built in proportion to his height and as straight as an arrow).

The journey took two days and when we arrived at the Pan, we were pleased to find that it contained a considerable quantity of water. Closer inspection quietened our enthusiasm as the water was a muddy green and had been contaminated by the hooves and urine of a large number of animals.

Walking around the pool one morning, studying the tracks of the different game that had used the pool during the night, I came across the spoor of a solitary buffalo bull. I followed the tracks with all the dogs and we were led to a small pool of water in which it was apparent that the buffalo had wallowed only minutes before. The dogs suddenly ran for a small clump of mopanes and had no sooner entered the trees when they gave tongue and reappeared chasing a huge, old buffalo bull. The animal made straight for the pool beside which I was standing, completely ignored my presence and turned to fight the worrying dogs. *Snap*, a bull-terrier cross fox-terrier, was trying to tackle the bull's nose. I stood there, reluctant to shoot the old bull and enjoying the spectacle of the fight and *Snap*'s aggressive cheek. Suddenly, *Snap* got a grip on the bull's nose and hung on. The bull swung the dog from side to side and up and down but the Determined *Snap* clung to the bull's nose. Finally the bull pushed its tormentor into the water and bringing its head up with a jerk, the dog's teeth were torn from their grip and the little white animal flew through the air. As the body descended, the vicious horns, with a mighty sweep, made contact and flung the dog yards outside the pool and onto the embankment. I shot the buffalo in the neck and ran to the aid of *Snap*. He was beyond attention and quite dead.

Everyone in the camp mourned the loss of *Snap*. C'wai's little daughter, especially, poured out her tears. The two had been great friends.

The Bushmen were surprised to find a buffalo at Sibannini as they had not seen them in this area before. The buffalo was very old, slaty black in colour, caked in mud and almost hairless. The bosses from which the horns developed were massive and covered the whole of the forehead. The horns themselves were thick and curved back and forward to upstanding points – not unlike the blue wildebeeste. He have weighed at least 1200 lbs. Against the ribs, on the near side, we discovered three slugs which must have been there for years. They had probably been fired from a muzzle loader with a black powder charge which had been too light to break the bones and penetrate deeper. I shot several elephant, giraffe and eland, from which slugs were retrieved in the same manner and the Bushmen explained that this was no rare occurrence when they were short of ammunition – though they usually stalked the animal to within a few yards.

Chapter Eleven – More New Arrivals

I returned to the camp and was dismayed to find that once again in my absence, we had been joined by more Bushmen. This time there were seven of them, one of whom turned out to be C'wai's father and a genuine aboriginal. In the reunion of father and son there was no demonstration of affection. C'wai's little girl (whom I have named Plover after the name of the bird in the Bushman language and which I could never get my tongue around to pronounce) approached her grandfather with slow, solemn steps and her eyes downcast. When she was within the old man's reach, he took her by the arm and, taking moisture from under his arms, he wiped the sweat-moistened third finger over the forehead of the child, repeating the application down her cheeks and around her neck! This peculiar ceremony was, according to Bankamakuni, the usual greeting of elders to their progeny.

As I watched the performance with interest, I wondered when and how the elders would show their relationship. C'wai's wife had been busy, with the help of the other women, grilling meat whilst the new arrivals sat with their heads bent, neither speaking nor moving from the positions they had initially taken. Eventually the women brought the meat heaped on platters of tree bark and placed it before the guests, murmuring a sing-song and clapping their hands. It was then, and only then, that the father-in-law spoke to his married daughter and nodded to his son. C'wai, who was grinning from ear to ear, then uttered the invitation to eat. This seemed to be the signal for a general recognition and there was great rejoicing. Washing and drinking water was brought with the obvious intention to please. Meat and fat vanished as if by magic. To my consternation, the women went on cooking whilst the men went on eating. How on earth was I to keep this crowd alive? There were now twenty mouths to feed.

Despite the problems they presented, my mounting troop of camp followers gave me a wonderful chance to study the Bushman and his customs. Only C'wai, his father, wife and daughter and two other families which I contacted later were true Bushmen and even in 1912, there were very few of them left. Today, I doubt if any of the race exist in a pure form, although there are supposed to be some in Botswana. They have interbred with the Makaranga, Bechuana, Moloswi and in a few cases with the Matabele. Consequently they have become taller, blacker, heavier-boned and more muscular. The only positive indication of their origin remaining is the unmistakable Mongolian features – the high-boned cheeks, wide eyes, small pointed ears and flat noses.

As trackers they were masters and despite the reputation of the American Red Indian, I could never see them beating these little men in the art of following a spoor. The Bechuana believed the Bushmen to be the first men that God created – hence their ability to go without water, without food and to follow a spoor like a wild dog. In the weeks that followed I was able to appreciate, having had much experience in the art of tracking, how these little people could tell with a glance how long it had been since an antelope, a lion, a leopard or a snake had left its time card on the ground. No two hoof prints were alike to them and once a wounded animal rejoined the herd, those particular tracks would be followed and sorted out from the hundreds of others left by the group. More often than not the wounded animal would keep to windward of the tracker, in which event the Bushman would leave the tracks, detour and rejoin the spoor further ahead. If no spoor was visible he would move in half-circles until he regained the tracks or found the animal dead or lying down. No wounded animal could escape their persistent and intelligent tracking. On one occasion at Gwaai, Trooper Rochard had returned from hunting bushbuck and remarked: "You know, this Bushman of yours can track a mosquito across a wooden floor. He is a positive genius."

Their hearing is also amazing. Whilst we were tracking a giraffe one day, C'wai stopped, listened and pointed in a certain direction. There was the giraffe and its presence had been revealed to the Bushman when he had heard the little red-beaked tick bird feeding on the giraffe.

Bushmen love honey and when food was plentiful they would go forth daily following the nondescript little brown honey bird. They seemed to understand the bird's excited chatter and would hasten to follow with whistles of encouragement. When the hive had been located and robbed the bird would be rewarded with a comb of half-formed grubs. Without this reward, they believed that the honey bird would lead them to the lair of a leopard or a lion! The Bushmen would climb recklessly for the honey, and although I have witnessed the robbing of a hive in such a way that the bees have not been disturbed, there have been tragedies. On one occasion on the Makahari Flats, the target was high in the hollow of a giant baobab. The bees made a determined attack, the Bushman lost his footing and plunged into the hollow tree. He broke his neck, the body was never recovered and the tree remained his grave.

Although they are unpredictable, unrepentant and often defiant as a race, I was shown such loyalty and sincerity by C'wai, having saved his life at Mangesi

Gorri, that had I told him to go and hang himself, he would probably have done so.

That evening, the reunion of C'wai's family was celebrated with an abandoned dance. Music and dancing are the Bushman's only recreation and then only when they have been well-fed and there is no indication of future privation. Their music is provided by a bow with a single strand of gut and a tom-tom. They clap hands and sing their "clicks" to imitate particular animals. They work up a terrific frenzy throughout the night and become so impassioned and excited to kill the imitated animal that they are quite dangerous in their delirium. Bankamakuni told me that he had witnessed dances which had resulted in deaths when the excitement of the dance had gone beyond control. The animal chosen for the charade on this occasion was the buffalo which I had shot that morning. The dance was followed by what can only be described as a Bushmans' Firework Display.

The women of the party had sought out several giant, dried-out mopanes. Invariably these trees have been hollowed out by several families of bush squirrel who eat their way up and up into the highest part of the tree as their families become larger. The Bushmen would start a fire at the base of the tree and train the flames into the hollow core through one of the lower entrance holes made by the squirrels. The tree then acts as a gigantic chimney and the fire roars up the inside of the trunk to emerge from the higher entrance holes of the departed squirrels in jets of fierce flame. Dry mopane timber is exceptionally hard and the six trees which were lit that night burnt for hours throwing off a glow from base to top. When the trees were almost burnt out they toppled with a mighty crash, scattering embers in all directions for hundreds of yards.

C'wai's little daughter, Plover, attached herself to me like a shadow in the camp. She was forever bringing me titbits – honey, cooked marrow bones, small bundles of green grass for the donkey that had carried her to the life-saving water of the Nata and collections of bones for the dogs. She was always on the move and it was a pleasure to see her dried-up, apricot coloured face, with its narrow eyes and perfect teeth, light up with pleasure when I showed my thanks for her thoughtfulness. One morning she brought me cakes of honey heaped on a bark platter. My thanks was profuse and clapping my hands in appreciation, I reached for the skin of the leopard which I had killed just after meeting the family at Mangesi Gorri. I presented it to Plover. Her excitement was heart-warming; away she ran – and she could run like a hare – shouting her joy to the world. She came back with her father and mother who repeated their daughter's thanks. C'wai said it would provide him with many charges of powder and shot as it was a valuable skin but, through Bankamakuni, I corrected him and told him that the skin was for clothing for Plover and her mother. I gave the mother a thick sewing needle and having examined it carefully, she burst forth with loud thanks, kneeling before me and bumping her head up and down on the ground. I don't think she had ever seen a needle and her delight and gratitude were touching.

That night the Bushmen held another dance and I heard them imitating dogs in their revels. Wondering what it was all about, I asked Bankamakuni for an explanation. He laughed and told me that they were braying the leopard skin, pretending to be dogs. They grabbed, pulled and twisted the skin, in the meantime barking and growling fiercely until the leopard was quite "dead". Sure enough, the skin was shown to me the next day and it was as soft as my handkerchief.

Late in the afternoon, Plover, with her finger in her mouth and eyes on the ground, obviously feeling very self-conscious, slowly approached my camp to exhibit her "new" dress. It was certainly an improvement on the "flap" which she had formerly worn and although the dress covered more than the previous garment, it was still very much of a "mini-skirt".

Very often ostrich eggs were brought to the camp and when my followers realised how fond I was of scrambled ostrich egg, the supply grew to an extent that transporting the shells became quite a difficulty. One day an egg was opened and out popped a chicken. Plover was delighted and in a great state of excitement, brought the wet, trembling weakling to me for inspection. With great care we dried the bird and kept it close to the warmth of the fire. Within 24 hours it was eating minced meat and within a week the ostrich was following Plover all around the camp. One day it swallowed a piece of bone which lodged in its neck. I operated and removed the bone and then stitched the wound carefully. Despite my efforts the ostrich failed to survive my rough and ready surgery and died with tears and heart-broken lamentations from Plover.

I mention this incident to illustrate that the Bushmen were not as sub-human as some people would have us believe. On the contrary, I found them to be sympathetic, inherently kind, friendly and capable of deep emotion. Their harsh life in the desert emphasised their deep comradeship and feeling for each other.

Chapter Twelve – On to Tamasetsa

Our supply of salt was exhausted and I did not look forward to a daily diet of meat without that very necessary condiment. I had heard of salt deposits in Bechuanaland but I had no idea where these were located. I questioned the Bushmen and they advised me that there were "mountains" of salt at the point where the Nata River vanishes into the Makahari Salt Pans. I asked for volunteers and five Bushmen agreed to leave at once. Supplied with a large quantity of meat for the journey, they departed almost immediately and such was their haste that I was given the impression that I would never see them again. Not that their desertion worried me – I already had too many followers and a few less would be all to the good. To my surprise, they returned within forty-eight hours, each carrying huge chunks of purple-pink rock salt. It was enough for many weeks and some could even be spared for the animals to lick. I was delighted. For my own use the Bushmen women cooked the salt and skimmed off the dirty brown scum in the process. When this smelly brown stuff had been completely removed, the residue was cooled, leaving clean white salt.

A wizened old Bushman, thin and shrunk to a shadow, arrived at the camp and reported that there were cattle at Tamasetsa – "As many as ants and lions are killing them all."

I made preparations to move in a hurry. Fresh meat was necessary for the journey and that afternoon I shot two tsessebe. I tried to shoot them from the saddle with one of the Bushmen's Martini Henry. What a hope.

This antelope is the fastest animal on four legs. When we closed in on the herd of seven they literally left the horses standing. Their fleetness and acceleration startled and dumb-founded me. Their action is peculiar and it seems as though the animal bunches its feet and hops through the air at an astonishing speed. I reined in the pony in amazement and decided to do the killing with the .400 Express which C'wai handed to me. Meanwhile, the herd had run for some distance, then stopped and turned and looked back at the horses. To my surprise they then came back in our direction! We sat and watched this inquisitive and curious performance and when they came to within 150 yards, I killed a bull with a well-placed shot in the chest.

The Bushmen explained to me that the tsessebe are very inquisitive and the Bushmen often approach the herd by covering themselves with branches, pretending to be "walking trees". The animals would stare and prance around, always approaching nearer, and when they were within range, they would be killed with an old muzzle loader or even with bow and arrow.

Hunting on horseback is exciting but extremely dangerous. One has to rely on the mount which must be in good condition, hardened and trained to the work. My venture in shooting the tsessebe from the saddle was for the sole purpose of conserving ammunition – not for the excitement. Apart from this, the hard gallops through the rough country took too much out of the horses.

Eventually we were on our way and having made an early start for N'guru, we managed to get to the pan late in the afternoon, having forced the pace and only given ourselves two outspans.

There was no visible water but ant-bears had dug several holes deep in the sandy bottom of the pan to get at the moisture. These holes were now cluttered with bird life trying to get a drink. The Bushmen, realising the trap in which the birds – especially the turtle doves – found themselves, attacked them and as they flew from the excavations, flayed them with leafless branches and killed hundreds. Amongst the carnage were several partridges which were presented to me and grilled for the evening meal.

We had left the mopane country soon after leaving Sibannini and were now in an area of msasa sand veld. Fresh tracks and elephant and other game were seen on our journey. As we had arrived late at N'guru, there was no time to construct the usual kraals for the animals. Instead, we collected a good supply of dry wood and kept the fires going throughout the night. I called Kleinbooi, Dubani and Bankamakuni to the fire and explained that we would meet up with the cattle at Tamasetsa. I said that I wanted them to enquire from the herdsmen if any cattle had left the herd since they had left the Zambesi and come on to the Pandamatenka Road. I would speak to the European in charge but I did not want any of them to reveal that we were a Police patrol. If they should be questioned, they were to say that we were going to Kasengula and the Caprivi.

At dawn we continued on to Tamasetsa.

I was reluctant to force the animals as I had the previous day and we camped at 10 a.m. in good time to prepare properly for the coming night. My biggest difficulty was in finding feed for the animals until Kleinbooi came to the rescue with something he had learned from the Biltong Hunters, for whom he had worked. His suggestion was that we should pulverise the Camel Thorn bean for feed and I was staggered at the results. The horses, mule and donkeys relished the change of diet and the women had difficulty in gathering enough of the beans to satisfy them. We tried other thorn tree beans with great success and I am sure that the protein content of these beans is high and compares favourably with other grains.

We reached Tamasetsa by mid-morning on the following day. Riding ahead with C'wai and Bankamakuni, I arrived at the Pan and there met a man by the name of Rademan who was in charge of some 600 head of cattle. Rademan was in a pitifully nervous state and was bordering on a complete mental breakdown. After we had introduced ourselves, the reason for his agitation, his irritableness and his constant state of fear was explained.

"Lions, lions and more lions plus hyenas and jackals! I think every lion this side of the Zambesi has followed me and the herd to this damnable spot. I had 800 head when I left Barotseland and up to now I have lost over 150. Each night the lions catch and kill three or four more and several head rush in panic into the bush never to be seen again. I cannot sleep, the herd cannot sleep and neither can they find time to rest or graze. Each time they get the smell of a lion they break into small groups and stampede in all directions. As soon as we have collected them together and try to set them grazing, they are off again. They are losing weight and will be worth nothing when they get to the Johannesburg market – if they get there at all!"

Whilst Rademan was pouring out his troubles I saw a herd of cattle running to the pan. They drank hurriedly and then left at a fast trot in the opposite direction to that from which they had come. Herd boys ran from all directions to try and turn the herd.

"You see," Rademan continued, "this happens all the time during the day. The poor animals must drink and when they come down to the Pan they get the smell of the lions and off they go. Of course, there are no lions to be seen during the day but the smell alone does the damage. The owners of the cattle will never believe what has happened and they will hold me responsible. If I move to the next water, I will lose the lot. I don't know whether to go on or to turn back."

Just then my caravan hove into view and seeing my donkeys he said: "My God! Donkeys! You will not have one left by tomorrow. Both my donkeys were murdered by lions at Pandamatenka. You must get busy right away and build kraals."

Needless to say, I ordered all hands to get busy on the enclosures. I selected what I thought to be a good camping spot near an ant-heap where there was an abundance of trees. The women were detailed to collect beans and to carry water for the night.

Rademan had a good supply of beef and he supplied me liberally. He explained that during the night the lions came from the windward side of the kraals and thus made the cattle stampede from the kraals when the predators would make their kill. The following morning he would collect the half-eaten carcasses and

those with only broken necks he would have skinned and cut for biltong.
Rademan told me to take as much beef as I wanted. That night was a most nerve-racking and sensational experience.

Chapter Thirteen – Lions

The enclosures for ourselves and the animals were completed by 4 o'clock. The brushwood, mostly thorn, was stacked high and wide and looked strong enough to ensure our safety for the night. A large quantity of fire- wood was also heaped in the centre of the enclosure – enough to keep the fires going until the morning.

From about 5 o'clock, until sunset, Africans brought cattle to the water, gave them a drink and herded them back into the kraals, of which there were four, big enough to take about 200 head each.

As soon as the cattle were safely kraaled and the gates made as secure as possible, the Africans laid heaps of firewood at equal distances around the enclosures. Shortly after sunset, Rademan gave a signal and the stacks of firewood were set alight. Unfortunately, the dry sticks soon burned down to embers and, although there were protruding pieces which if put back on the coals could have kept the fires going until well into the night, there was no one brave enough to leave the compounds, and to do this extra work. Consequently the fires later showed a red glow without any flames.

It was a bright star-lit night, without a breath of wind and, with the exception of an occasional "moo" from the cattle and the mumbling, under-toned voices of humans, the deep silence and calm were undisturbed.

Suddenly, a school of hyenas, with their long drawn-out mournful moans, raising to shrieks, gave tongue and immediately these weird howls were followed by the jackals; "Yaaah-ha-ha-ha" howls, repeated and repeated, breaking the silence of the night and producing activities in all directions!

Whether this was a pre-arranged signal or not I cannot say, but suddenly the bush became alive with the incessant laugh, howl, shriek, gurgle, cackle and grunts of hyenas and jackals. But not a sound or grunt to prove there were lions in the near vicinity. Pistol and the other dogs, with hackles erect, dashed from one side of the enclosure to the other, barking and snarling at invisible enemies. The cattle became restless, and those that had been lying down rose and joined the others in moving from one side of the kraal to the other. The more they became agitated, the quicker became their movements, accompanied by grunts and lowing.

The continual milling round and round the kraals promoted a thick dust which gradually moved in all directions like a thick foggy mist. Because of the stillness of the air, the muggy smoke-like cloud of dust increased and seemed to settle and cover the whole area in the valley, including my camp which was some distance away from the kraals.

One could only hear the commotion of the labouring cattle, their grunts, bellows and loud snorts. With the exception of an indistinct glow, the fires were invisible and completely covered by the increasingly accumulating dust.

A terror-haunted atmosphere was being produced by this hanging cloud of thick dust and the weird howls, moans and shrieks of the hyenas and jackals.

Altogether a weird, eerie African night. One that gave a feeling that something fearful was going to happen. No wonder one's marrow froze, wishing that the unknown catastrophe would happen, the sooner the better, so that the uncertainty would end. Not a grunt from the lions but we knew they were there; the cattle knew they were close; the donkeys and horses, breaking frequent winds, realised the cats were in the close vicinity.

Pandemonium in the kraals increased. One could hear the running hooves of the cattle as they milled in circles, bellowing, grunting, blowing loud snorts of fear and alarm.

The donkeys in our camp seemed determined to get right into the fires for protection. We had difficulty in calming their shattered nerves!

Suddenly, like a thunderbolt, there was a crash of splintering wood and the cattle from No. 4 kraal broke through the brushwood in panic, with loud bellows of terror, and stampeded in all directions, increasing the fearful blanket of thickening dust!

Within seconds came that awful, sickening, haunting sound of cattle being killed by lions. The lion gives several grunts and growls of pure satisfaction when he makes contact and catches the animal. Whilst the victim gives bloodcurdling bellows of anguish and fear, and spasmodically gives forth sounds of acute distress, like deep guttural sighs, which diminishes as the beast dies.

Apart from the sound of running hooves, which becomes fainter in the distance, complete silence reigns after the killing. An impressive and haunting experience not easily forgotten. Especially that blanket of dust which positively gave one the "cold creeps".

The cattle in the other three enclosures settled down. They seemed to know the lions were now satisfied and that they would not be disturbed again during the remainder of the night.

After the uproar, the shouting of the herds, barking of dogs, the dreadful commotion created by the stampeding cattle, a hushed silence and quiet calm followed. Even the hyenas and jackals were solemn and afraid to disturb the silent fear in the wilderness. Sleep was out of the question!

In contrast to their fear, terror and cowardly behaviour during the dark night, the African herders and my Bushmen showed considerable bravado during the day. Rademan called out all the herders to seek the cattle which stampeded and broke the kraal during the night. Strange to relate, most of the cattle, with the exception of seven, came back on their own. Obviously the animals realised the safest refuge was close to the humans and the water where they could slake their thirst.

The lions had killed four more cattle within four hundred yards of the kraals, and in the open vlei. At the carcass furthest away from the kraals, the herders disturbed five lions which slunk away into the bush on the approach of the Africans. This carcass was in fair condition and much meat was rescued for their consumption.

My determination to kill some of the lions grew as I walked round the watering places with C'wai and Bankamakuni, studying the general layout of the camps, water and kraals. I was sure that with trapguns I could kill quite a number.

Rademan, returning from the round-up of the cattle, was completely exhausted. His hair was tousled, his beard unkempt, his eyes red-rimmed, and he generally looked a muddled mess. I felt sorry for the man. He said, "You have now seen what happens every night since my arrival at this damnable place! What am I to do? Last night, with not a breath of wind to blow away that awful cloud of dust, has been the worst night I have yet had. I am lucky to have lost only seven animals – three might still turn up; we have only found four carcasses. That impregnable screen of heavy dust made the cats show more courage than usual. I am very worried and do not know what to do."

"Shoot them," I said.

"Shoot them?" he replied. "How in h… can one shoot these cats in the dark? They are never visible! Today, for the first time, the herders saw five, and they vanished into the thickest bush as soon as the Africans appeared. My rifle is only a single action .303 – a useless weapon with which to kill lions. I am sorry I did not bring a supply of poison. Of course, I never expected all this trouble with lions.

"After I opened up the water, the elephants gave me trouble by destroying the work I had done to get the water. Now they are not seen nor heard of. I suppose they have left, with all the disturbance going on here, but I would sooner they worried me rather than these lions. The cats are driving me mad."

"If you will give me some help," I said, "we will kill some of these lions tonight by laying trapguns at the water. Get your axe boys busy and let them surround the water holes with brushwood and leave two gateways to each enclosure. I will be there to supervise the work."

"What a wonderful idea! I will get busy right away and see everything is done exactly as you want it," he replied.

To have success with a trapgun, meticulous care and great patience must be exercised to get the trap set exactly right. At Tamasetsa the conditions were perfect for a setting. Lions must drink water and, there being no other water for many miles, the cats had to slake their thirst at these waters. There were three watering places and Rademan, with his Africans, had done some considerable excavation work to make sufficient water available for the large number of cattle. To enclose all these before sunset was quite a tough job. However, with the help of my Bushman followers and all the hands he could spare, the enclosures were completed by 4 o'clock in the afternoon.

The herders were instructed to bring the cattle in early, give them a drink, kraal them, and make the gates secure.

When everything was in readiness Constable Kleinbooi (who had previous experience with the "Biltong Hunters", in setting trapguns) and I, with the help of Rademan, started the setting of the traps.

The procedure is as follows: -

Two forked sticks are planted firmly in the ground on the one side of the gateway – spaced apart according to the length of the gun to be used as a trap.

The gun is laid in the forks, with the butt in the one fork and the muzzle resting in the other. The weapon must be level and securely tied in the forks to prevent the slightest movement.

A third stick is planted on the other side of the eight-foot gateway, in a direct line with the back sight and foresight of the rifle.

The muzzle of the rifle must be two feet from the ground. Consequently, the forked stick must be so regulated in height as to conform to this height.

A small stick, approximately six inches long and the thickness of the aperture between the trigger and the trigger guard, is inserted in this space.

To the end of the "trigger stick" (in which a groove has been cut) the end of a length of thin copper wire is twined and securely tied. The other end of the wire is led around the butt of the gun and then forward along the length of the rifle and tied, two feet off the ground, to the stick on the other side of the gateway.

Care must be taken that the wire runs along the length of the rifle, in line with the sight of the trap. This can be done with several loose ties round the weapon.

Slack on the extended wire must give approximately six inches. This six inch give is important if the discharge is to penetrate the vitals of the victim. The copper wire referred to is very thin. Years ago small rolls were obtainable from all stores by Africans for the purpose of making bangles. I had equipped myself with several rolls for the specific purpose of using them in traps.

In the one gate the trap consisted of an ancient Schneider rifle; in the other, a sawn-off Martini-Henry; and in the other three gates, muzzle-loaders acted as the traps.

Finally the traps were well covered with brushwood and made invisible.

It was almost dark when I joined Rademan in his enclosure for a cup of coffee and a chat.

He informed me that the cattle came from Barotseland, beyond the Zambesi, and were being loaded at Tsessebe Siding, in Bechuanaland, for the Johannesburg market. This was his first trip. Another man who had done the drive several times before was following with another herd, and a third herd was to follow the following month.

"Are the cattle all for Johannesburg?" I asked him.

"Yes," he replied, "the cattle dealers have been trying to find a market in Southern Rhodesia, but they have not been successful. I understand that no cattle are allowed to enter Southern Rhodesia from the north."

It was obvious from our conversation, unless he was telling me deliberate lies, that the cattle were on their way to Johannesburg. However, I decided to make sure and have the herds followed until they crossed the border into Bechuanaland.

With a parting "good-night, and I hope we are lucky and kill five lions tonight," I left his enclosure and walked over to mine.

Soon after I reached my enclosure, the hideous howling and wailing of hyenas and jackals broke the peace of the silent night. As if their "concert" was a pre-arranged signal, the first trap was discharged with a loud, re-echoing bang, followed by a muffled growl. An uneasy silence followed, and everyone, including myself, wondered if it was a hit and if we would find a dead lion in the morning. The second trap was discharged some hours later without the slightest indication that something had been hit.

Again that awful creepy stillness followed. An occasional "Yah-ha-ha" laugh from a distant hyena was the only sound that broke the deathlike silence. The intervals between the discharges from the traps were inexplicable and disturbing.

The Bushmen clustered round their big fires with alarm in their eyes. They were in mortal fear of the unpredictable and completely mute in comparison with their usual chatter.

This uncanny muffled night continued for several hours, when it was suddenly shattered by two explosions in quick succession, accompanied by several grunts and stifled coughs. Sleep was out of the question. We awaited the break of day with impatience and anticipation.

Chapter Fourteen – A Lion Hunt

Before dawn, the fifth and last crash of a rifle reverberated through the silent forests, followed by loud angry grunts and vicious snarls, which appeared to recede and diminish in the distance. Rademan shouted from his enclosure, "That one is wounded!"

At daybreak, and as soon as we could see, the Bushmen were instructed to tie the dogs on their leashes and follow me down to the water. On the way down Rademan joined us with several of his Maloswis. To our surprise and jubilant gratification, we found four dead lion, and the bloody tracks of one leading in the direction of the forest! Our success was indeed great! The results to this extent were unexpected, and the rejoicing of the Africans grand to behold.

In the one gateway we found an old lioness with a gaping wound through her vitals. She had died instantly.

In another gateway, we found a young lion, punctured through the lung by the Schneider bullet, with his head partly submerged in the water. He must have leaped three yards forward to get into the position in which we found him.

In the third gateway we found a young lioness lying on her back, outside the gate, with her neck shattered. At what angle she must have approached the trap wire to get the shot through the neck is inexplicable.

In the fourth gateway, also outside the enclosure, we found the "Grand-daddy" of all the lions! He was a huge brute, with a long black mane, bare scurvy patches on his skin, and fangs considerably worn. The charge from the muzzle loader had entered behind the rear shoulder and made an exit through the last rib on the off side. How he managed to throw his body back after getting the fatal shot is anyone's guess.

At the fifth trap, where the sawn-off Martini-Henry was set, we found pools of blood and the tracks of a lion, showing that the animal had gone round and round in circles before making off in the direction of the forest.

Leaving Constable Kleinbooi, who was an expert skinner, to remove the hides from the dead lions, Rademan and I made preparations to follow the wounded cat.

"Fools step in where Angels fear to tread", applied so far as I was concerned. Rademan remarked, "I know from experience we are now undertaking risky work. If the lion should attack you, I will stand and try and kill it, and you must promise me to do likewise if the cat comes in my direction." I gave my assurances. Being quite chilly early this morning Rademan had draped himself in a long sky blue German Military coat, which, he explained had been given to him by one of the German Police on the Caprivi Strip (in those days, before the First World War, Germany claimed the Caprivi Strip as belonging to the Reich; the British maps had it in red). I pointed out to him: "That coat of yours is rather long and may be troublesome if you should try to move in a hurry!"

All the dogs were on leashes with C'wai, holding on to an agitated Pistol, in the lead, following on the blood tracks. Approaching a large ant-heap well covered with undergrowth, and with flat bushy thorn scrub growing in the vicinity, C'wai said, "The blood is fresh and I am sure the lion is in that cover – better let the dogs go." I agreed and the dogs were released.

Pistol, with hackles erect, all his black points an ashy grey colour, moved gingerly on his toes in the direction of the cover. Suddenly he gave several short barks and dived into the thicket. Then bedlam broke loose! The lion growled and snarled and the dogs barked. At close intervals, one dog or another would dash out in a hurry, turn and go back to the attack.

The undergrowth was so thick and dense that it was difficult to see what was happening or to establish the exact position of the lion. Pistol and the Smokey bitch (from Mangesi Gorri) rushed in and out to the attack without fear, whereas the terrier remained some distance away, barking, snarling and growling with great agitation.

Aproaching nearer and nearer to the tumultuous commotion, searching for the whereabouts of the lion, I detected first the tail, switching from side to side, and then the body of the lion which lay with his head flat on the front legs, watching me! Kneeling on one knee to get a better view, I took careful aim and fired. Before I was fully balanced on my feet from the kneeling position, the lion appeared three yards in front of me on his stomach, turned over and, with a final grunt, died.

The bullet had entered on the side of the neck, travelled through the length of the body, and made a gaping exit high up on the off hind leg.

The only explanation offered as to how the lion covered nearly eight yards must be that it was poised and ready to plunge for me the same second that the bullet struck.

The charge from the Martini-Henry had smashed the point of one shoulder, presumably by touching the trigger wire on the trap at an angle.

From all points, Bushmen and Africans scrambled out of trees, where they had taken refuge, with satisfied grins and smiles on their faces. Rademan, approaching me with an impaired reputation, said: "I was close behind you when you aimed at the lion, and was ready for anything that might happen. But, God, the thing looked ugly when it broke from the scrub. There was no time to take aim, I turned and fled, tearing myself loose from those damnable thorns which seemed determined to hang on to me."

Indeed, as witness, pieces of the German military coat were hanging from several points marking the passage of his hurried retreat.

Bushmen eat lion meat, but only the hind quarters. The front quarters are taboo and strictly forbidden, because it may have eaten a human and killed the victim with the front claws! The lion's meat is a bright red and the fat a deep yellow colour. Much of the fat was rendered down for "muti" (medicine ointment).

Pistol and the Smokey bitch proved two wonderful lion dogs. Especially the former. He fully deserved his reputation as a "lion dog".

Cornelius van Rooyen had informed me that the establishment of this breed is strictly due to the importation of two grey–black bitches by Frederick Selous! These bitches were crossed with his ordinary "Boer Hound" hunting dogs, the result of which was eventually the "Ridge-Backed" lion dog as we know it today. He described the two "grey-black bitches" with curly hair over the body, and yellowish buff legs and points. From his description, I have an idea that the two bitches were Airedales. He also informed me that most of the litters from these two crosses were born with bobbed tails!

Pistol was born with a bobbed tail, and half the litter produced by Smokey, the Bushman bitch, of which Pistol was the father, also had bobbed tails! Some of these puppies I gave to Chief Sekoma, the father of the present Sir Seretse Khama.

The trapguns were set again that night.

Soon after 8 o'clock a trap was released, with an explosion that seemed to erupt a burst louder than any other discharge heard before. I suppose the quiet night caused us to imagine that it was a louder crash. Then followed terrible blood-freezing moans, grunts, howls and yelps. These convulsie sounds did not conform to the guttural grunts made by a lion. The Bushmen assured me it was a hyena making the howls and that he was wounded.

These moans continued for an hour or more when, suddenly, there came universal shrieks, crackling, and gurgles from what sounded like a pack of hyenas. The racket and uproar continued at long intervals right through the night.

Day was breaking, and visibility not quite clear, when we approached the scene. A number of hyenas were seen around one huge dog which was standing on his front legs whilst his hind quarters were on the ground. The pack moved away when we came nearer, and the wounded one struggled to follow in their line of retreat. His attempts, however, were frustrated by a broken back.

As I approached nearer with the intention of putting him out of his misery with the shotgun, he actually tried to rush at me, with fangs bared in a snarl. He was despatched with a charge of slugs in his head. The Bushmen were of the opinion, according to the tracks, that the pack tried to drag or kill the wounded hyena. The distance from the trap, where he was shot, to where we found him, measured 80 yards. He could not have covered this distance with a broken back without help.

We found spoor of lion which had visited during the night. The commotion and uproar created by the hyenas must have kept them away from the water. It was very noticeable, since the explosions from the traps during the last two nights, that the cattle rested in peace, and grazed without much concern during the day.

Rademan thanked me, and said, "If the cattle can remain restful and I can have a few night's sleep, I will make preparations to move on to the Nata River, instead of going back as I had fully intended to do until you arrived.

Constable Kleinbooi informed me that several of the herders in Rademan's compound had advised him that, the previous year, a number of cattle had been driven to the farm of a white man named Geise, on the Pandamatenka. This white man had his farm on the Rhodesian side of the border. They could not, however, say for certain if the cattle remained on Geise's farm or had been collected by subsequent drives to Tsessebe.

This was interesting information, and it was my intention to find out more. It was, however, several weeks before I managed to contact Geise. (Geise was the man who discovered the Wankie Coal Mine).

Chapter Fifteen – Rogue Elephant

Rademan and his herd of cattle remained at Tamasetsa for another week before Rademan decided to push on to the Nata River and thence to Tsessebe Siding in Bechuanaland where the herd was supposed to be railed to Johannesburg. Whilst the herd remained at Tamasetsa, the traps were set every night and two more lions and a warthog were shot and an eland cow had her leg broken.

The two lions were quite young and apparently from the same litter. They could not have been very careful when they approached the traps for they had both blundered square on to the wires and were shot through the vitals with slugs from the muzzle loaders.

The warthog, a massive old boar, had enormous tusks – the biggest I had ever seen – and had been dropped with a bullet through the neck from the Schneider rifle. The eland had struggled some 150 yards from the water and had then been set upon by hyenas. When we recovered the carcass it was in a mess, mutilated and torn, and the Bushmen retrieved very little of the meat.

After the success of the traps, it seemed that the lion was becoming educated and gave us a wide berth. Rademan had no more trouble and his cattle settled down to peaceful grazing and restful nights. When he finally departed with the herd, I told Constable Dubani to get two volunteers from the Bushmen and follow the cattle until they were over the border. The instructions were more easily given than executed: Dubani and the Bushmen were afraid to return on the Pandamatenka Road without protection. I relented sufficiently to provide them with the Schneider and the Martini-Henry – with one cartridge to each gun!

The cattle had not been gone two days when game, especially eland, elephant and sable, returned to the Pan to slake their thirsts. At first they came only at night but, soon afterwards, they could be seen at the Pan at any time. One day, a lone, old, tusk-less, bull elephant came down to the water in the middle of the day. I spied the monster from my tent and saw throw his trunk into the air, give several ear-splitting trumpets, curl his trunk under his chin and then rush at the donkeys who were standing close to the water. Without the slightest provocation, he repeatedly charged at the animals with screams of annoyance. The donkeys rushed in all directions and some of them stampeded straight for the camp, putting our lives in jeopardy.

I was reluctant to shoot the old bull, especially as he had only the stump of a tusk protruding. For a time I thought that he was just having "fun and games" and that, on tiring, he would have his drink and then clear off. It was apparently not so, but it was some time before I realised that the huge monster was berserk. After scattering the donkeys, the bull turned his attention to the camp, having obviously smelt the humans. Continuing his shrill screams of annoyance, he came lumbering straight for us. I fired and got him in the chest but the bullet failed to even slacken the charge. I fired again and luckily the bullet entered the forehead and penetrated the brain. The elephant dropped in his tracks with a huge crash and a cloud of dust.

Examining the carcass, it was evident that the old bull's condition had been caused by wounds which were still bleeding and obviously the result of shot from a muzzle loader. All the shot had done had been to penetrate the hide and crack a few ribs. Added to these injuries, the stump of the broken tusk was suppurating and gave off a sickening odour. The elephant had been suffering excruciating torture and the pain was responsible for his aggressive and angry mood.

At dusk, two elderly Bushmen joined the camp followers. They possessed an ancient, bugle-mouthed muzzle loader. Through Bankamakuni they explained that the elephant had charged them earlier in the day and having fired at it, they had followed the spoor in the hope of finding the animal dead. They had achieved this but my Bushmen were already at work, creeping into the huge carcass and hacking out large chunks of meat which they cut into strips and then hung out to dehydrate. In the meantime, their women were tending the fires, grilling meat and rendering down the fat which they would pass to the men to drink. The thick liquid seemed to act as an intoxicant as the men would laugh, jabber away in their "click" language and then go into raptures of delight at the slightest joke. The feet of the elephant were cut off at the joints, buried in the sand under the camp fires and left there for three or four days. When the cache was uncovered, each foot resembled a huge piece of charcoal but when opened there would be a large quantity of "condensed jelly gristle" which had a savoury flavour, was good tasting and quite agreeable to eat.

Bushmen are simple iron and stone-age people. Their reactions are in no way comparable to the Matabele, Makaranga or Mashona. When meat, their staple diet, is in abundance, they are like happy children.

Chapter Sixteen – Ivory Cache

The two new arrivals informed me that they knew the whereabouts of some buried ivory and offered to lead me to the spot. Leaving Constable Kleinbooi to look after the camp and the remainder of the Bushmen, we set out with all the animals in search of the tusks.

Some six miles from Tamasetsa, we entered a Mangwe (yellow wood) forest. These beautiful umbrella-shaped trees covered luxurious green, short grazing, there was ample evidence of game, and we soon saw large herds of eland, sable and gemsbok.

C'wai and the other two Bushmen guides who were walking in front of the horses, suddenly stopped and listened. The relative silence of the country was broken by snorts, as from a horse, an occasional bellow and then a thudding noise. Dismounting and following C'wai, we approached the area from which came the disturbance and saw the cause of the commotion. Two gemsbok bulls were fighting. What a sight!

The prancing of both animals, one of which had only a single horn, was something I had never seen before – or since. The one-horned animal was seeking refuge behind a forked mangwe tree and the other bull was milling around the other (who was obviously getting the worse of the fight) in flashes of great speed in a backwards and forwards, crablike motion. Both animals were far too concerned to be aware of our presence and we could thus witness the encounter to full advantage.

The single-horned animal was much bigger, heavier and older than his adversary and had a massive neck. Whenever the young bull charged, the elder would dive through the fork in the tree to the other side – and safety. As we watched, the younger bull made contact to arouse a bellow of pain from the other. Each series of charges was separated by a short interlude when the obvious victor would stand up straight, mane erect, neck arched, eyes rolling and triumphant snorts emerging from the extended nostrils. He was a well-proportioned, graceful beast and looked every inch a champion. Another series of attacks sent the old bull to his knees and his rival, giving no quarter, continued goring and slashing until the victim went on to his side. It was then that I shot the killer, for no other reason than in order to see what wounds he had sustained in the encounter. The old bull had no less than eight punctures through the stomach from which the recently eaten green grass was oozing. There were numerous long bleeding wounds in the hide of the neck and buttocks. The damage to the younger gemsbok was superficial – several long bleeding scratches on the off side only, none of which had gone deeper than the hide.

Giving Bankamakuni strict instructions to look after the skinning of the animals – gemsbok is the most palatable of all game, bar none – I continued on my way to the buried ivory with C'wai and the other Bushmen. Another six miles from our encounter with the gemsbok, the two guides indicated a giant Marula (Umgunu) tree and stated that this was where the ivory lay. I was agreeably surprised. We were only about twelve miles from Tamasetsa and I had reckoned on a much longer journey. The guides began digging and having excavated two feet of sand, there were the four tusks. It was difficult to find out from the Bushmen exactly how long the ivory had been buried. They were quite "dry", bleached and lifeless. When I returned to Bulawayo, the tusks were handed in and weighed 260 lbs. Some four months later I was pleasantly surprised to receive a cheque of £40 – a half share of the value of the tusks. The two Bushmen who had revealed their secret to me told me that they knew of another six tusks buried near Hendrik's Pan. We arranged to retrieve these at a later date.

On our return journey to Tamasetsa, we collected the gemsbok meat and arrived at the pan shortly after sunset, much to the delight of Kleinbooi and the remainder of the camp. They told us that during the day a herd of fifteen elephant had not only slaked their thirst in the pan, but had rolled, played and generally messed up our water supply.

Chapter Seventeen – More Lions

During the night, for the first time since the herd of cattle had left, we heard the roar of lions, the wailing of hyenas and the call of jackals. Towards daybreak, we heard the lions attacking an animal and distinctly heard the distressed bellows of an antelope in the throes of death. After this there was silence. The peace was broken by a sudden snarling and the noise continued with minutes of crescendo of intensified growling. This violent disturbance which continued past daybreak indicated that the cats were fighting amongst themselves. As soon as the visibility allowed us, we set out to find the cause of the racket.

C'wai carried the loaded shotgun whilst I was armed with the .400 Express. The constables were instructed to follow with the dogs, securely tied on their leads. The slight breeze which often follows the rising sun was in our favour. A mere 400 yards from the camp was a large ant hill. It was well-covered in vegetation and the continuing snarling and growling seemed to be coming from just beyond the ant-heap. C'wai approached the cover with stealth and extreme caution. Once he looked round with eyes popping: I motioned him onwards. With fear, bated breath and palpitating heart I followed until we reached the apex of the ant-heap. Through the foliage we witnessed an awe-inspiring spectacle: Two black-maned lions faced each other, walking as if on hot bricks round and round with never a second's hesitation. Like two professional boxers they sought an opening, whilst continually snarling. Some ten yards from the two protagonists, a lioness and three full grown cubs (one with the beginnings of a mane) were gorging themselves on the carcass of a dead eland. The cubs were covered with red "gravy" from their noses to their ears and clotted blood covered their legs and paws. The mother was clean in comparison, only her muzzle was bloody.

Such was the excitement of the scene that the fear and nervousness which had attacked me on our way to the ant hill subsided and was replaced with only an eager interest in the outcome of the terrifying combat. With louder, more intense growls and in flashing movements, the two lions sprang at each other, making contact in a vicious embrace and ripping each other with extended claws, murderous pointed fangs bared. The deadly embrace lasted only for the wink of an eye and then the disengagement was as sudden as the attack but whilst the two beasts were locked together standing on their hind legs, one could see the hair being torn from their respective manes. After the clinch the two animals resumed their threatening pacing; the snarls and growls became subdued. Meanwhile, the lioness and cubs continued to feed on their bloody breakfast, oblivious to the mortal combat of what might have been their fathers. Their only concern was in filling their already extended stomachs and they took not the slightest interest in the parental squabble.

The noisy battle between the two lions had started long before daybreak. It seemed quite possible that the struggle would continue for hours more; neither male seemed to get tired or be prepared to surrender or retreat.

Suddenly, the lioness jerked herself to her feet and with a blood curdling growl and her tail high in the air, she stared maliciously towards the ant-heap – towards us! In a flash I realised that our entertainment was finished and that immediate action was required. Taking quick but careful aim, I fired at the nearest of the two fighting lions and then grabbed the shotgun from C'wai's hands. The pride retreated towards the nearby forest with growling defiance. The male that I had hit followed the others more slowly. Before entering the trees he turned and faced us, gave several choking coughs and then subsided to the ground with blood pouring from his mouth.

The dogs flashed past with Pistol in the lead. Within minutes they gave tongue accompanied by roars, growls and snarls from the lions. I dared not follow. There were only a few rounds left for the Express and those had to be conserved for food. To go after the pride relying on a shotgun would have been folly. Reluctantly, we left the dogs to have their fun whilst we examined the dead lion. One cannot credit the damage which had been inflicted in those brief contacts of the two lions. The lacerations, despite the protection of the thick, heavy mane, had to be seen to be believed. The whole mane itself was a mass of clotted blood and fresh trickles dripping to the tips. The wounds were deep, as if they had been inflicted with a razor. The animal was simply torn to pieces and I presumed that the opponent was in a similar condition. Despite the escape of the other lion, I was sure that it would not live long. If his injuries were half as severe as the one I had shot, gangrene would finish him off very quickly.

The dogs continued to bark in the distance and the growling of the lions rose and fell as if they were chasing the dogs and then retreating. When we returned to camp, the dogs followed us in. They had no visible wounds and seemed none the worse for their play with the cats.

Chapter Eighteen – The Second Herd

Dubani and the two Bushmen returned that night having safely seen the Rademan herd across the border. At the junction of the Nata and the Pandamatenka Road they had met Lieutenant Morris (later Commissioner) and Dubani had a letter from him for me:

"Trooper Fairburn and I are camped on the Nata. If you can get here I shall be glad to meet you and if you need any help, we are here for that purpose. We will wait for two days after which we will return to Bulawayo via Plumtree. Constable Dubani has given me a report."

As my route was north, there was no point in returning to the Nata and so I did not see Lt. Morris until some 18 months later when he was in command at Gatooma (on which occasion, we arranged a raid on a professional gambler operating at the Cam and Motor Mine, Eiffel Flats). We were well supplied with meat – in fact we had too much and we were delayed while we allowed the meat to dehydrate. Four days later we moved northwards towards Pandamatenka.

Close to the Ngwasha, I was riding well ahead of the caravan with C'wai and Bankamakuni when we heard the shrill trumpet of an elephant. A few minutes later we heard the sound of galloping hooves and around a bend in the track, at full gallop, appeared a white man with a long flowing beard, mounted on a dun coloured horse. Our mutual surprise can be imagined. There we were, miles from anywhere, almost colliding. Reining his horse on to its haunches with a jerk, the arrival gazed over his shoulder and stammered:

"Elephant! An elephant, close by, chased me! A huge bull, must have been fifteen feet high!"

I am afraid that I greeted this outburst with laughter.

"You must have had a big fright to think the elephant was fifteen feet high. The record is only about ten and a half feet!"

This brief conversation seemed to settle his nerves to some degree although he continued to gaze over his shoulder along the track with frightened eyes. Further conversation identified the arrival as Smit and that he was in charge of 300 head of cattle being driven from Barotseland to Tsessebe. This was obviously the herd about which Rademan had told me.

Smit said that he had experienced no trouble with lions so far on the route although he had lost two cattle when a rhinoceros had charged the herd near Pandamatenka. Smit had started the drive with 300 head and he still had 298. Whilst he was still talking, the leaders of the herd appeared behind him, moving at a good pace with some fifteen or more drovers pushing them on. I explained to Smit what he could expect at Tamasetsa and warned him to get through there as quickly as possible, before the lions could concentrate and inflict the kind of damage that Rademan had suffered. Smit wasted no time and kept the herd moving past us. As soon as they were gone, I instructed Bankamakuni and two of the Bushmen to follow the cattle until they were over the border.

I camped at Ngwasha to await their return.

Chapter Nineteen – Snake in the Grass

The shortage of ammunition for the .400 Express became a serious worry. I only had three rounds left – not nearly sufficient to keep 27 humans and four dogs supplied with meat for very long. There were plenty of rounds left for the shotgun but at Ngwasha small game was very scarce and bird life almost negligible. It is very noticeable that where big game – elephant, giraffe and eland – are found, the smaller species are seldom seen. It seems that they do not enjoy sharing the same water. Elephants drink regularly and will travel long distances, as much as thirty or forty miles in one night, in order to get to water. They will even dig for it if it is not freely available. Eland and giraffe are less dependent on water.

The water at Ngwasha was not too good. After the elephant and rhino had bathed, it was quite a chore to get sufficient clean water for our own daily use.

One morning, C'wai and several other Bushmen went off after the call of a honey bird. Within thirty minutes they were back and reported that they had sighted a single "black bull" giraffe close to the camp. We hastened after the animal but were spotted by the giraffe which moved off. We followed the tracks but I was unable to get within range for a "sure" kill.

After several hours we arrived at a small "pan" which was over-grown with bull rushes and water grass. Feeling tired, I decided to forget the giraffe, have a rest under a sympathetic mopane tree and then return to camp later. Laying on my stomach, head on my arms, I was soon asleep. I had barely dozed off when C'wai awakened me and pointed to the other side of the pan. Looking up, I saw seven elephant coming down to the water. They entered the pan, started drinking and spraying each and then rolled in the mud with obvious enjoyment. C'wai, with great excitement in his eyes, handed me the rifle. To his surprise and obvious disappointment, I refused the rifle. The herd was composed entirely of cows and calves and I had no intention of killing a cow with a calf at heel. Abruptly the elephant ceased their play and with much grunting and noisy blowing, lumbered off in a great hurry. They had winded us and were losing no time in getting away.

Meanwhile, C'wai's attention had been held in the opposite direction. I could see nothing which warranted his agitation but as soon as the herd had gone,

C'wai dashed to the other side of the water, bent down in the thick water grass and produced a curling, twisting python! Holding the enormous snake with one hand C'wai tried valiantly to draw the long iron knife which was held in a sheath tied to his waist whilst the reptile tried, with more success, to wrap its coils around its captor.

I watched with interest. I felt sure that C'wai had known what he was doing when he had tackled the snake and that he was able to cope with the situation. The attempts of the snake to coil itself around the Bushman and the latter's one-handed efforts to prevent this, produced a spectacle that was full of humour. I could only laugh at the antics of the pair. The snake managed to get two coils around C'wai at about the same time as he managed to get hold of his knife. The Bushman started to hack through the crushing coils but was hampered by having little space in which to manoeuvre his murderous-looking knife. C'wai's right arm, in which he held the knife, was pinned to his side and he could only move his wrist up and down a few inches. During the battle the Bushman was shouting – as I thought, with excitement – but the shouts became guttural and suddenly changed to a wizened, dry sound. My amusement ceased abruptly and I ran in the direction of the fight to give what help I could. Before I reached the scene of the struggle, the coils abruptly relaxed and gave C'wai the chance to ram the long knife down the throat of the reptile.

If looks could kill, I should have died on the spot. The Bushman's anger and indignation at my behaviour showed with no uncertain fury in his face. I was rather mystified by the hostility.

Cutting the snake in two thus completing the unfinished hacking of a few minutes previously, C'wai dragged the two pieces – still twisting and coiling – to the mopane tree under which I had been resting. He prepared a piece of "tambo" from a neighbouring masasa tree and tied one length of snake, by the neck, to an overhanging branch. Having loosed the skin near the head and made a cut through the skin the length of the body, he inserted his fingers through two holes in the hide and with all his weight, dragged down to pull off the skin in one motion, leaving the white body of the reptile hanging on the tree and still twisting and curling. C'wai did the same to the other half of the snake.

During the whole of this operation, the Bushman looked not once in my direction nor uttered a single word. Having removed the intestines of the snake, he rolled the two lengths into tight separate bundles, tied them and vanished into the trees to return with a six foot pole. Placing the trophies at either end of the pole, he shouldered his burden and without a glance in my direction, stalked off in the direction of the camp in a frenzy of displeasure.

When we returned to camp, C'wai dropped his bundles upon the ground and launched into an irritable recital on the killing of the python with many gestures of annoyance and indignation directed towards me.

As we were unable to understand his performance, the constable and I could only guess at the reason for his displeasure. When Bankamakuni returned, having safely seen the Smit herd across the border, I instructed him to call C'wai to my camp to investigate his ill-feelings. The reason became obvious: "How many times have I saved his life? The blue wildebeeste would have horned him had I not been quick to bury my axe in the animals head. When the wounded lion charged, I stayed with him and did not run like the other white man. I stayed with him against my will when we watched the lions fighting. I remained at his side when the mad elephant charged the camp and the others ran. On each occasion, I was there to help and ready to save his life if necessary. And now, when I get into trouble, he laughs at me and refuses to help in killing the snake. I was in big trouble, my breath was leaving my body and if my knife had not killed the snake, he would have laughed to see all my bones crushed."

"But why did you tackle the snake?" I asked. "You must have known that you were likely to get crushed when taking on such an opponent."

"I thought he was only a small snake. When first I saw him in the distance, he looked small and in the water grass I did not see him properly. Had I known he was so thick and so long, I would have asked you to shoot him with the shotgun."

I went to great lengths in explaining to C'wai that I had been unaware that he was in trouble. I told him that I thought his shouts to be of excitement and joy at capturing such a delicacy. At this, the Bushman turned to Bankamakuni who was interpreting and his face lit up with a grin which turned quickly to loud laughter.

"He is right. It was my mistake."

All his grudge and hate against me was forgotten and we were firm friends again.

There was a great feast of python meat that evening. The Bushmen danced in celebration of the victory, imitating the snake in their contortions. It was an amusing sight but I would never forget the details of the capture they were re-enacting so joyfully.

Chapter Twenty – Hendrik's Pan

We moved north to Hendrik's Pan where, according to the Bushmen who had successfully located the four elephant tusks near Tamasetsa, there were another six tusks buried. Water at the Pan was scarce and so was game. However, the following day we set out in search of the ivory with six Bushmen and all of the animals. Our guides located the cache some eight miles from the camp but we were greatly disappointed to discover that the ivory had been removed within the last two weeks.

C'wai and the other Bushmen immediately started hunting for the tracks of the "robbers". Sure enough, within a few minutes, they had traced the spoor of several humans in the vicinity. To me, the tracks were invisible and only with the greatest difficulty and imagination could I detect them when they were pointed out to me. The Bushmen read them fluently and C'wai and the two original informants set out to follow the spoor whilst the rest of us returned to the camp.

We were still about two miles from the camp when we were confronted by a huge bull giraffe. In seconds I was ready with the rifle for a shot. The giraffe stopped and looked back in the direction from whence he had come and as he did so, I rested the rifle against a tree, took careful aim, fired and dropped him with a broken neck. He was an enormous giraffe – a real "black bull". The usual dark chocolate patches were black and the lighter blotches a dark brown, which made the animal appear completely black in the distance. A stench of sweet mush was predominant in the vicinity of the carcass.

C'wai and his two companions came running up. According to them, the tracks of the "robbers" ran parallel to the route we had taken towards the camp from the cache. They had seen the giraffe and it was their movement that had driven the animal in our direction.

I left the Bushmen busy butchering the giraffe and continued on my way to the Pan alone. When I arrived, I found that some of the Bushmen who had stayed in the camp were busy "grilling their sandals" – a most unappetising but apparently adequate means of satisfying their hunger.

It is surprising just what the human system will take when a person is in dire need of food and I had discovered how easy it is to dispense with items which are normally considered essential to good health. All my groceries had been finished weeks ago. It had been a treat to have a cup of coffee with Rademan at Tamasetsa but apart from honey, cooked berries (occasionally supplied by the Bushmen women) and the tubers of water lilies which are an excellent substitute for potatoes, my diet was purely protein – meat, meat and more meat. Despite this, or perhaps because of it, I was in excellent health – so much so that the Bushmen often had difficulty in keeping up with me. It was a different story with my clothes. They were patched all over with "brayed" duiker skin and my boots were in a very sorry state.

Whilst the giraffe meat was being dehydrated, the tracks of the "ivory robbers" were followed and led for several miles into Bechuanaland before I called a halt to the trail. It was the opinion of the two ivory guides that the owners of the tusks had heard how we had lifted the tusks at Tamasetsa and had lost no time in moving the second batch of tusks before our arrival. I had a suspicion that the two guides knew a deal more about the removal but were afraid to give any details for fear of repercussions from the owners.

Continuing north to Pandamatenka, we came across a party of Matonka Africans. I questioned them closely in regard to the movement of cattle in the area and invited them to a feast of giraffe meat to loosen their tongues even further. The cross-examination elicited nothing of value to me and the main purpose of my patrol. The only cattle movements along the Pandamatenka Road from Barotseland of which they had knowledge were the herds in transit for the Reef markets. They knew nothing of herds being smuggled across the border into Rhodesia on a permanent basis. The Matonkas directed me to the farm of a European known as Geise and we arrived there late in the afternoon.

Chapter Twenty One – Geise

This most interesting person was the discoverer of the Wankie coal deposits. Geise was a German, small in stature and with a moustache and goatee blond beard. His homestead consisted only of pole and dagga huts but the main living room was one of the largest that I had ever seen. The general impression of the place was certainly not one of affluence and I often wonder what recognition, in terms of hard cash, the man received for his vital discovery at Wankie. Despite the modest nature of the farm, Geise was most hospitable and entertained me lavishly.

I made further enquiries concerning cattle movements in the area and brought up the subject of a herd which I had been told had been delivered to Geise from the north. He remembered the occasion quite well and was completely frank with me.

"The European in charge of the drive suddenly realised that he had more cattle than could be accommodated in the trucks which had been ordered at Tsessebe Siding. He asked if I could look after the surplus 45 head until the next drive when they could be collected and taken on to the railhead. I agreed on condition that the herders would be entirely responsible for the cattle and in due course, they were collected and, as far as I know, were taken on to Johannesburg."

With the permission of Giese, I made camp close to his huts and, using this as a temporary headquarters, initiated patrols between the farm and the Zambesi. I sent Dubani and a Bushman off in one direction, Kleinbooi and another Bushman off in another direction whilst C'wai and I made the third patrol. The intention was to try and pick up the movement of cattle in any direction within a radius of fifteen miles and to gain information on previous movements.

The search was singularly fruitless. None of the patrols gleaned the slightest information that there was any cattle smuggling in progress or that, in fact, there had ever been such illegal movements.

In conversation with Geise one evening I asked him if there was any way of getting .400 cartridges for the Express at Kasengula as I was down to my last two rounds. Rising from his chair, he said: "I think I have some somewhere and as I have no use for them, you are quite welcome to them."

He went out and returned after a few minutes with a box of 25 rounds. He presented them to me with his compliments. I was immensely grateful. The ammunition took a great weight from my mind and represented meal tickets for the rest of the patrol.

Geise told me that there was a group of Matonkas living some 15 or 20 miles from Kasengula. Hoping that they would provide me with some information, I decided to break camp and move closer to the Zambesi. The going was pretty rough but numerous elephant paths helped us along our chosen course.

Late in the afternoon, we emerged from the dense jungle into a vast, half moon-shaped clearing which was dotted with clumps of gigantic trees. In the distance, in the centre of the clearing, we saw a herd of elephants playing in and around a big water splash. Dotted around the water and watching the elephant were clusters of impala, zebra and waterbuck. On the edge of the forest was a black mass of buffalo, grazing and browsing.

The elephants – forty, perhaps even fifty in all – had control of the water. The leader of the herd was a huge solitary figure with tusks yellowed with age. He stood there keeping watch over his wives and children like a great granite rock.

We retraced our steps to move back into the forest and I sent C'wai back to stop our caravan and set up camp on the fringe of the jungle. Here was a wonderful opportunity to replenish the larder and I decided to shoot a buffalo. Together with Kleinbooi and C'wai, I made a deep detour into the bush with the intention of stalking the buffalo herd on the far side of the clearing. C'wai, with his uncanny "bump of locality", conned our position from time to time until eventually he signalled that we were opposite the herd. We closed in and silently moved towards the unseen buffalo

There was a sudden stirring at the extreme edge of the herd nearest our position, followed by the noise of thousands of running hooves. We dashed forward to the fringe of the forest to witness a wonderful sight. Facing us was a mass of buffalo some 400 or 500 strong, a matter of only 200 yards from our position. They were on the alert, ears forward and heads erect, trying to get a scent with their distended nostrils. Some of the larger bulls moved with hesitating steps in our direction. They seemed to be investigating the cause of the herd's disturbance. Resting my rifle against a tree, I took careful aim and fired.

The report of the rifle was the signal for the biggest stampede of buffalo and other game that I have ever seen. The buffalo charged down the valley with a roar of thundering hooves like distant thunder. Some fifty buffalo emerged from the forest on our left and passed within 15 yards of us in their mad gallop to join up with the rest of the herd which was vanishing in a cloud of dust. It was a wonderful and awe-inspiring sight to see so many animals in their head-long rush. One would have thought that in their haste, many would have been crushed to death by the obstructing trees but they seemed to weave in graceful partings around anything in their path. About 400 yards away, the herd wheeled and the clouds of dust parted to reveal the guardian bulls turned and again sniffing the air in our direction. Meanwhile, the bull elephant had bellowed with a terrifying blast and had moved off in haste followed by his lumbering family.

When the powder-like cloud had settled, I saw my victim on the ground. He was not dead but badly wounded. Watching our approach with baleful red eyes, he snorted with hateful maliciousness. He made several attempts to get to his feet but was too seriously injured to be successful. With a final attempt, he managed to rise to his knees and then plunged forward and turned over, blood pouring from his nostrils. He was a fine young bull in the prime of life and with a beautiful set of clean symmetrical horns. (My inadequate transport prevented me from returning to Bulawayo with some wonderful trophies. Even my lion skins, some of which were outstanding specimens, had to be given to the bushmen.)

With so much game around, the presence of lions was to be expected and there was abundance evidence of the cats. C'wai was sure that we would have trouble during the night and, in consequence, we hurried with the butchering of the carcass and were glad to get back to the new camp before darkness fell. The camp was substantial and large quantities of dried wood had already been gathered together with a good supply of "beans" for animal fodder. Throughout the night we were worried by the loathsome hyenas and jackals. Although we heard no signs of lions, we found their tracks close to the camp the next morning.

Again, I arranged patrols in different directions in search of cattle movements but, as before, we had no success. After four days of patrolling, we moved camp again to a position even nearer the Zambesi. The surrounding country was infested with game of almost every description. A change of diet was provided when some of the Bushmen who had not been allocated patrols, went as far as the river and returned with large quantities of smoked fish which they had bartered for meat. Amongst the supplies were some monster bream which must have weighed at least 10 lb when caught. The fish was delectable and a wonderful variation from our normal fare of meat.

This camp provided no more information than had the previous ones and after considerable deliberations, I decided to return via the Pandamatenka.

Chapter Twenty Two – Narrow Escape

Our trek back to the Pandamatenka Road from the Zambesi was not without incidents which might have ended in tragedy had we not been favoured by our "Lucky Star" which had protected us on so many occasions on this momentous patrol through the wilderness.

Our first camp on the way back was made on the outskirts of a beautiful valley which was enclosed all round with thick jungle. Whilst all hands were busy making kraals for the night, we heard the calls and cackling of a flock of guinea fowl. The birds seemed very agitated and it sounded as if something was disturbing them. I left instructions that the dogs were only to be released when shots were heard and taking the shot gun, I set off with C'wai in the direction of the disturbance in the hope of bagging something for the pot.

The birds were in a thick "sinanga" (thicket). I could see some of the guinea fowl perched on the lower branches of a solitary tree growing in the centre of the sinanga and their agitation seemed to be directed at something below them. C'wai was leading and was concentrating intently upon the thicket. He stopped at intervals, listened and then continued with mincing steps. The impression I received was that he was stalking something other than guinea fowl. He stopped again and stared at the thicket with peculiar concentration before shaking his head and moving forward again. Abruptly he turned, faced me with bulging eyes and whispered: "Tau" – "Lion", in the Bechuana language.

I was not entirely convinced of C'wai's findings, but, to be on the safe side, I immediately unloaded the No. 6 bird shot from the shot gun and re-loaded with S.S.G. slugs. We were no more than fifty yards from the noisy birds and the thicket. Ignoring C'wai's warning, I advanced past him, on the alert and ready for anything.

Suddenly, a loud snarl followed by deep growls filled the air and a lioness padded out of the thicket right in front of me. She was a massive beast with a glossy coat and a tail that twitched from flank to flank. C'wai gave one shriek – promptly followed by the slapping of his bare feet as he ran from the scene at a terrific speed.

I stood petrified with horror. My heart missed several beats and my legs felt like rubber. I realised that the beast was about to charge! Within seconds she was rushing towards me with her head down and her tail stiff and erect. With only twenty yards separating us, I was staring death straight in the face and had the presence of mind to pull the trigger which released the choke barrel charge. The lioness paused for a second and then continued her mad rush. I fired the second barrel when she was only eight yards from me – I paced it off after the event – and the lioness executed a complete somersault and landed on her back, the brush of her tail hitting me on the leg. She was quite dead – the result of the mortal wounds in her head, thank goodness.

I sat down and was violently sick.

The shots had attracted the attention of the rest of the Bushmen and the dogs. They rushed past me into the thicket and a babble of excited voices and barking of dogs mingled with the cackling of the guinea fowl.

I took little notice of their activities. I was almost completely numb as reaction to the narrowness of the escape I had had from a terrible mauling and certain death set in.

It took me several minutes to recover from the panic and real funk which I had suffered and from which I was still suffering but the appearance of C'wai from the thicket restored my interest in the present. C'wai was holding in his hands a lion cub which he laid at my feet. The baby cat had been stunned and C'wai's excitement was obvious from his "clicks" as he returned again to the sinanga. I then became more aware of the excitement arising from the dense undergrowth and rising, I hurried towards the cause of the ferment. Before reaching the thicket, I was confronted by the Bushmen accompanied by the dogs and holding another three dead lion cubs. The Bushmen were highly elated with their spoils and were shouting with joy.

The cubs were about twelve inches high at the shoulder but for all their smallness, they must have been full of fight and viciousness in defending their lives. All the dogs were bleeding and even Pistol, the champion, had blood dripping from his cheeks and nose. The cubs had enormous heads in comparison to their size and weight of their bodies. With their enlarged heads, they seemed to be top-heavy. Their colouring was different from that of their mother – they were darker with brownish spots. Their claws were as sharp as razors and bloodied in what was probably their first and last battle.

I suppose that it was natural that I should feel more than a little remorse at the death of the cubs and I regretted their killing despite my own horrifying experience with their mother. As it was, they were perhaps better dead than alive as they would have been a nuisance and the chances of keeping them alive without a supply of milk was very remote.

The whole episode taught me several unforgettable lessons. Firstly, at close quarters the shot gun is more effective on lion than a rifle, in addition to the fact that the shot sprays whereas with a rifle one has but one bullet. Secondly, and although I had been frozen to the spot by fear more than any logical plan of action, it is useless to panic when faced by lion at close quarters: had I attempted to retreat, I would surely have been caught. Lastly, the old advice about keeping away from lions with young had been proved with emphasis. They are dangerous! It is peculiar how certain factors predominate on reflection after such a closeness to death. My outstanding impression was of the eyes of the lioness. They had seemed like bright electric bulbs, full of venom, hate and a malicious intent to protect her young at all costs. Had the lioness remained stationary and continued staring at me with those spiteful malevolent eyes, I am sure that I would have been hypnotized! I have often wondered since if, in fact, lions do mesmerize their victims.

The incident had given me a chance to turn the tables on C'wai, especially after our earlier altercation over the python. That night, with Bankamakuni interpreting, I asked him why he had run as he had.

"Because I knew there were small lions and the mother would kill us if we went near. When I told you there was a lion, you did not seem to believe me. When we went nearer and I heard the purring of the little ones and then the lioness suddenly appeared, I realised the danger and ran for my life." A remarkable tribute to the powers of the Bushman's hearing, but I could not resist the opportunity for a little "dig".

"So you left me to face the lioness as you thought I left you to fight the snake? I have the feeling that you did it on purpose to get even with me. Is it not so?"

The Bushman became very agitated at the suggestion.

"No! No!" he replied. "I swear by my god the Mamba (one of the gods of the Bushmen was the mamba snake) I never thought of the earlier time. I ran because when the death came, I wanted to get away before my knees went to water and my legs would not run!"

It was apparent that C'wai had experienced almost as big a fright as I had.

Chapter Twenty Three – Trouble with Father

Later the same day, C'wai reported that he could hear the guinea fowl at the water. Our earlier encounter had somehow removed all thoughts of "provisioning" from our minds. We quickly tied the dogs to their leads and went after the birds. We were fortunate in finding them clustered around the water, some having sand baths and others drinking. Stalking the birds to within range, I bagged four with a right and left barrel from the shot gun. Whilst we were collecting our supper, C'wai, whose eyes were forever reading spoor, showed me the tracks of a lion that had had a drink subsequent to the killing of the lioness. He told Bankamakuni that this was the father of the cubs and that he would track his off-spring in the evening and visit our camp!

Whilst grilling our guinea fowl for supper (they make a delicious meal when they are at the "black-head" stage, as these were) the dogs became restless. They snarled and growled and rushed from one side of the enclosure to the other in great excitement. The commotion continued right through the night, never once giving us the opportunity of closing our eyes and sleeping.

I was quite relieved when the dawn came and we could allow the dogs out of the enclosure.

It was now that I saw the true value of Pistol, the lion dog, not that I had ever doubted Cornelius van Rooyen when he had described Pistol as fearless and one of the best dogs he had ever bred to bale up lion, or that I had not witnessed Pistol in action before and been suitably impressed.

The dogs, with Pistol in the lead, rushed out in a direct line for a patch of scrub some three hundred yards from the camp in the open valley. No sooner had they closed on the patch of thicket when they gave tongue and a black-maned lion appeared snarling and growling.

The battle which ensued between lion and dogs was spell-binding. The strategy and cunning ruses of Pistol were amazing: at times he would be in front of the lion, hind legs erect, front legs almost straight on the ground with his head nearly touching the front paws as he barked in the face of the king of beasts, a mere three feet from the latter's nose. Pistol was like a coiled spring and the slightest threatening movement from the lion would see him flash away, faster than sound, only to start a fresh attack from another angle.

Meanwhile, Smokey, the Bushman's bitch and Patch, the terrier, were always on the opposite side to that from which Pistol attacked. The result was that the cat was simultaneously attacked from several directions and did not know which way to turn in order to escape the onslaught. Several times the lion plunged at one of the tormentors without the slightest success. Eventually he gave up all hopes of trying to get at one of the dogs with a run or spring. The combined cunning of the attack seemed to follow an expertly pre-arranged plan with its sole object that of tiring the lion. If he moved forward towards Pistol, the other dogs, especially Smokey, would rush in and nip his hind legs. Should the lion turn to snarl and snap at the dogs behind him, Pistol would be in and out before those deadly claws had moved. The dogs didn't seem to actually bite the lion – the whole battle was a masterly example of psychological warfare and the lion literally didn't know which way to turn.

It was only when the lion saw us approaching that he made a really determined effort to escape into the jungle. Summoning several loud growls and snarls, he plunged forward to scatter the dogs momentarily. He did not get far. Pistol moved in from the rear and nipped the lion's leg. The affront turned the lion with extended claws and he chased after Pistol for about 10 yards before giving up the hopeless pursuit and then laid down, ears flat, tail twitching from side to side and muttering angry growls in our direction. Without a moment's respite, his tormentors continued to worry and harass their victim.

I was forced to stand and watch. There was little chance of shooting for fear of hitting the dogs. The teasing continued as the muzzle of the Express followed the action. The shot gun was completely out of the question as the spray of pellets would certainly hit the dogs. Fortunately, it was early, before sunrise, and the relative cold enabled the dogs to keep up the battle without getting too tired. As the conflict progressed and it became warmer, it was apparent that my intervention must be sooner rather than later.

I approached the commotion with timidity and a fluttering heart – my fearful experience with the lion's mate was still fresh in my mind. The lion, seeing me draw nearer, gave several savage snarls, clawed frantically at the dogs in a parting gesture and dashed off. Before the scattered dogs could close in again, I fired at the running target and broke the lion's back. The impact of the high velocity bullet hurled him to the ground. He was up again in a second with a harsh rumbling growl which deepened to a murderous fury when he realised he was paralysed and unable to move his rear quarters. The menace issuing from his throat and the glares from his yellow extended eyes were enough to strike fear into the bravest. His savage ferociousness in his hopeless situation produced the typical image – the King of Beasts, noble, dignified and regal.

The dogs quickly realised that the animal was badly wounded and became even more daring in their attacks, actually nipping at the immobilised hind quarters.

The lion was down but far from out. He moved with such lightening speed on his front legs, that the dogs had no chance of making a concerted attack to overwhelm him. Finally the opportunity presented itself and I finished the battle with a charge of S.S.G. pellets from the shot gun into the massive head.

Our victim had truly been a magnificent specimen, splendid and superb in every respect. He had a clean, glossy coat, no cuts, not a single scar or blemish and a healthy black-brown mane on his well-fed body. The King's reign had ended in the prime of his life.

Chapter Twenty Four – Life in Eden

The valley in which we were camped was a veritable paradise. There was not a single visible trace that human habitation had ever invaded this green, silent haven of peace. One felt that since the dawn of time, the only creatures to be born here, to hunt, mate and make their homes in this wilderness, had been wild animals. The secluded valley had its own water and provided luscious green grazing.

Wild life was everywhere in abundance and it seemed to multiply with the rising sun. It was astonishing how quickly the area teemed with life. From every hidden lair, new families awoke in the morning and headed for the water and the green grass. Impala in their hundreds bounded free; herds of buffalo browsed; elephant, zebra, the handsome eland, sable and small families of roan antelope joined the grazing throng. Small herds of kudu, led by bulls with magnificent spiral horns, emerged. Only giraffe and wildebeeste seemed to be absent from the parade.

The Bushmen were not acquainted with the territory. They told me that they seldom moved further north than the Pandamatenka for fear of the lions and the aggressive Matonkas who hunted in the area. The occasional Matebele hunting parties were a further deterrent.

We stayed longer amid the beauty and wild life than was necessary. The reason was simply that I enjoyed being in the valley with its teeming game, the fresh spring water, honey for the asking, cooked berries, "potatoes" from the water lily bulbs and an almost unlimited assortment of meat. Even our animals appeared to be enjoying their holiday, the rest and relaxation. They were sleek and fit.

I sent out daily patrols in the direction of the Pandamatenka Road for more news of cattle. On one occasion, Kleinbooi together with three Bushmen did not arrive back in camp the evening after their patrol. They turned up the following morning to report that they had been "treed" by lions and had been forced to spend the night in the branches. The lions had left at dawn but six hyenas had remained on guard and had only departed well after the sun had risen.

One morning, a warthog sow, accompanied by four, well-grown piglets, came down to the water. Taking the shot gun and with the dogs on their leads, C'wai and I stalked the pigs to within twenty yards of where they were rolling, tossing and tumbling in the mud at the fringe of the water. The sow detected us and made off for the jungle with her brood. The dogs were hastily released and were off on the chase and in a few minutes had baled up two of the youngsters. The mother turned to the rescue of her young and with astonishing speed charged right into the dogs and with a vicious side swipe of her head, flung Smokey head over heels. Before the maddened parent could follow up her advantage, I killed her with a charge of slugs. The Bushmen rushed to slaughter the piglets before the dogs tore them to pieces. The freedom of two youngsters that had escaped was short-lived and the Bushmen returned from the chase in joyful high spirits with their spoils.

It was only then that I noticed that Smokey was bleeding from her side. Examining the dog, I was surprised to discover a four inch incision in the skin up against the ribs. One could hardly credit that the slight movement of the sow's head could have executed such a blow. Her tusks protruded only half an inch from the lower jaw but they were as sharp as razors.

On Kleinbooi's suggestion, a nearby ant-heap was excavated leaving a tunnelled hollow. In this "oven", a fire was kindled and kept burning for several hours after which time the embers were removed and the hole thoroughly cleaned out. The temperature of the oven was tested by throwing in dry leaves – if the leaves smouldered, the heat was too intense; if the leaves wrinkled like fish scales, the temperature was right for the roast. One of the small pigs, having been disembowelled, was placed in the oven with skin intact and the opening sealed with mud. After three hours the carcass was removed and the skin flayed from the body. The skin had acted as a casserole and had produced roast pork as luscious, savoury and palatable as any suckling pig ever roasted.

No small warthogs were safe in my vicinity after this feast. Sunrise another morning saw a family of four rhino file down to the water: two bulls, a cow and a heifer calf. The leading bull, on arriving at the water, suddenly started snorting and emitting squeals of annoyance, and turned with head lowered to meet the second bull. The latter stopped, squealed and then lowered his head and charged like a living avalanche at the other.

We were too far away to see what damage they were doing to each other but it was a sight to behold to see the two monsters flinging themselves together, part and then manoeuvre again to attack from the flank with upward thrusts of their deadly, single, sharp horns. Considering their enormous size and weight, it was surprising to witness the speed with which they spurted to a position of advantage. Suddenly, one bull did get into the flank position and with a sudden upward lunge, flung his opponent on to his side. He was soon up and running for the jungle, discretion and valour in the old story. The victor saw him off and then returned to the water with grunts of satisfaction to join the cow and calf in muddied abandon.

The peaceful bathing and playing in the water of the trio was of short duration. Out of the jungle lumbered nine elephant led by a huge bull with long thick white tusks. The bull elephant hesitated at the sight of the rhino and then resumed the parade to the water's edge. When the elephant were close to the water, the rhino bull faced the intruders, erect and aggressive looking. The rhino squealed and walked gingerly toward the bull elephant. The latter was not to be frightened by the cheeky "small-fry" and promptly gave a shrill trumpet blast and charged the "squealer". The rhino was quick to move from the path of the lumbering charge but seemed to have learnt his lesson and made off for the forest, followed by his family. The elephant, secure in possession of the water, sprayed themselves and each other with repeated dousings of water. The numerous species of other game watched the procedure with wonder, disdain or disgust – whatever animals of the veld think when their drinking water is so carelessly and flagrantly muddied.

We watched the panorama every morning for a week. Each day brought something new – a short or long battle among the species, strange antics of the different herds and the amusement of an extremely varied congregation assembling for "morning prayers". Not once did I tire of the daily spectacle. During the night and especially towards dawn, lions roared and grunted their muffled coughs. Hyenas emitted their weird howls and jackals laughed incessantly. We had become immune to these disturbances and slept restfully and contentedly.

Every member of the camp was reluctant to leave our Garden of Eden but Dubani returned from a patrol one evening to report that he had found fresh cattle tracks moving towards Tamasetsa on the Pandamatenka Road. We broke camp and left our haven of contentment. It had been a wonderful break despite my experience with the lioness.

We caught up with the herd of cattle on the Pandamatenka and trailed them unobserved to Hendrik's Pan, where I made our presence known to the European in charge, a man by the name of Van Zijl.

Van Zijl was an interesting character and had been in Northern Rhodesia for a number of years. Like Smit, one of the earlier trail bosses, he was an elderly but competent hunter. He had killed many lions north of the border and was a personal friend of the Barotse King, Lewanika, having saved many of the King's cattle from the predators. He told me that Rademan had returned and had related to him his experiences at Tamasetsa. On Rademan's advice, Van

Zijl had brought supplies of poison and with his 9mm. Mauser it seemed that he was equipped for any repetition of the Tamasetsa carnage suffered by Rademan.

We moved with the 360 head of cattle to Tamasetsa where we found that the water was completely covered with sand. Van Zijl's herders and my Bushmen had to work hard to dig deep enough to obtain sufficient water for the cattle. The lack of water had driven away most of the game and the lions as well. No spoor of the latter were to be seen.

Van Zijl assured me that his was the last herd for Tsessebe for this year and I decided to send an escort with him as far as the border and when the escort returned, to trek back to the Gwaai via Shekwanki, N'gwesha and Linkwasa.

I thought that the patrol was almost finished and that the dangers were all behind us. I was sadly mistaken.

Chapter Twenty Five – Thorny Problems

Van Zijl and his herd stayed for three days at Tamasetsa before I sent Kleinbooi and three Bushmen off with him for the border. In the three days that the cattle were resting at the pan, we saw no sign of lions, hyenas or even jackals. Game was scarce in the immediate vicinity of the pan and fresh tracks were non-existent. The country was now getting dry and the game had moved on to other watering points.

Food was getting low and I was glad when a Bushman party, returning from a search for honey, reported having seen fresh eland spoor near the Dubi Pan. We lost no time in moving off after the antelope and some four miles from Tamasetsa, near Dubi, we found fresh tracks and followed them for about two miles when we came across the herd grazing in an open space. I instructed C'wai and four Bushmen (who were driving the donkeys – our meat transport) to conceal themselves in the bush and I approached the herd on horseback, pretending to by-pass them on the right. To the rear and no more than two hundred yards on either side of the herd grew the thick thorn bush known in Afrikaans as "blouwverwag" – it grows into an umbrella shape and the branches intermingle from one tree to the next. The thorns themselves are half-moon shaped and range from the size of a tickey to that of a shilling piece. They are not unlike the renowned "wag-'n-bietjie" but are bigger, terribly sharp and the kind of bush which one is well advised to steer clear of.

My intention was to "turn" one of the big "blue" bulls of which there were two massive specimens in the herd. It was however essential to shoot and kill the animals before they entered the thorns for once they gained the shelter of that needle-like vegetation, all hope of following them was lost. The herd faced and watched me but let me approach to within 150 yards. From this short range, I made sure that the speed of my mount would take me into the eland for my kill before they reached the thorns. Stalking still closer to the herd, I suddenly swung the horse round and galloped flat out for the bull I had picked out. As I had expected, the eland scattered immediately for the cover of the thorns but I was right behind my target preparing to shoot from the saddle. Before I could push the horse on his flank to pull the trigger, the bull entered the thorns with the horse – and me – in his wake.

The next thing I knew was that I was suspended in mid-air having been lifted out of the saddle by the unruly, retentive and clinging thorns. I felt a burning sensation all over my body, face and arms. I felt exactly what I was, a worm on a hook, as I hung there kicking in the empty air and flailing my arms in an attempt to release myself. The thorns were deeply embedded and nothing would loosen their grip on me. Deliverance only arrived when the Bushmen arrived and literally cut me out of the thicket with their small hunting axes and removed those tenacious branches with care but not without adding to my already considerable discomfort.

When the eland bull had charged into the cover, pushing aside the thorn branches in his endeavour to evade the horse, the rebounding of the thorns had met the rush of the horse and me, the rider, with a terrific impact, causing deep and painful penetration of the thorns into my clothes and body. The eland did not get off completely unscathed. As he entered the bush, I could see the hair flying as the thorns raked his flanks.

By the time I had recovered from my initial discomfort, I was surprised to see that the herd had emerged from the thorns a mere 300 yards away and had stopped and were gazing at us and the horse as though inviting me to give a repeat performance. I discovered the rifle on the ground, covered in sand, and whilst I tried to remove the dirt from the falling block action, the antelope waited patiently. When the mechanism was working freely, I loaded and moved to a nearby tree where I rested the muzzle in the fork and brought down the bull with a bullet in the chest. I wished that I had used more discretion in my first attempt at the animal.

On my return to the camp, a bath – a paraffin tin of hot water – was prepared and Dubani played nurse and dabbed iodine on the painful cuts and bruises I had sustained. My whole body was burning fiercely and the pain was agonising.

The bull eland was a massive animal and must have weighed nearly three-quarters of a ton. The fat from the heart, kidneys and stomach alone would have filled a grain bag! The animal was in beautiful condition and the marrow from the bones was delicious. Eland meat is definitely the finest of the larger game species and very palatable, especially the undercut from the spinal column which is most tender and juicy. Still, I considered that I had paid a high price for my feast. I would have come off even worse if it had not been for my clothing. My khaki bush shirt and slacks had been so patched with brayed impala and duiker hide that the original material was unrecognisable. What my raiment lacked in elegance was certainly made up for in practicality. Even my hat was similarly patched and added to the brim were two flaps that covered the ears and tied under the chin – not unlike a scrum cap.

Chapter Twenty Six – Attempted Murder

At dusk that evening, three Bushmen with a flint-lock muzzle-loader between them joined the camp. They were from Bechuanaland and gave out that they were hunting for leopard skins. They remained in the camp for several days and then vanished as abruptly as they had appeared with no thanks for the food that had been given to them. The mysterious party were complete strangers to any of the Bushmen in the camp and Bankamakuni told me that they had been extremely inquisitive wanting to know where we had come from, our destination and our business in the territory.

A few days after the visitors had left, C'wai, Dubani and I went hunting for fresh meat again. Passing through thick bush in the same direction as we had seen the eland, we came across fresh kudu spoor. Following the tracks with C'wai in the lead, I noticed a slight movement on my left and, thinking it was the kudu for which we were searching, I flung myself from the saddle. Before my feet had touched the ground a shot vibrated through the air and a charge of slugs passed over my head like a swarm of angry bees. Looking in the direction from which the shot had come, I could see smoke hanging in the air and a man dodging and running on a zig-zag course away from us. Without a moment's hesitation, I took a quick aim at the fleeing figure and fired. The man threw up his arms, dropped his gun, staggered forward and then crumpled into a heap on the ground.

My blood ran cold and I was struck with horror at the sudden violence for which I had been responsible.

C'wai was speechless with awe, muttering incoherent words to himself and looking at me as if failing to recognise the person who had just dealt out such summary punishment. Dubani, who was behind us and had only heard the shots, came forward questioningly. Pointing towards the dark heap on the ground, I sent him forward to investigate. He hurried away but wandered off course and it was only then that C'wai found his tongue and shouted to the constable to move further to the left and then set off in his tracks. I sat down and considered with horror and dismay what I had just done. Dubani quickly returned and told me that the man was quite dead.

The bullet had shattered his spine and had blown his chest inside out. There was alarm in Dubani's popping eyes. I sent C'wai back to the camp to collect the other Bushmen and a shovel and mattock. Whilst Dubani and I were awaiting his return, the constable told me that the dead man was one of the Bushmen who had visited the camp recently. The weapon with which he had fired at me was the same flint-lock muzzle-loader. Unfortunately, Dubani was no more familiar with the Bushman language than I was, but Bankamakuni had told him that the visitors had not appeared to be as friendly and helpful with information as the other Bushmen who had joined my entourage at other times. There was no indication why the man had tried to kill me.

C'wai returned with the other eighteen Bushmen, two women and the digging implements. Before putting them to the task of burying the would-be assassin, I was determined to make a full investigation into the possible reasons for the attack. With Bankamakuni acting as interpreter, I questioned and cross-questioned each and every one of them. Hours of interrogation produced not the slightest tangible evidence of the reason why the Bushman had intended to kill me. The nearest approach to a motive was provided by the old Bushman who had reported the arrival of Rademan's cattle at Tamasetsa.

"You have blankets, you have knives, you have a shot gun and a rifle and many other goods they would have liked to possess. You have four elephant tusks which may have belonged to them or to their relations. They may have thought that by killing you, all these riches could have been theirs."

This suggestion of the old man loosened other tongues and they recalled having been asked: "How many lion skins has the white man? Has he only the four tusks? How many cartridges has he with him?" and similar questions. With no other evidence available, I was forced to accept this conclusion and my only consolation was that had I not been in the act of dismounting when fired upon, the Bushmen might now be digging my grave and perhaps also Dubani's, and even Bankamakuni's. My own shot had been an extremely lucky one and I hadn't reckoned to hit him although I admit that I had aimed at him. He had presented a very small target in the thick bush as he had dodged from tree to tree. The death of the Bushman had certainly not been premeditated.

I made a full description of the locality for the report which I should have to make at a later date. I showed the exact spot from which the Bushman had fired at me and the position in which he had died. The grave in the soft sand, where the man was buried with an assortment of logs half-way down to prevent hyenas and jackals disturbing the remains, was also shown on my map.

It was a long time before the horror of this tragic incident could be forgotten.

Chapter Twenty Seven – Rhino Rumpus

The news of the opening of the water hole for Van Zijl's cattle seemed to have been communicated to the wild life of the area in some mysterious manner. Game started returning to the water by degrees and one morning, among the bigger game, appeared two rhinoceros – a bull and a cow.

In my opinion, the rhinoceros is the biggest fool animal on the veldt. His very poor eyesight is offset only by his keen sense of smell and hearing. He seems to have a very dull and stupid intelligence, is completely senseless and will often act the complete imbecile. With his enormous strength and his fear (in his ignorance) of nothing, his addle-pated notions will often tempt him to tackle the impossible and try to remove ant-heaps that might be in his path. He has only to scent the slightest strange taint in his nostrils and his aggressive stupidity will imagine unseen enemies and he will attack roots and soil in paroxysms of fury. With hate in his small piggy eyes, he will charge his imaginary enemy like an uncontrollable avalanche with his stubby legs pummelling the ground whilst he gives voice in grunts, snorts and squeals like a steam engine. These aggressive tactics are not all bluff. He means to kill and he will kill – if he ever makes contact! His very unpredictability makes him dangerous but for all that, he is a likeable animal and can be a source of great amusement if one keeps out of the way of that single vicious horn of his.

On this particular day, the donkeys were at the water hole (the horses and mule were in the camp feeding on crushed camel thorn beans). When the pair of rhino appeared, the donkeys became alert, blowing through their noses and carefully watching the approaching couple. As soon as the bull scented the donkeys, he seemed determined to prove his valour to his mate. Without the slightest reason, he started pawing the ground and driving his horn under a small bush near the water. With snorts, grunts and squeals of fury, he made apparent his annoyance at the strangers that had dared to violate his water hole. Suddenly and quite unreasonably, he directed his massive body at the nearest donkey with an astonishing speed. The donkey moved quietly to one side and followed the rhino's charge with a look of disdain. The rhino, having missed his first target, charged in the direction of another donkey who likewise avoided the rushing bulldozer with nothing more than startled amazement. And so the game went on for fifteen minutes or more, the clouds of dust and the rhino's ill-temper increasing by the second. The donkeys were in fine fettle, fat and full of spirit and they seemed to enjoy the diversion. The rhino never managed to get near one of them and with a final charge, he gave up the chase, joined the cow who was wallowing contentedly in the mud and then trotted off into the forest looking as big a fool as ever.

On the way back to the Gwaai, between Shekwanki and N'gwesha, we had another experience with one of these unpredictable animals which was not at all amusing and which ended in tragedy.

I was now getting impatient, for Kleinbooi should have been back some days ago. In this wilderness, one could never tell what might happen, and when a patrol is overdue, the nervous system easily becomes agitated. The affair with the Bushman had not helped matters and when, by the third day, Kleinbooi and his party had not put in an appearance, I became more and more irritable.

That evening two Bushmen and a woman turned up in the camp. After our earlier experience care was exercised and they were closely questioned regarding their business and intentions. Some of my own camp followers were acquainted with the new arrivals and confirmed their story that they were hunting for leopard skins.

(Years ago, travelling through Bechuanaland by train, one was often invited to buy karosses made from different game and cat skins. The skins were supplied to the sellers, the Bamangwato, by the Bushmen. The former would supply the weapons and the black powder and send the Bushmen off on the hunt on the strict understanding that the hides were the property of the owner of the gun whilst the meat could be consumed by the hunting party.)

The arrivals produced two flintlock muzzle-loaders which they had concealed before entering the camp. I demanded the weapons be handed over to me on condition that they would be returned when the Bushmen decided to leave. They never did leave, but followed me to the Gwaai where they were settled with the others.

There were now around thirty Bushmen to feed, plus three dogs, two constables – when Kleinbooi returned – and myself. No one can have the slightest conception of how much these people could consume unless one has witnessed their feasting. There was no waste – even the skins were softened into blankets and clothing. Quite reasonably, they were of the opinion that they had never had it so good whilst they were with me and were quite content that this happy state of affairs should continue for ever. It was left to me to worry about the shortage of ammunition and where the next meal was coming from.

Kleinbooi was now four days overdue. I was worried, especially in the knowledge that he had the Schneider and the Martini-Henry. My faith in the

Bushmen had been shaken and I knew that there was little to prevent Kleinbooi's Bushmen from killing him in order to gain possession of the valuable rifles. The last cattle drive had gone through and now I was anxious to get back to the Gwaai and civilisation.

It was late in the fourth day, just before sunset, that Kleinbooi and his party finally arrived back. The constable was tired, hungry and full of woe. He made his report:

All had gone well until the herd had reached the Sibannini River. Here the old kraals had been rebuilt and strengthened to contain the cattle for the night and while this was being done, Van Zijl had gone off to hunt for fresh meat. He had shot two blue wildebeeste close to the camp and had then returned for help to butcher the meat and cart it back to the camp. Van Zijl had chosen to remain in the camp to supervise the work while Kleinbooi and his patrol of Bushmen and some of the cattle herders had followed Van Zijl's tracks to where the wildebeeste had been shot. They had neared the carcasses to find that someone had beaten them to it – there was a black-maned lion feeding off the meat! Kleinbooi had sent a message to Van Zijl post-haste.

The lion had seen the approaching party and made off into the nearby short mopanes. When Van Zijl had reinforced the party, they all moved after the lion but had no success in tracking the cat. The sight of the lion was not a good omen for the coming night and after the meat had been retrieved, the offal was also taken back, injected with poison and dumped close to the kraals. As was to be expected, the lion visited the camp during the night and succeeded in frightening the cattle to the extent that they broke out of the enclosure and stampeded. Investigation the next morning showed that the lion had eaten some of the offal and at the water they found his dead body. The animal was very, very old, with few teeth and a scurvy-ridden hide.

The next task had been to round up the missing cattle. Only seventy were missing after the first day and two more days brought the absentees down to three. Van Zijl ordered further attempts to find the missing trio but eventually gave up and moved on without them. On reaching the border, Kleinbboi and his Bushmen had left the herd to return. Before they reached the Nata River they had come across the missing cattle who were following in the tracks left by the main herd!

"We were very tired but I decided to take the cattle to Van Zijl and we caught up with him before he reached Tsessebe."

Van Zijl had been extremely grateful and had given Kleinbooi three golden sovereigns and he now handed the money to me for safe keeping.

And now an almost unbelievable fact was revealed to me; Asking

Bankamakuni to explain to Kleinbooi's Bushmen that Van Zijl had given them the money for finding the missing cattle, they replied: "What is it and what can we do with it?"

Further enquiries among my followers revealed that only two out of the lot of them had any idea of what was meant by money. Even in those days, this was something which amazed me.

I could not leave for Shekwanki the following day, much as I may have wished. It was necessary to give Kleinbooi and his men a rest and opportunity to feed themselves. They had covered several hundreds of miles and were footsore and dead beat.

It was three days later that we left Tamasetsa for the Gwaai. The patrol had been anything but routine up to now but the next stretch was to prove the most momentous of all.

Chapter Twenty Eight – Elephants

We left Tamasetsa three days after Kleinbooi had returned from his long escort of the cattle in charge of Van Zijl. Moving off from the camp which had been our home for so long, instructions were given to the Bushmen in charge of the dogs to keep the animals on leads. It was essential to keep them under control. Running loose, they were inclined to follow fresh game tracks and to chase any wild life that they saw with the result that their feet became tender and thin in the process.

C'wai, Bankamakuni and I were well ahead of the rest of the trek when we came across a herd of elephant. There were about fifty animals in the herd, feeding deep in the Msasa forest. The huge beasts were unaware of our presence and consequently we were given an opportunity of watching them at our leisure.

Elephant are destructive and devastating feeders. They wreck and ruin tree growth and leave a trail of desolation behind them like so many bull-dozers. Tons and tons of vegetation, regardless of its type and including the bark of trees, is eaten or wastefully trampled and destroyed. It is noticeable, however, that where forests have been destroyed by elephants in past years, the grass growth improves and this may be nature's way of compensating the ruined area by replacing and supplying succulent grazing for the smaller animals and antelope.

The endeavours of the big bulls to pull down some of the larger trees was both amusing and interesting to watch. One old bull in particular, with dark-stained, massive tusks, approached a fair sized Msasa tree, rose on his hind legs and reached with his trunk as high as he could. He gripped the tree with his trunk and started pulling downwards. As the tree was bent so he continued to lower himself, taking the tree with him. Eventually he sat and having exhausted the leverage of his weight, released the tree which catapulted backwards and forwards with considerable force. Apparently annoyed at his failure to uproot his meal in this fashion, the bull turned his attention to the roots of the tree and in slow motion and with great patience, he methodically began snapping them off by inserting one or both tusks under a buried root and then heaving upwards with all his strength. As each root snapped, the elephant grunted his satisfaction and moved on to the next. Having satisfied himself that he had considerably reduced the odds in favour of the tree remaining upright, the bull repeated his circus performance of getting on his hind legs, gripping the tree with his trunk and slowly subsiding into a sitting position. Not even the Msasa tree, with its amazing root system, could survive this sort of attack.

As soon as the tree had finally surrendered to the old bull and had thundered to the ground in a cloud of dust, the rest of the herd which had been browsing close by made a wild dash for the new supply of fallen fodder and milled around the tree with squeals and shoves and even exchanged blows with their trunks. Seconds after the mad charge, the herd scattered again in all directions to consume the morsels they had been able to rescue in the mad melee.

Two young bulls tried to strip the tree of its bark. When one had managed to tear off a piece, the other elephant rushed at him and knocked him sprawling to the ground. Seizing the prized bark, the attacker rushed off whilst his opponent regained his feet, screamed a shrill trumpet of rage and chased off with obvious determination to regain his "chew" from the thief.

Elephants are such intelligent creatures that there is endless interest and entertainment in observing their habits. We stood there watching and lost all track of time until suddenly the bulls began trumpeting and the herd turned in our direction with their trunks curled over their heads and their huge ears extended like the wings of monster bats. They had winded the arrival of the pack donkeys, the dogs and the Bushmen who were coming single file in our tracks. I signalled to the leaders to stop and to remain stationary whilst we continued to watch the elephant as they became increasingly restless. They gave voice in shrill squeals and loud trumpets and then eventually moved off in a great cloud of dust. It is surprising how quickly these enormous animals can travel. Within seconds the herd had vanished and there was not a sound to indicate their presence.

We continued our trek to Shekwankwi.

Chapter Twenty Nine – More Elephants, Much Trouble

Emerging from the forest and going down towards a small brak pan which I had named Idube (Zebra) on a previous trip, we saw ahead of us seven more elephant at the muddy pool. Amongst the herd was a big cow with a very small calf which I doubt was more than two months old.

The herd had seen us and was on the alert immediately.

For a reason that could never be explained to my satisfaction, Patch, a white bull-terrier cross fox-terrier, shot past my horse and made straight for the elephant calf! Then all hell broke loose!

Patch, who was one of my dogs, rushed in and tried to nip the calf. The calf quite naturally retreated and ran round and round its mother whilst the parent, alarmed and enraged at the sudden attack by this strange animal, let out piercing screams which drew the attention of the rest of the herd who came running to the rescue of the calf. Patch must have realised that the odds were against him and he scurried in my direction for protection. The mother cow, with blasts of annoyance, was determined to get at the elusive white tormentor that had threatened her off-spring and chased him with surprising speed.

On seeing the horse, the cow gave an extra-long drawn out scream, curved her trunk into her chest and came straight at me like an express train. I hardly had time to turn the horse and make for the protection of the forest.

It is relatively easy to avoid an enraged elephant among trees if one's horse is fit and accustomed to this sort of thing. The horse can manoeuvre much quicker than the huge bulk and weight of the elephant. I stipulate "trees". It is an entirely different story in long grass or in fine bush "sinangas". Here the elephant undoubtedly has the advantage: he can crash through with his weight and tough skin whereas the horse is completely hemmed in. The elephant was very close behind me as I entered the forest and I could smell the pungent odour that emanates from elephant when they are disturbed. As I entered the trees at a fast gallop, I looked around. This was an almost fatal mistake. With tremendous force my horse dashed my left knee against a tree and nearly unseated me from the saddle.

The slight hesitation caused by the impact in that mad gallop presented the elephant with the opportunity to sling her tusk past my right leg and press one of her tusks into the back of the horse and thus push both of us into the ground with a resounding crash.

I fell with my legs still in the saddle, on my right side and with my elbow buried in the sand. Fortunately my .400 Express was still in my hand with its muzzle pointing skyward. The elephant towered above me like a huge round granite rock, making guttural screaming sounds of satisfaction as she contemplated her victims and prepared to rub us from the face of the earth. The shock of the collision and the fall had not affected my immediate thoughts for safety. In a flash, I pointed the rifle upwards behind the off foreleg of the huge beast and pulled the trigger.

The cow gave a piercing scream, remained upright for a few seconds and then, in slow motion with her legs bunched under her, toppled over against a big tree trunk on the other side of the horse, quite dead and at an angle of seventy-five degrees.

The first living thing I saw from my awkward and increasingly painful position was the pathetic baby calf who, with his small trunk extended, was feeling at his mother's body and making low moaning whimpers of bewilderment.

C'wai was soon on the scene, his eyes bulging from his head in terror and his mouth wide open. As he regained his breath, he shouted at the top of his lungs for help. When he saw that I was alive, his shrieks and his dancing agitation increased. In no time I was surrounded by my entire band.

The horse was dead and to get me from under the lifeless body, I instructed the Bushmen to cut two long poles and by levering upwards, they finally dragged me from under the weight. My right leg, apart from being numbed and slightly discoloured, had nothing broken. The left leg was in a sorry state. The patella moved in all directions and the muscles, from ankle to thigh, were turning a purple yellow green colour. The pain was excruciating.

C'wai examined the leg, grunted and clicked and clacked in his Bushman language with great excitement, obviously issuing orders of some importance. Then he grabbed my shotgun and without even asking my permission, departed in a great hurry followed by two other Bushmen. I was too groggy and racked with pain to worry about what he was going to do with the gun.

Chapter Thirty – First Aid – Bushman Style

The instructions which C'wai had issued before his departure became quickly obvious. It appeared that he had told the others to disembowel the elephant immediately and, whilst the green wet dung was still hot, my leg was buried in the mess. This was done most expeditiously and, surprisingly, the heat generated by the stinking "poultice" was soothing and counteracted some of the sickening pain of the broken bones.

It was anything but pleasant lying there in the sun on my back under a heap of green steaming manure whilst the Bushmen butchered the elephant carcass. Two of them had crept into the frame of the ribs and were hacking and pulling and handing out long lengths of the huge intestines. They heaved, snatched, jerked and tore the huge heart, lungs and kidneys from the carcass with great enjoyment, oblivious to the way in which they covered themselves with blood. The large intestine, the colon, a huge chunk of fat walled with gristle through the passage, was heaved onto the live embers of the fire and grilled. The aroma from that grill would whet and stimulate the appetite of the dead and although I felt near that stage, I ate some. It was excellent.

We heard a shot in the distance and within ten minutes C'wai and his companions had reappeared carrying a white duiker! – obviously an albino.

The shooting of the duiker had a phenomenal effect upon the superstitious Bushmen. They clicked and clacked nineteen to the dozen, continually pointing heavenwards with expressions of the greatest awe on their faces. According to Bankamakuni, who interpreted their excited conversation:

"The death of the white duiker is portentous and is a gift from beyond the clouds. It will bring much luck to all of us who set eyes upon the dead animal while it was still warm. It brings particular gifts to the white man, proof of which we have already seen: the elephant could not kill him. And is not the dead elephant the fattest ever and will provide much food…"

C'wai, giving his account of the shooting of the duiker, said:

"The Spirit came directly at me with a leisurely lope, stopped, faced me and asked me to shoot. I did and the Spirit left him!"

The duiker was skinned and the belly part carefully cleaned. Whilst it was still warm the Bushmen sewed the skin tightly around my injured leg, four inches above the knee and six inches below. This operation kept the knee-cap in perfect position and in due course, when the skin had dried out a week later, it acted as a perfect plaster cast!

The opinion that Bushmen are sub-human does not coincide with my experiences of these little people of the bush. They have extraordinary veldt intellect and have the knowledge to produce medicines from trees, roots, berries, and as they proved in my case, even from the manure and hides of animals. This they do with complete success. How many white men would have thought of treating my hurts in the manner of the Bushmen?

The albino duiker was the only one I have ever seen in Rhodesia. Its colour was completely off-white with only the tips of the hair on its back having the more reddish tinge. All the points were black and the long hairs on the tail brush were a dark smoky colour. The horns were short and stubby and the teeth of the antelope were worn down to the gums. He was very, very old.

My horse had died as the result of a tusk penetrating the spinal column and unseating one of the kidneys. The wound had caused a deep gash from which the blood had gushed for a long time.

The bullet which had ended the life of the elephant and saved mine had travelled at a slight slant. It had passed through the length of the huge heart, shattered a portion of the spinal column and had left a gaping hole at the exit. It had been a very lucky shot considering the circumstances and it was no wonder that the cow had died instantaneously.

Chapter Thirty One – The Orphan

The elephant calf was my biggest problem and caused me to feel more than a little disturbed over his welfare. The little animal circled round and round the camp and could rarely leave the vicinity of the butchering of his mother. His mournful whimperings of distress as he held his small trunk on high, with his ears extended, were pitiful to watch. He wandered around aimlessly trying to trace his parent from the smell which was only too apparent. I ordered the dogs to be tied at all times to save a repetition of Patch's attack on the baby which had caused the whole sorry episode. Even so, they growled and their hackles rose whenever the calf came near them. The donkeys, the mule and the extra horse gazed on the orphan with both interest and suspicion. When he approached the animals, they would turn their backs, flatten their ears with the obvious intention of kicking him from their presence. We continually had to soothe, cajole and calm them in their agitation.

The manner in which the little orphan was rebuffed from every approach to the other animals was heart-rending. The Africans tried an approach without success. As soon as he got wind of the human odour, he would be off with as much speed as his stumpy flapping legs would allow, with audible expressions of fright. Minutes later he would return to his hopeless search with his heart-breaking whimpers of loneliness and desertion.

Despite my feelings, I realised that it was impossible to even consider keeping the little elephant. With what could he be fed? Milk was the obvious diet but where on earth could we get milk in this neck of the woods? He was much too small to share the donkey's diet of crushed camel thorn beans. After much soul-searching, I decided that the kindest thing in the long run would be to shoot him and, despite my injuries, I intended doing the killing myself with a well-placed shot rather than let the Bushmen hack him to pieces.

In the awkward and almost immobile position in which I found myself, it was very difficult to get my sights on the little animal and right up to sunset I tried without success. Soon after the sun went down, the fires were started for the night's protection. Immediately after the fires had been kindled, the distressing calls from the baby elephant ceased. Whether it was because of the fires or for some other reason, we did not hear or see the little orphan again.

During the night, however, the surrounding forest produced the usual drawn-out, mournful moans and shrieks of hyenas and the coughing and grunting of lions. I wondered if the little calf had met a quick fate at the claws of the predators.

Chapter Thirty Two – On to Shekwankwi

The water at Dubi was nothing but mud and green slime and it was essential that we move on to Shekwankwi, some four miles away. To move all the fresh meat and get myself into the saddle was a major operation. The Bushmen finally managed to get me mounted with considerable difficulty but not without causing me much pain and suffering.

At Shekwankwi a comfortable camp was made overlooking the big splash of water in the pan and where game were to be seen in their hundreds, especially eland and giraffe. The donkeys maintained a shuttle service between Dubi and our new camp with the meat. The last load arrived at the pan well after sunset.

The move had not done my leg any good. The pain was intense and sleep was right out of the question. In the morning, C'wai again came to the rescue by suggesting that I shoot another animal to extract a "poultice" from the stomach. From my bed, 200 yards from the water, I shot an eland cow and the hot fomentations were repeated without removing the "plaster cast". This was done by covering my leg with a soft brayed piece of gemsbok hide and the wet manure heaped onto the skin.

The treatment gave me immediate relief and I went into a deep sleep which lasted until late in the afternoon.

There was no possibility of continuing the trek to the Gwaai because of my condition and we were forced to remain at Shekwankwi for ten days until my injuries had partially healed.

The enforced delay at Shekwankwi was most interesting. A great assortment of game visited the pan daily. Giraffe appeared in large herds and the fighting between bulls of the different herds continued for hours and provided a wonderful spectacle. The animals would stand shoulder to shoulder, swinging their funny little "horns" at each other's chest until one of them tired, moved off and presented his opponent with a moral victory. If the bulls were well matched, the contest would literally last for hours and hours. I saw two bulls start their fight in the morning and only separate late in the afternoon. Straddling their legs so that they could drink would often bring their legs in conflict, promoting another fight forthwith and much kicking.

Elephants at play in the water were another great source of amusement. They seem to have a mania for water and would bath and spray themselves and each other all day long. As they immersed their huge bodies in the pan, one could almost hear the sighs of relief and enjoyment. It was remarkable to witness lions coming down to the water to drink in the presence of numerous species of antelope. The latter would merely give way, allow the cats to drink and watch them return to the forest whereupon they would continue their own interrupted watering. I saw this happen on at least two occasions during the ten days of our stay. The extraordinary behaviour of the antelope seemed to indicate that they knew the cats were not out to kill them.

Twelve days after my accident with the elephant, we packed up and moved on to N'gwesha. This, our last lap on the return to the Gwaai, proved to be the most disastrous of the whole patrol.

Chapter Thirty Three – Death and Near Death

The trek on to N'gwesha was uneventful – until we were in sight of the pan and the shimmering water. C'wai, Bankamakuni and I were in the lead and had just passed a thick clump of trees. The pack donkeys and the Bushmen followers were no more than 150 yards behind us. Suddenly we heard the grunts, snorts and excited squeals of a rhinocerous and I rounded my horse hurriedly to locate the animal. I turned just in time to witness the rhinoceros charge straight through the single file of Bushmen and donkeys. Somehow they managed to evade the first charge but when the cantankerous and highly irascible animal turned and came thundering towards the surprised caravan for the second time, he was successful in getting his long sharp horn into the stomach of a heavily-laden donkey. The poor donkey gave a snort of fright before it was heaved into the air sending its burden flying in all directions. The rhino, following up on his success, continued to gore the donkey. This all happened in less time than taken in the telling and by the time I had recovered and fired at the rhino, the damage had been done.

A well-placed shot into the thick neck of the attacker killed him instantly in the kneeling position as he mutilated the donkey. The latter managed to get to his feet and struggle away with his entrails and bowels dragging behind him. He did not get far before he fell to the ground and I put him out of his misery with another shot.

Once again, the suddenness of the incident had given us no time to think of the danger. Only afterwards did we realise how close death had been. Any one of us might have been the object of the unprovoked attack by the annoyed and irritated animal. Any one of us might have been disembowelled in the same manner as the unfortunate donkey.

Even though we were nearing the end of our journey, the event was typical of the surprises that can come upon one without the slightest warning in the bush. It also showed that one must never treat a rhinocerous with anything other than the greatest respect. He is undoubtedly the most unpredictable and therefore one of the most dangerous animals to be found in the wilds.

We were fortunate in that we were close to N'gwesha and water. We set up a comfortable camp and the carcass of the rhino was butchered for dehydration at our leisure. Cornelius van Rooyen had told me that rhino hide was ideal for making sjamboks and had told me how it was done. Kleinbooi was also conversant with the procedure.

The hide was cut into two to four inch strips, some of which were cut from the neck to the rump, to give an overall length of between seven and nine feet. The strips were then hung from branches and weighted at the ends. In the absence of large stones in the sandy veldt, heavy logs were used as weights. The whole idea was to stretch the strips of hide as they dried in the sun. By the time the task was finished, about 120 varying lengths of hide were suspended all around the camp.

At sunset that evening I had an attack of cold shivers and, thinking it was a touch of malaria, I dosed myself with quinine. The next morning, I was feeling extremely sick. I had a terrible headache, pains throughout my body, especially in my injured leg, and a temperature of 103. I felt like nothing on earth and could not care less about the future. All I wanted to do was to sleep and that was impossible.

The following day I had the utmost difficulty in passing water and the drips that did come away were blood-stained. I was afraid that I was in for a dose of black-water fever and, never having suffered from this disease before, I had no idea what to do other than to continue dosing myself with quinine and aspirin. The only other medicine I had with me was castor oil – which I added to my other medication.

What followed thereafter, I know not. The constables and the Bushmen said that I went mad, that I struggled out of bed, loaded the .400 Express and fired a shot into their camp. This demented performance gave them the fright of their lives and they ran into the bush and watched my antics from the safety of the trees. They told me that I then hobbled and struggled to the water where, bending down to drink, I toppled over and fell into the green slimy mud. I laid there until my followers mustered sufficient courage to approach my body. I was "dead" when they lifted me from the water, retrieved the rifle and deposited me back in my bed. When I did regain consciousness, the state of my clothes and the dried slime covering my body confirmed their statements. I enquired as to the whereabouts of C'wai, and Bankamakuni informed me that he and the older Bushmen had left to hunt for medicine and would return as soon as possible.

There was a festering sore on my left leg that had given me considerable pain since the involvement with the elephant. The wound had now become very inflamed and although I had covered the spot with a very good healing and drawing ointment (prepared for me by a chemist in Bulawayo), the wound became even more angry and inflamed day by day. I was unable to pass water and attempts to do so were accompanied by the most excruciating pain. This, together with my throbbing leg and a temperature soaring to the 104 mark, indicated that I was a sorry mess and very sick. Strangely, my knee in its "plaster cast" gave me not the slightest added inconvenience.

C'wai appeared late in the afternoon, inspected my leg, mumbled to himself and then took himself off again together with my shot gun. Whilst he was away Dubani, Kleinbooi, Bankamakuni and an old Bushman approached my bed and offered me some liquid in an ostrich egg shell. I tasted the stuff and spat it out immediately. It was as bitter as gall and caused the inside of my mouth to contract violently. They begged and begged me to drink the liquid but I was adamant in my refusal. When C'wai returned with the body of a warthog he had shot, the others told him that I had refused the medicine. He became very agitated and with expressions of great annoyance insisted that I drink the brew. To their combined relief, I was in no mood to argue further and did as I was told.

The hot contents of the stomach of the dead warthog were applied to my inflamed leg. The steaming dung gave immediate relief and the pain subsided. Throughout the night, C'wai and Bankamakuni sat in front of my bed, never speaking but watching me with an intense concentration.

At daybreak, I made further painful attempts to relieve myself and eventually, in a great bloody stream, I was successful. I was given more of the brew – more this time to my utter disgust – and by mid-day the medicine was working so effectively that I was passing water every ten minutes. The relief was so great and I felt so relaxed and comfortable that I fell asleep and did not waken until the following morning having slept for a solid eighteen hours.

When I finally awoke, "Doctor" C'wai was in attendance and I was again compelled to drink more of the terrible muti. If that was not enough further poultices of dung, warmed in boiling water, were slapped on my leg.

Chapter Thirty Four – The Last Lap

After eight days, still feeling very weak and looking like no other human being on earth, I decided that a move must be made. We trekked on to Linkwasa.

As we neared Linkwasa, a Bushman woman in an advanced state of pregnancy and carrying an elephant tusk overtook the caravan. She was obviously in a great hurry and C'wai and Bankamakuni spoke to her. I, of course, did not understand the conversation but Bankamakuni told me that the woman was about to give birth and was anxious to get to the water. I knew that the water at Linkwasa would most probably be covered by sand and that it would be necessary to dig for it. I urged the others to make haste so that we could get to the pan before the woman – she was in no condition to grovel for the precious liquid.

We arrived at the pan before the woman and, sure enough, it was covered. The Bushmen dug frantically and by the time the woman caught up with us again, she was able to scoop up some clean water into an ostrich egg shell before vanishing again into the jungle.

The rest of my party arrived about an hour later and two of the women detached themselves from the others and followed the mother's steps. Whilst everyone was busy making camp for the night, the three Bushmen women reappeared and the new mother was proudly carrying her baby! No more than two hours had passed – and there she was, full of smiles and hugging and nursing her little child who was making known his presence in the world with lusty howls.

I presented the proud mother with an old blanket. She took it as if it were cloth of gold.

My inflamed leg was not healing and the only way of getting relief was with the hot dung poultices. I was worried and decided to get back to the Gwaai with all speed where I could obtain medical attention. The following day we arrived at N'gamo and made our camp for the night close to the railway siding. At 6 p.m. I heard the rumble of the north-bound train for Victoria Falls. The Bushmen also heard the noise and wanted to know what it was. Bankamakuni explained. When the engine pulled into the siding with the normal clouds of steam and the noise of escaping pressure, the Bushmen scattered. Two of them started running and as far as I know they are still running. I never saw them again. Having followed me for hundreds of miles through the terrors of the forests, these two had seen enough of the outside world! The expressions on the faces of those who remained were something to be seen. None of them had ever seen train before and the utter amazement and disbelief was most amusing.

We continued on to the Gwaai and apart from soothing the nervous Bushmen whenever a train passed, the journey was uneventful. We arrived at the Gwaai Police Camp in the afternoon. I left the caravan there and without pausing, rode straight on to the Railway Station. Whitmore, the Station Master, told me that there was a train for Bulawayo that night. I asked him to contact Bulawayo and arrange for a buckboard to meet me at the Station the next morning when the train arrived at 7 a.m.

Chapter Thirty Five – Shopping Spree

During my absence on the patrol, traders from Nyamandhlovu (Messrs Green and Miller) had opened an African Trading Station on the Gwaai. A man called Ritch was running the place. (Ritch was a short, bow-legged, sandy-haired man. He was very shy and spoke with a slight stutter. A few months later, this meek humble individual, who had never been particularly strong on his legs, tried to get off a moving train one night. He lost his footing, fell under the wheels of the train and was killed instantly. Only the following morning was his body discovered on the tracks.)

Having made my arrangements with Whitmore, I returned to the Police Camp, collected all my followers and escorted them to the store. I told Ritch that I wanted to outfit the Bushmen, Bankamakuni and the two constables, Dubani and Kleinbooi. There was a difficulty in that I had only £3 in cash but this was overcome as Ritch was willing to give me credit until I returned from Bulawayo. The shopping spree got under way.

Apart from the constables and Bankamakuni, not a single one of the Bushmen knew what he or she wanted. They had never been in a store and their wonder and amazement as they gazed upon the display of blankets, dresses and shirts silenced them completely. They just stood and looked with wide-open, unblinking eyes. I picked out a gaudy, bright-red dress with animal heads printed on the material, a singlet and a blue blanket and presented them to Plover, C'wai's little daughter, who had been with the patrol almost from the beginning. I told Bankamakuni to instruct Plover's mother to dress the child in her new outfit. The poor little Bushman girl was terribly embarrassed as she was clothed in her "robes". The others looked on in astonishment whilst she kept her eyes riveted on her toe which was idly tracing patterns in the sand. After Plover it was the turn of the others and, one by one, women and children first, they each received clothing and a blanket. They took the gifts without a murmur or a single word of thanks. The "clothing parade" was finally completed and I spoke with Ritch whilst the Bushmen waited outside the store. (The purchases had cost £29 – a considerable sum in those days when £1 was worth its full value of twenty shillings Having finished my business with Ritch, I walked out of the store. I was greeted by a performance, neither rehearsed nor prearranged, which told me that the £29 had been well spent. As I emerged on to the verandah Plover pirouetted for a second and then fell to her knees upon the ground and thumped her head up and down on the sand. She then rose to her feet and uttered a shrill shriek of delight. This was the signal for a general "thank you" ceremony. Everyone, including the constables, shouted at the tops of their voices and accompanied their yells with abandoned whirlings and twirlings and spinning in all directions. The noise was deafening and continued on and on, as the party raised clouds and clouds of dust. Their gratitude was deeply touching.

Eventually I put up my hands for silence and explained to them that I was leaving on the train for Bulawayo that night to see a doctor. I told them that I would return as soon as possible but that, in the meantime they were to remain in the Police Camp and give no trouble and they would receive rations daily. I gave the £3 I had to Kleinbooi and told him to buy an ox from the locals if the party became hungry for more meat (although we never paid more than £2 for a large ox).

I asked the Member in Charge at Gwaai to look after the Bushmen during my absence, to treat them kindly, to feed them well and generally to make them feel at home until my return. I also asked him to take detailed statements from Dubani and C'wai regarding the shooting of the Bushman and to forward the statements to Bulawayo Headquarters.

The whole of my party were at the Station at 10 p.m. when I left for Bulawayo. They were most unhappy to see me go and the last glimpse I had of them as the train moved off, they were still on their knees and thumping the ground with their heads.

Chapter Thirty Six – The Aftermath

It was a terrible journey on the goods train that night. The excitement of the return to civilisation had overcome some of my aches and pains but as the train rattled on its way south, they returned with a vengeance. My leg was terribly inflamed and had turned all colours of the rainbow. I was feverish and running a high temperature when I reached Bulawayo and I had to be helped from the train by the coloured driver of the mulecart who met me and took me to the Memorial Hospital.

On reaching the hospital, I can barely remember being taken from the buckboard and being wheeled into the building. A man in a long white coat asked, "Good God! What's happened here?" and then all faded into oblivion.

I came round late in the afternoon and felt much better. The nurse asked me if I was feeling better and I was able to nod in the affirmative. She then took from the mantleshelf of the private ward in which I found myself, a jar which had a small stick, about an inch in length and a quarter inch in diameter, floating in a clear liquid.

"Dr Eaton wants to know how long you have had this 'beam' in your leg?"

Only the next morning did Dr Eaton allow me to explain and when I did so, he simply would not believe me!

"No human being can survive being shot at by Bushmen, being trampled by an elephant and an attack of blackwater fever!"

He confirmed after a very painful examination that I had indeed had blackwater fever. He was astonished that I was still alive to tell the tale. The only explanation I could give regarding the "beam" in my leg was that the splinter had penetrated when I had been dashed against the tree by the elephant. With all the other pains, I had been unaware of the injury in the soft flesh next to the shin bone. Dr Eaton had removed the "plaster cast" around my knee and was full of admiration for the rough and ready but thoroughly efficient Bushman treatment. The removal of the cast had precipitated the formation of "water on the knee" and a scotch dressing was applied. Dr Eaton was very anxious to identify the particular herb from which the Bushman cure for blackwater fever had been obtained. I had not been told by the Bushmen, whether intentionally or not. In any case, at the time of C'wai's doctoring, I had not been remotely concerned with the identity of the brew.

Having survived the rigours of the patrol, I wonder how I ever survived that stay in hospital. I was kept there for three months. The water on my knee would not clear up. Captain Murray visited me in hospital and told me that he had received the statements regarding the shooting of the Bushman.

As soon as I was fit enough, I was requested to report on the whole patrol covering the alleged cattle smuggling and also the attempted murder incident.

Regarding the "smuggling", I had already come to the following conclusions:

1. That there was no evidence to show that the cattle dealers had any intention of moving cattle illegally.

2. That the report from the Veterinary Department must have originated with the auctioneers on the Rand. Their suspicions had been aroused simply by the fact that the number of cattle arriving in Johannesburg bore little relation to the number dispatched

3. The auctioneers failed to realise that the deficiencies were entirely due to the predacious lions, other carnivorous animals and natural causes.

4. Had attempts been made to move cattle from the north or from Bechuanaland into Southern Rhodesia, the animals would never have arrived at their illegal destinations. Everything was against such movement: the country was too wild, water was extremely scarce and the distances between water too great as I had discovered to my cost even without a herd.

In the report I gave full details on the incident with the Bushman and his attempt to murder me. I emphasised that it had been a very lucky shot that had killed him. I became involved in lengthy correspondence with Leo Robinson, the Native Commissioner at Nyamandhlovu, concerning the prosecution of the Bushmen who had joined my party. None of them had the slightest idea what a Registration Certificate was or that they needed licences for the firearms they carried. If it was proposed to punish them, I was prepared to go to jail myself for contempt. I would have little success in the future in trying to bring more of the Bushmen back to civilisation if they were to be faced by a period in prison. It was months before the question was settled and, thankfully, the Native Department looked at the situation from my point of view. (This decision bore fruit on my second patrol into the area when, once again, I was joined by several Bushmen who returned with me to the Gwaai where they were happily settled).

I thought that I was never going to escape from the Memorial Hospital but eventually I was set free. Captain Murray and Sergeant Major Hough (God bless them) showed me the regulations under which I was able to claim all sorts of extra duty pay. Not having drawn pay for eight months, with the extra duty pay and the civilian clothes allowance, the total amount came to quite a fat cheque. My biggest surprise, however, was when I came to sell the sjamboks to one Van Blerk, a Bulawayo harness maker. He paid me £24 – an average price of four shillings each. He even asked for more as they were in great demand!

Without even applying, I was given fourteen days leave, to "relax" as Captain Murray put it. However, after only one week during which time I had seen everyone I knew in Bulawayo, life in the City began to pall. I asked Sergeant-Major Hough to let me cut short the holiday and return to the Gwaai.

He did, and I was happy.

GWAAI INCIDENTS

DURING the winter of 1913, I received a letter at the Gwaai Police Camp from Bulawayo Headquarters. It read:

> J.S. van Rooyen is reported to be living and squatting on Government land somewhere on the Gwaai River. His residence there is illegal and you are instructed to remove him unless he can prove satisfactory title to the land he is occupying. Report back as soon as possible.

There was nothing particularly startling about my orders but it sounded a rather unpleasant job. I decided to get it over with as soon as possible and began making preparations.

Riding animals for policemen in those days were mules. They were tough animals and a few of them even gave easy rides. However, I could never reconcile myself to riding them although there were occasions when there was no alternative. When these occurred, I always felt like Don Quixote…my feet nearly touching the ground, my rifle taking the place of the romantic's long lance and my pith hat perched where a visored helmet might have been as appropriate. There is no doubt that tall men looked as ridiculous on mules as do the present day policemen on their miniature scooters. As for the mule, only a few hands high and with a look of complete abject humility in his watery eyes, he might well have been saying: "why pick on poor me?" There were some mules, of course, half-bred things, which simply could not be trusted. With malice aforethought, they would buck before you were even properly settled in the saddle and viciously savage your feet in the stirrup irons – always presuming that you had been lucky enough to get the saddle on in the first place. More usually it was a case of chasing after a stubborn animal who, with neck erect, ears pointed and unfriendly snorts in your direction, seemed to be goading you into having another try at saddling-up. Many were the troopers who had travelled far…carrying saddle and packs in the wake of a recalcitrant mule.

I had very little respect for any of them – mules, that is. Such was my antipathy towards this mode of transport that I had a pony, my private property, somewhere in the vicinity whenever possible. Although this was strictly against Regulations, Captain Murray shared my love of horses and was an excellent horseman himself. He closed his eyes to many of my irregular happenings although not without reprimands galore and dire threats of being "put on the peg".

On my pony, *Dapper*, and followed by two pack donkeys (in contrast I loved and respected these little beasts), African Constable Kleinbooi and my batman, Ibhiza, we set off in search of Mr J.S. van ooyen. Beyond the M'sunguraala Vlei, where the old Falls road hugged a Guso belt, I came across the tracks of a vehicle with pneumatic tyres. I could scarcely believe my eyes and the spoor was certainly worth investigating. Following the mysterious imprints along the half-overgrown track which was the so-called Great North Road, I spotted a herd of sable on the fringe of the forest on my left. As I intended staying with Jim Chalmers on his farm Lynwoods for the night, I thought it would be a polite gesture to shoot a sable and "make my marble round" by presenting Jim with some fresh meat. Leaving the pack animals and the puzzling tyre marks, I rode off in pursuit of the herd. I was about to dismount for a shot when the sable winded me and dashed off back in the direction of the road. I followed as fast as I could in the thick forest and had just about got within range of the herd again when they suddenly split in two and stampeded in opposite directions.

Imagine my surprise as the twin clouds of dust receded to reveal the cause of the herd's sudden division. There, in the middle of nowhere, was a motorcar, with three Europeans in close attendance. I wondered if it wasn't some sort of mirage! The motorists were staring after the sable (who had stopped and were glaring back at the monstrosity which had invaded their privacy) and I was able to reach the group unbeknown to them. There was some satisfaction in surprising the trio from behind and, having introduced myself, all was explained.

This was the much-advertised Argyle Car Overland Expedition from Cape to Cairo. In charge was one Captain Kelsey and they had set out from the tip of South Africa weeks before. I had much admiration for them though I very much doubted if they would ever cross the Zambezi. The overlanders were stuck in deep, heavy, white sand and they were in the process of unrolling wire netting on the road in front of the car. With the netting in position, the engine was started and the car driven the length of the wire – some ten yards – before the whole process had to be repeated. The result of this painfully slow procedure was that the three adventurers were almost completely exhausted. They had the most wonderful equipment in the way of weapons, spares, camping gear and so on, but the best equipment in the world at the time would not have taken them across the white Guso sands of this particular area.

To me, the men appeared to be shy-painfully so – and it was a while before I realised that they were very pre-occupied and ill-at-ease. Their progress, or lack of it, was their over-riding concern. It was not until I suggested another way of traversing the sand that the ice was broken and then I was answered with a chorus of approvals on my suggested "magic carpet". I told them quite simply that they should have a breather while I rode on to Jim Chalmers' farm with a request for a team of oxen to pull the car over the obstacle. They were unaware that they were anywhere near a piece of civilisation. "Good God! A farm near here! That news deserves a drink. Come on, Kelsey, out with the hooch."

In no time the said hooch was gurgling down four throats with accompanying smiles of satisfaction. In the meantime, my pack donkeys and the two Africans had caught me up and I had sent them on to the farm. Reluctantly, I refused yet another round, mounted, and hurried in the wake of my caravan. Jim Chalmers was surprised not only at my arrival but at my news of the would-be motorists and was most helpful when I explained the expedition's difficulty. Quickly six oxen were yoked, extra chains handed to the two drivers and, with a leader, sent to the stranded motorists.

Jim and I were sitting on his verandah, awaiting the arrival of Kelsey and company when a most extraordinary incident took place. When Jim had taken possession of the farm, which had formerly belonged to the Susman Brothers of Livingstone, he had diverted a then-permanent stream which had flowed into the "Dibo-dibo" (the name the locals gave to the dish-shaped vlei into which the stream had emptied). Since its water had been diverted straight into the Gwaai, the Dibo-dibo naturally dried up and so, in turn, did the mass of vegetation deposited in the streambed over the years. When all was thoroughly dry, Jim had fired the former morass and had been astounded when the fire had burned for three months. When it had finally burnt out completely, he had been left with an ash pit which was very, very deep. Just how deep had never been discovered.

On this particular afternoon, with the sun setting in a deep red glow, a hundred of Jim's oxen which were being fattened for the market emerged from the forest in single file, moving in the direction of the ominous ash pit. We could see the animals clearly from our seats on the verandah and Jim remarked on the profit they represented. The leaders were about to pass the lip of the grey depression when we distinctly heard the grunt of a lion, followed immediately by low growls and excited shouts of alarm from the herdboys. The three front oxen dashed straight into the Dibo-dibo whilst the balance of the herd, with tails in the air, bellowed with fright and stampeded for the kraals. We both grabbed our rifles in one movement and ran to the stables where the alert stable hands were already saddling two horses. We cantered down to where the oxen had vanished with Jim's five dogs in our wake.

There was not a solitary sign of the three oxen. Only a slight depression in the ash marked their graves. (Even when we poked into the ash with ten foot long sticks the following day, we could find no trace of the missing animals.) Here indeed was a death trap. The approaching dark made it impossible for us to follow the lions that night although we heard the dogs giving tongue and answering growls. We returned to the homestead to wait for Captain Kelsey and his men.

We were just in time. As we reached the stables, the dust cloud produced by 24 hooves spread into the farm. In the still night air, the same dust cloud had submerged the identities of the expedition members. They looked ghastly – and admitted as much. Their eyes looked like raisins set in short-cake and their white dust-laden clothes gave them the appearance of a Ku Klux Klan trio.

It was quite some time before everyone had had their turn in the bathroom. When we were all settled on the verandah again, holding whiskies supplied by the sponsors of the expedition, we heard the story of the trials of the journey. Despite the expressions of hardships endured in every sentence, not one of the three men seemed to have any doubts that they would eventually reach Cairo. I had great difficulty in suppressing my own reservations.

Some weeks later, Chalmers told me that they had stayed with him for a full week before pressing on to Wankie. Months later, the Press revealed how the three men had split up in Livingstone leaving Kelsey to continue alone.

At Broken Hill, he went after leopard, wounded one cat but in the process was badly mauled and later died in hospital. So ended the Argyle Expedition. The car never reached Cairo.

Meanwhile, Chalmers knew all about van Rooyen and directed me towards the Ingulube River, a small tributary running into the Gwaai, near which van Rooyen had his settlement.

We arrived at the squatter's huts quite early – it was no more than nine miles from Lynwoods. Van Rooyen was surprised to see me and was naturally worried when I told him the reason for the visit.

"Remove me!" he exploded. "You'll never get me away from here alive but you can do what you like with my dead body! I'm staying here. These farms on the Gwaai have been laid out by the Government for the express benefit of the Pioneers, of whom I claim to be one. The damned Lands Department will not reply to my letters and I welcome a court case where I can really show up their inefficiency!" After this outburst, he gently uncrossed his knees, withdrew his gaze from the far horizon which seemed to have claimed him, and looked at me challenging. In a way, I sympathised with him.

"You may have right on your side, van Rooyen, but unless you can produce something in black and white, my orders are to remove you," I replied.

"The only documents I can produce are copies of letters between myself and the Department of Lands. They will prove to you that it is my firm in- tention to buy this farm in terms of the Pioneer Occupation Rights. It will also give you a damned good indication of the stupidity and inefficiency of those damned Civil Servants in Salisbury. The whole lot should be booted out tomorrow!"

"I'll look at the letters later. In the meantime I would like to camp here for a day or two. Where can I pitch my camp?"

"Right here by the huts under one of the big trees. I've nothing against you personally and I'll be glad of the company. Watch out for lion though, they've been troublesome of late so the nearer you are to the huts, the better."

No relation to the Cornelius J. van Rooyen or "Nellus" of giraffe-capturing fame I had earlier encountered, this van Rooyen was an educated man. Apart from his rolling "V"s, his English was perfect. But there was nothing prepossessing about his appearance. He had a most peculiar figure – short bandy legs and very long body, all surmounted by a long thin face adorned with a well-trimmed goatee beard. He was very fit and, I discovered later, could walk miles on those short hoopy legs of his.

Later, when he was showing me hospitality out of all proportion to the nature of my business, we had a long and fascinating conversation. He had the extraordinary ability of imitating the call of guinea fowl.

"At times when I'm very hard up, I sit for hours in the veld calling the birds," he told me. "When I have a good cluster standing around, I blast off with my shotgun and sometimes collect as many as fifteen at a time. I send the birds to a friend, Van Blerk, the harness and shoe maker in Bulawayo. He sells them on the market and to private customers and then, when he has accumulated a tidy sum, I go down and buy my provisions before coming straight back."

Apparently van ooyen had killed a hippo some years previously and this had resulted in serious trouble and a very heavy fine. I think more for my benefit than anything else he concluded:

"But I'm a good boy now and never shoot Royal game!" While a substantial camp was being constructed for the night, a grey haired old Matabele shuffled into the camp. News of the presence of the police at van ooyen's must have spread quickly.

"My daughter, Idada, vanished two weeks ago," complained the old man. "We have searched and searched but we cannot find her. Will the Inkoos please make enquiries around the Gwaai Station."

I told the man, Inkolo, that I would certainly do what I could. I asked at what time of day she had disappeared.

"It was in the morning," he said pointing his hand skyward towards the 10 a.m. sun. "Some of the children saw her walking in the direction of the water and that was the last that was seen of her. She had no men friends and she was a good worker who looked after me well. I miss her very much and I am worried that after an absence of nearly three weeks, she is dead."

There was little I could do immediately and I was as pessimistic about her chances as her father. All I could do was to repeat my assurances of such help as was within my power and send the bereaved old man back to his kraal. Late the same afternoon, I took my shotgun and walked down to the Ingulube River. Ibhiza followed with my 6mm Manlicher-Mauser. The river was scarcely worthy of the name being but a small spruit fed from a permanent fountain some three miles above van Rooyen's huts. The storm water of the rainy season had formed pools at intervals.

Having passed one such pool, I was brought to a halt in my tracks by Ibhiza's cry of "crocodile". I hurried back and, sure enough, there was a monster crocodile lying on the floor of a pool no more than four feet deep.

I exchanged guns with my batman and walked closer to the edge of the clear water. The croc made no movement, thinking perhaps he was sufficiently concealed under the water. I fired and he moved hurriedly towards the other end of the pool. When the mud of his progress had settled, I saw that he was in shallower water. A repetition of my actions drove him even further into the shallow water of the top end of the pool where I was able to get a bullet into the brain. The death convulsions of the monster sent water flying in all directions and brought him almost out of the water and on to the bank where, in a final spasm, he reared almost vertically before crashing back to the ground.

My shots had attracted several of the locals who were more than delighted to witness the end of the dreaded ingwenya. They asked my permission to disembowel the reptile in a search for "snuff-stones" – stones which the croc had swallowed and which are supposed to help in the mastication of his food. These smooth round stones are highly prized for grinding snuff.

The Africans struggled to get the monster completely out of the water. Finally he was dragged onto the grass and I was amazed at his size. He must have been very old, was black with age and had very worn teeth. The degree of size lay rather in the monster's breadth than length.

By the time the natives had hacked open the bowel, they were disappointed to find no stones. What was distinctly sobering was that they uncovered – with howls of astonishment – a native bangle, one of the white composition things sold in the stores for a few shillings. Closer examination of the bangle turned their amazement into horror and wailing. The bangle was identified as being that of the missing girl, Idada. Ikolo, Idada's father, was soon on the scene to confirm the identity of the bangle's owner by a shallow hole burnt into it by his daughter. His grief was amplified by the mysterious bush telegraphy which brought scores of other mourners to the edge of the water. The bereaved father asked my permission to burn the carcase of the croc in sacrifice. I consented, thinking that it might be some consolation to the old man.

When I dined with van Rooyen that evening, he was disappointed that I had not saved the skin of the reptile. He reckoned that it might have brought £4 or £5 which he would have shared with me – most considerate of him! After dinner, I examined the documents that he believed gave him claim to the land. To my mind, he certainly had a case and I requested the loan of the documents in order to attach them to my report. He made copies of the originals before handing them over to me on receipt.

I left van Rooyen's the following day and returned to the Gwaai via N'gamo. I saw no sign of the Argyle Expedition but of course I learned later that they were still at Jim Chalmers' place.

I received no further instructions regarding van Rooyen when I had forwarded my report. In many ways I was pleased since what had appeared to be a rather unpleasant chore had turned into a most interesting patrol.

LOST ON THE GWAAI

The telegram, delivered by the Station Messenger, came from out of the blue:

Reported no trace of ex-Sergeant Kennedy farming beyond Malindi. Proceed immediately and endeavour to locate him.

Kennedy had joined the Force after the Boer War. I had met him for the first time when taking a horse to Inyati where he was in charge. One of the troopers under his command was Teddy Hughes Halls. Kennedy had fallen foul of two rather prudish members named Lochner and Webber and the result of the disagreement was that Kennedy had been transferred to Wankie. He took his discharge from there and then started farming and trading on a section of the main Falls railway line near Dett, which became known as Kennedy's Halt.

The cryptic telegram and my own knowledge of the man were thin clues on which to base the search. How the devil was I supposed to trace this needle in the haystack? For fully thirty minutes I pondered over the message before deciding on a course of action. The best plan seemed to be to board the train from Gwaai to Malindi, taking with me the packs and saddlery and to wait up the line for the animals to arrive in charge of Constable Kleinbooi and C'wai. I sent a runner to call C'wai who lived some distance from the camp, and meanwhile set Kleinbooi and my batman busy with the packing for the trip.

By the time C'wai had arrived at the station, the packs were ready and had been taken to the station and stacked near the rails. Just in case Kleinbooi, my batman or C'wai should be tempted to delay things by taking a nap on the journey up to Malindi with the animals, I made sure the blankets joined the packs to be railed to our destination. Just before sundown, the three Africans left with the two pack donkeys and my horse.

Having seen them off, I made myself comfortable at the station to await the goods train which was due in the small hours of the morning. Whitmore the Station Manager, his foreman Anderson and Knowles, the ganger, joined me and introduced me to an extraordinary sundowner – absinthe. The drink, with its peculiar taste of a mixture of liquorice and aniseed, was definitely not to my liking. Still, after three helpings of the cloudy concoction, carefully prepared by dripping water drop by drop into the tot, I began to feel soothingly off-balance and very sleepy.

Anderson woke me at 3.45 a.m. when he heard the rumble of the approaching train and I heaved myself and my packs into the guard's van. Some six miles beyond Gwaai, the train travels on what is supposed to be the second longest stretch of straight line in the world but it was a most unpleasant journey with dust penetrating the van and getting into one's eyes, ears and nostrils. The van swayed alarmingly when the dead straight track allowed the locomotive to drag the train at a top speed of something in excess of 25 mph.

The train arrived at Malindi shortly after sunrise and having moved my packs to a shady tree, I awaited the arrival of my trek which I expected at about midday.

In front of the galvanised tin shack which served as Malindi's station, was a huge tuskless elephant skull which bore witness to the occasion when the train had collided with the elephant, which had to be destroyed. The story is told that every passenger on the train who possessed a firearm (including revolvers) pelted the poor beast until it was dead. The tusks were presented to, or taken by, Miss Going, the daughter of the only farmer in the area.

At about 9 o'clock, I had company. A European arrived on one of the strangest conveyances I have ever seen. Drawn by four blue-roan oxen with enormous horns and humps, the two-wheeled cart was just a flat platform with no rails. It looked most uncomfortable. The newcomer jumped off the vehicle and, assisted by an African companion, started to unyoke the oxen. The trek gear had hardly touched the ground when the man yelled to me enquiring if his wine and brandy had arrived. Without waiting for a reply, he charged over to the shack and re-appeared with a broad grin on his suntanned face. He showed perfect teeth between his clipped moustache and black goatee beard as he smiled in my direction.

"Hello, who are you?" he enquired as he approached me with outstretched hand. As he wrung my hand in a vice-like grip, he continued, "I'm Briers."

The rather one-sided conversation went on before I had a chance to speak. "Man, are we lucky! My old people at Paarl in the Cape never forget to send me a two-monthly supply of wine and brandy and as soon as I've cleared the stuff, you and me are going to have a long drink."

It was only then that I had a chance to introduce myself. Later, sprawled against my packs, tin mugs of dop in our hands and munching the rietbok biltong I had rooted from my supplies, Briers told me that he – or rather his father – had bought him a farm on the Gwaai from which he and his partner, Maurees, were trying to eke a living the hard way.

"And it's a damned hard way," he went on, "Mosquitoes, lions, leopards and even the birds trying to devour us and our cattle. My partner is all for giving up and going back to the Cape and his job as a lecturer at the University. Man, can you understand how anyone can give up this wonderfully free country for a bunch of sniffling students? Here it's a man's life offering wonderful opportunities to live in comfort and without women bothering one's peace of mind."

Without pausing to explain the contradiction between his first and last sentences, he went on: "I'm speaking from experience. Even the native here is a happy-go-lucky individual. Look at this one coming towards us. He couldn't care less how he is dressed and by the look of that serene and peaceful expression on his face, he has no women troubles either!"

The African referred to stood some distance from us, raised his knobkerrie and battle-axe in greeting, pulled the tattered duiker skin worn around his loins through his legs and sat down on his bare buttocks in the sand.

"What's the trouble, old man? Where are you going and where do you come from?" asked Briers with a smile.

"We are looking for Inkoos Kennedy…" and before he could complete the sentence, I was on my feet and questioning the native with an excitement which completely bewildered the old man. By dint of careful questioning and much patience, I eventually dragged sufficent information from him to indicate at least where we could begin tracking the missing man.

Briers, who had joined the interrogation, was most pessimistic. "You'll never find a man in that forest. It extends from the railway track for ten miles right down to the Gwaai River, and from the Sukoma Valley to only God knows where. It is one of the most extensive guso belts in the area and teems with elephant, buffalo, eland and herds of sable."

N'devu, the name of the old Matabele, was told to wait with me for the arrival of the rest of my trek and to then come with me in my search for Kennedy. He was quite willing and perhaps relieved that I had taken over the responsibility of the difficult search.

Meanwhile Briers, a born humorist and a man of exceptional vitality, hitched his team of oxen to the "carriage", tied the treasured barrels of liquor with rawhide reims securely onto the platform and threw a parting shot at me.

"These oxen are 'trotters' and they will have me back on my farm on the Gwaai within the three hours it would take a team of horses to cover the ten miles. The best of luck in your search and call in at the farm on your way back. I promise you a good bed, good eats and plenty of drink."

And with that he patted the barrels behind him with affection, raised his arm in salute, cracked his whip over the oxen and was off in a cloud of dust as the willing animals speeded him homewards.

I was not expecting my cavalcade before midday. The forty miles could not be covered at more than two and a half miles an hour. I faced at least another two hours of waiting, during which time my mind was fully occupied with the privations and distress which the poor Kennedy must be suffering. Having known the discomfort and pain of being without water, the swollen tongue, the swollen ankles and the semi-coma in which one dreams of fountains of clear running water, I could well appreciate the hell the unfortunate man might be enduring. To curb my impatience to be moving, I occupied myself by preparing a substantial meal for the Africans and animals when they arrived.

Shortly after 11 o'clock, I glanced down the line and, to my relief, spotted a small cloud of dust in the far distance. I was convinced that it was my caravan and I was right. They arrived within thirty minutes, tired and thirsty. I knew that both men and animals were tired but, having explained to the Africans that a man's life hung in the balance, they were satisfied to rest for only an hour before we packed, saddled up and moved off.

This part of the Gwaai was the domain of the Wankie police and I was not as familiar with it as I was with my own area. However, I am gifted with an appreciated "bump of locality" and, in the company of C'wai and Kleinbooi, I had no fear of getting "bushed" during the search. We plunged into the forest without hesitation although N'devu voiced the opinion that it would have been wiser to follow the railway track for some miles before entering the jungle. This would have meant extra mileage, which I felt we could ill afford.

We had covered some ten miles when C'wai's eagle eyes spotted vultures circling the tops of giant msasa trees. He hurried on ahead of us to investigate and a few minutes later we heard his "hyena" call. This peculiar cry was a product of our Kalahari travels and we had used it whenever we had become separated. We hastened in the direction of the call to find C'wai sitting on the carcass of a dead buffalo with a broad grin on his flat Mongolian face. He pointed his finger to boot marks in the red Kalahari sand. They were most certainly those of Kennedy.

The buffalo, a young bull, had been shot through the lungs not less than two days previously. The stomach was distended like a balloon and the legs pointed stiffly skywards. Hundreds of blue-bottle flies hummed around the carcass.

We made camp a few hundred yards upwind. C'wai was in his element at the gift of meat from the gods. Both he and the other three Africans considered the meat most palatable, despite the smell. Big fires were kindled and before long the appetising aroma of the grilled meat floated through the air. The four natives gorged themselves and then, after the long trek from Gwaai to Malindi and the forced march from there to our present camp, it was small wonder that they slept like the dead.

The following morning I roused them but it was with difficulty that they rubbed the sleep from their eyes. Two of our four canvas water bags were already empty and I dared not allow them even a little water to wash their sleepy eyes. Instead, I gave them a damp cloth for this purpose and the same cloth was then used to sponge the nostrils of the donkeys and my horse.

N'devu and my batman were left with the animals and I told them to cut the buffalo meat into strips while awaiting our return. C'wai, Kleinbooi and I then set out on Kennedy's spoor.

The tracks led north to a point about two miles away from the buffalo carcass. Then they started veering westwards. Further on the spoor took a southerly direction until finally we were almost back at our camp. Obviously poor Kennedy had been completely lost and was staggering around in circles.

We had a hurried meal and inspected the spoor for a second time, looking for the later footprints of the lost hunter. Like blood-hounds, C'wai and Kleinbooi hunted around until finally the Bushman gave a shout and indicated tracks leading off to the east. We followed hurriedly until we were brought to a sudden halt when the trail was obliterated by a herd of eland. It was frustrating and tiring work to try and pick up the trail again and, to make matter worse, it seemed that the herd was travelling in the same general direction as that taken by Kennedy. When we finally picked up his spoor again, it led us northeast and then started turning again in the direction of the dead buffalo. The exercise taxed my patience to the full but C'wai refused to take his nose from the trail and slowly and laboriously we made progress.

We reached a spot under a large tree where it was apparent that Kennedy had lain, perhaps even slept. His trail then moved northeast by east and had the poor man continued in that direction, he would have reached the banks of the Gwaai no more than three miles away. But again he deviated, circling to the left and then to the right. It was obvious that he was very tired, his steps were getting shorter and he took rests at frequent intervals.

We, the pursuers, were also getting tired, hungry and thirsty. It was now 3 p.m. and we had been on the move since before sunrise. The one waterbag we had brought with us was nearly empty and when anyone required a drink, I would only allow a small mouthful to keep the saliva in motion.

Kennedy's trail, which read like an open book to C'wai, was very obscure as far as I was concerned. The Bushman was positively possessed by an unearthly intuition which neither Kleinbooi or I could fathom. He would imitate almost every movement of the lost man, lay down where Kennedy had lain, crawl on his hands and knees where the signs were that Kennedy had done likewise, struggle from side to side with pretended weakness and then pull himself erect and then continue on tired and weakened legs.

C'wai's tracking was phenomenal and although I had seen him in action before, there was nothing to touch his ability on this occasion.

We were very disappointed when the tracks veered to the left again and I felt positive that we should shortly come across the dead body of Kennedy. The spoor, patiently explained by C'wai although it was becoming plainer as the demented thrashing increased showed that the man could not continue much longer.

Suddenly C'wai gave a whoop of delight and pointed to another track alongside the booted imprints of the hunter. The new footprints were barefoot and it was obvious that Kennedy had had the great fortune to be discovered by an African and that the two of them had then struggled in the direction of the river.

With the tension so suddenly broken, I felt overwhelmingly tired. C'wai and Kleinbooi thankfully joined me as I sat down with my back resting against a tree. It was 4 p.m. We discussed the new situation and decided that Kleinbooi should go back to the camp, cover the buffalo meat we had left there with branches, and then bring the animals to our present position. In the meantime, C'wai and I would continue in the direction taken by Kennedy and his rescuer. I was certain that our camp was no more than two miles away as the crow flies and if Kleinbooi moved himself, he would rejoin us at the river before dark.

Kleinbooi left immediately and C'wai and I set off on the trail again. The tracks led east-northeast towards the Gwaai and although a large herd of buffalo crossed the trail and erased all sign of the pursued, we had no difficulty in picking up the two pairs of tracks on the other side of the 200 yard path of the buffalo. We had not gone far when we realised that we were on a distinct slope and that the river was very near. The trail was now very clear and we arrived at a giant msasa tree where even I could see that Kennedy had taken a rest while his rescuer continued to the river and returned with water.

We followed on to the river and lost no time in splashing into the luke-warm water and slaking our thirsts.

Some fifty yards below the point at which we had struck the river, we came across the wheel tracks of a vehicle drawn by four mules. The spoor really puzzled C'wai and his clicks and clacks were most amusing as he tried to fathom the reason for such peculiar tracks here in the wilderness. We were soon to find out the cause.

We found ourselves on a broad footpath leading to an African village on the opposite bank of the river. Following the path, we came to the kraal to be greeted by several women and children. They explained that Kennedy had been found "dead" and they had sent word to the Police at Wankie. They had come post haste and had taken the lost hunter to Wankie Hospital on a buckboard.

Subsequent reports proved that Kennedy had very nearly lost his life and was in a shocking state when eventually discovered. He had been wandering in the wilderness for three and a half days.

Kleinbooi turned up with the caravan long before sunset and the women wasted no time in helping to cart in the rest of the stinking buffalo meat.

ELEPHANT GRAVEYARD

During the course of one of my patrols, I called in on the Townsends. They were new arrivals who were farming, or trying to establish a farm at the confluence of the Sekuma Valley and the Gwaai River. I had a great deal of admiration for them and thought highly of their sheer guts in attempting such a hazardous undertaking in an area which was then a complete wilderness.

Just to make life more difficult, the Townsends were being harassed by elephants.

"One night the brutes lifted the thatch from the rondavel in which we were sleeping," complained Mrs Townsend. "I was almost paralysed with fear and at the same time shivering in anticipation of the beasts' next move. I screamed and prayed that they would not trample the thin walls. Whether it was my bloodcurdling yell or my husband's sudden appearance in the doorway which gave the elephants a scare, I don't know, but they ambled off and silently vanished into the darkness."

I had no doubt concerning the truth of the tale. The area swarmed with game of every description. I promised to do everything with my very limited powers to see that the animals were kept at bay (small comfort to either the Townsends or myself). I then made my departure and moved further up the Sekuma valley and we made camp for the night on the edge of the forest.

The valley, which at this point varied in width from 100 to 400 yards, contained no visible running water at this time of the year. High water marks of the rainy season were, however, plainly to be seen on the slopes and the vegetation below was bleached and muddied. Now that the relentless sun had come down like a lid on the oppressive green waste, it was a frightening "valley of death". The only living inhabitants seemed to be the plagues of insects. All was silent and desolate. The only colouring was the sickening, over-rich greens and the dirty, decaying browns. The ground had become soggy, seeping mud, mostly rotting vegetation and treacherous quagmire. It was a lonely, desolate and intimidating place. The complete hush, the endless mire and coarse vegetation, the superfluity of obscene insect life in this wasteland was like nothing I had ever come across. Tramping over the thin grass covering, interwoven with decaying plant-life, was a real hazard. The crust would quiver several yards ahead of my weight and a sickening smell would belch forth from the bubbles that rose from the stinking depths.

Along the edge of the swamp, on a narrow ledge of relatively firm ground, I could see where game of every kind (and especially elephant) had ventured close to the morass to uncover the rusty, red water in which they had wallowed. I warned the trek that we were in for a very uncomfortable night. I ordered the making of fires which were banked with masses of wet leaves and branches – of which there was no shortage – and the dense smoke which resulted offered some protection for the pack animals and ourselves from the ravages of the swarming mosquitoes.

We tossed and turned beneath the clogging blanket until about three the following morning. The first shrill scream of a single elephant, followed by what sounded like a whole regiment of beasts, brought us out of our bed-rolls.

There was no peace thereafter. At regular intervals the elephant would repeat its cry and, as if it were a signal, the herd would thunder back their screaming, trumpeting chorus of pain, fright and fury.

It sounded as though the herd was right opposite our camp on the other side of the valley. Something was obviously disturbing them and the flapping of the huge ears against their bodies could be heard distinctly in the few pauses between the shrieking. On and on continued the frightful racket. Surely, I thought, it couldn't be that our smouldering fires were responsible for the elephants' intense agitation? But, unable to ignore the din, we were forced to listen and I longed for the first streak of dawn when we might discover the cause of the herd's derangement.

Dawn, when it came, did nothing to solve the mystery. The sky lightened to reveal an impenetrable mist completely covering the valley. There had been no let-up in the deafening anguish of the beasts despite the fact that some four hours had passed since we had been so forcibly made aware of the rumpus. As the sun slowly burned off the veil, we saw the dim outline of perhaps fifteen elephants on the other side of the swamp. We had to wait even longer before our curiosity was finally satisfied.

A young bull had ventured too far into the quagmire. He was floundering around up to his neck in the oozing slime, trying desperately to keep head and trunk above the mud. Each mammoth effort – and failure – to drag himself free from the relentless clutch of the stinking cesspit was accompanied by trumpeting and gurgling coughs. The bull's pathetic distress signal was recognised by the watching herd and they answered in a helpless chorus.

One big cow, with long, thin, tapered tusks and probably the mother of the trapped bull, tried to go to her off-spring's assistance with what seemed like soothing grunts of endearment. She was joined in the attempt by a massive bull with yellowing tusks who seized the cow's tail with his trunk and played "anchor-man." Slowly the mother edged into the swamp, moving forward cautiously until she was up to her belly in the rotting, soaking vegetation. But she couldn't get within range of the younger bull, realized her failure, and retreated to firm ground with difficulty and great screams of disappointment. The herd, which had paused in their bellowing while the attempt was being made, resumed their helpless cries of anger and destroyed trees and ant-heaps and ploughed into the ground with their tusks in frustration.

It was apparent that the herd would not leave the young bull until the end – one way or another. An audience of other game – sable and roan antelope, eland, a few tsessebe – had gathered and were watching with interest from a safe distance. Looking at the animals, with their ears forward, noses in the ear, barking and blowing their surprise, I wondered if animal instinct had gathered them together in an effort to assist in the rescue or whether it was just the morbid curiosity so often exhibited by supposedly higher forms of life.

If the herd had been unsuccessful in its attempts to rescue the bull from the slime since 3 a.m., I felt that it was most unlikely that further efforts at this late hour would be any more rewarding. I decided to shoot the trapped beast and put him out of his misery. My 6.5mm sporting Mauser was not the most suitable weapon for elephant hunting although it discharged a very high velocity bullet. The range was over three hundred yards and the target, though held fast in the vicious quagmire, was never stationary.

I made myself comfortable against the bole of a tree and aimed carefully at the waving head. The first shot thudded home on target but without any indication that it was a fatal blow. The report of the shot in the quiet morning air reverberated from the forest on either side and alarmed the herd to a renewed chorus of ear-splitting screams and more frantic excavation of the surrounding terrain. The big cow and her companion danced and shrieked their annoyance as if they, unlike myself, could see the effect of the bullet. The gallery of curious game stampeded in a mad rush for the safety of the dense forest.

My fourth shot had the desired effect and must have penetrated the brain. The trunk which had bravely waved in a vertical position for over five hours, suddenly collapsed with a distinct "flop" on the disturbed surface of the slime and the head slowly sank forward into the morass.

For fully thirty minutes or more the herd trumpeted their defiance. Finally, having received no response from their dead comrade, they slowly moved off into the forest leaving only the old cow and her male companion to stand over the scene of the tragedy. The couple remained for at least an hour after the rest of the herd and then, in complete silence, they trotted off in the tracks of the others.

I was considerably relieved to see the huge rumps disappear into the trees. Our eardrums had been pounded by the herd's racket since the early hours and the sight of an agitated elephant is hardly soothing to the nerves at the best of times. The silence, the deathly silence, was almost welcome – and seemingly very appropriate.

Determined to get a closer look at the scene of the tragedy, we packed and moved down the valley seeking a suitable place to cross. It took us an hour before we found a "bridge" which had been used by elephant and smaller game and was therefore safe for us to use.

We journeyed along the bank to the spot of the young bull's desperate struggles. There was no sign of him. The sinister brown liquid mixed up in the broken vegetation was completely tranquil and deceptively innocent. No one would believe that a few hours ago we had seen the long battle for life of a large elephant.

I paused and wondered how many other animals – and perhaps humans – had disappeared in this treacherous quagmire and in the other numerous swamps dotted all over Rhodesia.

THE TWINS

The sun was hot and my horse was tired as I drew near to the giant marula tree which threw its welcoming shadow close to the kraal of Matabele Chief Inyuku.

My approach scattered the score or so children, a herd of goats and several lean and hungry-looking dogs. The fruit of the marula, like a small plum, is much relished by the natives in that they make beer from it, as well as by almost every wild animal in the veld, including the elephant. Each fruit contains an edible seed or nut and it was obvious that the children and goats had been engaged in a feast before they saw the approaching horseman who had caused their flight.

The tree was close to the main entrance of the stockade which enclosed the "bee-hive" huts occupied by Inyuka, his seven wives and his numerous relatives. Under the tree were several logs that served as seats, for this was the spot at which the old chief and his headmen held their indabas.

No sooner had I lifted the saddle from my tired horse than Chief Inyuku appeared from the stockade with a broad grin on his ugly old face. He greeted me in his harsh, throaty voice:

"Good morning, Sigwanya (my native name meaning 'Crusher Jaws', itself derived from 'Crocodile Jaws'), I hope I see you well. You look tired and dusty. Sit down and I will send for beer and have your horse attended to."

He turned to face the stockade and shouted: "Isiza, Isiza, bring cold beer from the river and tell M'jongwe to come quickly and take Sigwanya's horse to the water."

Inyuku had been a headman in the time of Lobengula when the latter, as King of the Matabele, ruled the country. After the Matabele Rebellion and the death of Lobengula, Chief Inyuku and his wives and relations had established themselves on the Gwaai River. Inyuku was well into his sixties – tall, thin, muscular and very fit; his eyes were set deep within the folds of his cheeks; his lower mouth and jaw with its thick lips seemed enormous; his nose was flat with protruding nostrils and grey scraggy hair covered his upper lip and chin.

Within minutes of making ourselves comfortable on one of the logs, Insiza – the number one wife of Inyuku – appeared, followed by two strapping well-developed young girls carrying calabashes on their heads. With ceremony they knelt before us and carefully placed the receptacles upon the ground. They then clapped their hands in greeting, rose and returned to the enclosure around the huts. As the three women vanished from sight, I turned and faced the old chief.

"Inyuku, I see Insiza will soon make you a happy father again?" The old man poured the beer, brewed from kaffir corn and retrieved from an excavated tunnel in the black clay walls of the Gwaai River so that it was as cold as ice when served. He nodded his head and replied:

"Yes, yes, Sigwanya. The event is expected very shortly and the women have already begun to make preparations for the 'birth feast'."

I doubt whether it was Insiza's enormous protruding stomach that sent some unconscious thought to my brain but it was pure innocence and curiosity which prompted my next question. "Inyuku," I enquired, "the Matabele have certain tribal laws when twins are born. Would you explain them to me?"

The question seemed to frighten Inyuku and it was only then that I realised that the chief might have shared my unconscious brain signal.

"Sigwanya, that is an ugly question," he said sharply. "Why should Insiza have twins?"

I tried to gloss over the blunder I seemed to have made.

"No, no, Inyuku. I am not suggesting that Insiza is going to have twins. I ask only from interest." To further calm his agitation, I threw in a little flattery. "Who can enlighten me better than you who knows your tribal laws so well?" I asked, patting his skinny shoulder with the flat of my hand.

Inyuku looked hard at me and, apparently satisfied that I was merely making conversation, cleared his throat and, in a rasping voice, explained: "The Matabele have strong objections to the birth of twins. One of the two children is usually left to starve or is prevented from breathing by the attendant midwives. This practice is referred to euphemistically by saying 'lendisiwe' (she has been married off) in the case of a girl or 'laswela' by which it is understood that a boy has been quietly smothered. The body of the child is buried close to the hut inside the stockade and it is customary to place the surviving twin on the grave when it is sick or crying, to soothe its pain."

I was extremely interested in Inyuku's lecture and, realising this, he continued:

"The Amakalanga kill not one but both children, usually by piercing the brain with a needle through the fontanel immediately after birth. The Matabele do not recognise twins as ordinary human beings and allow no mourning for the one that 'dies'. The basis of the whole belief – with which you must agree in your wisdom – is that one of the twins is always weaker than the other and it is therefore better to destroy the weakling at the beginning of its life than let it linger on."

Despite Inyuku's compliment to my intelligence, I could not let him get away with the idea that I could support the killing of a twin under any circumstances.

I was brutal in my approach.

"Inyuku, have you ever seen a man hang with a rope around his neck?" I asked.

"Oh, yes!" replied Inyuku, surprised and failing to grasp exactly what I was getting at. "I have seen several such deaths and it is not a pretty sight. The dead man's tongue comes out a very long way I never knew that a man's tongue was so long until I saw that of a man who had been hanging from a tree by his neck for a whole night. Why do you ask?"

Smiling in order that the warning I was about to give would not sound too threatening, but inwardly very serious, I told Inyuku the consequences should he become involved in the sudden death of twins.

"I'm glad you have seen a man hanging, Inyuku, and that you agree that it is not a pretty sight. Just remember that you will look like that man hanging all night from a tree if your wife, Isiza, or any of your other wives, gives birth to twins and they are smothered at birth in accordance with your tribal laws. You are now under the law of the white man and the government will not allow the smothering of children at birth. We consider that to be murder and anyone guilty of murder must hang by his neck."

"Ah, ah, Sigwanya," replied the old chief, shaking his head from side to side in slow motion, "your talk is ugly talk. Why do we discuss such a subject? There will be no twins. The witchdoctor has thrown his bones and has taken blood from Isiza and I am to be the father of a boy. But I have heeded your warning and I promise that nothing will happen if twins are born."

At that juncture I dropped the subject, having no wish to antagonise the friendship of the old man whom I had known and respected for so long. We continued drinking the cool, refreshing and potent beer and it was only some three hours later that, with a very heavy head, I took my departure.

Ten days after my visit with Inyuku, I again had reason to pass close to his kraal. The welcoming shade beneath the marula tree was deserted apart from a few chickens, two mangy dogs and a few goats. The animals fled in alarm as I rode into the shadows. I off-saddled the pony and was placing the leather against the bole of the tree when Inyuku made his appearance. The Chief looked deep in the dumps and the usual cheery greeting was completely absent.

"Hello, Inyuku. You look as if you have just been to a funeral." I said, a most tactless remark as I was later to discover. "What's wrong, has your best bull died?"

"No, Sigwanya. It is not the bull," he replied in a woeful voice, shaking his head in sorrow. "We have great trouble in my kraal and I am completely heartbroken."

Being well acquainted with the African mind and demeanour, I did not press for further details in the knowledge that I would get the full story in due course. The icy beer was placed before us, my horse was taken for watering and I settled down on the log waiting for the explanation of Inyuku's sorrow. My host made no attempt to drink. After a long silence, the old chief gave a despairing moan and launched into his sorry tale. "Sigwanya, Isiza gave birth to twins last night and both children were born dead. The witchdoctor says that Isiza is witchridden and he is determined to hunt out the umthakathi."

The news silenced me, especially after our conversation of a few days previously. While I sat wondering what to do, Inyuku moaned and groaned beside me, his head squeezed between his hands.

I reasoned to myself that it would be many years before the tribal laws of the superstitious natives could be replaced with education and, until then, fear of the consequences would be the only way of stamping out the inhuman custom. As against this, I had no proof that Inyuku was not speaking the truth when he said that the children had been born dead. It was only my horribly suspicious policeman's mind going into action and, even if murder had taken place, it was going to be a damnably difficult charge to prove. Perhaps I was wrong, but I decided to put the fear of God into Inyuku, just in case the deaths had not been accidental and as a warning for the future.

Without a word to Inyuku who was still sitting on the log with head in hands, I shouted to M'jongwe to bring my horse. Saddling up I mounted and addressed the old man from the height of officialdom in a fit of pretended anger.

"Inyuku, listen and listen carefully! You are going to hang by the neck and will be like the man you saw with his tongue dangling down to his navel. I am going to report that I suspect you of having killed your two children – and may Heaven help you!"

And with that parting shot, I spurred my pony into a gallop and left Inyuku sitting dumbfounded in a cloud of dust.

Shortly after breakfast the next morning, I was sitting in my office trying to keep abreast of the paperwork when Impisi, a minor headman of Chief Inyuku, made an appearance and requested an interview. I invited him into the office. He entered and greeted me respectfully before sitting down cross-legged in front of my desk.

"Well, Impisi, you are early. How is Inyuku and what can I do for you?" I asked pleasantly.

Impisi sat there, his face working and perspiration glistening on his black cheeks. Finally, in a frightened voice, he answered my question.

"Sigwanya, Inyuku has a sad heart and he says that his heart will remain sad until he hears from me that you have accepted his present."

"Present! What present? I know of no present," I said in astonishment.

"No, Sigwanya. Of course you have not seen it. I have only just come with the present that Inyuku sends to you. They are awaiting word from you to come nearer."

"Well, go and tell them to come nearer, whatever or whoever they are!" I exclaimed.

Impisi was obviously feeling very uncomfortable and left the office hurriedly. Ten minutes later he reappeared driving six black heifers and assisted by two young girls aged about sixteen or seventeen.

The cattle were left at the door and the three Africans entered. The two girls were beautiful by any standards. Their unblemished skin shone like a pair of polished copper statues; the upper parts of their bodies were naked to reveal firm and perfectly formed breasts. Their only clothing consisted of mini – very mini – skirts made of carefully pleated, dark blue "German print". The abbreviated skirts showed off faultless legs to full advantage and, as they entered the office, the skirts swayed with a graceful motion that could not have been bettered by a professional Hawaiian dancer. I cannot recall having seen two more noble or perfect samples of African womanhood. My admiration was to be quickly replaced by acute embarrassment as Impisi explained the nature of his errand.

"Sigwanya." he said nervously, "Inyuku sends you the six black heifers as a present, to keep in your kraal and to breed from. O'dumisa here," pointing to the girl on his left, "and I'lilanda," indicating the other girl, "are to remain here in your camp, to cook your food, look after your chickens, clean your huts and keep your bed warm."

For several seconds there was complete silence. I was almost stunned by the nature of the "gift" and it took me some minutes to regain my composure. With difficulty I addressed the two girls.

"You, O'dumisa and you, I'lilanda, did you agree to this arrangement?"

Both girls were much too bashful to speak their assent but there was no mistaking the way they vigorously nodded their heads.

Once again there was dead silence. Having recovered from my initial shock, I tried to fathom out why Inyuku was attempting to blackmail me. The death of the twins was the only answer. Could it be that my suspicions were correct? I literally barked at Impisi with blazing eyes:

"Why does Inyuku send me these presents?"

"Inkoos," replied Impisi, fear in his eyes at my sudden change of manner, "who knows the mind of Inyuku? I am only carrying out his instructions and I gave you the message as I was told to give it."

My anger had almost caused the girls to rush from the office and now they stood there as if in fear of their lives. I felt sorry for them and for Impisi whom I realised was only Inyuku's messenger. At the same time I marvelled at the obedience Inyuku could exact from his followers. What hope had I of ever extracting the truth of the twin's death in the face of such authority?

My sympathy softened my tones and I told the trio to go into the kitchen and ask Cephas, my cook, to give them something to eat before returning to the kraal. After they had gone I realised that I would have to explain the refusal of the gifts in an idiom that would penetrate their uncivilised skulls.

I went into the kitchen and discovered Impisi and the girls squatting on the floor, tearing at lumps of bread supplied by Cephas. The latter could hardly keep his eyes off the girls and, not wishing him to hear the lecture I was about to deliver, I sent him off on some errand.

I addressed myself primarily to the two young girls.

"I am sorry that I cannot allow you to stay with me, but black and white do not mix, O'dumisa and I'lilanda. Have you ever seen the Sable antelope and the Roan antelope mix on the veld? You see them in large herds close to your kraal. Tell me, have you ever seen them mix?" The trio shook their heads in unison. "Ask Inyuku when you go back if he has ever seen the antelope mix. I think you know the answer you will receive. If the antelope of the veld keep to themselves, how can Inyuku expect black and white humans to inter-mingle?

"What colour will the children be? They will be neither white nor black. You, the Matabele, will cast them from your huts and the Europeans will want nothing to do with them either.

"Finish your food, rest yourselves and then return to Inyuku with the heifers. Give him my message and tell him that I will come and see him very shortly. Go in peace."

There was little doubt about the reaction of the two girls. They seemed visibly relieved although I was sure that they would have performed their "duties" without question had they stayed. Impisi was not quite so happy and and it was possible that he was apprehensive of Inyuku's reaction at the returning of the gifts. For myself, I could not cast off the worry caused by my suspicions over the death of the children and Inyuku's consequent generosity. Did the Chief have a guilty conscience or was he only trying to restore the friendship that existed before my abrupt departure from his kraal?

The problem plagued me for the rest of the day and even when I got to bed. I could not throw off the nagging worry. I tossed and turned on the mattress and sleep seemed impossible. Eventually I succumbed to tiredness and dropped off into a deep but not dreamless sleep.

In one of the most vivid and disturbing dreams I have experienced, I saw a tall, gaunt African struggling through a gloomy forest with slow heavy steps. On his shoulder he carried a heavy coffin. He trudged through the undergrowth with the deliberation of a funeral march and stopped under the branch of a tree from which a noose was suspended. With awful solemnity, the man lifted the coffin from his shoulder and turned. At that moment I recognised him. It was Inyuku. I tried to run towards him but my legs would not move. I shouted to him to stop but not a sound came from my throat.

I awoke from the nightmare suddenly, drenched in perspiration. I glanced at the time and saw it was two in the morning.

The illusion was so vivid and frightening that further sleep was out of the question. The reality of the horror was so disturbing that there and then I decided to go to Inyuku's kraal. It was only when I was in the saddle and some distance from the station that I began chiding myself for setting out on the journey in the middle of the night purely on the basis of a dream.

Dapper, my pony, was an easy ride with a fast gait and a comfortable triple. We covered the ten miles to Inyuku's kraal in good time and approached the rise on which it was situated as the red dawn was beginning to break.

Dawn – the time when the birds start twittering and prepare to welcome the new day; when the semi-opaque red light illuminates unruffled leaves; when all is hushed; when grotesque shadows slowly creep from beneath trees and shrubs, throwing long wraith-like patches before them. It was in this eerie, spooky environment that I drew closer to the marula tree, silhouetted against the reddening sky.

As I approached, all the horror in my dream returned in a rush. For the second time I was drenched in a cold, icy, sweat. Scarcely distinguishable from the shadow of the tree was the bone-chilling spectacle of a human form suspended from one of the branches. My fright conveyed itself to the pony in a sudden contraction of muscles and we were hurtling towards the tragedy at a mad gallop. As we galloped into the shadows, I saw that the hanging body was that of Inyuku. Yanking at the reins, I brought the frightened pony to a rearing halt and groped desperately for my knife. I slashed at the rope and the body dropped to the ground with a seemingly lifeless thud.

Dismounting, I ran to the old chief's side and my relief at finding him still breathing precipitated another wave of perspiration. I raised the alarm and within minutes we were surrounded by a multitude of the kraal's inhabitants. Brutally, I interrupted their amazement and confusion to demand water and, when it arrived, I splashed it over the head of the old man. He opened his eyes and, in a soft, innocent voice, asked, "Yini indaba?"

As Inyuku slowly recovered, I gave him "what's the matter" with both barrels in a sermon I guarantee he remembered for the rest of his life.

The Chief might have been successful in his attempt at suicide had he used a higher "drop". As it was, he had stood on a log no more than eight inches off the ground and had calmly stepped off. Instead of breaking his neck with a sudden jerk, he had only let himself in for a long slow death by strangulation. Thank God I had arrived when I did.

Inyuku forlornly explained his stupid actions with his head in his hands.

"When Impisi returned with the cattle and the girls, I thought that the police would soon be here to fetch me. I could not face the humiliation and degradation of the trial. I tried to take my life but now you have given it back to me."

Mindful of the tragedy so narrowly averted, I tried to console my friend.

"Inyuku, I will not report the matter provided that nothing like this ever happens again," I whispered confidentially.

Four months later Ijuba, Inyuku's fourth wife, gave birth to twins – and they lived. And to this day, I still wonder whether the death of Isiza's children was accident or murder.

SOUTH AFRICAN REBELLION

Illustration at head of first instalment in *The Outpost* of June 1971
Photographs: Generals De la Rey and Botha 224
Sir A. Milner and Lord Buxton 225

Returning from a long patrol in the Gwaai area in October 1914, I stopped in at the farm Lynwoods run by Jim Chalmers. He passed on to me casually the news that World War 1 had broken out and although I had heard vague reports from Africans and "tame" Bushmen that the white people were killing one another, I had treated the rumours as nonsense. When Jim went on to say that a rebellion had broken out in South Africa I became really apprehensive and felt like pushing on all the way to Bulawayo for first-hand information.

With all the impetuosity of youth I suppose I looked forward to all the thrills of being involved in a full-scale war. At the same time I realised that the news probably marked the end of the delightful solitude of long patrols. Perhaps never again would I witness the soft long shadows of the forest trees, the constant hum of insects, a friendly star-filled sky, roving herds of game, the scent of wood fires and the delicious aroma of meat being grilled.

It seemed as though the last chapter of a wonderful leisurely way of life had been written.

Late that night I devoured all the newspapers Chalmers had given me. I could not understand how the political assassination of an Austrian duke could be the cause of international war and lead to the disruption in the land of my birth. Having seen at first hand the brutality of the wild, I could not credit the reports of atrocities, of ruthless cruel slaughter on the European battlefronts. I did not believe that human beings could collectively be so cruel.

It was with renewed energy that I continued on my way to the Gwaai police station the following day. Late in the afternoon I arrived in camp to be met by an excited Trooper Rochard.

"Where the hell have you been? I've had runners out all over the country looking for you. Bulawayo wants you there as soon as possible. I've been rushing between the camp and the railway station just answering phone calls for your whereabouts. Just come and see what all the fuss is about."

I followed Rochard into the office. There were several letters, all signed by Major Tomlinson, who was i/c K Troop at the time, plus a number of scribbled messages routed through the Station Master who had the only phone in the area. The letters did little more than repeat Rochard's first greeting – that I was to go to Bulawayo immediately – and the messages were subsequent enquiries seeking my whereabouts.

The mystery of the summons was exciting, but looking around at the camp I had built on the riverbank, I was suddenly reluctant to leave. The grass huts were between the forest and the river itself which, like most Rhodesian rivers, were constantly changing. In the winter months there would be no more than a few pools and then the rain would come and a wide and swift-flowing torrent made a crossing almost impossible. Apart from the staff at the railway station there were no other Europeans in the immediate area. The loneliness of the place never bothered me though. When not engaged on extended patrols west of the railway line, there was always the attraction of a spot of quiet fishing or hunting along the riverbank. It was such a peaceful existence that I treasure the memories of those days.

And now, because of the inconsiderate assassination of some obscure Central European figure, I was to be wrenched from my Eden. Why?

There was a goods train for Bulawayo which passed through Gwaai at 2 a.m. the next day. I took the train and by 9 a.m. was facing Sergeant-Major Hough in K Troop office in Bulawayo. His welcome was typical.

"At long last – the elusive Pimpernel!"

Before I could reply to his ribaldry, Major Tomlinson emerged from his office next door. He greeted me with apparent relief and told me to come into his office.

Major Tomlinson was one of the most respected and well liked officers in the Force. A born gentleman and utterly deserving of this overworked expression, he was of average height with a black toothbrush moustache and a perpetual smile on his round face. Always well dressed and perfectly groomed he had that jaunty dapperness which revealed an abundance of energy.

"General Edwards wants to see you in Salisbury in civilian clothes as soon as I can get you there," I was told.

The summons was ten times as mysterious as that which had greeted me at Gwaai. The Commissioner this time, no less!

"Have you any idea why I'm wanted, sir?"

"No, I can give you no explanation. You will be on the mail train tomorrow night without fail. In the interim period you will make arrangements to store your kit and settle any outstanding private affairs. Corporal Stone will be at the station to see you on your way tomorrow and he will hand you an envelope containing further instructions. When you've packed away your kit you will not remain in camp but book in at the Carlton Hotel. If for any reason you leave the hotel tell the desk where you are going and for how long you'll be away so that I can contact you if necessary."

Major Tomlinson wished me luck and I was dismissed. In the outer office Sergeant-Major Hough gave me my pay cheque, a rail warrant and £5 for expenses. After my interview with the major, I made no mention of the NCO's "Pimpernel" jibe. I just did not know what to think – I was either about to be hanged or promoted to the dizzy heights of colonel!

Having stored my kit and packed some spare civilian clothes in a gladstone bag, I rickshawed to the Carlton. I was given a room with glass doors which opened onto the courtyard on the ground floor. My thirty-odd hours in the hotel almost exploded the obscurity obviously intended by Major Tomlinson.

In the room next to me was a character who shall be called Johnstone. He was a likeable fellow and we had several drinks together before dinner that evening, We shared the same table and had a liqueur in the lounge together after the meal. Soon after, Johnstone excused himself saying that he had an important appointment to keep.

With time on my hands I trotted along to the old Empire Theatre, thoroughly enjoyed a variety show and was back in my room ready for bed just before midnight. It was a typically hot and sultry, oppressive October night so I opened the glass doors, crept into bed and was asleep within minutes.

In the early hours of the morning – it turned out to be about 3 a.m. – I suddenly became aware of someone breathing laboriously in my room. Hardly knowing what to expect, I quietly crawled out of bed on the far side, braced myself and waited for something to happen. The events of the day and the business at Sarajevo can be blamed if my imagination went a little wild. Nothing happened except that the panting gradually subsided. I decided to chance the light.

"For God's sake, turn it off. He'll kill me."

I immediately switched off the light but in the few seconds of illumination the picture of my friend Johnstone standing in the middle of the room as naked as the day he was born and with blood all over his feet and ankles was etched in my mind. The expression on his face reiterated the fact that he was in fear of his life. Having poured a glass of water and offered it to my guest in the hope of calming him down, I drew the blinds, shut the doors and switched on the light again. Explanations were called for. Johnstone reacted by pleading with me to switch off the light again.

"Please let me stay here. He knows that I'm staying here and my room number. He'll kill me in my bed!"

I kept the light on but offered the poor man my dressing gown and the only chair in the room. He flopped down and again begged me to extinguish the light. This time I obliged and the darkness must have encouraged the confession which followed.

It transpired that Johnstone was in love, the trouble being that the object of his devotion was already married and living in a Bulawayo suburb. Conveniently the husband of the woman was employed on work which took him away from home for long intervals. The previous day the husband had informed his wife that he was off on a long trip, had asked her to pack his camping gear and buy sufficient food for him for several days. She had complied, told friend Johnstone of her anticipated solitude and the rest can be left to the imagination. The husband must have had some inkling of his wife's intentions and returned home in the middle of the night. The blissful occupants of the double bed had been rudely awakened by a hammering on the bedroom door. Johnstone, caught in the act as it were, grabbed his trousers and made for the window as the door panelling started splintering. He discarded his trousers in using both hands on the tight-fitting window and by the time he had reached the garden beyond, the enraged husband was in the room, at the window and firing revolver shots in the naked man's direction. Johnstone admitted that he hadn't stopped running until he reached my room.

I eventually went back to sleep leaving the intruder contemplating his sins on the chair. I don't know when he finally left my room but when I enquired from the desk on my way to breakfast, I was told that he had paid his bill and had left for South Africa at 7 a.m. That was the last I saw of Johnstone and I imagine his experience deprived the erring wife of his companionship for ever.

After breakfast I went to the barber and had my hair trimmed. A khaki-clad figure occupied one of the chairs but it was only after he had been shaved that I recognised Major Murray. He nodded in my direction and when I left the parlour he was waiting for me on the verandah outside. He wanted to know what I was doing and when I told him of the proposed visit to Salisbury, he nodded and said that now he remembered.

Hoping to find out more, for the major was my direct superior at the time as well as being an acquaintance of old, I asked him what he remembered. The only satisfaction I got was the cryptic comment that I would find out in due time in Salisbury. I was pretty sure he could have told me much more but he wished me luck and limped off towards the Bulawayo Club.

Much later I was to learn that Murray himself had plans afoot and was then making final preparations to take his famous column northwards. This was the last time I saw this very competent and highly respected officer. Had I not received my own mysterious instructions and had I been given the chance, I would have been one of the first to accompany him to East Africa.

For a number of years I had been under his direct command in Matabeleland. In that time I found him reasonable, logical, exact and fair to his subordinates. Whatever others in the Corps may have thought of him, as certain as is the sun rising on Rhodesia is the fact that the name of Murray, his deeds and his aspirations will live as long as men of the B.S.A. Police take pride in their work. To me he was a wonderful example of an excellent policeman and an intelligent soldier.

I was on the platform of the station in good time to catch the mail train at 9 that evening. Corporal Rodney Stone handed me the letter Major Tomlinson had referred to and wanted to know what all the mystery was about. When I told him that he knew as much as I did he just didn't believe me.

After the train had pulled out of Bulawayo I opened the letter. I was instructed not to proceed to the Police Camp on arrival in Salisbury but to go to the Avenue Hotel where Room No. 12 had been booked for me. There I would receive further instructions.

Reduced to a cliché, the plot was thickening. Comfortably settled in Salisbury's Avenue Hotel, my further instructions came with a member of the C.I.D. who asked me to accompany him to Police Headquarters. There I was ushered into the presence of the Staff Officer, Major Phillips, who greeted me politely and wanted to know why it had taken me such a damned long time to reach Salisbury! However, my explanation was accepted and he asked me to be seated while he enquired if the Commissioner was ready to interview me.

He was away for several minutes and when he returned he asked, without preliminaries of any sort, if I was loyal. I was taken aback for a moment but after thinking for a few minutes, I replied in the affirmative. Then he wanted to know from which part of South Africa I came, whether I had any family alive in the Union, what their reaction would be to the war and so forth. It was difficult to reply with definite answers on all the questions put to me but I did point out that my father had been on friendly terms with General Botha, the South African Prime Minister, long before the outbreak of the Boer War, that he had been a member of the South Africa Party which had been established by Generals Smuts and Botha and, further, that during the Boer War, when no schooling was available in Pretoria, my brothers and sisters and I had joined the Botha children across the road to receive education from their governess, a Miss Meatly. (After the war had been in progress for some months, Miss Meatly, who was English, was put across the Natal border because of her nationality!). I was unable to speak for my four older brothers, all of whom had fought against the British in the Boer War, on the question of their side in this latest conflict.

Major Phillips again made his excuses, left me alone for about ten minutes and then returned to usher me into General Edwards' office.

The Commissioner greeted me, enquired after my health and said that he hoped I was fit enough to undertake a very onerous job. In a conversational manner he pointed out that there was rebellion in South Africa, a revolt which the South African government was attempting to suppress. While he had every confidence that they would be successful in stemming the rebellion, General Edwards explained that there was no reason why Rhodesia should not take the precaution of preventing the flames of rebellion crossing the Limpopo.

"For this reason I want you to go to South Africa, via the Limpopo, and try to find out if the rebels have any intention of crossing the border from the Transvaal to start something here in this country. I have no definite suspicions on the matter but as we are involved in a world war, we must be on the alert. I suggest you start your enquiries at the Messina copper mine. If you hear anything of interest, route your report through Mr Delasso who's in charge of intelligence at the Limpopo Drift. There are a number of policemen already at the border under Major Essex Capell's command but try to avoid them by going straight through to Messina. Remain under cover as far as possible. And remember, although we have some information regarding the rebellion, any additional knowledge on the causes of the revolt would be most useful.

"And now," continued the Commissioner, "I want you to start your duties by attending a meeting here in Salisbury at the Dutch Reformed Church Hall tomorrow at 8 p.m. Afrikaners from all over Rhodesia will be attending as delegates of their respective districts and I want a full report on what is discussed. Don't make yourself conspicuous and don't reveal your identity unless you are specifically requested to do so."

The mystery of my journey from the Gwaai to the Commissioner's office was now fully explained. I was dismissed by General Edwards and Major Phillips took me in hand to arrange the practical details. The first subject was money and when I declined an offer of advance expenses, assuring the major that I had more than enough cash in my pocket for the proposed investigation and that I would claim such expenses when it was all over, he smiled and remarked that I was much better off than he was. Transport, however, was not quite as simple. I could get to Bulawayo by rail and then on to West Nicholson but the hundred-odd miles on to Messina was something else. Eventually I suggested a bicycle with especially strong tyres and substantial carriers back and front. Such a machine was delivered to me at the Carlton Hotel as I paused in Bulawayo en route to West Nicholson. However, I anticipate. There was still the business in Salisbury to be transacted.

There were about forty delegates at the meeting in the DRC Hall.

It was a rather strange assembly of farmers who had gathered to put their views and voice their complaints to the other members of their community. A Melsetter farmer named Maarten was voted to the chair and no time was wasted in getting down to brass tacks.

The chief cause of dissension was the Rhodesian government's action in relieving Afrikaners of their rifles and ammunition. Delegates, especially from the border areas, were particularly bitter and pointed out that they were at the mercy not only of indigenous Africans, but marauders from outside the country too. One speaker hotly announced that, in company with several of his countrymen, he had crossed the Limpopo as far back as 1891, had remained in Rhodesia and had taken the oath of allegiance. But now, because of a rebellion beyond the border with which they were not even remotely connected, they were being forced to swallow the insults of the government.

Up jumped another Afrikaner, even more obviously ill-humoured.

"Rhodesia has always belonged to the Boers and we have always resented its occupation by Rhodes…" He would have gone on smearing the government had not the chairman heeded the remarks of one of the saner minds who said that comments like those of the previous speaker and others with equally intolerant opinions were probably the main reason for the government's action. There was a very noticeable murmur of agreement in the crowded hall and the next speaker had an extremely attentive audience.

"I have listened with grave attention to the outbursts from certain delegates but we must view the problems of today in the same light as they are viewed by a worried government. Since we are all Rhodesians and have to make our living here in this country, there are a few points which I would like to emphasise.

"Let us be firmly resolved," he continued, "not to sacrifice what we have achieved here by wayward action. In Rhodesia we are on solid ground whereas to the south things are beginning to crumble. I do not think anything will come of the so-called rebellion. Some of us here went through the Boer War and we cannot easily forget the privations we suffered then. Why should we interfere in favour of the rebels when we have everything to lose by such a course of action? I think the time has come when it can only be to our advantage to support the government of the Chartered Company to the hilt. But as loyal Rhodesians," concluded the speaker, "we have every right to possess rifles under licence, in accordance with the law, for our protection. I suggest that a deputation be appointed to interview the government on this subject."

The vast majority of those present were in full agreement with this sensible address. There may have been a few hotheads who thought otherwise but they were soon convinced of their mistaken short-sightedness and fell in with the majority decision.

A few less-significant matters were discussed before the meeting was brought to a close. I left hurriedly before anyone could question my presence.

Late into the night I prepared my report on the meeting, pointing out that it would be most unwise to continue the ban on Afrikaner arms and that they should be returned immediately, especially to those living on the borders. If the rifles were not returned, it could be just the thing to cause discontentment and perhaps drive otherwise loyal Rhodesians into the arms of the rebels. At present there was almost no support among them for the South African revolt. On the contrary, they were law-abiding citizens and many of them had already volunteered for active service.

The next morning, after I had handed in my report, I spent my time window-shopping. I was surprised at the number of men on the streets already in uniform – and not a few of them were obviously Afrikaners. I believe that nearly 70 per cent of the men under the age of 45 ended up on active service. Some went to England to enlist, others joined up in South Africa to be incorporated in the South African Forces as Rhodesian units. Two European regiments and one African regiment went to East Africa. The Chartered Company itself sent units of the British South Africa Police to assist in several campaigns and many policemen received temporary commissions.

Salisbury's hotels and bars were cluttered with khaki uniforms knocking back drinks in abandoned farewell to friends to the accompaniment of lusty songs about what they were going to do to Kaiser Bill. Poor devils, little did they know what was really in front of them and that many of them would never again see sunny Rhodesia.

Ten years later, I walked into the Salisbury Club one evening and noticed Mr Huggins (Lord Malvern) speaking to a tall white-haired gentleman at the bar. When the doctor saw me he nodded in my direction and beckoned me over. He introduced his companion as Mr Maarten who, taking my hand, remarked that we had met before. I shook my head – for the life of me I couldn't remember. Then Maarten reminded me of the meeting in the DRC Hall, the meeting which he had conducted.

"I want to thank you," he said, "for being partially responsible for persuading the government to return our weapons back in 1914. I'm only sorry you had to wait so long to receive the Afrikaner community's thanks."

He went on to say that when the deputation appeared before the government's spokesman, my report was on the table in front of him.

That night I boarded the mail train to Bulawayo, the first leg of my journey to Messina.

I arrived in Bulawayo from Salisbury at 8 o'clock and on making enquiries was told that the Gwanda train would be leaving an hour later. Figgard, a Hollander, who ran a taxi business in Bulawayo, took me to the Carlton Hotel where I collected my spare clothes and a bicycle which had been left at the Hotel addressed to me.

Returning to the station in the same taxi, clutching my new bicycle which had been loaded on the running board of the car, I was just in time to get a seat on the Gwanda train. In the compartment allocated to me I found Bishop Bevan who was also travelling to Gwanda. What a charming old gentleman he was and I was very fortunate to have such an interesting companion on that slow journey. I think Bishop Bevan was one of the greatest champions of the British South Africa Police. He seemed to know every individual and had a good word for every one of them. I was sorry when the Bishop left the train at Gwanda, leaving me to continue the journey to West Nicholson by myself.

The train arrived there fifteen minutes late, at 1.15 p.m. and I had planned to stay the night at the local hotel and leave for the Limpopo Drift early next morning. But my luck was right in when I met a chap named Deverux having a beer in the bar. He asked me to join him on the journey south. During our conversation he informed me he was a commercial traveller on his way back to South Africa by car, and when I pointed out that I was on the way to Messina by bicycle, he suggested that I keep him company on the journey and tie the bicycle on the running board of his car.

Immediately after lunch we packed the car with our luggage and secured the bicycle with a hank of rope I had scrounged from the proprietor of the hotel. The car, a 1913/14 model Napier, had a canvas hood which was supported from the windscreen by two two-inch straps buckled to the top of the mudguards. The bodywork and mudguards consisted of solid steel sheeting. It was as well the body-work was substantial – it had to withstand the frightening jolting we were to endure during the hours of darkness on that memorable journey.

Shortly after two o'clock and a substantial lunch, we left West Nicholson via the main road to Messina and the Limpopo. The distance was no more than 100 miles, but the road was no better than a sandy track and it was impossible to average more than 20 miles an hour. However, Deverux know his car and drove with care to avoid the many pot holes, sandy patches, sudden turns, loose stones, razor backs and the protruding stumps which might have smashed the sump of the low engine casing. Bumping up and down on my comfortable seat I enjoyed the scenery, especially the new red, bronze and green leaves appearing on the msasa trees. The country was dry and very hot and one could well imagine how in earlier days men had struggled with their wagons through the merciless bush and granite formations. Their difficulties must have been tremendous.

It was getting dark and we were still some distance from the Limpopo. Eventually it was necessary to switch on the lights and our speed consequently decreased. Some distance further on we saw numerous eyes in the thick bush on either side of the road. We had no sooner seen the eyes when we were in the middle of a large herd of impala. Whether the animals on the right of the road tried to join those on the left, or vice versa, I do not know, but the buck seemed to jump over the car, making incredible leaps in their efforts to clear the lights. Before Deverux could bring the car to a stop one big ram became entangled in the off-side leather strap supporting the hood and came down with a mighty crash on the bonnet. The impact was terrific and alarming. The animal struggled with horrible bleating sounds to free itself, but without success. I could not get out of the car on my side because of the bicycle laced across the door. Deverux, scared out of his wits, did not attempt to move until I told him to get out. The impala continued to bellow mournfully when I grabbed its nose. I pulled back its head and cut its throat with my sharp pocket knife. After the carcass had been pulled off the bonnet there was no sign of a dent in the bodywork. I was p positive that everything would have been smashed to smithereens after that dreadful impact. During the few moments we were involved with the herd it was incredible to witness the height and distance the animals reached in order to clear the lights of the car. In the dusty light the colouring of the animals appeared to be white instead of a reddish-brown, giving them the appearance of ghost-like phantoms floating through the air.

There was insufficient room in the car for the whole carcass, so I proceeded to cut off the two hind quarters and it was only then that I realised that the animal's back had been broken in the fall. No wonder he'd no strength left to kick himself off the bonnet.

To my surprise, when I cranked the engine the old Napier spluttered, coughed a few times and roared into life as if nothing had happened. We continued our journey and at nine o'clock we were on the banks of the Limpopo, our lights showing the wide expanse of dry, sandy drift which we had to cross. It was many years later when Beit Bridge was constructed on this very spot.

Deverux pressed the rubber bulb of his python-shaped hooter, explaining that it was impossible for us to get through the drift under our own power. Draught animals were usually in attendance on the other side of the river. He again pumped the hooter and a voice from the other side responded. Some fifteen minutes later a team of eight donkeys appeared from the other side of the drift and stumbled slowly in our direction.

At any moment I expected the troops guarding the border to approach and question our presence but we saw no one except the donkey team leader and the driver, both Africans. I asked them if they had seen any troops on the Limpopo and their answer was negative. This was strange as I had been asked to make my report to Delasso who was supposed to be stationed on the border.

With the judicious application of brakes, Deverux free-wheeled down the steep embankment until he was level with the track on the bed of the river and the eight donkeys making up the team were hitched to the bumper of the car. In slow motion, the inadequate little team struggled and stumbled on the rough track, kept going by menacing shouts and flicks of the whip from the driver. Several times the team was halted for a breather, while Deverux and I sat comfortably in our seats smoking cigarettes. I never thought then that the vast expanse of dry sand would be covered with water within a few weeks and that I would be struggling for my life in the angry flood waters!

The donkey team was too weak to pull the car up the steep incline on the far bank, but by placing stones behind the back wheels and starting the engine, the donkeys were helped to draw the car out of the river bed and eventually on to the level road leading to Messina.

I paid the donkey driver the ten shillings fee he demanded, and we proceeded on our way to the copper mine only eight miles on. We arrived at the Messina

Hotel before closing time and made our way to the bar to ease our parched throats. The room was packed with a large joyful crowd of miners and men in uniform drinking both beer and spirits. Deverux and I elbowed our way through the crush and squeezed our way to the counter for service. A man behind the counter, with scanty hair on his abnormally large head, broke off his conversation with another customer, moved in our direction and took our order for two beers. Having served us he returned to continue his conversation and I heard him say:

"It is much too much! A pound to castrate one bull is an excessive charge even if he is a veterinary surgeon and has got to travel from Louis Trichardt."

"I'll do it for half the price," I said jokingly.

Sudden interest appeared on the barman's face. He turned round to face me and asked "Can you castrate bulls?" Having convinced him, he then asked me if I would save him money by operating on over a hundred young bulls.

This conversation over the bar counter was the beginning of a firm friendship between myself and Sacks, the owner of the Messina Hotel. The proprietor was an extremely intelligent man and, as our acquaintance grew, I realised he was a born philosopher and also a valuable source from whom I would possibly be able to get much information regarding the rebellion. I promised to operate on his bulls the next day. I told him I was staying on in Messina for some time but that Deverux would be continuing his journey.

This was the cue to arrange our accommodation. Calling to his assistant behind the bar, a man named Fisch, Sacks told him he would not be long and asked us to follow him. At the side of the hotel was a row of bedrooms and we were allocated one each for the night. He apparently knew Deverux as a traveller, but had never seen me before and, when I was in the room, asked me straight out what was my business.

"I am a cattle speculator, Mr Sacks. My line of business on the Rhodesian side isn't very profitable at present and I thought that now the railway line has reached Messina, I might try my luck over here."

"I don't want you to think I'm being inquisitive – I'm acting under instructions from the police," replied my host. "They want to know details of everyone visiting here."

That concluded our conversation for the night and I was not slow in getting my head down after the long journey. After breakfast the following day Sacks again brought up the question of the castration of his bulls. Confirming my earlier promise that I'd do the job, I pointed out that the sun was hot and that the best time for operation would be after four o'clock in the afternoon. At the appointed hour all was ready and, as fast as the African servants pulled down the animals,

I operated. It was almost dark by the time I had attended to all of the 104 bulls.

Back in the bar after the dusty job in the dry cattle kraals, Sacks displayed a delighted grin on his face. He gloated over his saving of £52 and independence of the veterinary surgeon from Louis Trichardt. Pushing pen and paper in my direction over the bar counter he asked me to make out my account. I burst out laughing and told him I was only joking when I said I'd do the work for half the price.

"But," he frowned, not understanding my humour, "you give me two legs of venison, castrate 104 bulls, which would have cost me £104, and say you want no payment. That's not good enough. I must pay you something." In earnest I asked him not to embarrass me by insisting on payment for a job which had taken no more than a few hours and which I had done as a favour to my host. Further, I added, one of these days I would probably ask a favour in return. Sacks never referred to payment again but he refused to charge for my accommodation or my beers in the bar!

Constable Winston who was temporarily in charge of the South African Police at Messina informed me that a sergeant and another constable had been called to Pretoria because of the Rebellion. Messina was in fact a three-man station and Winston was alone there for the time being.

During the first few days in Messina I made it my business to sound out local feelings on the Rebellion. I solicited the views of both men who sympathised with Hertzog, the chief trouble maker, and those who supported the Government, Botha and Smuts.

I was passing the private apartments of the manager of the hotel, Mr Sacks, when he invited me to join him on the verandah for tea. I was then introduced to his wife and also to a youth named Dreyer who was a fair-haired, blue eyed student of Stellenbosch University. The conversation was soon on the usual topic for discussion – the Rebellion: no one ever seemed to talk about anything else. I remember asking this youth what he considered to be the reasons for the rebellion.

In Dreyer's view the rebellion's history went further back than the Boer War. He started his explanation for the rebellion by mentioning that in 1792 the Colony of the Cape was already bordering on being one and half centuries old and was composed of Hollanders, who had served under the East India Company, and Huguenots originating from France. The Afrikaner evolved from the mixing of these two peoples. Some of them were known as Boers (farmers) but they were all blessed with a strong independent spirit and they were very religious.

Sometime in 1814, the British occupied the Cape on the pretext of the Dutch alliance with France, known as the Treaty of Paris. The British Governor, Lord Charles Somerset, was one of those autocratic individuals who could not help himself becoming unpopular. Then in 1816 an incident occurred where a certain Mr Bezuidenhout was summoned to appear in Court for ill-treating his African servant. Bezuidenhout failed to attend Court. Bezuidenhout was killed by the Native Police. It was then that relatives and friends of Bezuidenhout rebelled. The ring-leaders were hanged at Slachter's Nek. This incident and the name of Slachter's Nek was for many years a symbol of Afrikaner defiance of British authority.

During 1820 some 5 000 British farmers and artisans immigrated into the Cape. The influx of the Britishers brought with it a keen London Missionary Society who took a great interest in the lot of the native. In 1833 slaves were freed throughout the British Empire. This affected the Afrikaner who had the Slachter's Nek incident fresh in mind as well as the discovery that English was replacing the Dutch language which resulted in his decision to trek north. They had heard from Pioneers that there was fertile land with plenty of grazing ready for settling. Thus in 1835 the Afrikaners trekked northwards leaving behind the Britishers and Missionary Societies. In ox wagons they trekked over the great Kei, the Orange and the Vaal Rivers until they finally reached Natal, the Orange Free State and the Transvaal to settle. This was not done without loss of life, however.

They experienced skirmishes and battles with Zulus, Basuto, Bechuanas Xhosa, Matabele and Bushmen. The treacherous massacre of Retief and his party by the Zulu King Dingaan was avenged by Andries Pretorius and his small party of men on December 16, 1838, which became well known as Dingaan's Day.

The Afrikaner Voortrekkers who had conquered Natal, the Orange Free State and the Transvaal made sure that they were free from the British Yoke and could live an independent life enjoyed by their fore-fathers. The British Government, however, held the view that the territory "conquered" by the Afrikaners was British and, in 1842, asserted influence in Natal. The Afrikaners loaded their weapons and trekked from Natal to the Transvaal. The Orange Free State and Natal, now vacated by the Afrikaners, became British territory. The Transvaal was too far north for the British, so the Afrikaners were allowed to retain their independence. Two years later, the Bloemfontein Convention recognised the autonomy of the Free State and the Cape received its Colonial Constitution. The independent Transvaal was recognised by the British through the Sand River Convention in 1852. Now when diamonds were discovered near the Orange River people flocked to the area from all parts of the world. These precious stones caused a certain change in policy from the Cape, reversing the annexure of Afrikaner states to bringing those states more under the influence of the Cape. Paul Kruger resented the change of policy. He, Paul Kruger, was a member of the Volksraad and spokesman for the Conservatives. With civil war threatened in the Transvaal, Lord Carnavon, representing the British Government, ordered Sir Theophilus Shepstone to proceed into the Transvaal. Sir Theophilus did so with eight civil servants and twenty-five policemen and proclaimed its annexation to Britain.

The Proclamation guaranteed that the Transvaal would continue to legislate its own laws under a separate Government annexed from Britain. Sir Theophilus did not, however, call a representative assembly and this resulted in a restlessness among the Afrikaners. Paul Kruger went to England to demand independence but this was not granted and the Transvaalers became bitter with resentment. In view of the disregard for the Sand River Convention and the failure to gain independence Paul Kruger held a plebiscite, much to the annoyance of Sir Theophilus. The result gave Paul Kruger overwhelming support but made no difference to the British.

When William Gladstone came into power in Britain in 1880 Paul Kruger tried again but this was no more successful than his previous attempts. The Boers decided on war.

During 1881 the Afrikaners engaged British soldiers in a battle thereafter known as the battle of Majuba Hill. The Afrikaners out-manoeuvred the British. Half the British soldiers were killed or wounded and the remainder were taken prisoner. General Collie was shot through the head. British reinforcements were on their way to South Africa although Gladstone decided to restore the concept of an independent Transvaal. The Transvaal became independent. To Germany, however, it seemed that the freedom had been achieved by force of arms. For a number of years there was an uneasy peace between the Transvaal and Britain. The defeat at Majuba was fiercely resented by the British.

Cecil John Rhodes came on the South African scene in 1880. At the age of twenty-seven, Rhodes founded the De Beers diamond company and amassed an enormous fortune. His money influenced many, one of whom was Jan Christian Smuts who shared the view that the Colony of the Cape should be extended into the interior. In 1884 Britain proclaimed Bechuanaland a Protectorate. In the same year South West Africa became a German Colony.

Rather like the attraction diamonds had on the world, gold, when it was discovered on the Rand brought a rush of people from all over the world to South Africa and soon the Witwatersrand became cosmopolitan. The cosmopolitan community, known as Uitlanders, became the focus of attention of both Britain and Cecil Rhodes who had ideas of toppling Paul Kruger in his administration of the Transvaal. Claiming that this community was living in "intolerable" conditions there were hints that Britain would have to intervene. Dr Jameson thought that he was acting on the right lines by attempting to "rescue" the Uitlanders. He discovered his mistake, however, in finding that there was no internal revolution and found himself surrounded by the Afrikaner commandoes who forced him to surrender. Dr Jameson had disobeyed Cecil Rhodes' instructions in his raid on Witwatersrand and was subsequently handed over with his colleagues to Britain to face criminal proceedings.

The Jameson Raid united the Boers and tension mounted among the Uitlanders. Sir Alfred Milner, High Commissioner and Governor of the Cape, was set on the idea of nullifying the independence of the Transvaal and in the course of a conference in Bloemfontein with Paul Kruger rejected any concessions Kruger suggested. British troops arrived from India and Britain in support of the Governor's demands on the President of the Transvaal, Paul Kruger. A letter was sent to the Governor to emphasise the concessions the President was prepared to make and that a state of war could be presumed if there was no assurance that the British troops would be removed from the borders with the Transvaal. Needless to say, there was no reply and war was declared.

By 1901, Paul Kruger had fled to Holland, farms had been burned and concentration camps set up. Lord Kitchener proposed to General Botha that hostilities should cease, so they met at Middleburg. The British demand was that of an unconditional surrender which was unacceptable to General Botha and thus hostilities did not cease. A year later, with the situation growing bleak for the Boers, peace was declared at Vereeninging in May 1902. This youth by the name Dreyer estimated that the Boer War had cost Britain some £250 million, and 22,000 officers and men killed. Dreyer stated that 3996 Boers were killed in battle, 1,081 died of wounds and 1,700 men, 4,200 women and 20,000 children died in concentration camps. He said 31,000 Boers were made Prisoners of War and taken away from South Africa. These were allowed to return on their swearing an oath of allegiance to the British Crown. Some 116,500 Boers and 10,000 natives were homeless whilst 60,000 Uitlanders were providing homes for them as they made their way back to countries from whence they came. Dreyer regarded Britain as a Big Bully but then Sacks prevented Dreyer from becoming heated on this subject and suggested a visit to the bar for a drink. This was most welcome.

Events in South Africa after the outbreak of the First World War and my arrival in Messina towards the end of October should be related to appreciate the detail which led to the tragic rebellion which involved so many outstanding men in the Defence Force and members of Parliament of the Union. Within fourteen days I had made my acquaintance with many men and women in Messina, but nowhere could I hear – not even a whisper – the intention of anyone going over the border to start a rebellion.

Many people, both English and Afrikaners, enquired from me conditions for a settlement in Rhodesia and I was not backward in blowing the trumpet for Rhodesia. In the minds of the English-speaking community and those who supported Botha and Smuts, the Union of South Africa was on the side of England. Another large section of the community had the opinion that the Union was only involved in so far as her own safety was concerned, but there was a further section of the community who felt that the opportunity existed to break away from Britain and the Union would become a Republic.

General De la Rey
Photograph by courtesy of National Archives.

Photograph by courtesy of National Archives

Sir Alfred Milner

Governor-General Lord Buxton.
Photograph by courtesy of National Archives.

I was in the house of a Nationalist when I heard that a group of commando rebels were at Mara, on the Sand River, making preparations to attack and occupy Louis Trichardt. The town of Louis Trichardt, some sixty miles from Messina, was where the Government-trained men of war were assembled. I decided to go to Louis Trichardt.

The train journey was very slow. Apparently the track was new and there was a danger of boulders breaking loose from the mountains and rolling onto the track. In the rainy season boulders rolled onto the track fairly frequently and in some cases had to be blasted away using dynamite. It was midday when I eventually arrived at Louis Trichardt. A wagonette with four mules and driven by a coloured was ready to take passengers to the hotel. I booked in at the hotel and, after lunch and a rest, went for a walk around town.

On seeing a sign "Botha Kritzinger Estate Agents" I decided to enter the office to find out if the Mr Kritzinger was a certain man I knew who worked for a firm of attorneys Sim and van Velden of Pretoria at one time. It was indeed a pleasant occasion when we both recognised each other and naturally I told him what I was doing – it was no use pretending I was a cattle buyer. With his ears protruding and his gimlet piercing blue eyes he listened to my story as though he was reading my thoughts. He first of all wanted to know if I supported the Botha/Smuts Government Party or the Hertzog Nationalist Party. I told him that I belonged to neither as I was a Chartered Company man belonging to "the only peaceful country in the world" – Rhodesia. I hoped that I would support the Botha/Smuts Government Party.

I then told him of the rumour going around Messina that rebels were going to attack Louis Trichardt and that a commando unit was now at Mara. Excitedly, Kritsinger said, "I must inform Stops at once" and left the office. Stops was the local Magistrate.

At sundown, Kritzinger came to see me at the hotel. Over a beer he told me that Stops had passed on the information to the Military.

After our beer we walked to the gaol because the gaol had been taken over by the Government men of war in training. On hearing drill orders being given in Afrikaans I passed the remark that although I was a Boer the sound of "left right" seemed better than "links en regs".

According to Kritzinger, Botha and Smuts had decided without hesitation to support the British – their old enemy – when the Great War was declared. Through the offices of the Governor-General they cabled the Colonial Secretary assuring him that Britain could feel free to remove the troops from South Africa for services elsewhere, while the Defence Force of the Union would take up respective duties. Some days later a reply came from London accepting the offer and also suggesting that the South African Government might consider taking portions of South West Africa which would give them command over Swakopmund, Luderitzbucht and the wireless stations in the interior. Smuts, as Minister of Defence, issued the following statement: "At the suggestion of the Union Government after the outbreak of the War, His Majesty's Government decided to remove the Imperial troops at present in South Africa and the Union Government at once undertook the responsibility of safeguarding the defence of the Union in every possible way. In order to carry out this undertaking, it now seems necessary for the Union to organise and equip a force for this purpose. The Government proposes not only to rely upon the Union Defence Force proper but to afford an opportunity for other suitable citizens not at present belonging to the Defence Force to volunteer for active service in South Africa during the present war. Notice in regard to this important matter will be issued from the Department of Defence in due course. At the proper time Parliament will be called to consider the action of the Government and to make provisions for the extra expenditure. In the meantime the Government are taking every precaution to ensure the continuance of normal conditions within the Union, and to deal with the numerous special problems which are arising. They feel assured of the active support of the people of South Africa, of whatever race or political complexion and hope that the result will be the safeguarding of the abiding interests of our common country."

In issuing this statement to the public, General Smuts was clever in withholding hostile intentions towards German South West Africa. His obvious intention was to keep the German forces in that country guessing, pending his consultation with Parliament. More important still was the certainty that a section of the Afrikaner population, particularly the Hertzog supporters, would be bitterly opposed to such action. And, further, Smuts could not be certain of the temper of the entire Defence Force. Two things were clear to Botha and Smuts – their desire to show loyalty to Britain and secondly, to tread gently.

Beyers and others knew of the intention to move against German South West Africa and, through them, rumours were already spreading amongst the backveld farmers, who clung to the belief that Britain's difficulty was the opportunity for the Boers to take back their independence.

General Beyers, who was well-known to Kritzinger and myself, was a well-respected attorney, practising in the Alexander Buildings, Church Square, Pretoria. To Kritzinger, who was a strong S.A.P. supporter, came the bitter news that Beyers was a Hertzog supporter, strictly against the invasion of German South West Africa and advising men in the defence force not to follow Botha and Smuts in their intention of invading the German territory. In Pretoria, the English-speaking people were loyal and impatient. Recruiting depots were going apace both in Pretoria and on the Rand – a sizeable force was concentrated at Booysens. At this time, according to Kritzinger, the Germans attacked a party of Boers at Schuit Drift on the Orange River and forced the Boers to take refuge on an island. Apparently the Germans had crossed the border at Nakob and dug in on Union soil. Early in September, a special ten-day session of Parliament was called. Hertzog, with all the words he could command, vehemently defended Germany who, he said, had committed no act of aggression and he saw no legitimate reason why the Union should invade German West.

In the meantime, Maritz was already at Upington, thirty miles from the German border and from there he sent a secret emissary to Beyers to say that all was going well and that the German Governor Seitz was expecting him sometime during the middle of September.

About the middle of September, Beyers resigned as Commandant-General and Smuts appointed himself, with the concurrence of Botha, to the post of Commandant-General. Kritzinger was sure Beyers and other leaders who had rebelled, would come to a sticky end. He was very puzzled, however, over the actions of De la Rey and the little town of Louis Trichardt. De la Rey felt himself committed to aid his people in a bid for freedom. This he hoped to do with the help of Botha without shedding any blood.

The son of Jan Smuts wrote in the biography of his father: "A pathetic figure of the rebellion was General Koos De la Rey, now grown old and perhaps not so clear of mental perception. Oom Koos was the old Boer type who had always at heart remained a Republican. He had entered into the spirit of Union because of his great affection for Botha and my father. My mother says three closer friends could not have been imagined. My father venerated De la Rey almost as a parent and there was nobody, with the exception of Botha, for whom he had closer feeling. In his confused mental state, De la Rey now came strongly under the influence of the prophet, Niklaas van Rensburg. This shrewd seer had served under him in the Boer War where he had done some very creditable 'seeing'. People knew De la Rey's weakness for van Rensburg. In the national interest, his son-in-law, Bennie Krige, tried unsuccessfully to keep them apart…"

In the opinion of many, De la Rey had gone out of his mind under the influence of a maniac. Through his followers, who saw him right up to the end, one sees De la Rey completely sane but bewildered, when it was brought home to him that Botha and Smuts would not, and could not, take part in his bid for independence. Botha and Smuts could not tell him before as they needed his support and, as his support and influence was of considerable value to the leaders of the Union Government, they deliberately deceived De la Rey for the sake of a great United South Africa. More than one old man had to be sacrificed for the common cause – and their hearts bled for their old friend.

Van Rensburg, the prophet, had given De la Rey a vision of two bulls fighting, which was to the effect that Britain would go under and Germany would win the war. Botha, he could see, would be returning happily to his people, but Jan Smuts would go overseas and never return. He had also seen the figure "15" with De la Rey and a carriage and a cloud of dripping blood.

After the declaration of war, De la Rey sent for two of his trusted officers, Wolmarans and Izak Classen and ordered them to organisé a meeting at Treurfontein near Lichtenburg, on August 15th. On this day – the great day – De la Rey intended to restore the independence of his people. He had visions of riding up to Pretoria followed by his men in their thousands. At Pretoria, a great meeting would be held and then delegates from the meeting would be sent to fetch Botha. Carried on their shoulders, their Commandant of old would be acclaimed State President, and the people of the new republic would be happy again.

Egelenburg, in his biography of Louis Botha, had this to say:
"General De la Rey sent round messengers with the customary order for the burghers (of Lichtenburg) to meet at Treurfontein, on August 15th, mounted. De la Rey was a senator, although he had all the while filled public offices he had never been able to reconcile himself to the loss of Boer independence. The outbreak of the great war had affected his mind to such an extent that he could no longer think logically. It is well-known that his own son-in-law had ceased to regard him as accountable for his actions in those disturbed days and considered it necessary to have him looked after. Botha called his old comrade-in-arms to Pretoria and, assisted by General Smuts, Schalk Burger and Mr N.J. de Wet, KC, he succeeded in calming the distraught old man. The discussion was a painful one for all present, but especially to De la Rey himself. It was a sad disappointment to him to find that neither Botha nor yet any of those had for a moment contemplated leading a movement that – in view of Britain's difficulties – could end only in an attempt to restore the two republics. Throughout the night (August 12) Botha wrestled with De la Rey."

That night (August 12) was one of the most dramatic in the lives of the three great men. General Smuts tells about it himself: "Then there was the occasion at the beginning of the Great War when the rebellion among his (Botha's) Boer comrades was on the point of breaking out and he (Botha) and myself and a couple of friends were striving far into the night to persuade General De la Rey to keep out of mischief that was afoot, and to use his great influence against it. General De la Rey was labouring under the deep religious impulse that made him hear the call of God for the release of the Boer people from the bondage imposed on them at Vereeniging. The argument with him therefore necessarily took a religious turn and it went on for a long time, until Botha at last said to De la Rey, 'Oom Koos, it may be the will of God that this nation shall be free and independent, but nothing will ever convince me that this shall be brought about by treachery and dishonour.' And more to that effect, his very language at the time reminding me of one of the greatest passages in the Book of Job."

De la Rey eventually surrendered. "But don't you invade German South West", he admonished Botha. Then he went to bed too shattered to know what to do next with Botha's words ringing in his ears, "I have sworn my loyalty to the British Government", clashing with his own "I have sworn my loyalty to the Union of South Africa."

On August 13, De la Rey saw General Beyers and the latter advised him to cancel the meeting at Treurfontein called for August 15. On August 14, De la Rey arrived back in Lichtenburg and advised his trusted officer Izak Classens that the meeting at Treurfontein would still be held as planned, but that none of the burghers were to come armed. On August 15, 800 men assembled unarmed at Treurfontein while all kinds of rumours were flying through the Transvaal. Beyers had advised that Government officers would attend the meeting. The meeting was conducted in an orderly manner and a motion was unanimously adopted in which confidence was expressed that the Government would deal to the best of their ability with South Africa's interest in the world crisis. All was peaceful and in order. Loyalty was expressed to the Government. The fearful August 15 had passed. General Kemp remarked: "One can gauge the fear for that day from the fact that, although martial law had not been proclaimed, the newspapers were requested not to publish a word about the meeting."

De la Rey began to realise what others had already seen for some time – Olive Schreiner for one – the possibility of a rebellion, of civil war. The prospect was terrifying. What had Niklaas van Rensburg, the prophet, meant by the black cloud over Lichtenburg and the number 15? The fifteenth of which month? What did a month sooner or later matter in God's time? Could it possibly be the fifteenth of September?

Consideration must be given to the influence General De la Rey had over thousands of Boer families and burghers who loved and respected him. Generals Botha and Smuts can be forgiven their seeming weakness, to reconcile De la Rey's thoughts to their way of thinking. They knew that should De la Rey follow Hertzog and Beyers their task of quelling a rebellion will be great indeed. From this point of view it is necessary to follow the further actions of this remarkable man before the outbreak of the rebellion.

De la Rey's days which should have ended in peace took on an increasing turmoil. There were signs that the country would be torn about and for the time being he would fight and beg for unity, but what had God in mind for him? He knew that something was going to happen in which he will be directly involved. Did not the prophet, van Rensburg, say so! Did God mean him to lead his people to independence in spite of Botha and Smuts? He was no longer sure and restlessness possessed him.

De la Rey attended the National Party Congress on August 26. De la Rey was asked to speak on the threatening split of the South African Party. He advised them not to split and pleaded for unity. "My heart is torn," he said in a moving speech, "I have asked God to take me as a sacrifice, but God has not found me worthy. In the whole world today right and justice have collapsed. What rules today? Might!" He paused and continued, "I call upon you, do not divide…" He went on and it was clear that he had not hardened against Botha at all. He pointed out that President Kruger and General Joubert, in spite of their differences, had always been loyal to one another. In the same way, De la Rey will remain loyal to Botha. "General Botha and General Hertzog are both great men and both of them are my friends. In these troubled times it is imperative that we all stand together. Let us not divide, let there be no rifts, let unity be maintained …" After his speech, De la Rey left the congress, accompanied to the door by the leaders and the whole gathering rose to pay tribute to De la Rey as "A Botha man"! Out of the hall, De la Rey was heard to remark, "I refuse to fight under a German flag, nor will I fight under an English flag, only under my own flag."

De la Rey made preparations to attend a special session of Parliament, a session at which the fateful decision would be decided whether to invade German West or not. Two nights before his departure, General De Wet made one of his unexpected calls. According to Harm Oost, de Wet told him, "I had discussions with Oom Koos. He told me he had finally made up his mind that if German West is attacked, he would at once leave the Parliamentary Session, return and call up his people to prevent the Government from executing their plan. At the same time, he would raise the Vierkleur."

Kritzinger was of opinion Harm Oost was telling a story or that de Wet told a deliberate lie to Harm Oost. Privately and in public De la Rey had pleaded for unity and the importance of standing together, how then could he plan to pull the country apart? A few days later at Potchefstroom De la Rey addressed members of the Defence Force, mainly the De la Rey Riflemen of whom he was the Honorary General, and urged them to pledge their loyalty to their officers, especially at that difficult time. Ever since his battle with Botha and Smuts, when he first saw the possibility of rebellion, civil war and its inevitable bloodshed, De la Rey pleaded for unity. As far as his own plans were concerned he did not know what to do. A man of his intellect and far reaching experience was not going to do anything until he knew Parliament's decision about German South West.

Early in September, General De la Rey kissed and said goodbye to his wife and left for the Cape to attend Parliament. Little did he realise that it would be the last goodbye he would ever again say to his wife! At Potchefstroom, he left the train and visited the training camp of General Kemp. Here he addressed the young men and asked them to remain loyal. He spent the night with General and Mrs Kemp and discussed their plans. Kemp had been in close touch with General Beyers who had told him he would resign as Commandant General if an attack on German West was definitely planned. Kemp had assured him, Beyers, that he would also resign. Their intention was made known to Botha and Smuts, who threatened a court martial. There was no evidence that Beyers planned rebellion, but on Kemp's own admission he would rebel at the right time. Kemp and Maritz were waiting for a German victory which would make their plans run smoothly. As much as Botha wanted De la Rey for the unification of the country, Kemp and his followers needed De la Rey to call up the people! De la Rey was obviously used by both sections. Where did his duty lie – with Botha and his British commitments, or with Kemp and his rebels or freedom for his people? Two days later De la Rey continued his journey to the Cape.

Parliament re-opened on September 9. Before that, decision had already been taken, at the caucus of the South Africa Party where MPs and Senators had gathered, that the attack on German South West had to take place. The members of the other parties, with the exception of a dozen Nationalists, supported the decision. In the opening address in Parliament, the Governor-General, Lord Buxton, on the opening of the 9th, announced that Parliament had convened in order to legalise the mobilisation of the Defence Force for the defence of South African interests "and in order to co-operate with His Majesty's Imperial Government in the defence of the well-being of the Empire."

At the second session later that day, the Prime Minister made a long speech in which he underlined the gravity of the times, the fact that South Africa, as part of the Empire, was automatically involved in war with a common enemy. Only two courses were open to South Africa: that of loyalty, duty and honour, or that of disloyalty and dishonour. The Imperial troops were being withdrawn from

South Africa to serve elsewhere and it was now up to South Africans to see to the defence and protection of their country. A section of the Defence Force had been mobilised, not to be sent to any specific region, but as part of a defensive programme. Subsequently, the Imperial Government had notified the Government that certain military operations in German West were regarded as strategically important and that it would be considered a great service if South Africa could deal with them. The Union Government had decided to accede to this request in the interest of both South Africa and the Empire, as the Government had been notified there was considerable activity on the border, that they had in fact crossed into Union territory at Nakob and had taken up positions in the area (according to Johannesburg papers this was later proved to be fiction), and as the Germans had forced the war on England, the Union, as part of the Empire, was in honour bound to give its support and protect itself.

General Hertzog (according to the Rand papers) reacted at once by saying the Union is asked to declare war on Germany, for that is what it boils down to, and is honour bound to do so. None of the other Dominions had been asked to undertake an act of aggression, but South Africa is expected to do so and, for what purpose? He supported the defence of South Africa, but any offensive against German possessions would not be in the interest of South Africa nor in that of the Empire. Smuts, in support of Botha, attacked Hertzog by saying he spoke like a "German Advocate" and a "blanket patriot".

The vote was taken at 9 a.m. There was tremendous tension among the members, the Press representatives and members of the public. The result was twelve votes against ninety-two in favour of action against South West. The majority of eighty came to their feet and sang the British National Anthem. In the Press Gallery, Harm Oost banged his fist on the desk and shouted, "This means rebellion!" He was not alone in his feeling of outrage: there were many who agreed with Hertzog that now it would take fifty years before Afrikaans and English-speaking South Africans would ever come nearer unity. Johannes Meintjes tells us, it was a mere formality for the Senate to approve the resolution. Later, in the cloakroom, De la Rey met Hertzog and said, "Barry, they have done it now. There is nothing left for us to do. We must return to our homes – if we can reach them..." (they both knew that they were constantly watched by detectives). And that was their last chat.

De la Rey spoke quietly and forcefully. He pleaded for toleration, words said in anger could lead to trouble, even a civil war. At all costs unity had to be preserved. He added, not surprisingly, that he would not vote against the Government's motion, but wished to make it clear that he did not feel himself duty bound to participate in any war that England choose to wage. The Prime

Minister had said there was no question of neutrality. To that this was his reply...in a hush of intense and absorbed interest, De la Rey went on, "When I signed the Treaty of Vereeniging, the thought never occurred to me that my signature would bind my country to a war should Britain be involved in one. The people of South Africa can do very little when it comes to a world war, so why must the people be endangered? Since the Treaty of Vereeniging, the people had not been guilty of a single disloyal act against the British flag... It would be quite a different matter if a German force should attempt to take South Africa. Then I, for one, would do my utmost to defend our country. But the Germans would hesitate before they did so, as we are now four Provinces and a united South Africa. It would take them longer than three years to conquer us."

He was always and at any time ready to render his services for the defence of his country. Anyone who had gone through what he had experienced would understand his objection. Many people looked up to him for guidance and he had a responsibility to those people.

Johannes Meintjes reported on De la Rey's speech...This dignified speech, delivered by such a legendary figure (about whom wild rumour was then in circulation) was followed with close interest. All eyes watched as De la Rey, having finished his speech, took up his hat and left the Senate. There was a thrill of excitement when Louis Botha was seen to leave his seat, obviously in pursuit of De la Rey. Two other men had left at the same time as De la Rey, wishing to consult him and it is on their authority that the following scene has been recorded. They were Niklaas Serfontein and Jan Brand Wessels, Free State members of the House of Assembly. They spotted De la Rey and followed him, unaware that Louis Botha was doing the same. De la Rey walked towards the northerly exit, down the steps on the left, when Botha suddenly appeared. The two Free Staters fell back. They were then out of the Houses of Parliament and stood to the left, behind the wall of the stoep. De la Rey was between the statue of Queen Victoria and the porch. As Botha lumbered down the stone steps he called out, "Oom Koos, wait a bit, I want to see you."

De la Rey halted and turned, facing the porch and Botha came up to him. The two generals were about six paces away from the two men who were watching unseen.

"Oom Koos," Botha said with grave concern, "what are you going to do?"

De la Rey looked at him in quiet contemplation, his eyes dark and miserable. "Louis, now is the time to go through with the solemn agreement made by you and me and de Wet at Vereeniging to take our freedom."

Botha said nothing, his eyes fixed on the hawk-like face before him. Then he faltered. "Oom Koos, I'll see you later." Louis Botha turned to go back, De la

Rey filling his pipe, and at that very moment a cameraman hidden in the shrubs took a photograph and fled. Both generals looked startled, Botha in forward motion, De la Rey with both hands around his pipe, seeming to follow Botha. Actually he was on his way out of the grounds.

That same afternoon De la Rey was at the station to board a train for the Transvaal. As De la Rey located his compartment, he looked along the platform as there was a stir among the assembled people. It was Louis Botha, well-known and impressive. De la Rey's eyes lit up in a flood of warm emotion.

Botha, his strange blue eyes misty, his ruddy face darker than usual, came up to the old man. The bell was ringing, the train was leaving. De la Rey put his arms around Botha and kissed him on the mouth. Then he boarded the train which started moving out of the station. Tears shone in the face of Botha as he watched the famous head of De la Rey with its hawk-like features gradually going out of sight. It was a fitting farewell. De la Rey had his destiny with death; Botha had to lead his country through the most difficult and heartbreaking phase of his career.

Johannes Meintjes continues to tell us that at De Aar, De la Rey was joined by Piet Joubert, one of Manie Maritz's young men, on his way to Pretoria to interview General Beyers on behalf of Manie Maritz. Piet Joubert had fought under the command of Manie Maritz in the Boer War at the age of 15. He took up farming in German West and had become pro-German, the same as Maritz.

General Smuts, who was feeling most uneasy about some of his officers, wanted Beyers at Upington. A three-pronged attack on South West had been devised, one led by General Tim Lukin, a second by Colonel Beves and the third, consisting of Maritz's young men, was to be led by General Beyers. Maritz also wanted Beyers at Upington on September 15 for quite a different reason than the one Smuts had in mind. Maritz and Joubert had been having discussions already with German officers for co-operation in a bid for South African independence.

Joubert boarded the train in which De la Rey travelled for the purpose of sounding the old man and coming to some arrangement. His talk to De la Rey was frustrated by Hendrik Mentz who joined them, a firm supporter of Botha and the invasion of South West. Joubert must have made some indiscreet observations, for Mentz wasted no time in reporting him as a "traitor" in Pretoria and up to mischief.

Nobody has been able to tell us exactly or convincingly what De la Rey was planning to do now that South West was to be attacked, and perhaps for the simple reason that De la Rey did not know himself and was waiting for the course of action to be revealed to him. The next day would be September 15, the day he had now every reason to expect was the day Niklaas van Rensburg had prophesied as the day of blood and the day on which he hoped he would be sacrificed. Constantly at the back of De la Rey's mind was the warning by N.J. de Wet, the Minister of Justice, "Oom Koos, you must behave yourself; we will have to impose the law on you; treachery will be smashed."

De la Rey decided to give the detectives the slip by not changing to the Pretoria train at Germiston, but to go on to Johannesburg. Joubert got out at Germiston and took a train for Pretoria, with a message from De la Rey to Beyers. De la Rey left Park Station and went to the Victoria Hotel where he was given room No. 15. Yes, September 15 had dawned and to De la Rey it must have seemed like any ordinary day, although he suspected that it was not so.

General Beyers showed his letter of resignation to Joubert. Condensed, the letter was as follows:

"Since August, I have verbally informed you and General Botha that I disapprove of sending commandoes to German South West with the purpose of conquering that territory. I was then on the point of resigning but decided to wait the result of the special session of Parliament. The Government must be aware that the majority of Dutch-speaking inhabitants of the Union are against sending troops over our boundaries where we have no provocation to do so. Great Britain is said to have become involved in this war with Germany in order to protect the independence of smaller nations and to uphold treaties. History has taught us that where it suits her, Britain does protect smaller nations; and on the other hand, when it suits her, abuses the rights of smaller nations, ignoring independence and treaties – as has happened in our country. It is said that war is being waged against 'barbarism' of the Germans. We have forgiven but not forgotten the barbaric acts committed by Britain in our country. You have said Germany has plans for the annexation of South Africa; in my humble opinion, aggression from our side can only expedite such action on her part. The statement in Parliament that Germans have already crossed our border has been proven untrue, not a single German soldier has crossed our border. This European war hardly affects South Africa at all. If Germany should be triumphant and should decide to attack us, we would, even without British help, have the noble and honourable duty to defend our country to the utmost. The force of 8,000 German troops at present in South West would not dare to attack us. I have repeatedly stated, as at Booysens recently, that in any attack on us, Boer and Britain will stand side by side to defend our country and no one would have considered it a greater honour than myself to lead our men in our defence. I accepted the appointment of Commandant-General for the defence of our country, as laid down in the first article of Defence Law, and such an article cannot be changed by an informal decision of Parliament. By aggression we may start a fire which could be disastrous to our country. For me, there is only the way of belief, duty and honour towards my people, such as General Botha has always asked, and I accordingly have no alternative but to hand in my resignation."

General Kemp says that Beyers expected that the shock of his resignation would move all the other officers in the Defence Force to resign also, causing the collapse of the Force, but this did not happen. Only a few men, including Kemp, resigned and their arrest was imminent.

There was a call for De la Rey and when he went to the lounge he was surprised to meet Mrs Beyers who had come from Pretoria to fetch him. De la Rey at once collected his bag, paid his account and followed Mrs Beyers to her car which was parked some distance from the hotel to avoid suspicion. It was an open Daimler, registration number TP 24. The car was driven by General Beyer's chauffeur, Mr A.J. Wagner.

At about five that afternoon, they arrived in Pretoria and were taken to "Beyerheim" on Walker Street, Sunnyside. This was the house of Piet Beyers and De la Rey walked into the house. Gert Maritz at once took De la Rey to the room where Beyers was waiting. From five o'clock until six-thirty they talked. What they discussed no one will ever know for certain apart from the fact that it naturally involved the resignation of Beyers and some sort of plan on procedure.

At 5.30 p.m., Mrs Beyers took some coffee to the two men and Beyers told her, "Oom Koos wants me to go with him to Potchefstroom and he wants me to go this evening. I've told him that I have refused all requests to leave Pretoria." (Beyers expected to be put under arrest). Mrs Beyers glanced at De la Rey, who spoke up at once, "Look, Tilly, you need not worry about your husband."

"No, Oom Koos, I'm never worried about him. But we can't go apart just like this. I would like to hear your plans. What are you going to do?"

"We are going to save our people and want to prevent bloodshed. Sir James Rose-Innes tells us, A man who wanted to prevent bloodshed could not possibly be planning rebellion or civil war." Beyers and De la Rey talked in the bedroom until they were called to supper. Beyers looked worn out, whatever had been decided or planned between them was clearly not of Beyer's choosing. But De la Rey was elated. Beyers put down his knife and fork with some weariness.

"Look, Oom Koos," he said, "it is late. Let's rather wait until early tomorrow morning – then I'll go with you as far as Potchefstroom."

De la Rey started with impatience, "Krisjan, we've decided to go tonight. I promised Jan Kemp to be there." He did not add that the prophet van Rensburg had seen them together, that the date was the fifteenth, that it was a windy and cloudy night outside. When supper was over, prayers were said. Beyers looked miserable, but prepared to leave. Outside in the street the Daimler stood waiting. The chauffeur, who had been told to get ready for the trip to Potchefstroom was also waiting. The generals descended the stoep and walked towards the car.

The wind roared through the trees and the sky was black.

Editor's Note.
The sixth instalment of South African Rebellion was published in the November, 1971, issue of *The Outpost*. It ended as above, with the following editor's note to conclude:

> The next instalment will give a detailed account of the Foster Gang which was, indirectly, responsible for the death of General De la Rey that same night. Harm Oost, the editor of Het Volk, suggested De la Rey was murdered! The reader can decide for himself whether this was so or not.

(General De la Rey was shot by a Policeman that night in somewhat mysterious circumstances.)

No next instalment was received. Eben Mocke died in February, 1972, so the tale was unfinished. Some further details may be found in the National Archives Submission in Part Four.

Illustration at the head of the first instalment of The GAMBLERS
in *The Outpost* December,1967

Sergeant-Major Hough poked his ruddy-complexioned face around the door of my room where I was lying on the bed having a rest after lunch. "Major Brundell wants to see you down at the town office. I don't know what it's all about and he won't tell me. You had better look sharp about it!"

Only two days previously I had bought a brand-new B.S.A. Motorcycle and, having had my rest so rudely disturbed, within ten minutes I was roaring off with the throttle wide open and with the express intention of annoying those who were fortunate enough to be enjoying their siesta. After all, why should they rest while I had to work.

Punctually at 2 p.m. at the Bulawayo Town Station, I reported to Major Brundell who was known to be a very competent investigator. He was quite extraordinary handsome – very tall, long in the leg, clean-shaven with prominent features and piercing dark eyes. He moved with speed and suppleness.

Major Brundell opened the conversation in a rich baritone which had pleasing inflections and the faintest hint of an accent I was unable to place.

"There's been a spot of trouble on the Cam and Motor Mine at Eiffel Flats near Gatooma. The management have complained that…but here is the file, look through the correspondence for yourself."

He passed the papers across the desk to me. There were several letters from the Mine management complaining that the younger employees were finding it difficult to pay for their board and lodging and that they were squandering their money at a local gambling school. They had tried to uncover the whereabouts of the gambling school without success and now they were asking the police to trace and put a stop to the activities of the card sharps. I passed the file back to Major Brundell who said:

> I want you to go to Eiffel Flats, try to trace the gamblers and if the management's suspicions are confirmed, charge them and bring them to Court under the Gambling Laws. Lieutenant Morris is in charge at Gatooma and if you need any assistance, get in touch with him from Hartley. I don't want you seen with the police in Gatooma under any circumstances. I am sending these papers off to Lieutenant Morris today to let him know that you are making investigations and I will arrange with Captain Murray that you are seconded to the CID for the time being.

I wasn't all that keen on CID work but I felt that here was a wonderful opportunity for a long ride on my new toy – the motorcycle. I asked Major Brundell with breezy aplomb if the Government would pay my expenses if I made my own way to Eiffel Flats. He foresaw no difficulties about this and agreed that it would be a decided advantage if I had my own transport on the case. Having warned me not to risk my cover by being seen in Gatooma once again, Major Brundell dismissed me.

Early the next morning, with a Gladstone bag packed with extra clothes on the carrier, I was on my way to Gwelo. The roads at that time were hardly suitable for two-wheeled transport. The hazards of stones, sand, ruts and mud made travel on a motorcycle anything but a joy ride. The Bembesi and Shangani Rivers gave me much trouble in crossing and altogether it was a very tiring journey. I was only too pleased to arrive in Gwelo at 6 p.m. and to book in at the "Horseshoe Hotel".

The "Horseshoe" was owned by that peppery and interesting character, Major Hurrell, who was well known for his brave and reckless exploits during the Matabele Rebellion. His son, Dave Hurrell, was the first-born of Gwelo and was given the farm Foxton by Cecil Rhodes. Dave Hurrell died recently but the farm is still occupied and worked by his family. The "Horseshoe" was later bought by Tom Meikle, demolished, and the present Midlands Hotel erected on the site.

The following morning, with dark heavy rain clouds evident in all directions, I was on my way to Que Que. If anything, the road conditions were worse than on the previous day. Heavy rain had fallen during the night and motorcycle travel was about the world's worst form of transport. My cup of troubles was overflowing by the time I arrived at the Que Que River and found, to my utter consternation, that the river was in full flood.

There were a number of Africans on either side of the river patiently waiting for the water to subside before crossing. It was obvious to me that a crossing was completely out of the question for many hours if not for the whole day. I was in no mood to sit and wait and, soliciting help from the Africans, I made my way down river about three miles, where the railway bridge offered a solution. It was quite an exercise to get the heavy machine up the high embankment but with the Africans pulling and pushing we eventually succeeded. Slowly and carefully, we managed to push my valuable motorcycle to the other side.

I continued my journey slowly along the side of the railway track as far as Gobo where the main road crossed the line. Once on the road again, I had no further trouble and at 4 p.m., cold, tired, wet and hungry, I arrived at the Que Que Hotel. A steaming hot bath and a brisk rub down and I began to feel better.

I made my way into the bar for a drink before dinner and was accosted by a short, thick-set, old gentleman with a walrus moustache and a voice like a subway train putting on brakes. "Have this one on me," he grated, and I obliged and had several more – on him and on me. This was John Austin, known locally as "Honest John". He was the owner of the large general store and local butchery and, during the course of our conversation, I gathered that he was of Finnish nationality and that he had journeyed to Africa "before the mast". His pride in the sea, his former profession, was more than apparent and in front of his home, which was close to the hotel, he had a high mast anchored with stays and with the Union Jack fluttering at the head. When he heard that I was in the market for slaughter cattle (my own idea of a "cover" story) he laughed and rasped in his concrete mixer voice: "You won't find any cattle around here. I have the greatest difficulty in getting beef for my butchery and to maintain supplies to the Globe and Phoenix Mine."

Our friendship strengthened glass by glass and we adjourned to the verandah of his huge homestead. He led the way to a small room at the end of the stoep which he referred to as his "den". Here he produced a bottle of John Crabbe whisky, remarking as he drew the cork: "I import this whisky myself direct from the distillery in Scotland. It is the mildest whisky on the market – try it!"

I tried it – several times – and it was harsh and strong and far from "mild". Later that night when I had parted company with the old man, we had agreed that he would buy any cattle I was able to purchase at the ruling market prices – 17/6 to 27/6 per cwt, dressed weight.

("Honest John" left £50,000 in his Will for the purpose of building a battleship. This was hardly sufficient even in those days and the sum was added to the overall expense involved in the construction of the *Matabele*.)

I continued my journey the following day – with a heavy "John Crabbe" head on my shoulders. The Sebakwe River was flowing strongly and the water was again too deep to get across on the motorcycle. I enlisted the assistance of eight Africans who carried the machine across hitched to two long poles strapped on either side of the petrol tank. I crossed in a "cradle" propelled by hand and suspended from a too-thin wire rope. It was a sensation that I did not enjoy. The next hazard turned out to be the Umniati, which turned out to be a roaring torrent. There was no hope of crossing by the road bridge and once again I made use of the bridge so thoughtfully supplied by the Rhodesian Railways and once again I was fortunate to find willing hands to help me although the embankment was much higher than that at the Que Que River. By the time the machine was across, I was so drenched in perspiration that I might just as well have swum across had the current been more obliging. The final obstruction on this unforgettable journey was the Umsweswe River – a wide expanse of water, though not too deep, flowing over the stony drift. Again it was a case of carrying the machine whilst I "cradled" myself across. By this time I was sick and tired of the motorcycle and wished that I had never seen, let alone owned, the contraption.

My relief that there were no more rivers can be imagined and I was truly thankful when I rode into Gatooma. Without stopping I continued on to Eiffel Flats and towards the Cam and Motor Mine. Some two miles from my destination I arrived at a small wayside inn. I stopped, booked in for accommodation and a bath and had a reviving drink. I was almost dead on my feet to say nothing of my posterior, which had patiently borne the brunt of my bouncing progress from Bulawayo.

Before dinner, the little bar of the hotel was filled with a number of people who arrived only to drink. Soon it was packed with men enjoying their sundowners. The crush increased so much that the man next to me sidled up closer and closer to make way for the newcomers and our proximity was such that we could hardly ignore each other. My neighbour identified himself as Petersen and he had a distinct foreign accent:

"The Mine Club is getting so overcrowded these days and it looks as though this place is getting to be just as bad. Are you staying here?"

I told him that I was and asked if he knew where I might buy slaughter stock.

"Strange you should ask me about cattle. Only this afternoon I saw sixteen really fat beasts belonging to the farmer who owns the ground adjacent to the Mine. He tells me he has several buyers interested, but they won't give him the price he is asking. Perhaps if you go and see him, you might make a deal."

We continued talking and after a few more drinks Petersen made his excuses and walked to the door. His parting invitation set my heart throbbing.

"Feel like a flutter?"

"A 'flutter'? What do you mean, a 'flutter'?"

"A 'speel' – a gamble!" he replied testily, scorning my pretended innocence. "There's a game going tonight and if you want to come with me, I'll pick you up after dinner."

"Yes. Thank you very much," I replied as off-handedly as I was able. "I've got nothing to do, the night is long and I will be only too happy to go along with you." Here was the perfect break, as the Americans say, and although I would have preferred an early night after my tiring journey, here was an opportunity of being introduced to the gamblers – an opportunity I just couldn't afford to miss.

Petersen called as he had promised and we set off down the road in the direction of the Mine. As we strolled along, Petersen gave me a warning: "Where I am taking you is strictly *sub rosa* and between ourselves. The Mine management is opposed to gambling and is trying to put a stop to it. I can't understand their attitude – it's our money so why should they worry."

It was a rather dark night and it was only at the last minute that I saw the building that was our destination. We stumbled around the structure to the back door, Petersen knocked, the door was opened and in we went.

Petersen introduced me to one Dave Harrison. He was an Australian Jew and I was greeted in a distinctly Australian drawl. I later discovered that Harrison was the owner of the tin shanty which he also used as a hair-dressing saloon.

A long table was set in the centre of the room and around it were already gathered several other men. A huge Miller paraffin lamp hung over the centre of the table and a green shade reflected the light directly on to the table. Talk was general until others arrived to complete the school and Harrison then produced a new pack of cards from a box, broke the seal and began to deal individual cards on the table. The game was Faro – definitely a game of chance and played by betting on the order in which certain cards appeared when taken singly from the top of the pack.

The "speel" went on and on and it was only at 2 a.m. that the game finally wound up. Counting up, I found that I was £11 to the good. I was delighted. During the game there had been considerable sums of money lying on the table – sometimes as much as £150 or more.

As the school broke up, Harrison, in a hurt voice, said: "You ginks" (an expression he used in all the years I subsequently knew him) come back on Friday night and give the Bank a chance to get back tonight's losses."

The following day, I motored over to Hartley, interviewed Captain Stephenson and then telephoned Lieutenant Morris in Gatooma. The latter told me to hang on and await his arrival when we could go into the situation in detail and make arrangements for a raid.

When Lieutenant Morris arrived, we had a long discussion and decided to make the raid at about 11 p.m. when the gambling would be at its height. I was to be in at the opening of the game and remain until the raid was completed.

I returned to Eiffel Flats and visited the farmer Petersen had mentioned. I bought the cattle for £8 per head on condition that John Austin paid the railage from Gatooma to Que Que and that the farmer drove the cattle to the Gatooma siding. I then phoned "Honest" John who agreed to the deal on condition that his weights were accepted after slaughter. I later received the account plus a cheque for £15 – my profit – and Austin paid the farmer direct for the beef. There were advantages in being attached to the CID but for the moment everyone on the Flats knew that I had bought the cattle and my "cover" as a cattle buyer was assured.

On Friday night, accompanied by Petersen, I was again in the school, with Dave Harrison holding the Bank. As the game progressed, more and more patrons appeared until the room was packed to overflowing. By 11 p.m., my nerves were taut, awaiting the arrival of the raiders. By midnight, when they had still not made their appearance, I was getting hot and bothered. What could have gone wrong? To make matters worse, the pile of my winnings was getting larger and larger and the heap of sovereigns and silver accumulated at an alarming rate. I was worried that in the event of a raid, all my money would be confiscated! As time wore on and there was no change in my luck, I began to get more and more infuriated with Lieutenant Morris and his non-arrival.

Eventually at 2 a.m., Dave Harrison called a halt to the proceedings:

"Well, you ginks, that's enough for tonight!"

There were long and loud protests. The punters wanted to go on for another hour, but Harrison was adamant.

"I must have some sleep and you ginks have to work tomorrow. You can have another 'go' on Tuesday."

I counted my winnings and found that I had won £47. I welcomed the end of the game and was rather relieved that the anticipated raid had failed to materialise.

After breakfast that morning, I went over to Hartley to find out what had gone wrong. Captain Stephenson was sympathetic: "I can well imagine you had an exciting night," he said anxiously. "Lieutenant Morris was on the phone this morning and he is on his way over here to see you. Better wait for his explanation."

Lieutenant Morris was obviously disappointed and apologetic. "The four men on bicycles managed to lose themselves completely and were unable to find the hairdressing saloon. They stumbled and struggled through the mud until well after midnight before returning to Gatooma in the early hours of the morning."

We made arrangements to stage another raid for 11 p.m. the following Tuesday. Lieutenant Morris's parting words were that he hoped we would have more success on this occasion.

Tuesday night saw me back at the gaming table in a state of some excitement. As before the shanty was packed to capacity and money changed hands with reckless abandon. The gamblers seemed to have no idea of the value of money. Bets of £5 on one card were nothing out of the ordinary. I played with studied care and, once again, met with some success. Actually I was beginning to enjoy the game – no skill or the exercise of one's intelligence was required and it was essentially a game of pure chance. Had I lost, I have a suspicion that I would not have enjoyed the game as I did and it would have become monotonous and boring. But winning definitely had its interest value!

As the appointed time drew nearer, I again became tense and nervous.

The insides of my hands were wet with perspiration and the least unexpected movement gave me the jitters. Fifteen minutes before the chosen hour, I surreptitiously transferred my cash from the table to my pocket leaving only a small heap of silver in front of me.

At 11.15 there was a sharp knock and the back door opened to allow three men to make a hurried entrance. One of them said loudly, with frigid politeness: "Police! Keep your seats, gentlemen, and no nonsense, please."

As he spoke he moved forward and grabbed the four corners of the tablecloth to scoop it up with the cards and cash inside. The other two then got on with the "documentation" and recorded the name and address of each person present – including mine! Then we were all warned to appear in Court at Gatooma on the following Thursday. The police left, taking with them the money and the cards as exhibits.

There was a profound silence for several minutes until someone in the audience exploded viciously: "The bastards!" I joined in the abuse, feeling about as low and treacherous as man can become. Harrison was about the only one who sat there saying nothing.

"Dave," yelled a man from the side of the room, "don't look so damned humiliated and defeated. We'll all club together for your fine."

"That's nice of you ginks," replied Harrison humbly. "I appreciate the offer but what really worries me is all the damned publicity!"

Someone else chipped in and suggested that we all went for a drink and the entire assembly moved down to the hotel. As quantities of beer and spirits were consumed, the louder and more heated the threats of revenge against the so-and-so who had given the game away. I spent money – my winnings – lavishly.

The atmosphere in the Gatooma Magistrate's Court the following Thursday was brittle and thorny when I went into the witness box to give evidence against Dave Harrison. If looks could kill I would have died there in Court. The vitriolic antagonism was plain to see on the face of everyone in the courtroom.

The outcome was that Harrison was fined £50 and all the stakes found in the shanty were confiscated. I trucked my motor-cycle back to Bulawayo and left on the first train.

A few days later, I received a copy of the Gatooma *Times* and in the Personal Column appeared the following: "Constable M. Please return to Gatooma, your friends await you."

I decided that CID work was most certainly not for me.

THE SEQUEL

Many years later, it must have been 1923 or '24, a Gymkhana meeting was staged at Gwelo. I had long been out of the Force and had entered two ponies which I used as hacks on my farm. In the second race I had entered my nomination, Patrick, and in the same race was the mount of Saddler Sergeant McDermott. His horse was a fine black gelding with white points, broad-chested, groomed to perfection, and showing a lively clean and alert eye. I decided that the black looked the winner and ignored my own entry to back Sergeant McDermott's horse.

The only bookie on the course was none other than my old adversary, Dave Harrison, who had opened a hairdressing saloon in Gwelo. As I was walking up to his stand to place my bet, the chiming voice of a woman asked: "Is your pony going to win?"

I turned and found Miss Cynthia Stockley immediately behind me with her race card in her hand. (Miss Stockley, the novelist, was rather plain but had a very attractive voice.)

"No, no, Miss Stockley. I think the black looks a likely winner and he will be carrying my money"'

"In that case," she replied in her melodious voice, "I shall follow your example."

I laid a bet on the horse which would have netted me £60 and Miss Stockley £20 if it came home first, but to my consternation and distinct embarrassment, it was my own pony, *Patrick*, which won the race. Nobody on the course was more surprised than I although I did notice that Sergeant McDermott was examining his mount's legs with an almost equally bewildered expression. Unfortunately, I did not speak to him during the meeting.

In the fourth or fifth race, *Patrick* and the black were again matched and I persisted in my faith in the latter despite the earlier disastrous result. In the hope of regaining our losses, both Miss Stockley and I backed the former loser.

"If he wins," said Miss Stockley, " the champagne supper is on me!"

He did win – with ease, and as we went to collect our winnings, Dave Harrison asked me, as a favour, if I could wait until Monday for my money as he could only afford to pay Miss Stockley. In the company of a lady, who had already promised me supper, I could hardly make an issue of the debt and agreed.

Some ten days later, I went into Gwelo on business and went to Harrison for a haircut and to collect my winnings.

"You know," he said uncomfortably, "I felt sure you had forgotten about your money. I thought you had decided that it was a small repayment towards the losses I had back at Eiffel Flats eleven years ago. You ginks here in Gwelo are too smart for me. I went down a couple of hundred pounds at the races. How about calling it a day'"

"No, Dave," I replied apologetically. "If you want a refund on your losses at the Cam and Motor I suggest you apply to the Government."

"What!" he exploded. "Do you think those Civil Service ginks will have the slightest consideration for me? Not on your life. My only salvation is good fellows like yourself and those ginks on the Flats who helped me to pay the fine."

"I'll meet you halfway, Dave," I replied. "Give me half my winnings and a haircut and we'll call it quits."

"I knew you were a good fellow," he said smugly. "Here's your £30 and sit down and collect your haircut."

If I had but known at the time that Dave Harrison was quite well off, he would never have "conned" me out of that £30.

But it was some salve to my conscience that Dave finally had the last laugh on me.

"MONGOOSE" and the GUTU PATROL

Author's Note: Gerard McClement (1661) is very mistaken in his letter to "The Chronicler" in February's *Outpost*. There are a couple of his comrades on the Gutu Patrol who are still very much alive. Teddy Hughes Halls (939) still keeps himself very actively engaged in looking after the interests of those old-timers creeping into their eighties, and I too am still in the land of the living, having narrowly escaped the slow journey to Warren Hills. I can remember most of the facts surrounding that "historic" patrol and, after Monty Surgey's entertaining efforts last month, perhaps I can be allowed to recount the adventure which I think took place in 1912 and not, as Mr McClement says, 1913.

I was making preparations for my second patrol into the Kalahari (see Kalahari Patrol) when word came through that I was wanted at Headquarters. Sergeant-Major Hough was as blunt as usual when I arrived at his office in Bulawayo.

"Your Gwaai trip is off. There's trouble in the Gutu area and you will be accompanying a contingent leaving here tomorrow. I shall be going, as will every man who can be spared. We shouldn't be away for long and when we get back you can charge off to your wilderness."

I was very disappointed but there was no point in arguing with the Sergeant-Major. I asked him which horse had been allocated to me.

"I have decided to let you have *Mongoose*. He can carry a ton so your weight shouldn't affect him."

Unenthusiastic about the change in plans, I strolled down to the stables to make friends with my chosen mount. *Mongoose* was a grey and looked more like a carthorse than a riding animal. Long-bodied, broad-backed and with short thick legs, he had a huge head with "roman nose". The mule-like ears were pulled back as I patted him. Offering him one of the sweets which I invariably carried to stop me from smoking too much, *Mongoose* shot his big ears forward, sniffed the object in my hand, wobbled the thick lips and neatly plucked the bull's-eye from my palm. He crunched and out of all proportion to the size of the morsel and then moved head up and down, asking for more. It seemed that he was one of those "horse-sense" animals who would react according to the treatment he received. He proved to be a lovable old character and we became firm friends.

The men from K Troop (if I remember rightly) were Lieutenant Lockwood, Sergeant-Major Hough, Sergeant Birbeck, Corporals Teddy Hughes Halls and Tim Law and Troopers Harmer, Dyer, Zeederberg, Harveyson, Rochard,

Mathison, Jones and myself. Le Ruille went as saddler and O'Grady as farrier.

Rumour was rife on the reasons for this sudden excursion. A full-scale war with the natives was high on the list of "possibles" and we were all sure that there would be blood-letting. Excitement ran high.

We were allowed only the minimum of kit-blankets, ground sheets, billy cans, saddlery, raincoats and our "British warms". The following day we loaded our kit on a buckboard drawn by mules, rode to the railway station, unloaded our kit and saddlery into a truck and bedded the horses down in enclosed vans for the trip to Umvuma.

The railway journey was one of the slowest I have ever experienced. The driver was taking no chances. Every culvert or bridge he encountered was crossed in slow motion. Even so, the leisurely journey had its compensations. Slowly the scenery unfolded: wooded areas gave way to wide open spaces with waving tall grass and the blue hills in the distance; water seemed to be in abundance with every little dip, spruit or river flowing with clear water. It was an attractive picture to the eyes of youth.

Lalapanzi station on the Great Dyke, where chrome would be mined extensively in later years, was passed, the name itself conjuring up visions of the exhausted Pioneer Column sleeping in a makeshift fort on a nearby hill; Iron Mine Hill, the next stop, provided the ore which Umvuma's Falcon Mine mixed in the gold and copper smelting process; on through the ancient hills which hugged the railway line and where the old native workings, from which had come the ore for assegais and battle axes, were still visible; until finally we reached Umvuma.

We were met and joined by the Mashonaland contingent, mainly new recruits fresh from Depot who looked very young but full of energy. No time was wasted in getting the troops away from a town bustling with the activity associated with the construction and extension of the Falcon Mine.

Captain Gus Myburg was in charge of the expedition with Lieutenant Lockwood second in command. Dummerick was our medical officer with Breeden in charge of the commissariat assisted by Trooper Johnny West. Sergeant-Major Schlacter – a real veteran who had been an 1890 Pioneer and who had fought in the Boer War – looked after the transport wagons.

It must have been an impressive sight as we streamed out of Umvuma with the officers at the head of the column, behind them the Salisbury troops, then the Matabele contingent and finally the wagons bringing up the rear. We were off into the "unknown" to put an end to the "troubles".

We took the old Fort Victoria road along the Umvumbi River (also known as the "Blinkwater") and passed over the farm "Elands-vlei" which I would buy many years later. Late in the afternoon we out-spanned where there was good grazing and running water. The horses and mules were released to drink and then mustered for nose-bag feeding and grooming. With the animals bedded down for the night, we prepared our own meal. Corporal Hughes Halls drew the rations for K Troop and with our flour we received a minute quantity of baking powder – hardly sufficient to make the dough rise. The result was tough on one's stomach but it did stick to the ribs for a long time! With coffee, sugar and bully beef, there was little doubt that we would survive.

We were off at dawn the next day after the horses had been fed their ration of crushed yellow maize and we had swallowed our coffee. We rested from 10 a.m. until 2 p.m. before readying ourselves for another couple of hours in the saddle. It was when the animals were being mustered for the resumption that it was discovered that Sergeant Schlacter's chestnut mule and Trooper Harveyson's bay pony were missing. Myburgh and Lockwood came down the line, spotted me and the former spoke:

"Here, you! I want you to go after the missing horse and mule. Find them and then catch us up. Take a man from your section with you." Hughes Halls volunteered to come with me and as soon as his pony and *Mongoose* had emptied their nose-bags, we saddled up and rode in the direction of the spot at which the animals had grazed. I had no difficulty in cutting the tracks of the mule and horse. They had grazed in a semi-circle until they reached the road from Umvuma and then, without turning right or left, they had made for the town. We followed the spoor quickly; the sun was dipping fast and speed was a necessity. *Mongoose* had the trot of an ox and the canter of a camel and he gave me a very rough trip. In the failing light, the tracks continued towards Umvuma and when it was no longer possible to see the spoor of the truants, we rode on into the town to find the mule and horse awaiting our arrival.

There was no point in setting out after the patrol that night so we made our way to the hotel in search of food and beds. The place was packed with men from all parts of the world – Australians, Canadians, Afrikaners, Englishmen and Jews. The two of us in uniform drew immediate attention and we were showered with questions on the reasons for the patrol. Such was their thirst for knowledge that we were pressed into drink after drink although we protested that they knew as much about the affair as we did. It was only with the greatest difficulty that we escaped from the throng to stagger in the direction of the dining room. A delicious meal of mutton stew, vegetables and milk tart, followed by several cups of black coffee, restored our senses. We prepared to leave and, knowing of no other exit, I made for the bar.

"No, no! Not that way! They'll kill us with booze!" cried Teddy. "Let's go out through the kitchen."

We groped our way around the pots and pans and eventually found our way outside where we breathed deep gulps of the cool night air. Finally we found our beds and slept like the dead until coffee was brought to us next morning.

I was determined to have a look at the construction work going on at the mine before we resumed our travels and with difficulty managed to persuade Hughes Halls to accompany me. The hill was a beehive of activity. Groups of men seemed to be working in every direction; machinery was scattered in gay abandon all over the place and it was inconceivable that the various bits and pieces would ever be assembled correctly. Some distance from the mill site, miners were already hauling ore from a shaft by means of a steam hoist. Plumbers swarmed about the place constructing steel tanks of all sizes while masons, with the help of numerous Africans, were laying bricks, mixing cement and concrete and adding to the overall hue and cry of the construction.

Little did I dream then, as I gazed on the activity, that in the distant future I would be involved in treating the yellow dumps which would rise as the result of the mining operations.

Our pursuit of the slow-moving patrol was made easy since we had four riding animals between us. By changing mounts every hour we soon covered the ground. It was a real treat to ride on the back of Schlacter's mule after having been bounced around on *Mongoose*.

We caught up with the patrol approximately where Chatsworth is today. Myburgh was most complimentary and Schlacter and Harveyson were pleased to see their mounts again. When we had off-saddled and camped for the night, Captain Myburgh sent for me.

"From tomorrow I want you to scout ahead of the column. Should you see any gathering of natives, you are to return immediately and report. Don't get more than three miles ahead of us. We don't really expect any trouble – but we must be on guard."

This was the official hint of the cause of the excursion and proved the exaggeration of the earlier rumours.

The next morning, as soon as the rest of the patrol was on the move, I rode ahead through attractive country dotted here and there with granite out-crops. As I rounded one of the kopjes there was a sudden outburst of yodelling from a crowd of native women and children. *Mongoose* didn't like the sudden chorus and stopped in his tracks and would have swung round and made off had I not held him. I dismounted and dragged him after me up the hill towards the huts. Silence fell on the assembly as I approached and offered a greeting. The reply came in a language I could not understand and there was an embarrassing pause until my eyes fastened on a heap of majodas and pumpkins. I plunged my hand into my pocket and drew out a heap of small silver. By dint of much gesticulation and waving of hands, the vegetables were brought and laid in a pile in front of me.

More waving of the hands produced an axe with which I cut open one of the majodas and then offered a slice to *Mongoose*.

The ice was broken. *Mongoose* crushed the fruit between his massive jaws and asked for more, to the delight of the women and children. One little girl bravely came forward and stretched in front of my monster with a piece of majoda on her palm. *Mongoose* leaned towards her and, as delicately as he had sucked the bull's-eye from my hand at our first meeting, took the little girl's offering. The game was on. The children squabbled among themselves to feed the horse and, as for *Mongoose*, he enjoyed every minute of it until I had to stop the milling youngsters for fear that even his long barrel would eventually burst.

Eventually I left the kraal with two chickens and two pumpkins tied behind the saddle while the children screamed their farewells on all sides.

When I returned to camp that evening, Hughes Halls told me that two Native Commissioners, Messrs Blackwell and Bazeley, had joined the column and that Captain Myburgh wanted to see me. I made my report to the Captain (the absence of men in the kraal I had visited rather countered the friendly treatment I had received there) after which I was told to be more careful on the next day.

"We are entering an area where we might experience trouble with the Africans. It might be serious, although we anticipate no real difficulties. If you see any number of Africans together, return immediately and report...and be careful!"

Although I was prepared to be cautious on my scouting trips, my own opinion was that we had gone to a lot of trouble for nothing.

During the night a picket guard was posted ahead of the patrol. The rest of us slept soundly until I was roused from deep slumbers and caught one of our number filching condensed milk from the one and only tin we possessed. He dropped the tin like a hot coal when the first curse shattered the night.

After *Mongoose* had breakfasted on his ration of crushed maize, I set out ahead of the column for another day's scouting. At the first kraal I came to, I was treated to another screaming reception and, after Myburgh's warning of the previous day, I wondered if the yelling was a warning to other kraals or merely a friendly greeting. *Mongoose* thought it was an invitation to another majoda feast and I had difficulty in getting him past the kraal.

At about 9 a.m. the horse picked up his ears and quickened his pace. The reason for the sprint was soon revealed. As we rounded a corner of thick bush, there in our path was a large gathering of Africans. The squatting horde was so close and so utterly silent that I had thoughts of turning tail and reporting back immediately to Myburgh. Before I could turn, however, one of the natives in the centre of the group stood up and slowly raised his hand in greeting before squatting down again as though I was already gone. The hushed gathering and the complete disinterest in my presence was totally foreign to my experience and, with a creepy sensation in my spine, I quietly turned the horse and casually left the indaba.

As soon as I reached the column I reported to Captain Myburgh. Together with the Native Commissioners and other officers, he went forward to see for himself.

What transpired at that meeting, the rest of us never knew. Apparently they were able to convince the Africans of the justification for the increased hut tax – which we discovered was the cause of the heightened tension – and the "war" was over. It would be unfair to say that the whole expedition was a waste of time and energy: the sight of a large, disciplined body of men must have had a salutary effect on the unhappy natives.

But the showing of the flag was not yet over. Having come so far, it was decided that we should pass through Gutu and on to Fort Victoria. As we approached the latter, as some salve to our disappointment and celebration of the overall success of the mission, an ox was purchased and slaughtered. The issue of fresh meat was welcomed.

In retrospect, I must have had some nerve when I asked Captain Myburgh if I could leave the patrol in order to have a look at the Zimbabwe Ruins when we were camped near Fort Victoria. He didn't throw a fit when I made the request but considered it thoughtfully.

"I'm afraid not – the journey is quite impossible. We are returning the day after tomorrow and it is too much to expect your horse to cover the 40 miles there and back in time."

"But, sir," I remonstrated, "*Mongoose* is fit, I will take care of him and see to it that he is properly fed."

"And where will you get the grain with which to feed him?"

"Majodas, sir. He loves them almost as much as he likes sweet potatoes." And I went on to tell the officer of my mount's previous indulgence.

Myburgh smiled at the story but he would not change his mind.

"We're supposed to be under active service conditions and you must continue with your scouting when we leave here."

And so it was not until 1922 that I saw the ruins for the first time.

Our return journey was made along the Pioneer Road through Felixburg to Enkeldoorn. There we parted company with the Mashonaland contingent, who

pressed on to Salisbury.
The men of K Troop rode off to Umvuma, where we entrained for Bulawayo.

MAKAHA CONTENTS

Map	257
Chapter One Posting to Makaha	258
Chapter Two Witchcraft	266
Chapter Three Goldmines	273
Chapter Four The Makumbi Rebellion	278
Chapter Five Reinforcements	285
Chapter Six My African Cook	292
Chapter Seven Detection and Inspection	299
Chapter Eight Blackwater Fever	302

Southern Rhodesia

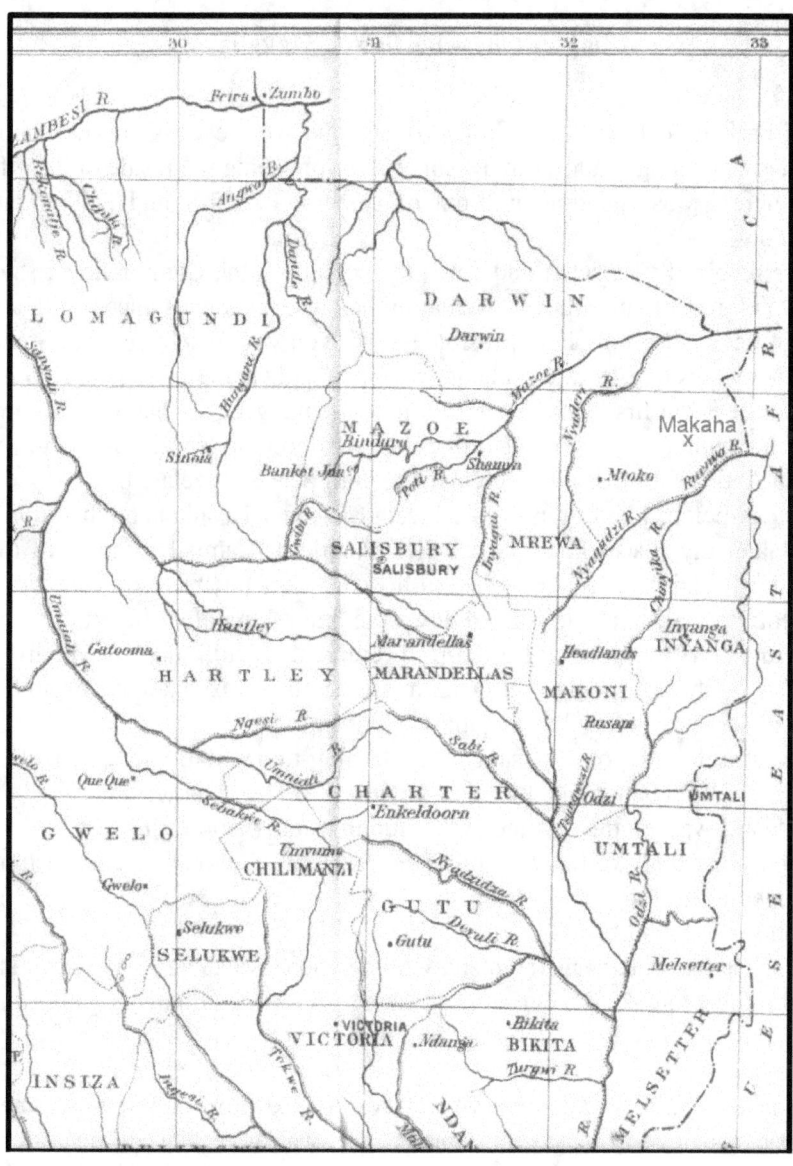

MAKAHA

Chapter One – Posting to Makaha

Even back in 1916, there were few of us who were ever given the doubtful privilege of riding in the Commissioner's car or seeing the inside of his office. But there I was, standing in front of General Edwards and feeling rather rebellious.

"I've received your letter and noted the contents," the Commissioner said to me. "You must realise, however, that in the present circumstances, with a war on our hands, it is simply impossible to give you your discharge. Every single member wants to go to war without giving a thought to the defence of Rhodesia. The Force is our first line of defence and I dare not give discharges to men who are time expired, especially now that there are no new recruits available. You are on Active Service and will remain so until peace is declared."

The day before I had been released from Salisbury Hospital and that morning had taken my place on the usual Sick Parade at Camp Hospital. All of us outside the Dispensary had been surprised by an unexpected inspection by General Edwards. He had walked down the line asking after the health of each individual. After asking if I was up to returning to full duty, to which I had replied in the affirmative, the Commissioner had gazed at the ground for several seconds before looking me straight in the eye.

"I want to talk to you," he said. Then, turning to his Staff Officer, Lieutenant Phillips. "We'd better take him down with us to Headquarters."

So there I was, on the mat and in the Commissioner's office, no less.

Having listened to the Commissioner's stern but sympathetic lecture, I appealed to him to send me to a station where I could be alone – as far from Salisbury as possible.

"Yes, I can do that. In fact, I intend sending you to Makaha, a one-man station on the Portuguese Border. Once there, you will attend to your duties properly and I'll hear no more about wanting your discharge from the Force."

On the train to Macheke, from where I was to ride to my new station, I met an American Missionary, Doctor Gurney. He was a red-faced, clean-shaven, white-haired little man who was most friendly and who invited me to accompany him to Makaha (where he was in charge of the Mission and

Clinic) in his Model "T" Ford which was two years old. I jumped at the invitation and sent the riding mule and pack donkeys on to Makaha by road.

The journey from Macheke to Mtoko in the Model "T" was anything but a joy ride. The roads back in 1916 were little more than rough tracks – rocky, sandy, and zig-zagging sharply to avoid protruding stumps and ant-hills. I was thankful when we arrived at Mtoko and were offered tea by Mrs Morkel, the wife of the Native Commissioner.

While we were politely sipping tea and chatting with the Native Commissioner and his wife, I noticed a thin, tired, bone-ribbed pony struggling to nibble the short grass at the side of the bungalow-type "Residency".

"What's the matter with that horse?" I asked Morkel.

"I just don't know. He's been lethargic for days and is completely off his food. I got him from a Chief who had no use for a horse and had no idea what to do with the animal. He has never been ridden here and I don't know if he had been broken to harness. He's quite tame and something of a pet of my wife."

"Send him to Makaha," I suggested, "and I'll try and get him into condition provided you let me have the use of him for a time."

"That's a good idea. I'll be only too happy to let you have him. As a matter of fact, the Native Department interpreter happens to be here and I'll let him lead the pony back when he returns."

Dr Gurney and I continued our journey to Makaha and arrived there at about 4 p.m. I took over the Police Station from Trooper Deane who was returning to Salisbury. Together we punished the bottle of brandy supplied with the "medical comforts" and the next day I had to replace the liquor from the local bottle store. I wonder how often the medical comforts, kept strictly in case of illness, came to the rescue of an unexpected sundowner? The Police Camp was situated against a range of hills overlooking the Makaha Valley. One had an uninterrupted view of the countryside and the several houses dotted in the ravine. The existing buildings were no more than beehive huts – not at all to my liking – and I immediately applied for and was granted the princely sum of £22 for improvements. With the money I started making Kimberley bricks and engaged a local African builder to erect a three-roomed house with a toilet some fifty yards from the establishment. I had so much money left over from the grant that the next step was a Court House with a raised platform and two witnesses' cubicles. When it was completed, I used the Court House as my office.

The Trooper-in-Charge at Makaha had many duties. He was Pass Officer, Issuer of Cattle Permits, and Public Prosecutor besides having a vast area to patrol. In addition to these formal duties, which swelled the monthly income by sixpence, a shilling and two shillings respectively, one was constantly involved in hearing, arbitrating and adjudicating in the complaints of the local natives. Seldom was there a free day, especially when the locals became involved in their numerous witchcraft practices.

One of the biggest problems in those days was sorting out their complicated marriage laws. Believing that a payment for the bride led to a happier and more stable marriage, the lobolo system was exclusively practised. But the system often went wrong and then the fun would start. The harassed trooper would think he had the matter satisfactorily unravelled and settled and then an unknown voice would enter the arena to claim that such and such a beast belonged to his father although it died thirty or forty years ago and that the said beast had sired so many calves during the years and what had become of the progeny? Unless the animals were returned immediately, the marriage would be bewitched. Such investigations were never ending.

The pony from Morkel arrived as prearranged and I wasted no time in dosing him with "Bots". The medicine was a great success, the pony thrived and we became the greatest of friends. The pony followed me like a dog and would whinny with delight when I approached the stable. He would squeal with annoyance if I withheld the sugar loaf too long. He had a lovable disposition and, if anything, became too friendly. On one occasion he marched into the dining-room looking for his "sweetener". After Court, some two months later, Morkel asked after the pony. "How's the horse getting on?" "The horse? Which one do you mean? Oh, the one you sent over from Mtoko. He died weeks ago – I told you over the phone, remember?"

"Must have slipped my mind, but I'm not surprised to hear he didn't make it. Always a sickly animal and I had my doubts when you reckoned you could pull him through his ailments."

"Yes, it was a pity. Still, I have another in the pink of condition. Come and have a look."

Morkel accompanied me to the stable.

"By Jove!" exclaimed Morkel in admiration. "What a beautiful animal. Where did you get him?"

"He was loaned to me by one Ernest Morkel Native Commissioner of Mtoko, who is so blind that he can't even recognise his own horse!"

The Native Commissioner's face was a picture of surprise and delight.

"He's yours," he said, "for as long as you stay at Makaha."

A chap named Daniels who had claims near the Olympus Mine was leaving the area and begged me to take over 30 head of mixed cattle at 13s. 6d. per head. I beat him down to ten shillings and he accepted the offer. I thus became the proud owner of a small herd of cattle to which I added from time to time. Cattle were cheap at Makaha and I concentrated on breeding stock in order to get milk from the cows. The local animals were very poor milkers, but thirty cups in the morning and the same at night were sufficient for my needs and those of the African constables and prisoners. Both the latter were extremely grateful. As far as the prisoners were concerned, it made them more amenable to their "hard labour".

The tennis court at Makaha was in poor shape and the local inhabitants asked if I could do something about it. On the premise that idle hands could be more easily tempted towards criminal activities – and from less "high-falutin" motives, I made use of the prisoners and witnesses and any Africans awaiting judgement on civil actions in restoring the tennis court. In the latter cases I passed judgement myself which naturally gave me a suitable period of grace in which to come to a decision as well as the benefits of the punishment of guilty parties in certain cases. Morkel, as Native Commissioner responsible for Makaha, objected strongly to this unofficial procedure and reprimanded me on several occasions for usurping the functions of the Native Department. On the quiet, I knew that he was envious of my restoration project and required labour to improve his own tennis court at Mtoko!

Officially, I made no judgements in civil cases. I merely "advised" and made peace in the family squabbles. The more frivolous criminal cases were settled likewise, to save the Native Commissioner the long journey from Mtoko. When he did come to sit in judgement, the sentenced prisoners had to be escorted to the gaol at Mtoko.

After one particular session, there were a number of prisoners destined for the Native Commissioner's tennis court. But I was still short of labour with my own sporting problems so I decided to delay their departure. The next morning brought a frantic call from Mtoko.

"What's happened to the prisoners?"

"Sorry! No escorts available."

"Look here! I'm not a fool! Send them in with the Native Department messenger. I need that labour urgently!"

"I'm sorry to have to disappoint you. I cannot be left without an African interpreter."

Words failed poor old Morkel and I imagined him stamping in anger after he had crashed the receiver down.

The following day the tennis court was completed to the delight of the Makaha community. The prisoners were dutifully despatched to the Native Commissioner.

At a subsequent meeting Morkel remarked: "You know, the way you flout the regulations will find you in serious trouble one of these days."

Quite seriously I replied: "Regulations are made to be broken. Can you honestly say, crossing your heart, that you have never broken one of the Commandments." He grinned and admitted that he had never looked at it from that point of view. Tennis was our only recreation – as may have been gathered – and on Saturdays after tennis there was a standing invitation from the local storekeeper, Willie Kaplan, to sundowners and dinner. Wright, a man from England, was Kaplan's butcher and he saw to it that the best beef roast appeared on the table, roasted as no one's mother could ever roast sirloin. These were strictly male gatherings – the only white woman in Makaha was Mrs Kalwait, the wife of a timberman on the Radnor Mine. She did not participate in our sundowners.

Years later, long after I had left Makaha, our jovial butcher Wright was brutally murdered close to the tennis court when his head was bashed in with knobkerries.

The toilet which I had built was some fifty yards from the main buildings and had no door. A half-moon thatched hedge covered the opening. At sunset one evening I was sitting in the PK when I heard the African herdboy bringing the cattle into the kraal. He was whistling and talking to the animals as Africans will, trying to persuade them to enter the narrow gate into the kraal and calling them by their respective names as he did so. Suddenly my pleasant rural contemplation was shattered by a crash and the bellowing of stampeding cattle. The boy gave a primitive scream and in a cracked voice yelled "Lions, lions!" He passed the PK at a speed that must have surpassed the existing sprint record.

I jumped from my seat, clutching at my trousers and desperately trying to fasten my belt with trembling hands. With every nerve stiffening, I rushed to the house for my rifle. Before I reached the gun – or the house – the predictable happened. My trousers slipped to my ankles and flung me full length, face down, on the hard, gravelly, red earth. Blood spurted from my nose and tears welled in my eyes.

Fortunately my cookboy, Joe, had the sense to realise what was happening and hurried into the living quarters for the gun. He handed it to me – by which time I had safely secured my trousers. Wiping the blood from my face, I rushed to the cattle kraal.

The cattle, bunched together in panic, were standing some two hundred yards from the kraal, looking in my direction with white-walled eyes and ears quivering. I tip-toed forward but saw no sign of the lions except their pad-marks showing distinctly in the cattle tracks.

Unfortunately the sun had dipped behind the range of mountain in the west and, as dusk gathered, it was far from the best time for tracking. Constables, prisoners and witnesses appeared on the scene and I quickly gave instructions for the frightened cattle to be rounded up. The herdboy, having regained his courage, reported that he had seen at least five lions after the cattle had caught their smell and stampeded. He had looked around for the cause of the disturbance and had been confronted by the quintet of tail-twitching predators. That was when he had decided to attempt the sprint record.

Marley Brothers, who had the contract to supply firewood and timber to the Radnor Mine, were in the habit of allowing their trek oxen to graze in the valley during the night. I sent a hurried note warning them of the threat and advising them to kraal the animals. They replied that it was too late, the oxen had already been released. All that could be done was to kindle huge fires here and there and hope that the lions would be scared by the flames. Later, when I was having supper, I heard cattle stampeding again and the unmistakable noise of the Marleys' first ox being pulled down. The bellowing of the poor beast as it struggled in the murderous claws was of mercifully short duration. In the short interval between the time when the claws made their first grab on the victim and the last neck-breaking clout, the poor beast must have suffered terribly. One can imagine the rolling eyes, hoarse bellowing and heaving jerks as it tried to escape the clutches of the evil-smelling murderer. Wild life is beautiful but it can be unmercifully cruel.

I swore to put an end to the lion menace the very next day. How I longed for Pistol, my lion dog of Kalahari repute. At Makaha I didn't even have a domestic cat on establishment and I made up my mind to get a dog, or dogs, as soon as possible.

Before sunrise I was off in the direction of the kill, followed by several Africans and a scraggy-ribbed, long-nosed, brindle kaffir dog which belonged to one of the witnesses in a pending witchcraft case. One of the Marley brothers told me later that the lions had taken a really big ox, a remarkable front leader and almost irreplaceable. They must have been hungry as most of the carcass had been eaten. We scattered and looked for pugmarks, my companions showing a marked tendency to search in close proximity to myself and the rifle! The dog, whose hackles had risen at the first whiff of the cats and hadn't yet calmed, was even more nervous than the Africans. It was difficult tracking in the long grass and trying to find the padmarks on the sun-baked red ground. Finally, we latched on to the direction taken by the predators and from then on the dog was a big help. He seemed to gain courage as we progressed and he actually released his tail from between his legs and allowed his hair to flatten. Suddenly he gave a yelp, a short bark, and fled to the rear of the followers – from which safe position he barked long and loud.

I advanced with the rifle and entered the shadows beneath a large tree. Apparently the lions had lain there until fleeing in the direction of a nearby hill at our approach. I wasn't going to attempt to track the lions further through the rocky kopje and decided to return to the carcass, erect gun traps and hope that the lions would return to their kill in the night. Two Martini-Henry's were set up with care at the site of the dead ox.

There were no sounds of exploding rifles in the night and, with the dawn, I discovered why. Willie Kaplan sent a message to the effect that lions had killed a cow at his other store eight miles away, and that his brother, Maurice, wanted me to come and shoot them! I wasn't keen to go after the cats again without trackers or dogs but I told one of the constables to take the two unfired rifles from the trap and meet me at Kaplan's store. I followed later on *Swift*, the name I had given to District Commissioner Morkel's horse.

Poor old Maurice Kaplan was in a high state of agitation as he told his tale:

> I had just turned in and was lying in bed reading when I heard bellowing and stampeding. Next morning there was a hammering on the front door of the store and Africans yelling "Lions" on the other side. I dived out of bed and unlocked the door to admit five pop-eyed frightened Africans in such a case of nerves that they couldn't give a coherent account of what had happened. We listened for further sounds of lions on the rampage but heard nothing. Even then the natives were afraid to leave the store so I let them stay there for the night. I didn't get much sleep myself after the excitement either. This morning we discovered the cow that had been pulled down and savaged.

The cattle enclosure was no more than a hundred yards from the store and the carcass of the cow only a short distance from the kraal. Under my supervision the natives dragged thorn branches around the carcass leaving only two entrances. To cover these openings I placed the two rifles carefully in the bush, laid the trip wires and waited for dusk.

At seven o'clock Maurice and I were enjoying a sun downer when both rifles went off, the reports echoing and re-echoing across the valley in the still night. Then there was dead silence – no grunting or angry roars to indicate that we might have killed at least one of the lions.

We could scarcely wait for dawn and the chance to inspect the results of the ambush. In one of the openings lay a lion with a heavy mane that had just turned black. He had been dropped in his tracks by a bullet that had bulls-eyed in his heart. Fifteen yards further away from the trap was a lioness, a beautiful specimen lying on her stomach with front legs out-stretched. The bullet from the other gun had passed through her lungs.

Africans appeared from everywhere, the usual phenomenon, until there must have been fifty or more. There was no lack of volunteers to cut long poles in the forest and cart the two dead cats back to the police camp.

The two skins, at a later date, were presented to Lady Chaplin, the wife of Sir Drummond Chaplin, who was Administrator of Rhodesia at the time.

Two days later, a couple of Africans reported that they had been chased close to Makaha by a wounded lion with a broken shoulder. This puzzled me and I wasted no time in looking into the matter. I set out with my two informants – and my dog. (I had bought the brindle kaffir hound for the mammoth sum of 10/- from the African witness.)

As the scared Africans had indicated there was the spoor of the lion. I followed the tracks for about fifty yards along the main road after which the animal had turned off into the bush. Releasing "Non" – the contraction of "nondescript" which I had bestowed on my dog – he sniffed the grass, gave a low growl and... fled! How I grieved for Pistol as I cursed my new acquisition. He allowed me to approach and I managed to get a lead fastened to his collar. Then I quietened him and coaxed him back on the trail but still he yelped his protests with hackles in the air and tail between his legs. I gave up in disgust and handed him to one of the Africans. Then, with my shotgun at the ready, I walked carefully into the grass.

I quickly excused Non of his misgivings. No more than a few yards into the bush, I heard a low growl and a full-grown lion cub tried to rise in front of me. I spattered his head with a charge of slugs from my cannon. The animal's shoulder was shattered and gangrene had already set in. Later we extracted the .450 bullet from a Martini-Henry. The only explanation I could offer for the rifle wound was that the cub had been in direct line with one of the adult cats shot near Maurice Kaplan's. I was pleased to have been able to put him out of his misery but he would have been a very dangerous animal to come across, despite the shoulder injury.

I returned to camp and was met by a native woman. Her blistered hands told their own story of the boiling water ordeal.

Chapter Two – Witchcraft

The African woman who waited for me in camp when I returned from the lion hunt was distressed both mentally and physically. Her hands were a frightening mess, blistered and swollen as a result of the primitive and horrible witch-hunting torture of immersing the hands in boiling water. Tearfully she related her story.

With her parents, her husband's parents, her sister and her own four children she had fled from the Masanga area of P.E.A. They had camped on the Rhodesian side of the Ruenya River. The reason for their flight was that they were afraid of being involved in the war between the Portuguese and the Makumbi rebels. When the husband rejoined the party after about a week, he was extremely angry with his wife and accused her of being unfaithful to him in his absence. She denied the charge but her husband was adamant and told her that the witchdoctor had confirmed his suspicions. Although both her parents and those of her husband supported the wife's innocence, the husband would not be convinced. Finally, and apparently after further consultation with the witchdoctor, the husband insisted that his wife submit to the boiling water test under threat of death.

The poor woman had little option. The pot of water was placed on the fire, brought to the boil and the wife duly plunged her hands into it. The torture must have been horrible, but all the husband had done was to get up and leave the hut. The woman had no inkling of his further intentions. She had come to me for protection, not – strangely enough – to charge her husband with the vicious assault.

It was a real job getting the story from the girl. I had to rely on Joe, my cook from Portuguese territory, to interpret for me but he was up to the task. Both my African constables were out on patrol. The first thing to be done after hearing the story was to get the woman's injuries treated. I escorted her to Dr. Gurney's clinic myself. He saw me coming and came to meet us. He glared from beneath a shelf of bristling eyebrows.

"I hope it's not more trouble. I have my hands more than full already. What's wrong with that woman's hands?"

I told him the story and he took a cursory look at the girl's injuries.

"Come along with me to the surgery. Those wounds need attention."

The girl and I followed the doctor into the house. Suddenly he stopped.

"On second thoughts, we will not go into the surgery. There's a dead African on the table. It might give her too much of a shock. Actually, I was on the point of sending for you to witness a post-mortem. Bring her into the kitchen."

Doctor Gurney puffed and grunted his way between us in the confines of the small kitchen. He gently wiped the girl's hands, smeared them heavily with a white ointment and then bandaged them securely. The woman looked down at her hands and then at the doctor with an unusual depth of feeling in her eyes. Gurney yelled for his orderly and told him to feed the girl and give her a bed in the compound. I wondered what would have happened to the woman had she not found medical attention so promptly.

"And now," said Gurney, "let's get on with the bigger job in hand." He led me to the surgery. "This African died in the night after he had been sent in by Irvine, the manager at the Olympus Mine. I'm afraid I'm not altogether satisfied with the manner of his death. The post-mortem will clear up things, one way or another."

The dead body lying there on the deal table in front of me made me most uncomfortable. I suppressed a shiver, steeled myself to look at the corpse and tried to avoid inhaling that inexplicable, nauseating smell of death. Post-mortems were definitely not my cup of tea. I felt like vomiting when the seemingly blunt knife sawed through the tough skin of the dead man. Gurney seemed quite at home. With snorts and grunts and perspiration beading his brow, the doctor hacked away until the knife touched the outside rib. Eventually he had hacked away a vee-shaped section of skin. And so it went on – even today the memory is far from comfortable.

"Ah!" exclaimed the doctor, "can you see that black streak across the lung?" I forced my gaze from the open doorway to the object at which he was pointing. "Yes. What does it mean?"

"It confirms the report I had received that this man was involved in an accident at the mine and died as a direct result. When Irvine sent the man in, he merely said that he had been unwell for some time. It's downright man-slaughter and it's about time you did something to improve safety measures at the mines. This sort of thing has been happening all too frequently."

"What evidence do you have? Who informed you of the accident?"

"I can't tell you that. If they are involved they may refuse to give me further information."

I sighed. The doctor was obviously not going to pass on to me whatever other details he possessed regarding the suspicious "accident". No wonder Gurney was so thoroughly disliked by the small-workers. It seemed that he had snoopers in the compounds and quite naturally the miners didn't take kindly to this kind of spying.

"Alright, Doctor, I'll interview Irvine and let you know what transpires."

With business over, Gurney's expression changed. His stern look was replaced with a bright smile and he promptly invited me to stay for lunch.

"And you must see the wonderful present I have just received from America!"

I was more than pleased to get away from the death-filled surgery. I followed the doctor through the dining-room into his small and stuffy office. On his desk was a cloth-draped object. He whisked away the covering with a flourish.

"There! Have you ever seen such a magnificent present?"

I'm afraid I was unable to get quite as enthusiastic as the doctor about his new microscope.

"Let me show you some blood slides. It will be both interesting and instructive. This series of slides has been taken from a fever case over a period of six days."

I groaned inwardly, but at least this was better than messing around with the innards of the gentleman in the surgery. I prepared myself for the lecture and then found that I was completely absorbed.

"With the patient's temperature at 100 degrees, the blood corpuscles reveal little black spots; at 101 the spots on this next slide are more noticeable; at 102 the spots become larger and start growing legs; at 103 the blood is teeming with small 'crabs' and at 104 the tentacles of the crabs look like vicious claws. And now I will show the effect of quinine on the poison the mosquito has injected into the bloodstream. The first slide shows how the 'crabs' have diminished after 30 grains of quinine…"

The slides showed the degeneration of the poison as graphically as the earlier samples had illustrated its growth. I was impressed.

"What happens to the black spots and those terrible-looking crabs when the quinine destroys them?" I asked Gurney.

"It's essential to give the patient opening medicine every morning until the poison is flushed out of the system."

"While on the subject of malaria, Doctor, is quinine the only remedy? I ask because in India I was dosed with calomel and calomel only. My Indian doctor reckoned that quinine was outdated and much too drastic in comparison."

"It just shows how opinions differ," said Gurney. "I am convinced that calomel is too drastic and the cure is a much longer process. But whatever remedies we use here in Rhodesia, let nobody convince you that whisky keeps the fever away. The only 'doctors' to recommend that kind of measure are the whisky distillers themselves. The sundowner custom is a disgusting habit and one which I strongly despise."

I didn't have the courage to disagree.

The smell from the surgery was very much in evidence as we sat down to lunch. Even worse, from my position at the table, I could see the deal table on which the dissection had taken place. When Gurney's servant brought in a dish of pigeon squabs, it was too much. The idea of eating baby pigeons before they had even grown wings, and especially being offered such fare in that mortuary-ridden atmosphere, turned my stomach. Hurriedly, I refused the dish.

"Thank you, but no meat for me, Doctor. I'm not hungry – had too big a breakfast this morning."

"Oh, but you must! These squabs are delicious. I breed them specially and have so many now that I can have at least six a week. Do change your mind."

"No, thank you, Doctor. A slice of bread and butter with cheese will be more than sufficient."

Abruptly the doctor attacked the squabs. I watched with amazement, and it was no longer any surprise to me that the man was so fat.

I was glad when the ordeal came to an end and I could take my rolling eyes from that horrible deal table. The fresh air outside the doctor's residence was a breath of new life and I inhaled deeply all the way up the incline to the camp.

There was no point in postponing the unpleasant interview with Irvine. I saddled Swift and called in "Non", the ugly kaffir dog which was now in fine condition. As I arrived at the Olympus Mine, the skip in the main shaft was being hoisted to the surface and Irvine emerged covered in mud from head to foot.

"Hello, what brings you along here?" he asked with a smile, peering through the covering of mud. "Hell! It's hot down there. I haven't connected up the ventilation shaft as yet and the temperature down at the dead end is killing. I'm completely dehydrated. Come and have a whisky and soda before I die of thirst."

Irvine led the way to his living quarters and his African servant was obviously well trained. The drinks were ready as we entered. The mine manager lost no time in charging the glasses and downed his first drink in one gulp.

"Help yourself," he invited, "while I have a bath and jump into some clean clothes." My host was a New Zealander, a man well over six feet, in his thirties, fair, red-faced and clean-shaven. His inclination towards flabbiness was probably due to his liking for whisky. He reappeared shortly, looking quite different after the bath. He made for the bottle again.

"I've had one hell of a week. Everything has gone wrong. First of all, a broken cam and then, of all things, the camshaft itself went. How a five-inch solid steel axle can break is beyond me. Thank goodness I had a spare but it meant removing all the cams and the refit hung up the mill for two whole days. And all the time the wages bill was piling up and the employees were eating me out of house and home. Running costs seem to escalate the moment the battery stops and there is no gold coming over the plate. And now, to make matters worse, I strongly suspect that some of the employees are stealing the gold. What can you suggest?"

It looked as though my day's troubles were mounting. From the relatively simple but serious incident of the African woman's scalds had come Gurney's carefully contrived allegation of manslaughter at the mine and that in turn had now brought me to the apparent theft of gold. I hoped Irvine was wrong in his suspicions.

"Don't you think that with all your other troubles you may have been mistaken about the gold?" I asked soothingly.

"Not on your life! Last week we struck a rich patch in the mine and when the ore from the area came across the plate I noticed the build-up of amalgam. So much so, in fact, that I had to scrape the table twice a day – and later – three times a day. Each time I collected 30 ounces of amalgam. Suddenly, the scraping came down to 20 ounces in the whole 24 hours and yet the same class of ore was being fed to the mill. To make sure the thief, or thieves – there must be more than one – could not get to the copper plate, I had a frame made of half-inch netting wire and locked this over the plate with steel rods. Last night, at four-hourly intervals, I dressed the table and each time scraped off 25 ounces of amalgam. Do you still think I'm imagining things?"

I was forced to agree with the manager's suspicions.

"The only thing I can suggest," I countered, "is to put a detective on the job. Someone who is no stranger to mining but is not known in the area."

"That sounds a good idea. I would be more than grateful if you could help. The worry is driving me potty. I would take on another European for the night shift except for the fact that this mine is very lenticular – it's not often we strike a lens or kidney as rich as the recent one. The overall output does not warrant extra white supervision."

"From what you tell me, being the owner of a gold mine is not all beer and skittles," I replied.

"You can say that again!" exploded Irvine. "It's anything but a bed of roses. Everything connected with mining is expensive, especially here at Makaha. Transport costs of ore to the railhead by ox-wagon and spares the other way by mule-cart are killing me. It took weeks to land the plant here from Salisbury, the 40 HP boiler was a load itself, the mill another and other essentials a third. Can you imagine what's involved if the mine doesn't come up to expectations and everything has to be moved? When you've got a few months to spare, try dismantling a five-stamp battery and a boiler of this size, transporting them to an alternative site and setting the whole thing up again. One must have a reserve for such emergencies but how can I build up a reserve when the profits are being filched from under my nose. I'm sorry I ever took up gold mining. The Rhodesian public has no idea what the poor struggling small-worker has to contend with."

We sipped our drinks in silence for a few minutes. Much as I hated upsetting the miner further, I had not come for his whisky. I broached the subject quietly.

"Had any serious accidents lately?"

"No...nothing serious at any rate, and certainly nothing worth reporting. Why?"

"Doctor Gurney tells me..."

"That gormandising, blow-gut Arizona Buffalo Bill! I'll shoot him if I see him round here!"

Irvine was off again. The subject of "accidents" I had raised was about as popular in the manager's estimation as all the other delights of gold-mining generally.

"And that goes for that stub-nosed orderly of his," Irvine continued. "He snoops around the compound and everything he sees or hears which he thinks will round his marble gets reported to that interfering Justice of the Peace. I won't have him prying on my mine!"

"I'm sorry to tell you that the African you sent to the clinic with a minor complaint died last night. I was there when Gurney did the post-mortem. In addition to the internal injuries I witnessed myself, there's talk that he'd had a nasty fall underground which caused the injuries."

The news really hit poor Irvine. His mouth fell open and his breathing was suddenly short and strained. Shock kept him silent for a few moments. He was very quiet when he spoke again.

"What are you going to do about it?"

"I'm afraid I've no option. I'll have to summons you before the magistrate and let him decide the outcome."

There was no doubt that the death of the African had touched Irvine deeply. I felt extremely sorry for him, especially after he had impressed me so with the hardships endured by the small-workers. We consumed more liquor and by now Irvine was pouring treble tots into his glass with a trembling hand. Despite the bombshell I had dropped, he insisted that I stayed for dinner. We sat down to a delicious meal – in very definite contrast to the lunch meal. Canned pears, cheese and "Royal Coffee" followed roast beef, roast potatoes and green beans. I was hungry and did full justice to the excellent dinner of Irvine's cook.

The steam hooter blasted forth at 10 p.m. to signal the time for dressing the table. Irvine invited me to go with him. The security screen covering the copper plate was removed and the African in charge of the mill produced two hard brushes. Irvine took one of the brushes and then he and his employee, one on either side of the table, started brushing the silvery amalgam from the bottom part of the table to the top. Most of the amalgam had settled near the 600-battery screen where the water splashed the grit on to the mercury-covered copper. With a square piece of hard rubber, Irvine scraped the amalgam into a heap and then placed it in a porcelain container. More mercury was added to the scraped table and thoroughly brushed into the plate until it shone like a mirror. The five stamps, each weighing over half a ton, were dropped and the grinding of the ore continued through the night.

Irvine led me to his office where he produced a square of calico. He poured the amalgam into the cloth and squeezed out the residual mercury. We were left with 20 ounces of amalgam that Irvine reckoned contained about 45 per cent sponge gold. At the end of the month, all the sponge gold would be melted into bars and taken to the bank. The bank would pay out depending on the fineness. Olympus gold averaged about 750 fine, compared with pure gold at 999 fine.

For the second time that day, I was impressed with what I had seen of other occupations. But I was not tempted by either medicine or mining. "From what you've shown me, Irvine, I think the trooper's life is preferable to being the owner of a gold mine! We might get only five shillings a day, but at least we know that at the end of the month there will be so much in hand. You chaps never know whether you're worth a million or a penny."

"That's true," replied Irvine, who seemed to have recovered from the shock I had brought him. "It is the uncertainty of the gamble for big stakes that makes gold mining so interesting and exciting."

I was in the saddle and almost on the way back to Makaha when he again raised the subject of my visit.

"I'm damned sorry about all this. I should have reported the accident but at the time I honestly didn't think it was that serious. I only hope they don't hang me."

I was caught in that peculiar circumstance which every policeman faces. My sympathies were with Irvine but I couldn't express them. I trotted off back to Makaha.

Chapter Three – Goldmines

Before continuing with my chronicle of police life at Makaha in 1916, it might be of interest to offer a short geographical summary of that almost inaccessible area more often known in those days as the Kaiser Wilhelm Gold Belt which formed the north-eastern portion of Southern Rhodesia. The area lay principally within the administrative district of Mtoko but the gold belt extended across the Ruenya River into the northern portion of the Inyanga district. The Mtoko Native Reserve straddled the western edge of the belt, Crown Land – in which most of the active mining was situated – in the centre and Lawley's Concession astride the Ruenya River to the east. Evidence of mining activity from the earliest times was evident in the Makaha district. Native grindstones and the foundations of granaries could be seen on almost every piece of level ground which was reasonably near permanent water. The ruins of a few terraced gardens existed but the occurrence of these was rare when compared to the stepped slopes of the Luangwa Hills north of Inyanga.

Without terracing, the steep and stony hillsides of Makaha offered small encouragement to agricultural pursuits. This left only mining to attract African activity and their ancient workings potholed the area. Every mine in the district had been pegged over one or more of these old attempts. Fortifications crowned some of the hills and a fine example was situated on the southern peak of the Sequesa range overlooking the Ruenya. This ruin had a circular wall about eighty yards in diameter and was probably of native construction. On the other hand, a square fort situated on flat ground less than a mile from the Inyamsizi was attributed to the Portuguese pioneers of the early 17th Century. The Portuguese were trading in gold at that time and had a station at Luanze, probably somewhere near the present location of Mtoko.

Karl Mauch (of Zimbabwe fame) visited the Makaha region in 1872, discovered or rediscovered gold and claimed the ground for Germany as the Kaiser Wilhelm Goldfield. The name was retained until well into the 1920's. Mauch returned to Germany hoping to raise capital for the development of his claim, published his valuable book telling of his travels and then died a few years later in poverty and disillusionment. In 1895 Cecil Rhodes granted to A.L. Lawley and George Pauling the right for each to peg a concession of 75 square miles. This was their reward for their efforts in constructing the Beira railway.

Pauling staked his claim in the Kaiser Wilhelm field and at once transferred his rights to Lawley. In 1898, the concession was acquired by Monomatapa Concessions and they crushed some ore in the Sequesa Range between 1909 and 1911. They didn't make a profit! In my time at Makaha (1916), the concession was owned by Sir Thomas Cullinan and the only mines active were the Olympus, the Radnor (the biggest producer) and the Koodoo. Other mines – Non Pareil, Craig, Sultan, Mount Newman, Old Umbella, the Chipenguli West Extension and several others – had stopped producing and were lying derelict. In those days they were non-paying but the increased price of gold might have made a difference in later years. I wonder?

Morkel, the Mtoko Native Commissioner, sent word to me that he had received complaints that a hippo was destroying the gardens of Africans on the Ruenya. Would I investigate, confirm the reports and, if necessary, destroy the beast? I was glad of a break in the routine of issuing registration certificates and adjudicating in African family squabbles so I made preparations to leave immediately.

Riding down the Makaha Valley on *Swift*, my pony, and accompanied by an African constable, my batman and the nondescript dog I had acquired, I was more than thankful to be out of the office with the prospect of breaking in a sizeable chunk of new territory.

My first stop was the Koodoo Mine. Two Australian brothers were working the place and had this and the Found Mine on tribute. O. W. Kelly, the elder, had lost his arm in a nasty accident on the mine. It seems that he was wearing an old torn sports coat when he entered the engine room. As he examined the oil gauge, a loose piece of his coat was caught in the belt and he was dragged bodily into the fast-moving machinery and almost certain death. Fortunately he had the presence of mind to fling his free arm around a substantial wooden post supporting the roof of the room and hung on... literally for grim life. The other arm waswrenched from its socket and fed into the machinery. Hence he was known as "One-Armed Kelly" and his brother referred to as Captain Kelly.

Working for the brothers was a former member of the Force, ex-Trooper Crossland. I think he was overanxious to show off the secrets of his new employment and he suggested that I accompany him underground. Climbing from one level to the next on home-made wooden ladders, swaying at the end of equally rough rope ladders and skidding and sliding down open slopes on my backside was anything but interesting. I'm convinced he took me to almost inaccessible spots just to show me what a wonderful miner he was and how hard was the life of a small-worker. I was not impressed!

Some months later I had to descend from a catwalk into an 80 foot void to examine the body of an African. The man had missed his footing in the gloom and dived headlong to the bottom of the excavation. One side of his head was crushed like an eggshell and his neck was driven deep into his chest by the force of the impact. Rails should have protected such dangerous spots, in terms of the mining regulations. So also moving machinery should have been guarded. The Kelly brothers were later fined £25 for their negligence.

When discussing Irvine's problems of the theft of amalgam at the Olympus Mine with the Australians, they told me that they suspected similar happenings at the Koodoo. They readily agree to look for a reliable African from their own mine to act as detective at Irvine's place on some sort of reciprocal basis.

I continued my journey down the valley and into the increasingly lush tropical growth that flourishes at this low altitude. I passed the original Kaiser Wilhelm workings and glanced at the piles of rusting machinery, memorials to the endeavours and vanished optimism of those who had sought riches in the banded ironstone.

Late in the afternoon, we reached the river, found a suitable spot and camped for the night. Neither of my companions was familiar with the area and there were no Africans in the vicinity – probably because of the stony nature of the terrain. I left the problem of finding my bearings until the next day.

Despite the absence of kraals, game was scarce. We caught sight of a small herd of waterbuck, a few zebra and a kudu bull. The animals were wild and we could get nowhere near them. In the small hours of the morning a lion roared in the distance.

We set off up the river the next day in search of native settlements. The going was rough and although we had found nothing of the kraals, the animals tired rapidly and I called an early halt. No sooner had we off-saddled than two Africans made an appearance. They were fleeing from the violence of the Makumbi Rebellion in PEA and this was the first confirmation I had received of the outbreak. Two other Africans pitched up soon afterwards and although they knew where there were hippos, they knew nothing of the existence of crops that might have been ravaged by the wildlife.

We moved on up the riverbank until a steep face overhanging the water confronted us. The only way through was over the hills but the climb was worthwhile in terms of the view from the summit. Standing on a ledge overlooking the river, I was able to gaze straight down into an enormous pool of clean, clear water bordered by tall reeds, bullrushes and water-grass. A shoal of fish swimming lazily near the surface fascinated me. Suddenly, without the slightest warning ripple on the water, a massive hippo bull surfaced beneath the ledge and blew a spout of water from his nostrils before submerging once more. For several seconds I could see his huge body moving through the depths. A few minutes later, he surfaced again and the circus performance continued, apparently for my sole benefit, accompanied by the grunting noises of a domestic pig. The comedy was heightened by the ugly, ponderous proportions of the beast – large square head, long tasks and massive neck showing high above the surface of the water.

Later, just before sunset, three cows and a small calf entered the ring. The new arrivals kept well away from my vantage point on the ledge but the bull showed no concern at my presence. When "Non" barked at the monster, he became almost aggressive in his performance and was determined to upstage the cows to the point at which his frolics were repeated closer and closer to the ledge on which I stood.

More Africans appeared as if from nowhere and immediately begged me to shoot the hippo. He was known, they said, as a "bad one" and quite capable of attacking humans. I tried to explain that I had no intention of despatching the bull unless I was given visible evidence of his troublesome nature. I asked the new arrivals if they knew of maize fields in the vicinity. They did, but they were a considerable distance away. The Africans were convinced that this was the hippo with the reputation of destroying those same crops. If I destroyed him now, no more damage would be done to the gardens.

I discovered later that the Africans, all eight of them, were refugees from over the border. Not one of them owned crops on the Rhodesian side and their enthusiasm for killing the hippo was difficult to understand. The inconsistency, added to my own deep reluctance to take life unnecessarily, saved the day for the hippo bull. Even today I remember the elephant, rhino and giraffe I killed during those years, especially during my Kalahari Patrol, with the deepest regret. Every instance stands out vividly and is recalled with sorrow and at times a knot in the throat. One cannot forget the fear or the helplessness in the eyes of an animal before it dies. I knew that if I killed this playful hippo, I would be miserable for the rest of my life. I decided to return to Makaha the following day and, during the night, the hippo family seemed to be celebrating their reprieve by a series of loud splashes as if they were diving from the banks of the river.

Early the next morning I walked down to the edge of the water looking for game tracks. Following a wide footpath made by the hippo through the dense reeds, I nearly stepped on the ugly triangular head of a python. The reptile's head was the size of a dinner plate and his thick shining body sprawled in my path seemed to have no end. He might have been dozing in the weak morning sun or digesting an enormous midnight meal but when he became aware of my presence he reared up until the horrible head was level with my own. Then he twisted backwards, showing his white underbelly. Yards and yards of snake passed before my popping eyes as he sought escape. I was frozen stiff with horror until I realised that the reptile had vanished, leaving only the crackling of reeds and waving undergrowth as a reminder of his presence. I have no idea of the girth or length of the python. In any case, my frightened condition would have probably doubled the actual size. Be that as it may, he was certainly the granddaddy of all the pythons in the vicinity. I have never been able to scrape up any enthusiasm for snakes and bees – one seems to have no protection against their sudden and unexpected attacks.

On my way back to Makaha, I stopped again at the Koodoo Mine for a cup of tea with the Kelly brothers. I told them of what I had seen. In turn they told me the story connected with the original rediscovery of the workings at the Kaizer Wilhelm.

A narrow adit into the hill was found and when this was widened and a blockage cleared of fallen rock, the main shaft was opened up. At the face of the workings was a fairly large chamber in which were the remains of two human skeletons. The moment air got to the remains, the bones crumbled into fine dust – so much so that nothing could be retrieved. It was suggested that the bodies had been there for many years and that the miners had suffocated when the adit had been closed, either by human agency or by sudden heavy rains. Apart from some stone implements, there was no evidence of wood or iron tools. It is common knowledge that the earliest miners heated the gold bearing rocks in fires and poured cold water over them to reveal the cracks containing the ore. The gold was then scraped out for further treatment. It is quite possible that the ancient miners had been suffocated after their fires had exhausted the oxygen in the blocked tunnel.

An urgent note from Doctor Gurney awaited me and, when I had dumped my kit, I wandered over to see the old missionary. He was in a high state of excitement over the hundreds of refugees streaming over the border. He reckoned that we were about to be attacked and wanted a meeting of all the Europeans in Makaha so that we could plan our defences! He claimed the right, as Justice of the Peace, to take charge until such time as the Native Commissioner or someone from Salisbury could be sent to take over. I tried to calm him down, told him that such a meeting would only arouse the fears of the population and that I would contact Mtoko and Salisbury for advice.

Chapter Four – The Makumbi Rebellion

The extent of the exodus from across the border in the van of the Makumbi Rebellion and Dr Gurney's fears on the subject were undoubtedly exaggerated. To some degree, I shared his misgivings but neither of us had any definite information on which to base the "laager" precautions insisted on by the missionary. Knowing how primitive natives tend to make mountains out of molehills – understandable when one considers that their lives rarely offered anything in the way of real excitement – I was wary of making a fool of myself by sending an SOS to Salisbury. Even an urgent message to Morkel, the Mtoko Native Commissioner, might create the same unnecessary alarm and despondency.

As I left Dr Gurney's clinic, the imponderables of the situation weighed heavily on my mind. Rather than act in haste, I decided to sleep on the problem.

That night was one of the most miserable in memory. I tossed and turned in my fitful slumbers and dreamt of black and white humans hacking and slashing at each other with assegais to inflict gaping wounds from which blood refused to flow. From 3 a.m. further sleep was out of the question and the vividness of my dreams had frayed my nerves to the extent that I was almost beside myself. The "bloodless battles" and Gurney's dire predictions merged almost to reality. It was just possible that such a conflict could be precipitated upon the small community at Makaha. Groping in my befuddled mind, I suddenly hit on a solution.

I had already made the acquaintance of Senor Maldanado, the Civil Commissioner for the Masanga area just across the border. I had visited his camp where I had been lavishly entertained with excellent food and many glasses of a light red wine. Maldanado was the most logical person to consult on the true extent of the rebellion and his local knowledge placed him in a position where his advice would be invaluable to me.

It was 4 a.m. when I decided to pay the Portuguese Commissioner a visit. It was about thirty miles to Masanga and I intended to spend the night in the Portuguese camp and return to Makaha the next day. For this reason, I took only the minimum with me – a 6mm Mauser and a canvas water bag. I discarded even a blanket in my haste to be under way and make the best possible time to Masanga.

Before leaving the village I called in at the clinic to tell Gurney exactly what I intended doing. His fears about the local situation had grown to the extent that he was convinced I was riding to my doom. His explosion at my plan of action came as no surprise but he swore that if he had any authority over me he would have expressly forbidden my departure. I tried to tell him that as far as I could see, there was no danger even in a horde of fleeing refugees. He was taking the whole matter far too seriously. Finally, I played my trump card by telling him that it was just possible that he would be held responsible for the financial loss if his panic forced the closure of the mines. I left the missionary while his face was still drooping at my warning.

The sense of novelty and adventure with which I rode away from the village was refreshing after my worried night and the argument with Gurney. Instead of making for the main road to Tete – which in any case was only a track – I went past the camp of Marley Brothers, the timber contractors to the mines, and took an open footpath around the foot of the Zodonia Hill in the direction of the Ruenya River and Masanga.

As soon as I had left the gold belt formation behind me, I was in the typically granite terrain with rocky kopjes rising out of the msasa forest. It was attractive country and I kept my eyes peeled for game. Although there were easily seen tracks of sable, waterbuck and eland, I saw nothing moving.

About three hours and thirteen miles after leaving Makaha, as I was lounging comfortably in the saddle, deep in thought, while *Swift* ambled along, we were jerked suddenly from our oblivion when a flock of guinea fowl took to the air in front of us. Despite the fright the pony and I received, the presence of birds was an indication that there was water close by. Sure enough, after another few hundred yards, we came to a narrow deep ravine with a pool of clear clean water at the bottom. From the spoor around the water it was apparent that herds of game used the pool.

It was as good a place as any to take a breather. I off-saddled *Swift*, laid the saddle under a big tree that offered ample shade and led the pony to the water where he slaked his thirst greedily. I was in the act of knee-haltering the horse when, for the second time within a few minutes, the peace and quiet of the countryside was rudely disturbed, this time by the sound of a shot and quite close at that. Moreover, the report indicated a muzzle-loader, which is very different from the noise of a breech-loading rifle.

I hurried for my own weapon, which I had left with the saddle, and loaded it. Within five minutes a herd of seven waterbuck crashed through the bush into the glade. As the lead bull saw *Swift*, he led the charge in a sharp turn and the mad rush continued down the ravine in a cloud of dust to vanish in the distant forest.

I put down my rifle and was untying the water bag from the saddle when I noticed that *Swift* had one leg raised, his head was erect and his ears were pointing in the direction from which the herd had first appeared. Looking in the same direction, I was surprised to see a huge waterbuck bull struggling along on three legs in the tracks of the herd, the off hind dangling loosely. As soon as the bull saw *Swift* he stopped, held his head high, and blew through his nostrils at the pony. It was at that moment that I squeezed the hair trigger of the Mauser and the high-velocity slug struck the buck in the neck and dropped him in his tracks.

As I walked towards the dead animal I received a further surprise. Three natives carrying assegais and hunting axes appeared, followed by a fourth African with an ancient muzzle-loader on his shoulder. On seeing me, they stopped and were uncertain whether to approach in response to my waving arm or turn tail back into the forest. I could see them discussing the point and eventually they drummed up enough courage to walk up to me with puzzled expressions on their worn faces. They were far from fit and were obviously leading a hand-to-mouth existence. They gazed at me with fear in their white-walled eyes.

"Who shot the Isidumuka (waterbuck in Ndebele)?" I asked with a broad smile on my face. There was no reply. They obviously understood not a word of what I was saying. Then followed the deaf and dumb language of much arm waving, gesturing and wiggling of fingers. Eventually my question was answered when the man carrying the gun laid the weapon on the carcass and pointed to himself. I might have guessed!

Leaving the gun lying on the dead buck, the quartet indicated that they were thirsty and moved on to the pool. I examined the ancient muzzle-loader and surreptitiously removed the firing cap from the nipple and then eased the hammer home. I replaced the gun on the carcass. The natives returned and three of them immediately started skinning the beast while the fourth (and fittest-looking of the group) grabbed his axe and hurried in the direction from which they had come. I understood that he was off to fetch the remainder of the hunting party.

Within half-an-hour fires were kindled and the aroma of grilling meat saturated the glade. I helped myself to half of the liver and started my own grilling operations. Of all game meat, waterbuck tastes the worst. It has a smell of its own and, even after thorough cooking, the fat seems to stick to the roof of the mouth and can only be removed with the exercise of a finger. This particular waterbuck was a massive bull and must have weighed close on 400 pounds.

About an hour later, a string of Africans, including women and children, followed the messenger into the clearing. There must have been about forty of them in all. I then received yet another shock in this day of surprises One youth – he must have been in his late teens although it was hard to estimate with any kind of accuracy – wearing almost nothing in front and precious little behind, approached me with a broad smile on his very black face and said: "Dag baas!" in perfect Afrikaans. My amazement to be greeted thus in this wilderness by a naked aboriginal had me tongue-tied for the moment. I recovered to return the greeting in the same language and ask him where he had been taught Afrikaans. He told me that he had been born at a school on the Nyasaland-Mocambique border at Mwanza where missionaries of the Dutch Reformed Church had penetrated. Apparently, he had stayed at the mission for most of his life until his mother (who had been employed there) died, after which his uncle had taken him back into Portuguese territory.

Here was the obvious opportunity to get first-hand information on the rebellion, the reason for my journey. I questioned the youth and he replied that although he and his family had not been involved in the uprising, they were afraid of being murdered on one hand by the rebels and on the other by the Portuguese soldiers. This was the reason for their flight across the Ruenya. "We are not the only ones, more are following and should be here soon," concluded my informant.

There and then I decided to postpone the journey to Masanga and await the arrival of the rest of the refugees. If I could obtain all the news I was after from them, my journey to the Portuguese Commissioner would be unnecessary and I would be able to return to Makaha and then forward my information to Salisbury much sooner.

The refugees, who looked most unhappy, tired and depressed, spread themselves at the pool and began washing their faces and tired swollen feet. Their toilet complete, they settled down to a feast of grilled water-buck. And what a feed! They were obviously starving and devoured the half-raw meat with grunts of satisfaction as fast as they could shovel it into their mouths.

Late in the afternoon a further score of refugees arrived. These were all elderly, some extremely so and stricken in years. One doddering, bald and grey-faced old man seemed to give all the orders and was immediately obeyed with respect. This could only be the headman and the one to question, once I had allowed him to rest and satisfy his hunger from the dwindling remains of the waterbuck.

The headman was in such a state of exhaustion and the sun was dropping so fast in the west that I resigned myself to spending the night at the pool. Wiri, my newfound interpreter, was asked to help me make myself as comfortable as possible. He and a couple of his pals axed down a pair of six-foot poles, laid the logs side by side with a space of about two feet between and filled the hollow with soft grass. Here was my rough and ready, but amazingly comfortable bed. The trio also gathered dry wood and kindled a fire a few feet from my "two-poster".

Sitting on the bed with my arms about my knees and waiting patiently for the headman to recover, I received the biggest fright in a day of many surprises. A streak of yellow brindle flashed into view and knocked me flat on the bed. My face was then treated to a scrubbing broken only by whimpering whines and howls of delight. I had been found by Non, my kaffir dog who had tracked me all the way from Makaha. The poor thing was almost berserk with pleasure – he wet himself, jumped and bounced all over me and even seemed to be laughing at my amazement.

My cook told me later that he had kept the dog tied up until midday, as I had instructed. Joe had fed the animal at noon and then released him. But he had appeared again for his evening meal and only after six in the evening had Non taken it upon himself to set out after me. It was incredible that he had been able to follow my cold tracks after so many hours. Poor old faithful Non, he was to suffer a murderous death only a few days later.

The stars were well into the heavens when I had finished another snack of liver and washed the food down with a long drink of cold water from the canvas bag.

I summoned Wiri and asked him to bring the headman to me. He came without delay, accompanied by four equally elderly Africans. They settled themselves on the other side of the fire and Wiri squatted next to me. The interrogation began.

I questioned the men long into the night. With the usual difficulties of interpretation, the following story emerged.

The Portuguese were engaged on the widening and reconstruction of a broad road from Macequece to Tete and for the necessary labour force had relied on Africans living near the road who would benefit from the new line of communication. However, if the stretch of road happened to pass through a relatively uninhabited area, labour was recruited from further afield. The conditions under which the labour force worked were extremely severe. The workmen had to supply their own food, their own tools – mostly badzas and axes – and even receptacles in the form of baskets or clay pots in which to cart earth and stones. Hunters, specially appointed for the purpose, were supposed to supply meat for the workers' rations but, as often as not, there was little game to be seen over long periods. For as much as a week at a time there would be no meat ration.

The small quantities of food brought by the respective families were soon consumed and, in the absence of a meat ration, they were forced to live virtually off the country – and if the hunters could not find game, what hope did the workers have of success in their "spare time".

The work itself was very tough and, although hundreds of natives might be employed on the project, progress on the wide straight road was painfully slow.

Matters came to a head when the workers on the project rebelled against the worsening conditions under the leadership of one Makumbi. Immediately there were casualties among both workers and overseers, troops were called in and the violence snowballed into a full-scale uprising. Even Africans who had been unprovoked by the road-building operation were drawn into the conflict by Makumbi, who intimidated them into taking up arms against the authorities. Some joined the rebels but others fled in the hopes of escaping the violence of the opposing factions. Some sought sanctuary to the north in Nyasaland but many crossed the Ruenya into Rhodesia.

In many respects I could not help but feel sorry for these people, the innocent victims of understandable violence on the other side of the border. But what advice could I offer them? For them to stay where they were, unregistered and carrying arms for which they had no permits, was out of the question as far as I was concerned. The only thing that I could suggest was that they made their way to Masanga and interviewed Senor Maldanado. I knew him for a conscientious man and a sincere friend of the local Africans. He was the best intercessor to plead the African cause to his superiors in Tete.

One of the more junior elders who suffered the disfigurement of an ugly scar across his cheek answered my suggestion. "Senor Maldanado may be alive no longer. One gang of rebels planned to peg him over an ant hill and let the ants feed on his naked body."

The calmness with which the man disclosed the rebel threat was some indication of the state of affairs over the border. The information shook me but I countered that they should attempt to warn or rescue Maldanado. I gave them little alternative. I would not allow them to stay in Rhodesia unless they agreed to be registered and handed over their weapons. Furthermore, the "British Lion" would not allow them to shoot his game!

There was dead silence at the ultimatum. Eventually the headman, with a tired, faded expression in his eyes, said: "I know Maldanado, he is a friend of mine. Your suggestion is a good one and we will go to Masanga as you have advised."

I was more than a little relieved at the acceptance of my ultimatum. I expressed my gratitude on their agreement, both for their own sakes and that of my Portuguese acquaintance across the border. I sincerely hoped they would arrive in time.

I turned my attentions to *Swift* who had been surfeited with green leaves gathered from the reeds near the water, and gave my faithful pariah dog a further supply of bones to see him through the night. Then I climbed between the logs and made myself comfortable with the saddle numnah over my shoulders and the saddle beneath my head. It was a restless night. Non insisted on gnawing his bones next to my ear to which symphony was added the sound of *Swift* breaking wind every few minutes as the green leaves fermented in his stomach. I was glad when dawn came and I could move to the fire to thaw the aches and pains from my joints.

When all the refugees had left with the faithful promise to go straight to Masanga and Senor Maldanado, I saddled *Swift* and mounted, my mind already struggling with the details of my report for Mtoko and Salisbury.

Chapter Five – Reinforcements

AFTER my long interview with the refugees from across the border, the early morning ride back to Makaha was singularly uneventful. On reaching the village, I rode straight to Dr Gurney's home. The old missionary, I knew, would be anxious to hear first-hand news of the "dangers imminent" as a result of the rebellion in Portuguese East Africa.

Gurney's cherubic red face lit up as he greeted me. Almost in one breath he invited me in for breakfast, asked if I had discovered anything, if I had experienced any trouble, informed me that he had already held a meeting to discuss the emergency and that another had been scheduled that afternoon at which my presence was imperative. The questions poured out like mealies from a punctured bag. I ignored them all except the invitation to breakfast. There was an inner man to be satisfied before the curiosity of the panicky maiden American missionary.

The meal was delicious and I did justice to everything laid before me. As I emptied the plate before me, I became more sympathetic to Gurney's all-consuming fears. In my absence he had received reports that refugees were literally flooding into the area. I quickly countered this exaggeration with my own experiences and I think the doctor was almost disappointed when I told him that there was no cause for alarm. And then I reached that part of my narrative dealing with the rebels' threatened treatment of Senhor Maldanado – that they planned to spreadeagle him naked over an ant-hill. I thought Gurney would have a fit. His eyes widened and his face turned a brilliant crimson.

"There you are," he spluttered. "What did I tell you? We must flee or get troops in to defend Makaha before we too are pegged out over a nest of white ants."

I chided myself for over-dramatising the situation by mentioning the unsupported rumour, just when my intention was to calm the worst of the doctor's fears. The damage was done however, and I left the clinic with its supervisor in a worse state than when I had arrived. I by-passed the police station and headed directly for Willie Kaplan's store-cum-post-office.

(Editor's Note:
A new $65,000 bridge over the Nyadire River was opened on 16 March 1970, and named the "Barney Kaplan Bridge" by Mrs Sadie Kaplan, widow of the "father of the Mtoko District" who died three years ago. Barney Kaplan

arrived in Mtoko in 1911, started a general store and later the first hotel in which the original "rooms" were grass huts. Barney Kaplan had two brothers: Willie, who ran the store in Makaha, and Maurice who operated a similar store at the Olympus Mine, some eight miles from Makaha.)

Barratt, who ran the post-office side of the business and also helped Willie with his book-keeping, tried at my request to get through to Morkel, the Native Commissioner at Mtoko. The telephone was a very dubious line of communication in those days. The single wire was carried across country on relatively short wooden poles and the hazards of grassfires, and the natives who found the telephone wire ideally suited to the manufacture of snares meant that the line was as often out of use as operational. Now, in an emergency, I was almost sure that the line would let us down as usual. But I was wrong. After repeated attempts, I managed to speak to Mrs Roche, the wife of the NC's clerk, who was also the Mtoko postmistress. I carefully explained the position to her and I asked her to pass on the message to Morkel and to Corporal Sutton at the police camp there. I told Mrs Roche that I would be waiting for a return call in response to my report.

As I stood waiting for a reply from Mtoko, everyone who entered the store wanted a full report on the so-called "invasion". Clark, the manager of the Radnor Mine, was among them but his interrogation was broached with a broad grin. After I had put him in the picture on my interview with the fleeing Africans he burst into roars of laughter.

"I thought as much," he grinned. "The only person in Makaha scared out of his wits is the honourable Doctor. He demanded that we should all attend an emergency meeting yesterday and we are supposed to attend another session this afternoon. Now I have heard your report – which is just about what I expected – there's no point in stopping work for a second day in succession. I hope our absence will be an indication to Gurney of just how ridiculous are his fears."

It was a full hour before the call came through and, when the message did come, it was hardly worth waiting for.

"Await further instructions!"

I made my way up to the police camp where Joe, my faithful old cook had already got wind of my return and had a steaming hipbath with which to greet me. He was even more pleased to see that Non, my dog, was with me, having anticipated a tongue-lashing for allowing the hound to escape.

After my bath I relaxed and tried to get down on paper as much as possible of my interview with the refugees while the story was still fresh in my mind.

On the following day my further instructions arrived in the persons of Major Spain, OC District, and Mr Taberer, Chief Native Commissioner for Mashonaland. A Native Department retinue – two interpreters and a messenger from Mtoko, further swelled the ranks of the visitors. My first reaction to the VIP invasion was to wonder how on earth I was to accommodate, feed and entertain them "in a manner befitting". Joe rose to the occasion like a veteran and appeared before our guests in spotless white trousers, white shirt, red belt and red fez. I had no idea that he even possessed such uniform.

He further excelled himself by producing a tray with cups and saucers and a pot of tea. How my old cook had so quickly realised that we were hosting "the quality" from Salisbury was explained when he later told me that the Native Department messengers had tipped him off on what might be expected as soon as the party arrived.

Between sips of tea and mouthfuls of Marie biscuits, Major Spain explained that he had no intention of imposing himself upon Makaha for the night. He and Taberer wanted to camp nearer the border (near a prominent kraal) to which all refugees would be directed for personal interrogation "at high level". I had to confess ignorance of the kraal's location but the Mtoko messenger seemed to be familiar with it.

I gave Major Spain the full report that I had written the day before and, while he and Taberer were actually poring over it, more refugees arrived in Makaha. In the group were three Coloureds who had been employed in the Post Office at Tete. Armed already with my information, Major Spain and the Chief Native Commissioner gathered the new arrivals in the office and immediately started to question them. The exercise was considerably easier than my struggle with Wiri and his broken Afrikaans. However, the information obtained was little different to that which I had discovered. My main cause of worry, the plight of Senhor Maldanado, was not relieved. The men knew nothing of his whereabouts or whether the rebels had carried out their threats on the Portuguese official.

I was convinced that the Makaha "Chief of Staff" would confront my visitors from Salisbury before long and, sure enough, as Taberer was interviewing the three Coloureds, Doctor Gurney puffed up the hill and demanded a hearing. He was shown into the office in due course where he spluttered and stammered and offered all sorts of advice which, it was made plain, was not required. Finally, Spain politely told the missionary that all the matters causing him such trepidation would be attended to and the American was dismissed. He left the office like a pricked balloon.

Although Major Spain had said he intended moving further east as soon as possible, the questioning of the refuges took time and I realised that I should have to provide lunch. Once again Joe rose to the occasion and, when we returned to the quarters, I was staggered to see the dining-table laid with a new white table-cloth, new crockery, new cutlery, new serviettes and, in the centre of the table, a large plate containing a hunk of delicious corned brisket and a large bowl of potato salad covered in mayonnaise. (Joe excelled in making mayonnaise from egg yolks, salad oil and vinegar.) Even dessert had been remembered and on a side dish were eight cooked apples with cores removed and filled with sugar. I was not prepared to spoil the feast by asking where the food had come from and my guests, as surprised at the spread as myself while mumbling excuses about not really intending to stay for lunch, tucked in and cleaned up the dishes. They were loud in their praise of old Joe and followed up their delight by each tipping him half-a-crown. I watched Joe accept the money and wondered exactly how much the meal had cost me! After lunch Major Spain outlined his future plans. They were to set up camp close to the border and, with the help of the local natives, bring all the refugees to their post. Then Taberer would lecture the immigrants on the laws of Rhodesia, specifically that they should obtain Registration Certificates, surrender or destroy their firearms, be prepared to obey local chiefs and headmen, etc.

In my own capacity as Pass Officer, I was instructed to issue passes without the usual charge and also make out the necessary Registration Certificates, again without charge. All mail for the officials would be delivered to Makaha and arrangements were made for one of the messengers to collect this and return with one of my native constables. Thereafter, it would be my responsibility to ensure that the mail was delivered daily by the constable, once he knew exactly where the official camp was located. Major Spain's parting shot shattered any illusions I had about the removal of responsibility in the emergency.

"By the way, five or six troopers are on their way here and I trust you will be able to feed and accommodate them until other arrangements can be made."

As soon as the guests had ridden off I sought out my cook. First things first!

"Where on earth did you manage to rustle up such a magnificent lunch?" I demanded.

Poor old Joe, whose eyes were constantly red and whose skin was never without a covering of fine white ash from the smoky kitchen, spluttered and mumbled and finally came out with "Baas Kapilen (Kaplan)". It seemed that Joe was fully aware of the precarious state of the larder when the visitors had arrived. I was very busy so he had taken it upon himself to run down to the store and explain our plight. He had poured out his troubles to "Kapilen" and "Light" (Wright – Kaplan's butcher) and it so happened that the fare we had so thoroughly enjoyed had been intended for the two men's lunch. With typical generosity, they had allowed their midday meal together to be commandeered and, for good measure, had thrown in the brand-new table linen and crockery from the shelves of the store.

The dessert was a story on its own. For some time I had been receiving weekly consignments of apples from the Rhodes Fruit Farms at Inyanga. The first unsolicited paraffin case of fruit had been most acceptable and I had promptly sent off £1 by return in payment. The money came back with more apples and a note.

"We will not accept payment from you and further supplies are here for the asking."

When I told Joe that we could expect another half-dozen mouths to feed, his jaw dropped. All he could mutter was "Skoff?" with a very obvious question mark. As host, I shared his consternation. My batman, in charge of three native witnesses, was despatched to Inyanga with money and a request for two more cases of apples. It would take them two days of fast walking to get there but I tried to impress upon the batman the urgency of the mission.

Meat was problem number two. I summoned one of the Coloureds from Tete and, with Non on a lead, set out for the hills behind the camp with the intention of trying to bag a kudu. Less than a mile from the quarters, I was lucky enough to see a solitary old bull browsing from a tree. Although his head and neck were well covered by leaves, his body was almost broadside on. It was an easy target and I made sure of a heart shot. The report of the rifle echoed through the hills, the buck reared on his hind legs and crashed down the hill through the undergrowth. Following the blood spoor, I was convinced that at any moment I would come upon the dead bull but, to my surprise, the tracks went on and on. I paused and motioned to my companion to do likewise, hoping to hear the thrashings of the wounded animal. Non was whining to be released but, after quietening him, there was dead silence. A very faint "hoo-hoo-hoo" call of wild dogs I put down to my imagination but nothing could be heard of the wounded kudu. Finally I decided to release Non, hoping the dog would lead us to the wounded bull.

No sooner had I unleashed the little kaffir-dog, who sped off in the tracks of the bull, than I realised that the wild dogs I thought I had imagined were very much a reality. The "kak-kak-kak" of the pack almost submerged the unmistakeable bellowing of the wounded buck. I chased down the path in Non's wake to the scene of the commotion. As I pushed through the heavy undergrowth, a scene was revealed which beggars the imagination.

Poor old Non was lying outside a ring of a dozen or so wild dogs, covered in blood and with his stomach and entrails ripped from his body. He was quite dead. The stinking odour of wild dogs was everywhere as they fought over the carcass of the dead kudu, tearing great chunks of bloody meat with their massive jaws. The power of those teeth and the disgusting way in which the pack swallowed the meat without even pausing to chew on it was frightening in its utter abandon. Seeing my poor, faithful, inoffensive pet lying dead at the edge of the carnage and the once magnificent bull being torn to ribbons by the hideous carnivores, released a torrent of rage and vengeance within me. I aimed at the largest dog in the pack which was trying to gulp down a massive piece of meat and fired a bullet into the ugly head. The sound of the shot interrupted the disgusting feast. The pack mustered to one side of the carcass with much conversational, almost bird-like twittering. The dogs faced me, their rounded black ears straight up but their bloodied jaws still working on their spoils. A second shot at another large animal in the stinking pack seemed to make them aware of the new danger. They retreated in all directions – but not for long. The bolder and more aggressive members of the pack circled the dead bull, lifted their heads high and slowly advanced on me.

I cursed into the evening air. There were only two cartridges left in the revolving magazine of the 6.5 Manlichter Mauser and the chase had taken me some three miles from camp. It would have been utterly foolish to have emptied the gun into the loathsome pack, especially as the sun had vanished below the horizon and dusk was setting in fast. Reluctantly I backed away from the stinking horde and returned to camp, cursing both my lack of foresight and ammunition. I would have butchered every single member of the pack and enjoyed the slaughter. Of all the wild animals in this country, the wild dog must be the most hated. The packs hunt and bring down live prey, pursuing their victim and all the time tearing great mouthfuls from the living flesh. They are quite capable of turning on their own kind and treating their mates in the same vicious and sickening fashion. I have never heard of another carnivorous species being so cannibalistic as wild dogs.

It was quite dark when I reached the camp. Joe's reaction to Non's death was touching and his cup of sorrow was overflowing when I told him how our larder had been robbed of the massive kudu bull. I was equally distraught and in my anger decided to sacrifice one of the heifers from my herd to feed the expected troopers. This decision had a consoling effect on Joe. I think he was almost as worried as I was about ensuring that our guests were well fed during their stay. Other problems piled up on each other in the course of the evening.

A note from Gurney told me that the woman who had suffered the boiling water torture was ready for discharge – could I ensure that she was not subjected to a repetition of her husband's brutality? The mail brought a Court Summons to be served on Irvine to answer charges of neglect resulting from the death of one of his employees in Gurney's surgery. Captain Kelly was sending me an African who would try to uncover the mystery of the amalgam thefts from the Olympus Mine. Non's death, the sacrifice of one of my prized heifers and this mountain of police work, all added to the overall worries of local involvement in the Makumbi Rebellion, combined to make that evening at Makaha one of the most miserable of my life.

Chapter Six – My African Cook

Despite the worries of the previous evening – feeding my expected guests, the police work which was piling up because of my involvement with the rebellion, and the brutal death of Non, my kaffir dog – I had a good night's sleep and rose to face the new day in a much brighter mood. I was resigned to the slaughter of one of my precious heifers but storing the meat presented its own problems. Although I owned a small charcoal safe, a whole carcass would not fit into it by any stretch of the imagination. Having reluctantly decided to sacrifice one of my private herd, I had no intention of seeing the meat go bad. I decided to approach Wright, the butcher at Willie Kaplan's store, with the idea of coming to some "arrangement".

The butcher was a typical Yorkshireman with a broad accent, a joyful character and the epitome of the "hail fellow – well met" type. One always found him smiling and showing an even set of teeth under his blond moustache.

(Some years later I met Willie Kaplan in Johannesburg and he explained that hard times had hit Makaha and the store no longer justified the presence of two Europeans. He had journeyed south to start a furniture concern on the Rand leaving Wright to look after both butchery and store in Rhodesia. I was staggered when Willie related how Wright had gone for a walk one night, had been attacked right next to the tennis court at Makaha where we had enjoyed so many hours together, and had been brutally murdered by two Africans who had smashed the butcher's skull with knobkerries. Willie had not had the heart to reopen the store after the tragedy.)

Wright was busy cutting meat into two-pound parcels for the Radnor Mine when I entered the butchery. He looked up and beamed forth with his bright and sunny smile.

"And what can I do for the policeman today?" he asked.

"I want to donate one fat healthy heifer to the business…" Wright's howl of laughter cut me short.

"Since when have you been a philanthropist? This sounds damned good I can't wait to hear more."

I voiced my proposal. He would supply the meat requirements for myself and to feed the troopers who were expected from Salisbury at any moment. When the reinforcements had left Makaha, I would hand over one of my heifers to be slaughtered and Wright could then reimburse himself, pound for pound, for the meat supplied to the camp. If the weight was in his favour, I promised to make up the difference at a fixed rate of sixpence per pound.

"...And I want none of your compound meat in exchange for the tender beef of my heifer," I concluded sternly.

Wright was more than pleased with the arrangement but Joe, my cook, was less enthusiastic. He reckoned that the butcher would get the better part of the deal by retaining the "fifth" quarter – the head, skin and intestines plus the liver plug and kidneys!

The grocery problem solved, I turned my attention to my police duties.

Court was held in Makaha every two weeks and the next session was only three days away. Apart from a stack of charge sheets against the usual tax defaulters and pass law offenders – there were more than a dozen of these – I had decided to bring Irvine before the magistrate to face a negligence charge arising out of the death of one of his employees at the Olympus Mine. If I could manage to get through all these cases, I would be left with a clean slate and be able to concentrate on the repercussions of the Rebellion, including the intimidating presence of Major Spain in my area.

The African sent to me by Kelly to act as a "trap" and put an end to the amalgam pilfering at the Olympus Mine was sent off with a note addressed to Irvine, accompanied by two genuine work-seekers. I had briefed my amateur detective thoroughly and hoped that he would bring back results.

I spent the rest of the day completing the dockets, expecting the troopers from Salisbury to arrive at any minute. There was no sign of them by late afternoon and I still had to warn Irvine of the pending case against him which would be heard on the coming Tuesday. I saddled *Swift* hurriedly and rode out to the Olympus Mine. Although Irvine greeted me with a smile, it was obvious that he guessed the real purpose of my trip. He invited me in for a drink and we had no sooner charged our glasses than he voiced his apprehension.

"For God's sake tell me when my case is to be heard! That Arizona cowboy (Dr Gurney) has been spreading tales around that I am really in for the high jump and I'm sure – if the verdict depends on his evidence – that I face the gallows."

Perhaps unsympathetically, I laughed at his fears, pointed out that there were no gallows at Makaha and that, if it suited him, I intended calling him before the magistrate on the following Tuesday.

"The sooner the better," was his reaction. "This waiting for the summons has really been getting me down."

I produced the summons, filled in the date and handed the document to him. With this side of the business concluded, Irvine seemed to relax slightly. He claimed that the setting of a date for his execution was reason enough for another drink and proceeded to pour two more stiff tots of whisky into our respective tumblers.

As we were drinking, Irvine's cook entered and handed him a note. It was the introduction I had given to my "detective". The miner eyed the note, turned round slowly and looked me up and down.

"Well, I'll be damned!" he said seriously. "You remembered your promise on the other matter. This calls for another drink!"

By the time we had finished "another drink" – and another – and had consumed an excellent three-course meal, Irvine had forgotten all about his hanging, his scheduled trial, Arizona Bill and the theft of his gold! By the end of the evening, we were the best of friends. With some difficulty, I mounted and rode back to camp clutching the pommel of the saddle before staggering into bed. It was surprising that I could concentrate on domestic matters when I awakened the next morning.

Doctor Gurney had given me a considerable number of Rosella plants soon after my arrival at Makaha and these had now grown into six-foot high trees bearing a prolific crop of buds. Gurney had let me into the secret of preparing "rosella jelly", a jam that compares favourably with red currant being particularly delicious with game dishes. Harvesting, I had been told, should take place when the buds – a deep red-purple colour – were on the point of breaking into their triangular petals.

Before crossing to the office and the daily routine, I instructed Joe to pick all the buds that were mature, sort out the necessary petals, wash them thoroughly, weigh them and then bring them to me for inspection. The crop weighed ten pounds, according to Joe, so I then gave him an order on the store for twelve pounds of sugar and told him to get on with the cooking. My chef, who reckoned he was one of the best cooks ever born, called me early in the afternoon to inspect the concoction. I was surprised to find that the mess had started to "jell" much sooner than Gurney's recipe had given me to understand. The saucepan was removed from the fire and the contents strained through a muslin cloth into a dish. The dish was placed in the charcoal "cooler" to set. Inspecting the jelly later, I was horrified to find that it had set into a hard black mass on which no knife could make an impression. I was mystified, as I had followed Gurney's recipe accurately. One thing was quite certain – my expected visitors would not be offered rosella jelly.

Later in the afternoon, I joined the Makahaites for our customary game of tennis. Following the game, we all joined Willie Kaplan at the store for sundowners and, in the course of general conversation, Willie asked me why I had ordered twelve pounds of gelatine that morning. "Ever since this store was opened I have had that carton of gelatine in stock and when your cook asked for some I gave him the lot as a present!"

The mystery of the concrete "jelly" was solved but poor old Joe never lived down that one big mistake. Later he became an expert in cooking the jam.

My visitors from Salisbury arrived the next morning. The five troopers had no special orders and had been told merely to wait at Makaha for further instructions. There was only one spare bed in the camp and that was devoid of a mattress. However, there were plenty of empty grain bags of which the visitors made full use to supplement the bedding they had brought with them.

Joe was the busiest man in Makaha following the invasion. I caught occasional glimpses of him as he dashed back and forth from the store before vanishing again into the depths of the kitchen. For dinner that first night, he produced a delicious beef stew and well-cooked rice, followed by a dessert of cooked apples. Black coffee with thick cream rounded off the meal and the troops did full justice to Joe's efforts.

The Native Commissioner, Morkel, arrived early for court the next morning and, while we were going through the charge sheets, Irvine rode in from the Olympus Mine and Gurney puffed up the hill from the clinic. Irvine was to be charged under the Mining Regulations for neglecting to make a report on the accident to an employee, the maximum penalty for which was a fine of £25. Irvine gave his evidence in a straightforward manner and pleaded guilty to the charge. It was a different matter when friend Gurney took the stand.

As the doctor gave evidence, he became increasingly agitated almost to the point of insulting the magistrate. At one stage, I even interrupted the proceedings to plead for a warning on contempt of court. Morkel was unmoved however, and seemed fully aware of the missionary's excitability. My appeal sobered up the doctor to some extent and he quietened down eventually. Morkel reached his verdict and fined Irvine the expected sum of £25.

Gurney was by no means satisfied. According to him, the proceedings had placed a value of a mere £25 on a human life. Carefully, I explained to the American that the case would be sent for review by the High Court and, that if the Reviewing Judge found that there had been a miscarriage of justice, the case would be reopened. I repeated my warning in court and tried to impress upon the missionary the necessity of respectful conduct in the presence of the magistrate. I gave up trying to suppress his mutterings about there being no justice in Rhodesia, left the old fanatic still mumbling to himself and proceeded with the hearing of the other cases.

The tax defaulters – there were five of them, mostly foreign natives – were fined £1 or one month's imprisonment for each year in default. The Registration Certificates of some of the offenders had to be referred to the Fingerprint Bureau. This department was under police supervision and even in 1918 was extremely competent and of invaluable assistance to prosecutors. No tax defaulter had any hope of getting past the Bureau if once his finger-prints had been registered. It was quite amusing to see the expressions on the defaulters' faces when presented with proof of the exact date on which they had entered the country and the place of their immigration.

After lunch – Morkel had his with Doctor Gurney and I did not envy the magistrate's subjection to another of the missionary's tirades – the balance of the pass law cases was heard. The day's business was finished by 4 p.m., Morkel was on his way back to Mtoko and I was left with a clean slate – with the exception of the woman who had been through the boiling water torture. She was still at the clinic but was awaiting her discharge.

Mail was accumulating for Major Spain and Mr. Taberer and I was uneasy at not having heard from them. I was on the point of making arrangements to contact them when a native constable turned up with a note asking for their mail and any further news I might have received at my end about the rebellion.

Major Spain wrote that most of the refugees had decided to return to Portuguese territory, that he had no evidence of the rebels themselves crossing the border and that he had heard that Senhor Maldanado had reached Tete safely. I was very relieved to hear this last piece of news.

More good news came in the form of the return of my batman and two witnesses from the Inyanga orchards. They brought with them two cases of beautiful apples – one case for cooking and the other for eating. My visitors descended on the latter with relish. They had little else to do with their time other than spend it exercising their jaws!

It was Joe – hard-working, perspiring Joe – who became the chief source of the visitors' amusement, although their laughter in no sense belittled the cook's efforts to make their stay as pleasant as possible. The script of the comedy appeared something like this.

"What is there for lunch, Joe?"
"Stuul and lice – gooda stuul !"
And, "What have you got for dinner?"
"Stuul and lice – gooda stuul!"

There was little variation – in the conversation or in the menu provided for the simple reason that there was nothing else to cook. The troopers fully understood the position and were most appreciative of Joe's stews and rice. They were equally appreciative of his attempts to speak English. But Joe had the last laugh on more than one occasion.

One evening, after we had consumed the usual "stuul and lice", Joe appeared from the kitchen with a plate on which reposed a round mould of brown dough about the size of a football. All eyes were riveted on the cook and explanations were demanded. A half-moon smile appeared on Joe's black features but he wouldn't be drawn.

"Gooda puddin. Me gooda cook!"

And what a good pudding it was! It turned out to be a wonderful apple dumpling – stuffed with pieces of suet, thin slices of apple and the whole as light as a feather. The sweet vanished rapidly with the accompanying rosella jelly and golden syrup. Licking their lips, the troopers demanded to know where Joe had been taught to make such a "gooda puddin". We gathered that at one time he had worked for a farmer across the border and that this was one of the results of his tuition by the lady of the house. With the present turmoil in Portuguese East Africa, I quietly hoped that Joe's teacher and her family had eaten equally as well and in comparable safety.

One afternoon I bagged a duiker. My batman was in the process of skinning the buck when Joe appeared, his eyes widened and he poured out orders and instructions to the other servant. I had no idea of the import of the one sided conversation until the following evening. "Stuul and lice'" was noticeably absent from the menu when Joe set before us a steaming oblong object which looked anything but edible. Despite our questions, Joe maintained that this was just another of his very good "stuuls". There was no alternative but to taste the questionable dish.

I offered the point of the carving knife to the object and we all jumped back in alarm at the resultant frightening hiss and whistle of escaping steam. When the object had been deflated to a state of seeming safety, I widened the incision and revealed – both to our eyes and nostrils – the most appetising steak and kidney pudding.

Joe explained. The stomach of the duiker had acted as a large casserole into which he had placed an ox kidney and the duiker kidneys, two pounds of diced beef steak, a piece of ox colon, liver, four large onions and three cloves of garlic, pepper and salt. Some of the meat had been obtained from Wright – I might have guessed that Joe would not let the butcher get away with all the offal of my promised heifer – and the rest had been rescued from the batman's cooking pot. The combined ingredients had been placed in the thoroughly washed duiker stomach, securely tied and then immersed in boiling water for several hours.

The result was delicious and one of the troopers was loudly acclaimed when he said that no mother born could have provided a better meal. The troopers' enthusiasm extended even to a quick collection and Joe was presented with five shillings and promoted from "gooda cook" to "Number One Cook" on the spot.

A final pleasant note to the evening occurred when a messenger from Major Spain arrived to say that the officer considered that he was wasting his time out in the wilds and intended returning shortly to Makaha.

It seemed that the Makumbi Rebellion had missed Makaha in its tide and that everything would soon be back to normal. I hoped so – and so, I think, did Joe.

Chapter Seven – Detection and Inspection

The quiet interlude, interspersed only with the excitement of Joe's culinary adventures, soon came to an end. Irvine, the manager of the Olympus Mine, sent a note reporting some progress in putting an end to the theft of amalgam from the mine. It seemed that my "secret agent" had been able to solve the mystery of the missing gold.

I made my excuses to the troopers from Salisbury who were becoming increasingly bored with their days of inactivity and rode out to the Olympus. Irvine greeted me with a broad smile.

"Your detective has really shown me something of the art of pilfering gold. You won't believe just how cunning the thief is until you have seen for yourself. Come down to the mill for a lesson on the 'ignorance' of the African."

As related earlier, Irvine had locked a wire cage over the table when first he had realised that someone was stealing amalgam. Frustrated by the grill, the thief had evidently cut strips of copper wire, quick-silvered them and hung the strips inside the box. Although the returns would be nowhere near the earlier profits of crime, over a period the strips would gather enough gold to make quite a ball of amalgam.

My detective had certainly earned his keep but, by the time he had reached the bottom of the affair, the thief had realised the game was up and had flown. My man identified him as a Portuguese African and, although I circulated his description and registration details, he was never apprehended. However, the thief's modus operandi was passed on to all the other small-workers in the valley and no further pilfering took place in my time at Makaha.

Irvine invited me in for a "sip" and dinner but having tasted the New Zealander's hospitality to the point of excess in earlier dealings, I decided to forgo the invitation, made my excuses and returned to camp. Joe, very definitely promoted to "Number One Cook", produced a delicious dinner consisting of marrow bones on toast, brisket stew, rice, sliced majodas sweetened with sugar and apple pie. The majodas were something quite new and a welcome change in the absence of other vegetables.

After dinner, someone suggested a game of bridge and we played cards until daybreak. Fortunately it was Sunday and we were able to sleep until lunchtime. When I eventually opened my eyes, Joe was standing at my bed clutching the lead of a slate-coloured pariah cur so thin one could count the ribs. Under the cook's arm was a puppy of the same colour that looked like an underfed rat.

"Plesant for you, baas," he smiled with an ear-to-ear grin on his ugly face. "Him name Non!" He dragged the ugly bitch closer to the bed. "And this one," he continued, "him name Joe!" I was handed the rat-like puppy. "Me buy for five shillin in Radnor Compound."

I was on the point of chasing both Joe and the curs from the room when it struck me that the cook must have spent all of the five shillings he had been given by the appreciative troopers to replace my kaffir dog Non who had been killed by wild dogs. How could I turn down such innocent generosity? Gracefully, and with as much enthusiasm as I could muster after the all-night session, I accepted the gifts, told Joe to tie the bitch in the kennel and to feed her and the pup. When I saw the two animals again their stomachs were extended like balloons. It was a real effort for the mother to wag her tail but wag away she did. Non the Second, Joe the pup and I became firm friends. The two dogs became very obedient and proved to be mighty hunters and very persistent trackers on a blood spoor.

This was the third time that I had become involved with pariah canines and indicated that even the meanest-looking cur can give the most loyal service when treated firmly with kindness and good feeding. Many years later I met the famous lion hunter, Yank Allen, and mentioned to him my enthusiasm for the ordinary whippet-like kaffir dog. He felt exactly the same way as I did and told me that he used no other dog when going after lions.

A note from Major Spain told me to send the troopers back to Salisbury after arranging for their transport. This was done and, two days later, my reinforcements were gone leaving Makaha Police Camp a very lonely and forsaken place. It took me several days to adjust to the solitude.

The following week, just as I was getting ready to leave to attempt to trace the husband of the woman who had suffered the ordeal with boiling water, Major Spain and the Chief Native Commissioner returned to the settlement. They reckoned that no good purpose would be served by remaining out on the border and both were satisfied that the Makumbi Rebellion had fizzled out and that very few, if any, refugees would attempt to enter the country.

The officers arrived back on a Friday and stated their intention of remaining for the weekend in order to meet the inhabitants of Makaha. This gave me a headache – I could hardly offer them the rough and ready accommodation available in the police camp. Finally, I suggested that I make arrangements with Clark, the Radnor manager, for the two officers to stay at the cottage on the mine which was often used by the company directors when visiting the area. Clark readily agreed.

Everyone except Doctor Gurney turned up as usual at the tennis court for the normal Saturday afternoon game the next day. Imagine my surprise when Clark arrived with Major Spain and Mr Taberer, both of whom were in full tennis kit. The Native Commissioner, at that time and for many years after, was the Rhodesian Champion, and Major Spain, six feet, big-boned and heavy, was also a star performer. In a foursome, in which I partnered Mr. Taberer against Clark and Major Spain, the Chief Native Commissioner confided that I could become a most useful player if I rectified my faults. Then and there he proceeded with my tuition and by the time he had shown me how to use my wrist when serving, taught me the whip stroke from the back line, how to spin the ball and the backhand stroke, I was convinced that I would be soon challenging my tutor's title. The standard of tennis at Makaha improved tremendously after that weekend and enthusiasm for the game was greater than ever before.

After tennis, Willie Kaplan invited us to the store for a sundowner. Thanks to a generous host and with wonderful snacks prepared by old man Wright, the Makahaites enjoyed themselves to the full – and so did our two guests. In general conversation, Taberer and Spain told us all they had about the rebellion and stressed that there was no cause for alarm. This information tended to increase the consumption of whisky and eventually we went home in a very warm state of mind.

On Sunday morning, Major Spain mounted a surprise inspection of the camp, looked through my books and once again reprimanded me on the subject of my retention of Morkel's horse. The censure had no sting however and was given with a smile. Later he congratulated me on the animal's condition and it was at this moment that one of the African witnesses placed a basket of crushed camel-thorn beans outside the stable door. My Officer Commanding asked about the concoction and I told him how Cornelius van Rooyen had given me the tip at Makalola. It was wonderful feed for horses, mules or donkeys and, whenever I had spare labour, I organised the collection of the beans. Major Spain was very interested and asked a number of questions on the subject.

Passing the kennel on the way back to the house, Joe's two "plesants" growled at the officer.

"Whatever do you want with mongrels like those?" inquired Major Spain. I explained how I had been given the curs, stressing Joe's generosity in spending his tips from the troopers for my benefit. I think the Major was as touched as I had been by my cook's kindness. Anyway, he delved into his pocket and presented Joe with six shillings before leaving the camp.

Major Spain and Mr Taberer departed for Salisbury the following morning, Monday. The camp and the settlement at last reverted to a normal routine.

Chapter Eight – Blackwater Fever

Doctor Gurney provided me with yet another headache in his self-imposed capacity as the guardian of Makaha morals. This time he complained that prostitutes at the Radnor Compound had become a menace to the health of Africans in the valley. He told me that it was my duty to arrest the scarlet women.

Now this was a very delicate subject and one to which I had formerly turned a blind eye. The mine owners accepted the presence of the women as one way of keeping their employees content. On the other hand, the missionary had a point in that the uncontrolled spread of venereal disease was a growing problem, especially as many of those afflicted were ashamed to report their sickness. To avoid an unpleasant confrontation with the mine managements, and at the same time in an attempt to control the spread of the disease, I asked Gurney if he would be prepared to treat those cases which I could round up and bring to the clinic. For a moment I thought the American was going to throw a fit. His face turned a bright red, he spluttered and rolled his eyes and accused me of enlisting his help in breaking the law.

"No, no, Doctor," I replied with a smile. "I am merely asking you to help me in my dilemma. I'll have the miners up in arms if I arrest the prostitutes. They look upon them as a necessary evil and their presence is not uncommon wherever large numbers of unmarried Africans are employed.

We argued on the subject for several days until eventually I won the missionary over to my way of thinking. The business with Irvine and the African who had accidentally been killed at his mine had, I think, made the American realise that there were practical problems about maintaining the strict letter of the law in an isolated community such as Makaha.

The mine owners were equally sympathetic when the position was explained to them and, with their help, I managed to round up about fifteen women and deposited them at the clinic. They were kept there until they were cured and meanwhile we managed to get a number of afflicted African males to the clinic where they received injections before returning to their compounds and eventually to their work.

The whole project snowballed. The prostitutes soon realised that they could be easily cured of the unsavoury disease and the men too realised that they could have their cake and eat it. Africans appeared of their own volition at the clinic, not only from the mine compounds but from the outlying districts as well. Such was the demand for Doctor Gurney's services that he had to introduce a small charge to cover his expenses. Still, his patients were undeterred. It was quite amusing to think that Gurney had now joined those who were making money out of prostitution1

The mine owners were equally enthusiastic about the operations – for two reasons. Firstly they received the benefits of a healthy and contented labour force and, as Gurney's old rival Irvine remarked, the project kept the missionary so busy that he had no time to poke his nose into other people's affairs. Clark, of the Radnor Mine, was most congratulatory towards me for succeeding in putting a halt to the spread of venereal disease in Makaha. He reckoned that the Africans were equally appreciative. So ended my foray into the realm of public health and public relations.

Intending to arrest the husband of the wife who had been put through the boiling water ordeal, I left the station early one morning on Swift, accompanied by the victim, an African constable, my batman and a pack mule. We made for the Ruenya River, the place at which the woman had left her husband and family. It was slow going – the woman was not used to the normal pace of a patrol and had to stop frequently to rest.

Early in the afternoon, we reached the spot at which I had shot the waterbuck and had the indaba with the first lot of refugees. Game spoor abounded and among them were the tracks of an elephant cow and calf. This was most unusual but later it was explained to me that the upheaval of the rebellion across the border had driven large quantities of game into Rhodesia.

I was resting on my bed, prepared for me by my batman, and the Africans were down at the water getting ready for the night when I heard something moving in the grass behind my head. Resting on my elbow, I listened intently but the sounds of movement had stopped. No sooner had I returned to the horizontal than the mysterious noises resumed. This time I got to my feet and walked carefully towards the waving grass from which the activity seemed to emanate. I came upon an extraordinary sight. Two long cobras had a third slate-coloured snake in their respective mouths. The tail was well down the throat of one cobra while the head was deep inside the other. I called the African constable and my batman; we killed the two cobras and extracted the victim from their throats. The subject of this extraordinary feast was about three feet in length and about one foot had been consumed by each of the two cobras. That left another twelve inches or so to be consumed. I have often wondered what would have happened when the jaws of the two cobras met!

Moving on the following day, we saw several herds of assorted game – sable, waterbuck, zebra, eland – and caught a glimpse of the cow elephant and her calf wandering in the same direction as ourselves towards the river. By midday, we were on the banks of the Ruenya and at the point that the woman said she had run away from her family. There was no sign of them although there was abundant evidence that they had been there – hastily built huts which had already been partly demolished by the elements.

I ordered camp to be made for the night, hoping to track down the brutal husband the next day. During the hours of darkness, the woman rose from her makeshift bed near the fire and explained to the constable that she was going into the bush to relieve herself. That was the last time any of us saw or heard of her. She just vanished like a needle in a haystack. In the morning we traced her steps to where she had obviously crossed the river to return to Portuguese territory. I sincerely hoped that when she rejoined her husband she would not be given a flogging and her hands put back in the boiling water.

Bad news greeted my arrival back at Makaha. I was told that Percy Marley, one of two brothers who contracted for timber for the mines, had been taken to Salisbury to have his leg amputated. The story behind the removal of the limb was almost incredible. Percy owned a small bulldog puppy and the animal had been left outside the brothers' house when they retired for the night. A sharp cold wind sprang up during the hours of darkness and the puppy had howled to be let into the warmth. Percy left his warm bed, opened the door and searched for the puppy, but before the dog could be found, the cold wind had wrapped itself around Percy's legs. He retrieved the puppy and climbed back into his bed. A few minutes later a sharp pain in his right leg made him shout to his brother Sidney, for help. Examining the leg, it was discovered that it had turned purple. Dr Gurney had been consulted and had rushed his patient to Salisbury hospital in his Model T Ford where attempts to save the leg were in vain.

Good old Willie Kaplan decided that the Makahaites could not stand around doing nothing in the face of such unexpected tragedy. He organised a fund and a small utility cart and harness were purchased for the unfortunate Marley when he was released from hospital. Most of the money, I might add, came from Willie's own pocket.

I fitted the harness to a mule belonging to the brothers and the population of Makaha turned out in force on the day of the presentation. Percy was completely overwhelmed and, when he got up to thank everyone, Willie in particular, he burst into tears. Such was the tremendous spirit among the Europeans at Makaha.

A report from an African that white hunters were shooting game on the Ruenya sent me off to the river on patrol once again. Before I could make contact with the poachers, however, I went down with a severe dose of malarial fever. Although I pumped quinine into myself, the attack became worse and I only just managed to get back to Makaha and my bed, with a temperature of 104. Dr Gurney examined me and diagnosed my second bout of black-water fever. He was right and for several weeks I struggled to keep alive with the American missionary's help. I will never forget how the little doctor, despite the altercations we had had during my stay at Makaha, nursed me day and night and poured gallons of barley water into me.

When the crisis came, Gurney remained at my bedside for a solid 48 hours, watching me intently and never once falling asleep. When at last my water cleared and I was able to move, the American gave voice to a masterpiece of understatement when he told me that I had had a close call. The graves of fellow policemen throughout Rhodesia were mute testimony to those who had succumbed to the dreaded fever.

I was like a skeleton after the attack and Doctor Gurney continued to nurse me until I was fit enough to be transported to Salisbury Hospital.

When I was released from hospital, I was detailed to help Sub-Inspector Quinton with paperwork in his Salisbury office. Trooper Small took over at Makaha and many years were to pass before I again set eyes on the rolling valley. So ended an exciting chapter of my life – on the surface just a few months of routine police duty, but in reality, an education all of its own.

The Devil's Cataract

by

Pioneer

The major events portrayed in this story actually happened but the period in which they took place and the names of those involved have been changed.

Illustration at the head of the page in the January, 1968, issue of *The Outpost*. "Pioneer" was a nom-de-plume used by Eben Mocke.
Photographs: pages 312-313

Sergeant Jackson sat in his office at the Victoria Falls Police Station and wondered what the day's crop of tourists' complaints would provide in the way of business. The oppressive heat, the humidity and the never-ceasing roar of the Zambesi in its abandoned descent were quite enough to add to the daily routine of police duties at a busy border station. The additional burden of outraged visitors only too conscious of the fact that it was their money which provided most of the income of the village's permanent residents and who had left a large slice of their holiday budget in the hands of the smart-alec hawkers selling "genuine African curios" at exorbitant prices or had lost their precious cameras to the marauding baboons, would have tried the patience of a saint and Sergeant Jackson's three stripes were no substitute for a pair of wings. The tourist influx had certain advantages but the trouble was that the pretty faces never stayed long enough to lastingly brighten the policeman's outlook. Another dust-laden car rattled past the door of the office. Sergeant Jackson sighed and prayed that it would be an uneventful day. His prayers were not to be answered.

Two of the policeman's transient charges stood in the middle of the Victoria Falls bridge and admired the magnificence of the 650 foot steel structure and the rampaging waters in the gorge 360 feet below. Mrs Hilda Caine of Bulawayo, a tall, well-preserved, good-looking woman in her late thirties was showing her niece Rhodesia's prime tourist attraction. Dorothy, the niece, was a visitor from the Cape and had Sergeant Jackson been privileged to meet her before the events which later transpired, he would have concluded that Victoria Falls had certain other scenic attractions. She was no more than twenty and sparkled with the fire of youth. Her deep blue eyes set in a sensitive and intelligent face and her trim figure carried erect upon long shapely legs would have endeared her to the lonely bachelor Member in Charge. When she voiced the thoughts of the wondering eyes, her husky tones completed the picture of attractive youth.

"But however did the builders of the bridge manage to get those heavy girders across the gorge in the first place, Aunt Hilda?"

"As you know, Dorothy, your Uncle Tom was an engineer and the last time we were here he went into all the details with the pride of a Rhodesian and an engineer.

"According to your uncle, it would have been much easier to have built the bridge further up the river above Kandahar Island where there was a drift used by wagons. Rhodes, however, insisted that the passengers on the trains should be able to feel the spray from the Falls as they crossed the Zambesi – which does happen at certain seasons – and this romantic idea gave the engineers many headaches. First of all, they fired a light line across by rocket, pulled across a heavier rope and then a steel cable. A cradle was suspended from the wire and this was used until the bridge was completed to transport the workmen and their stores and equipment across the gorge."

Dorothy, listening intently with her elbows resting on the rails of the bridge, shuddered as she gazed down into 350 feet of emptiness.

"I'd never cross this chasm in a box suspended on a wire rope even if my life depended on it!" exclaimed the girl.

"Your life would depend on it," quipped her aunt. "The spans of the bridge were pushed out from each bank in sections of 25 feet. They slung a net beneath the spidery frame, but not one of the engineers ever fell off. The only casualty throughout the operation was an African who was killed when a girder was lowered into position.

"On April Fool's Day, 1905, the time came to join the two sections and close the gap. This was done, a temporary track was laid and a light shunting engine pushed two trucks across the bridge to establish the most impressive and also the most beautiful of links in our whole railway system."

The two visitors remained enthralled by the sight before them and Dorothy thought how even the mighty bridge seemed an insignificant human gesture when viewed in the midst of the mighty channels which the river had torn through the earth in its rushing travels. It was the elder of the two who finally suggested that it was time that they moved on.

They left the bridge and, on reaching the road, turned off to the right along a path. As they neared the Falls and the continuous rising cloud of spray they put on the raincoats they had been carrying. They stopped at the edge of the cliff and gazed at the roaring waters opposite.

"This is known as Danger Point," said Mrs Caine.

"And a very appropriate name at that," replied her niece. "This precipice might be the edge of this world and beyond the mist and spray, another land."

"From here," continued Mrs Caine, "one has perhaps the most glorious view of the whole expanse of the Falls. To the right is the Arm Chair and Eastern Cataract, on the left are the Rainbow Falls, the Horseshoe Falls, Livingstone Island and the Main Falls. Just look at the way in which the rocks have been carved by the rushing waters. Down there is the depression that looks like a giant footprint which has been given the name 'Eve's Footprint'. From here we'll walk along to the edge of the ravine where you will get a grandstand view of the largest curtain of falling water in the world."

Dorothy was entranced. The majesty of the view from the bridge was now being replaced by the terrible violence of the close-up sight of the roaring Zambesi. The two women picked their way through the pools and mud towards the Devil's Cataract. They stopped finally immediately opposite the foaming torrent. Mrs Caine, shouting now to be heard above the roar, continued her travelogue.

"More water passes through the Devil's Cataract than over the main falls. The local Africans attach great significance to this place. They believe that it is haunted by a cruel malevolent god and make offerings of beads and trinkets which they fling into the abyss with frightening incantations quite in harmony with the awful deity of the place, to appease the spirit."

Dorothy was hypnotised by the rushing torrent. She had a peculiar impulse to throw herself into the chasm to be swept downwards to certain death in a sacrifice to the omnipotent river god in contrition for man's puny attempts to tame the wilds. She could scarcely overcome the feeling of abject humility when faced by the roaring wall of water. Finally, in a voice almost silenced by the awe-inspiring sight, she said: "It has a very frightening beauty."

"Yes, it is beautiful," echoed a flat unfriendly voice behind them. The women wheeled in shocked surprise. Completely absorbed in the vicious splendour of the cataract, they had been completely oblivious to the presence of the intruder. A middle-aged African in an inconspicuous garb of khaki stood a few yards behind them. The initial shock of his sudden appearance was in no way lessened by the blazing eyes which seemed to stare right through the women to pierce the roaring curtain of water at their backs. The peculiar fixation of the eyes and the twisted inhuman grin on the face which had abruptly emerged from the gloomy dripping undergrowth, coupled with the wrath of the river pounding at the rear turned the atmosphere of innocent tourist enthusiasm into one of sudden threatening nameless danger.

"It's time we were getting back," said Mrs Caine as calmly as she could. "Lead on, Dorothy."

Dorothy retraced her steps along the narrow slippery path now blocked by the African. His eyes remained fixed on the foaming backdrop. She edged past him and hastened her steps to get away from the gallery which had so quickly become charged with menace. A few paces past the African and Dorothy halted in mid-stride. A sudden startled cry from her aunt made her wheel around fearing the worst. The African had his hands around her aunt's throat, struggling to throw her to the ground. Mrs Caine's frantic attempts to ward off the attacker and the panic in her eyes sent Dorothy sliding and scrabbling to the rescue. In desperation she flung herself at the native and grabbed the collar of his shirt. With all her might she heaved to release her aunt from the grip of savage fingers. A strangled oath burst from the African's lips as he succumbed to the tightening pressure around his throat. Releasing Mrs Caine, he turned and swung a vicious blow at Dorothy's head. The clenched black fist missed the girl's face by a fraction but the sudden movement ripped the shirt from the man's back and Dorothy went sprawling in the slippery mud.

The African, having momentarily disposed of the annoying interruption, turned his attention again to his victim. Mrs Caine, in her brief respite, had rolled away from her attacker but nearer to the 350 foot drop into the foaming torrent. As she struggled to regain her feet on the greasy slope, her assailant dived on her, flattened her to the ground and once again locked his fingers around her throat.

Dorothy lay on the ground a few yards away, frozen by the horror of the suddenness and the obsessiveness of the attack upon her aunt. A choking cry from Mrs Caine released her niece from the grip of the nightmare and she scrambled to her feet and staggered towards the struggling pair. Seizing the belt below the glistening back Dorothy tugged with all her strength, her panic-stricken cries being lost in the frenzied roar of the cataract.

The madman, hampered again as he held Mrs Caine by the throat with one hand and tore at her dress with the other, released his hold and turned his attention once again to the younger girl. This time there was no mistake about the accuracy of the blow that he threw at Dorothy. She reeled back and the instant before her head struck a rock, she saw her aunt rolling away from the rapist, nearer and nearer the edge of the chasm. As darkness descended, Dorothy heard the blood-curdling shriek of her aunt as she vanished from sight into the mist-filled ravine.

Dorothy regained consciousness bewildered and at a loss to her surroundings. The blood dripping from her head and the glistening skid marks in the mud before her soon brought her back to horrible reality. Fearfully she looked around for the attacker but he had vanished as suddenly as he had appeared. She was completely and desperately alone. She tried to shout but her voice was an inaudible croak.

Painfully, Dorothy crawled to the edge of the abyss and looked down through tear-glazed eyes. There was no sign of her aunt. All she could see was the boiling foam almost obscured at the bottom by the rising spray. The reverberating thunder of the water was a crashing reminder that there could be little hope for her aunt.

Heaving dry sobs from her tortured chest, Dorothy stumbled to her feet and up the path towards the road and help. Her exhaustion and nervous shock filled the journey with punishing knee-grazing fall after fall.

It was a tear-stained, bleeding, forlorn young woman who staggered up to the hotel – a far cry from the smart young lady who had partnered the elegant widow as they set out on their sight-seeing tour earlier that morning. The casual loungers on the hotel stoep rushed to her assistance in alarm and the dreadful and almost incoherent tale poured from her sobbing lips.

Sergeant Jackson, an assistant and the local Doctor were at the hotel within a few minutes of receiving a report of the tragic affair. The Doctor, having attended to Dorothy who had been put to bed by two sympathetic guests, gave the Sergeant as much information as he had been able to extract from the hysterical girl. It was decided to throw a cordon around the Falls in an attempt to bottle up the accused before he could make good his escape. All fourteen male guests at the Hotel volunteered to help and were posted at strategic points. Two African constables were sent to guard the Falls Bridge whilst Sergeant Jackson and his trooper set out for the scene of the brutal assault. At the Devil's Cataract, they systematically searched the undergrowth in the hope of finding some clue to the identity of the attacker. Their search was fruitless. The only evidence of the calamity was the churned up mud.

Late that evening, helped by a bright moon shining in a cloudless sky, the two African constables continued their watch on the bridge. An African suddenly appeared walking nonchalantly towards the place where the policemen were concealed at the end of the bridge. The African fitted the vague description given by Dorothy and the two policemen tensed as he drew nearer. As he passed the centre of the bridge, the man stopped and looked down at the fast-flowing waters of the gorge. The guards remained motionless. Having inspected the depths, the figure glanced around as if to satisfy himself that the coast was clear. He continued his leisurely approach to the end of the bridge. As he drew opposite the two policemen, they stumbled out of the undergrowth and yelled at the man to stop. Instead of obeying the command, the African gave one startled glance in their direction and was off like the wind. He raced along the top of the gorge until he arrived above the Silent Pool. He stopped, casually looked round to make sure that he was still being followed and, as the guards raced up to him, calmly stepped off the precipice and dropped silently from sight. Peering over the edge of the cliff, the two constables searched the almost vertical slope. To their surprise, they saw that the cliff dropped sheer for about thirty feet to a ledge. It was on this ledge that their victim lay, squirming and groaning in pain. With one man left to keep an eye on the murderer, the other constable rushed off to report to Sergeant Jackson.

Within fifteen minutes, Sergeant Jackson, Trooper Seekings and four African constables had arrived by car with ropes. The news that the perpetrator of the vicious crime had been trapped spread around the village and through the hotel like wildfire. Soon there was no absence of willing hands to help lower Trooper Seekings over the cliff so that he could bring up the injured accused.

Well-secured in a make-shift harness, Seekings started the hazardous descent. It was not an easy place to attempt the descent as the cliff was almost vertical and there were no foot or hand holds in the rock to assist him. The thirty foot drop seemed almost like three hundred feet and Seekings sighed with relief when his feet finally reached the ledge.

The African was still conscious although one leg was obviously broken. He squirmed on the narrow projection and snarled at his rescuer. As Seekings bent to tie a second rope around the wretch he struggled and spat and shrieked to be left alone. Seekings can perhaps be forgiven for his harshness as he swore to deliver the murderer to the hangman. It had been a long hard day and the tragedy had left its mark on everyone connected with the case. Seekings tried again to secure the rope under the man's arms and the victim squirmed like a worm to make the task almost impossible. Suddenly, with a super-human effort,

Top: Victoria Falls Bridge
Bottom Left: Devil's Cataract
Right: The Silent Pool

Victoria Falls Police Camp 1925
Photos from the album of Tpr William Albert Smith (2066/2431)

he twisted on to his back, placed his healthy leg against the side of the cliff and pushed himself off the ledge to fall headlong into the gorge. The animal shriek that accompanied the seemingly floating descent froze the blood in the veins of the watchers.

Seekings was hauled to the lip of the precipice and the Silent Pool never gave up the secret of the identity of the madman.

The matter did not end there. There was still a remote possibility that the bodies of Mrs Caine and the African would be located. The police, the Warden and the hundreds of visitors to the Falls joined in the gruesome search. Every inch of the gorge was explored with binoculars and guards were placed at various intervals in the hope that the bodies would eventually be seen floating down the gorges.

Four weeks after Mrs Caine had disappeared over the edge of Danger Point, the Warden detected an object immediately opposite the place at which the struggle had taken place. It was impossible to be sure that it was the body of Mrs Caine. The spray acted like a dense smoke screen and it was only at intervals, when the wind was blowing in a certain direction, that the Warden could get a momentary view of the "thing" lodged on a ledge below the roaring curtain of the Devil's Cataract. The Warden referred his find to Sergeant Jackson and the two of them, after much discussion and inspection, came to the conclusion that the object was probably Mrs Caine's remains.

The next problem was how to retrieve the body. No human being had ever ventured into the cauldron of seething water and anyone attempting such a descent would be drowned in the foaming spray or beaten to death against the rocks. There seemed to be no practical solution.

It was then that Sergeant Jackson suggested that they invite the opinion of the chief engineer at the mine. In the meantime, it was decided to keep the find from the public to prevent hordes of blood-thirsty sightseers descending on the slopes of Danger Point. Two days later, the Chief Engineer, Mitchell; his assistant, Sims; Sergeant Jackson and the Warden assembled on Danger Point. Each strained his eyes to find the object and, having placed the position of the body, stood back to await the verdict of Mr Mitchell.

"I don't see any real difficulty in lowering a box down to where the body is, but who is going to undertake the task of actually bringing the body up? The man, or men (I think it will have to be two) might get drowned in the process. If we can find someone brave enough to give it a go, I propose that we erect a derrick and hoist right here and bring in an engine rather than rely on manpower. We will have to have several rehearsals with the cage unmanned and at exactly midday when the sun is shining straight down into the gorge. As I said, the real problem is finding someone to volunteer to go down in the box."

"I'd like to go down. I think it would be an interesting experience," offered Sergeant Jackson.

"And I will be your partner," said Sims, the assistant. "I do suggest however, that we take a small looking glass with us so that we can signal to you up here."

"That's a splendid suggestion, Sims," replied Mitchell. "The signals will give you some measure of safety and three quick flashes and we'll have you back up here in no time."

Having decided on the method, the two engineers returned to the mine to make the necessary arrangements. Within thirty-six hours the machinery had arrived at the Falls and had been placed in position.

It had already been decided to hold the first trial at noon and, at the appointed hour, a large box five feet square and four foot high, with numerous two-inch holes drilled in the flooring, was slowly and cautiously lowered into the chasm. All went well until the contraption was down some two hundred feet when it started swaying from side to side alarmingly. Realising that the crate could not be landed with any accuracy, the Chief Engineer ordered it to be raised.

Two lengths of wire rope were attached to the bottom corners of the crate and then passed over the gorge to Cataract Island where two men, some distance apart, controlled the pendulum motion of the descent. Again the box was lowered, this time with complete success, and the crate reached the bottom almost on top of the body. As it was too late to attempt a rescue, the first manned attempt was postponed until noon the following day.

The next day, Jackson and Sims, clothed in waterproofs and with long rubber gloves covering their arms, prepared to enter the crate. In the box they had placed a roll of waterproof sheeting with which to wrap the body.

Mitchell gave the men their final instructions in a subdued but excited voice:

"Remember to flash the glass at frequent intervals and if you get into difficulties, give several flashes in quick succession and we'll have you up immediately. Don't take any unnecessary chances, the best of luck and have a pleasant journey!"

The box was swung out over the chasm and lowered very gently. It was Sims who broke the silence as the two men began their precarious descent. "Good Heavens! What an astounding sight. Just look at the thousands of rainbows. Never have I seen anything so beautiful!"

Jackson joined the chorus of wonderment as the box sank lower into the gorge. The clouds of spray and the noonday sun shining vertically into the chasm provided a myriad of rainbows of different sizes. It was as though the two men were sinking into another world.

As the skip went lower, the brilliance of the view became clouded and the pair found themselves passing through a more threatening but no less eerie stage of their journey. "Rain" was falling in torrents and conversation was drowned in the roar of the falling water which sounded like the passage of giant locomotives in a narrow tunnel. Still descending, the eardrums of the two men were all but shattered as the intensity of the deluge increased. The thunder was even accompanied by "lightning", as the sun's reflection projected bursts of blinding light through the heaving curtain. A storm of hail was the next frightening experience, the hail being provided by showers of small black pebbles. The basalt formation on which the waters pounded was continually being eroded by the tremendous pressure of the cataract. It was easy to believe that another gorge would eventually be formed as the water ate its way through the rock.

Suddenly the deafening thunder ceased. The roar of the locomotives passed into the distance and the men realised that they had passed through the curtain and were beneath the arch formed by the rushing water. A few seconds later the cage grounded and the engineer and the policeman emerged from the box to find themselves almost on top of the remains of Mrs Caine.

It was not a pretty sight. The corpse was headless and only the poor woman's corset continued the battle to contain the swollen flesh. In haste, the two men unrolled the canvas and attempted to wrap the remains in the sheeting. They were unsuccessful. At the slightest touch, the flesh parted from the bones. With care and patience, not helped by the revolting nature of the task, the men finally succeeded in sliding the sheet under the body, brought the two ends together and lifted the canvas and its gruesome contents into the cage.

Sims, looking upwards at the face of the cliff, spotted a white object resting on a small shelf. Stumbling and slithering up the gradient, he reached the ledge and retrieved a canvas shoe. It was apparently the property of the deceased and must have been wrenched from her foot during her fall.

Sims and Jackson joined the mortal remains of Mrs Caine in the skip, gave the pre-arranged signal with the glass to those at the hoist and started on the return journey. They reached the top without incident.

The Devil's Cataract continued its rushing, roaring, foaming descent and the success of the two men who stepped out of the cage near Danger Point seemed a very hollow victory.

ZAMBESI DUCK HUNT

Trooper 1437 undertakes a trip in 1968 which is a far cry from his Kalahari Patrol of 1912. Some things do not change however......

I accepted the invitation to accompany my niece, Joyce Thomson, her husband Tommy, and Polly Paine on a duck-shooting expedition on the Zambezi with mixed feelings. Having charged all over Rhodesia in the last sixty years, the prospect of a boat trip on one of Africa's greatest waterways offered excitements which I had never yet experienced and after many months of very inactive "retirement", I was raring to go. I was also curious to see again the river which in these days has assumed such a news value to the world press and perhaps a third motive which prompted me to accept the invitation was the determination to prove that, at 79, there was life in the old dog yet.

At 2 a.m. one Friday morning early this year, Tommy's Land Rover, in charge of one of his drivers and loaded with all the necessary camping gear and trailing his massive boat with its 80 hp Evinrude, started out on the 200-mile trip to Chirundu. Four hours later, Joyce, Tommy and I left Good Hope on the outskirts of Salisbury and drove to Polly's establishment where we boarded the latter's Jaguar. Polly had his own smaller boat on its trailer behind.

The Great North Road is fully tarred and, at a steady sixty miles an hour, Joyce and I were able to settle down to reading the morning's newspaper. It was many years since I had travelled this route and as we sped over the attractive pass on the Great Dyke, I was reminded of the unfortunate loss (those many years ago) of several hundred pounds invested in a chrome-mining venture. It was still early when we passed through Banket with its miles of green mealies which looked quite healthy despite the drought, and then we were at Sinoia in time for breakfast.

We continued northwards after breakfast. More mealies on either side of the road looked quite capable of supplying Rhodesia with "sadza" for the coming year and then we were through Lion's Den and past the turn-off to the Mangula Copper Mine. On we sped until we were delayed by a long convoy of new vehicles bound for Zambia. The sudden gradients and the long string of dirty new cars kept Tommy on his toes as we overtook the convoy one by one. When I thought of the convoy's destination, I found myself lost in the curious paradox of relations between the two countries.

We paused in a small village and a police patrol informed us that Tommy's Land Rover was some three hours ahead of us. We passed the turnoff to Kariba and the road took on much more of a switchback nature. Hairpin bends and steep gradients slowed our progress. We were descending the Zambezi Escarpment and as we rounded one razor-edged bend, the whole of the wide and endless Zambezi Valley flashed into view. The scenery was fantastic and the colouring of the mountains on the distant and unfriendly shore in Zambia was magnificent beyond description. Down, down and still further down we zig-zagged. Polly's boat on the trailer behind us gave me the creeps. The other passengers were oblivious to the appendage but I felt sure that on one of the sharp turns, the contraption would turn over and drag us from the dizzy heights in the process. I worried needlessly. It was remarkable how the little trailer followed its "mother" and hugged "her" with the greatest confidence without the slightest skid or slip.

We paused in our descent at the Wild Life Management Camp at Morongora – an attractive building erected by the Department of Wild Life and National Parks. We reported to the man in charge, Tommy's rifle was sealed, and licences were issued for the shooting of duck – and duck only – at Camp F, our destination.

Leaving Morongora, we continued on the descending road to the floor of the Valley until we were on the straight, fully-tarred road to Chirundu. With all the windows of the car open, the heat was becoming oppressive and we were soon removing the warmer clothes we had worn from the highveld of Salisbury.

At this time of the year, with the bush in full leaf, it is extremely difficult to spot game. Apart from elephant droppings on the road, we saw no sign of wild animals. We paused again at a roadside motel and filling station, refreshed ourselves and refuelled the Jaguar, and then turned off on a dirt track leading directly to the river. Within two miles we arrived on the banks of the Zambezi to be greeted by Tommy's driver and servants who had reached the river some hours before us.

The Zambezi never fails to impress me. It rises as a tiny stream in the forests of the north-western tip of Zambia, wanders through Portuguese West Africa (Angola) and re-enters Zambia to flow southwards through the vast Barotse plain. Seven hundred and fifty miles from its source, it thunders over the Victoria Falls and then rushes through a series of gorges until it is tamed in the vast Lake Kariba of over two thousand square miles. Through the turbines at Kariba, it continues to flow to Feira and into Portuguese East Africa (Mozambique), and finally, after a journey of 1,725 miles, it reaches the Indian

Ocean.

Normally the Zambezi reaches its highest level at the end of March, but this year, perhaps due to the heavy rains upriver, three of the sluices at Kariba had been opened. At Chirundu, we were seeing flood conditions with the water deep from bank to bank. The opening of more sluices could have been disastrous to wild life and agriculture down the river in PEA.

Our temporary camp on the banks of the river was a beautiful spot. Enormous shady trees protected us from the beating sun and a natural gully had been flattened into an improvised but adequate launching site. Joyce produced a large tin of assorted sandwiches and, washed down with beers which seemed miraculously cool, we satisfied our appetites. Whilst we were eating – and drinking – Polly suggested that before setting out for our final destination down the river, we took time off to inspect a piece of ground, just below the Chirundu Bridge, he intended hiring from the Government. He wanted to set up another fishing camp at this place.

Tommy's boat was soon in the water with the owner at the wheel, myself beside him, and Polly in one of the back seats. To my consternation, Joyce, wearing dark goggles and a green jockey cap, perched her graceful figure astride the bows of the craft with her bare legs dangling in the water. Thinking that perhaps I had robbed her of her seat next to Tommy, I offered to move but she smiled with an inner excitement and argued that she always occupied the seemingly precarious bow station. The engine coughed twice and then roared into life. There was a bubbling froth under our stern and we began to move backwards. As we slid into clear and deep water, the engine note rose to a crescendo, the craft pivoted in a tight arc, lifted its nose clear off the water, frothed the awakened water with its propeller and away we shot like a bat out of hell. I felt that I was suddenly minus stomach and heart and my blood started racing in aged veins which had accepted a sedentary life for too long. My excitement was added to by my concern for Joyce who sat on her pinnacle like the figurehead of an ancient sailing ship with the gale of our progress pressing her clothes against her delightful figure and streaming her flowing fair hair in imitation of the bubbling wake behind the boat.

Like a torpedo we shot beneath the Chirundu Bridge. My eyes were not appreciative of the magnificent engineering of the span – they were still riveted on Joyce whom I felt sure was about to tumble from her perch to be cut to pieces by the propeller to provide a minced meal for the crocodiles! Relief came when Tommy was forced to throttle back to hear and obey Polly's directions. I was very relieved!

Our more comfortable but swift progress brought us quickly to the shore and

Polly indicated his plot. I admired his foresight. It is easy to visualise that in the near future houses will be built on the banks of the Zambezi to accommodate tourists and visitors to this wonderful area. The weather is ideal in the winter and many Rhodesians will flee from the cold highland winds to enjoy the terrific range of aquatic sports offered on the river. Both Tommy and Polly are of the opinion that the river at Chirundu offers even more facilities than Lake Kariba which is more of an inland sea and can be dangerous for small boats.

We returned to the launching site at the same mad speed with which we had departed. Being a little more used to the headlong rush, I was able to appreciate the Chirundu Bridge and admired the wonderful suspension. Polly told me that the cables had been manufactured on the spot as the weight and thickness of the wire ropes would have prevented their transport by road across the escarpment.

Back at the launching site, no time was wasted in removing the camping paraphernalia from the cars and loading it into the boats. When everything had been properly packed, Tommy embarked his three African servants, Joyce again took up her position on the prow and the boat roared off down the river. Polly and myself boarded the slower boat and followed at a more leisurely pace.

Polly's 40 hp boat had two very comfortable swivel seats equipped with arm and back rests which gave one a sense of security over the vast stretch of turbulent water. The swish-swish of the water slipping past, the cool wind of our passage on my face and the deck throbbing beneath us provided an atmosphere of exhilaration. We were on our way at a steady – and after the ride with Tommy, sedate – 25 miles an hour.

On our right we passed the derelict pumping station of the Chirundu Sugar Estates and in the far distance we could see the high brick chimney of the refinery where the cane had been treated in the days when the huge fields, now under grass, had rippled with sweetness. It was a sad sight and one could well imagine the thousands and thousands of pounds that had been spent on the venture before the world slump in the sugar price had closed down the scheme.

Just beyond the confluence of the Mwangu, we saw the Chikwenya (Tommy's boat) streaking along at full speed between the islands with water cascading from her bows. It needed little imagination to sense the way in which Tommy was enjoying every move, how he gloried in every turn, or how he smiled in satisfaction as the *Chikwenya* came to heel at the slightest twist of his wrist. Suddenly he spotted us and changed the course of his craft in our direction. On he came, straight at us like an outraged rhino and at a speed which threatened to cleave our smaller boat in two. When he was so close that I could see the diabolical grin under his black Charley Chaplin moustache, he swerved, and just about swamped us with his bow wave as he passed. Polly and I were thoroughly drenched.

"Gunpowder and witches!' exploded Polly in a voice like a subway train putting on brakes and with his little semi-grey beard curling in anger. "What the hell d'you think you're doing, trying to wreck our boat?" In only a slightly more modified tone, Polly confided to me that one of these days he would personally duck "that man bloody Thomson", and feed his fat carcass to the crocs. My own thoughts were unprintable! The cold and sudden dampness induced by our shower should have destroyed my excitement. But it had the opposite effect. Within thirty minutes the wind had dried us thoroughly and our two boats continued to throb gracefully down the mighty river, planing like dolphins around the islands and forcing new life into our nicotine-cluttered lungs. This was the life!

The range of mountains hugging the river on the Zambian side were grey, heavy-looking and ominous. When we altered course, their colour changed. Sometimes they were grey and then green and then completely shadowed to give the impression of a monstrous scaled dragon.

At the mouth of the Rekomitje River, the Zambezi became almost an inland sea with its vast expanse of silent running water. Tommy had grown impatient with our modest progress and the *Chikwenya* was merely a speck in the distance, trailing a milky wake. We motored on with the current, enjoying the peace and the scenery until suddenly we saw the *Chikwenya* at anchor and I realised – to my disappointment – that we had reached Camp F, our destination. It was a delightful spot, right on the riverbank and taking full advantage of the welcoming shade of the enormous trees. The buildings were erected at equal distances of some thirty yards apart. In the centre was the dining room, with one complete wall into which had been built shelving and a cubicle which contained the paraffin fridge. The other three sides of the structure were open with pillars erected on a three-foot wall supporting the roof. The floor was of cement and the outsides of the walls were camouflaged with a most attractive mosaic pattern. The two bedrooms were of the same structure. The bathroom and toilet – with flush system – were completely enclosed with the necessary doors. At the back of the dining room was a kitchen with built-in cupboards and a wood-burning stove. In all the years I have spent in the bush, I have never seen nor heard of a hunting camp such as this! There was only one snag. It cost all of £4 per day!

At such a rental, one might be forgiven for expecting that everything would be in working order. Unfortunately, the paraffin lamp working the fridge was unserviceable and a 300-gallon tank supplying water for the bathroom and toilet was empty – the engine and pump which filled the tank had been removed! Polly's beard again curled with anger and Tommy's protests were loud and long. The African in charge of the camp was the convenient butt of their wrath and he charged around all over the place, making himself very useful in a desperate effort to make amends. Once we were settled in, I received yet another pleasant surprise which proved that Tommy and Polly had left little to chance. They unearthed a cache of liquid refreshment plus oils, grease and petrol which had been brought in before the rains. They had thought of everything – particularly the beer which was so welcome after a day's hunt in the heat.

We rested up for a while and then, despite the journey we had undertaken since dawn, at five o'clock we went after duck. Joyce did not go with us. True to her nature, she dislikes seeing anything killed unnecessarily and she preferred the less violent sport of fishing from a suitable spot near the camp.

We set out in Tommy's boat – I had yet to learn my lesson. Some five miles from the camp, we spotted the first flock of duck and several schools of hippo. Tommy was perched on top of the driver's seat, hatless, with his unbuttoned shirt billowing around his neck and his bared back straining forward like a hunter taking a fence. The throttle was wide open as we skimmed after our quarry. The duck, startled at the screaming approach of the boat, suddenly turned and the mad Thomson, oblivious to the limitations of the boat in the thrill of the chase, swung *Chikwenya* in such an abrupt turn that the boat tilted at a crazy angle and very nearly dipped my elbow in the racing water. My vertebrae turned to a stack of ice cubes and when the boat desperately sought an even keel, I loosed off several rounds from my shotgun. I harmed not a single feather of the flock!

Pointing his arm in another direction, Tommy gunned *Chikwenya* and was in pursuit of a second flock leisurely flapping their way across the water. They saw the screaming demon after them and increased speed. We followed suit although I had hoped the boat would go no faster! I glimpsed a school of hippo on my left and a new fear tightened the muscles of my stomach and sent shivers down my spine as I visualised the aftermath of hitting one of the monsters. The bewildered duck broke formation, I fired both barrels and, despite the state of my nerves, had some success. The sudden cutting of the motor brought welcome relief and I mopped the sweat from my forehead. I had been dead scared and felt ash-dry fright on my rolling tongue.

It seemed that my fervent prayers had been answered when Tommy suggested that Polly take over the driving to give him a chance at the sport. I lowered my gun and took up a position in one of the back seats overlooking the stern. If we were to have a repeat performance of the mad scramble from one side of the river to the other, I was quite content to experience the thrill of the ride alone. Shooting was for the birds! Tommy was relentless. He bellowed instructions to Polly and we were off again – streaking after a flock of knobnoses. The boom of his gun reverberated across the water which glinted in the setting sun. I hung on for dear life but was spellbound by the seething waters churned up by the engines.

There was a sudden silence as Polly cut the engine and nosed the boat on to a sandbank. Tommy climbed over the side to retrieve the bag and it was then that I saw another flock about to overfly our position. I hurriedly rose and took a pot shot. My jellied knees could not withstand the recoil and I fell back into the boat, barking the skin of my arm from wrist to elbow in the progress. Tommy and Polly were not at all sympathetic.

On our way back to camp – and thankfully Tommy was moved sufficiently to respect the peace and tranquillity of the great river at dusk – we spotted a flock of birds coming down the river in typical duck formation. The birds were silhouetted against the reddening sky when I cracked off with both barrels. The birds casually broke formation and, once again, not a single feather flew. I put down my gun and was greeted with roars of laughter from Tommy and Polly. Their laughter was not aimed at my shooting prowess but at my failure to recognise that the birds had not even been duck! I was the original "greenhorn" at this game.

Beer, glorious beer, gurgled down my dry throat back at the camp and I was soon fully recovered from my experiences of the afternoon – and ready for more. In turn, we bathed from two buckets, one containing hot and the other cold water. I endorsed my hosts' complaint on the empty water tank. A much-needed and refreshing shower would have been welcomed.

More beer – I will not say how many – and a delicious dinner quickly made us ready for our beds and we retired at an early hour. The call of a hyena woke me at 2 a.m. The animal's howl is one of the weirdest sounds of the African night; that long, drawn-out, mournful moan, rising to a shriek makes your blood curdle unless you are used to it. It's a loathsome beast. At intervals, I could hear the loud grunting moo of the hippos, their noise amplified across the placid moonlit water. Although my bed had been covered with a net, I heard not a single mosquito. I had thought that the Valley would have been infested with these noisy and irritating insects.

The following morning we rose early to resume the duck shoot. Again I was relieved when it was decided that Polly and I should venture forth in the former's smaller boat, leaving Tommy to wreak havoc by himself. The cavortings of the larger boat acted as a beater although before very long we heard Tommy's shots echoing across the water and saw the duck flying in all directions. Polly picked on a particular flock and we chased after them. It was a hopeless task in the smaller boat so we devised a new strategy. I was marooned on an island which had fair cover whilst the two boats throbbed away in opposite directions. As the engine noises receded, I heard shots and looked expectantly for the duck to come my way. I waited and waited in vain. I was beginning to wish that I had stayed with the boats in spite of the palpitations they aroused and then, for my sins, Tommy's boat arrived and ended my isolation. No sooner had I resigned myself to another death-defying session of rocketing about the Zambezi when a flock passed directly over my island. We downed a few and our bag was added to the trophies Tommy had already shot.

Perhaps Tommy had something of a hangover from the previous night, or perhaps he was loath to poach too much from the beauty of the early morning, or again, perhaps I was becoming accustomed to high-powered flight, but our river excursion was wonderful in every sense. We curved round and round numerous small islands within sight of schools of hippo, and then abruptly two spurwing geese appeared speeding along the river bank. Both our guns exploded simultaneously and both birds fell. Before Tommy could correct the course of the boat, one of the dead birds ran foul of the propeller and the corpse was considerably mangled when we dragged it from the water.

The sun was climbing high in the sky and it was getting hot by the time we decided to return to camp for a combined breakfast-lunch. After the meal, Tommy and Joyce wandered off for some fishing, Polly resolved to have a siesta, and I decided to have a shave. While scraping the stubble from my tender and sun and wind burnt face, I nearly slit my throat in surprise when four giant "snails" with houses on their backs staggered into the camp waving sten guns in my direction! On closer inspection, the "snails" turned out to be humans clad in nondescript camouflaged uniforms and, as I put down my razor, their leader came forward and introduced himself as Inspector Roy Townsend, of Salisbury. He introduced the remainder of the patrol – Patrol Officers Wiggell, Bush and Crook – and all four slipped the "houses" from their backs and sank to the ground; tired, footsore and obviously aching in every bone from weariness and the heat. One man removed his boot with a sigh of relief to reveal a blistered and raw foot. Our hearts went out to them and for my part, my mind flashed back over fifty years to the privations I had suffered on patrol then.

Even in those days, such hardships had been the exception rather than the rule, and it was with real sympathy and genuine gratitude towards the quartet that I suddenly realised how much the Rhodesian public owed to these unpublicised, unsung watchmen of our borders.

Our cook needed no bidding to brew a pot of tea. The four policemen, having rested for a few minutes, wearily discarded their clothing and one after another made for the river and a refreshing dip in the water. They seemed oblivious to the dangers of hungry crocodiles – exhaustion and weariness to the marrow of their bones outweighed any such thoughts.

They returned from the water naked but for towels around their waists and gulped down the welcoming tea. As they achieved some measure of relaxation, they quietly passed the time of day. I felt almost guilty as I listened to their travels. Here was I on a carefree holiday, in total ignorance of the hardships being experienced by those with the duty of protecting us. If I ever hear a conversation in the Mess along the lines of "things ain't what they used to be", or that in the old days "men were men", I offer fair warning that I will react to the defence of today's policemen with all the vehemence of my aged bones. These four men had trekked from Camp E to Camp F through water, mud and slush; they had plodded through senanga infested with tsetse fly and with the damnable mopani fly crawling into their noses, ears and mouths. As if the hike was not enough, they had undertaken the journey bent almost double under the terrific weight of their packs.

In my ignorance, I wondered why it was not possible for the patrol to be assisted by carriers to lighten their loads. With all their equipment, their ammunition and their weapons, their chances of protecting themselves against the sudden onslaught of a nervous and highly irascible rhino would be small. If a naughty rogue elephant got their wind and decided to attack them, the packs would be a severe handicap. I can understand a man carrying a heavy pack on level ground, but to lug this weight through dense and muddy jungle, the haunt of vicious and malicious animals, seemed to be asking too much. A further suggestion is the issue of a suitably prepared mosquito netting round the brims of their hats as a protection against tsetse and the crawling mopani flies.

The four policemen retired with their leaden packs for a well-earned rest. Joyce and Tommy had returned from their fishing with the catch of the day – a 60 lb vundu and a 14 lb tigerfish. It was the first time I had seen one of these hideous, ill-shaped, repugnant vundu. Later we departed on another duck-shooting adventure during which Tommy nearly collapsed from exhaustion in his attempts to get waterborne after he had grounded his boat on a sandbank.

That evening, the policemen joined us in a gulp of beer and a delicious stew of wild duck. Later, around the camp fire, we chatted and, during the general conversation, two of them revealed that they had taken their discharges, tasted civilian life, and then rejoined the Force. One had been the manager of a hotel and the other a salesman. They had done quite well, but civilian life had become a bore. They claimed that work in the police is much more interesting, accommodation for married men is excellent and, if no accommodation is available, the allowances are very liberal. They were very glad to be back in uniform (and I wondered at their sentiments after days of lugging those heavy packs!).

The patrol was off the following morning and we embarked on another duck-shoot. After "brunch", it was decided to visit Camp G near the Mana Pools and indulge in some fishing.

The distance to Mana Pools was about twelve miles and we arrived there to be greeted with tea from the resident warden, Hans. His quarters consisted of three Cator huts in which, I am sure, one could have baked bread. The huts were ovens and I sympathised with the warden who had been marooned for three months. Rather a lonely life, I thought, although Hans seemed happy enough.

We continued up the channel and eventually anchored the boats in promising fishing waters. Polly acted as my "gillie" and prepared the tackle and rods for I know sweet nothing of the art. Finally the hooks were cast and we sat in the blistering sun waiting for the expected bite. As time passed our excitement and patience faded and we settled for a more positive catch – a bottle of beer. We invited Tommy and Joyce to join us but we should have known that Tommy, with knowledge aforethought, had brought his own supplies and was at that moment emptying his second bottle.

Suddenly we saw Tommy's boat moving and his rod bent in a semi-circle. He pulled, relaxed, and pulled again; the rod bent and quivered almost to breaking point; the boat moved faster in the direction of the taut tackle. I was sure he had hooked nothing less than the biggest fish in the Zambezi. The battle continued with the boat moving further and further from us. At last, Tommy rounded a corner and was lost from sight. Some ten minutes later, we heard his engine start and he reappeared with another vundu, as big if not bigger than the catch of the previous day. He was as proud as Punch and his catch won him the pool that I had suggested in a moment of madness. I should have known better. Polly and I, sad at losing our money, sought solace in another bottle.

The following morning, Polly and I prepared for our return to Salisbury. Tommy and Joyce had decided to remain for another two days and to go back with the Land Rover.

All good things come to a speedy end. It was with a heavy heart that I left Camp F. In a crowded lifetime, I have had considerable experience of hunting and, in the process, enjoyed exciting moments. On lakes in India I have shot duck, but never, I repeat never, had I been so thrilled, excited and stirred as on this trip. Polly and I left in his boat soon after breakfast. Apart from seeing more hippo, the journey along the river to Chirundu was uneventful. Once in the Jaguar, the boat loaded on to its trailer and hitched to the back of the car, the road was ours. We paused at Makuti, had a few drinks, went on to Sinoia where we posted the mail Hans had given us, and then continued non-stop to Polly's farm where we had a refreshing cup of tea with Mrs Paine. I was back at Good Hope by 5 o'clock and I felt rather lonely when Polly pulled away. As I climbed into bed that night, I thought of four other men, far away in their loneliness and far from comfortable – and I offered a silent prayer for their safety and for the safety of the others like them.

A footnote to this story appears on page 311 of Volume Three of *The History of the British South Africa Police*:
There is a sting in the tail of the Zambezi meeting: Some months later, Roy Townsend, who had spent four years in the Parachute Regiment with service in Malaya and Palestine before joining the Force in 1948, was involved in the interrogation of a captured terrorist group. One of them remarked that he had seen Roy before and when asked where, and under what circumstances, replied: "You were on a patrol with four others. We were hidden in ambush about ten yards away from you but we did not fire because then we did not want anyone to know we were in the country."

COMMENTARY

TROOPER 1437 arrived at *The Outpost* just before me. His "Biltong Hunters" appeared in my first magazine when I introduced myself editorially as a mere town policeman, "unfamiliar with the business of the bundu". The new contributor soon corrected this shortcoming and America's Virginia Trooper shared the lessons, assuming its highwaymen readers knew what biltong was. Before the year ended, Eben had taken his fans on patrol in the Kalahari and I was regularly on safari at the Ministry of Information's Photographic Section, hunting the Big Five and other game and aiming to match the ircumstances of our contributor's text.

Intruding on both Eben's memoirs and mine, a recent television programme showed giraffe capture in Kenya which employed none of the safety measures so carefully explained by Eben in his Kalahari dealings with Cornelius van Rooyen (in Trials of a Giraffe). Another interesting fact passed on to us by our readers is that van Rooyen Senior is generally accepted as being the person responsible for the introduction of the Rhodesian Ridgeback – referred to in the story as the "hunting lion dog".

Perhaps Kenya's giraffe have become a bit more stiff-necked than their ancestors down south but, quite apart from SPCA concerns, this almost immediate response to the first episode of what was to be one of *The Outpost's* longest serials was of great support and encouragement to the new editor – and, of course, the new contributor.

But there was the odd jarring note. In *Old Comrades* a year later (September 1967), the columnist – "The Chronicler" – noted that Mr Frank Elliott (1766), having correctly identified his 1437 colleague, reckoned the latter's story had been published in *Police Review* fifty years earlier when it had been taken with a pinch of salt by the author's fellows. (A search for it in *Police Review* was fruitless.) "The Chronicler" emphasised how popular the serial had become, particularly among the younger serving members. What he didn't mention was that although readers stuck on an *Outpost* crossword clue often phoned the Editor for help, Kalahari Patrol provoked the first ever enquiry as to what was to happen in the next instalment! In the face of criticism, the old timers rallied to support Trooper 1437's cause and a double spread of their letters appeared in the following November issue, traditionally the month in which more historical content was customary. Their team spirit added much to the "tribal knowledge" of time and place.

The letters follow:

Cecil Napier (1421) 1911-1916
The Editor, *The Outpost*
Dear Mr Stock,

In *The Outpost* of September 1967 under "Old Comrades", a Mr Elliott refers to Kalahari Patrol by Eben Mocke as having been taken with a pinch of salt by readers back in 1912. I was stationed at Mtetengwe, on border guard, during Mr Mocke's patrol, and knew all about his movements and heard of many of his adventures from Bushmen and local Africans. Some years later, when I was a game hunter, I hunted in and visited nearly every part of the country mentioned by Mr Mocke and I found that he was still well remembered and several incidents related in his story were verified. Also, Cornelius van Rooyen a friend of mine and who was a well-known hunter, related to me that Mocke had been involved in several dangerous incidents which I can well believe knowing the country as I do and having myself written several stories and radio plays set in the Kalahari and the Nekati far up the old Hunter's Road. I cannot recall ever having read his story in *The Outpost* before and had it been published, I am not likely to have forgotten it.

It is always easy for doubt to be thrown on the veracity of a writer, especially by someone with a scant knowledge of the country and people around whom the tale is woven. I wonder if Mr Elliott has ever in his life been further than Plumtree – certainly not into the vast waste that is the Kalahari – and I question his authority to criticise.

C. C. J. Napier.

Monty Surgey (1860) 1914–1948
The Editor, *The Outpost,*

Dear Alan,

... Page 43, the criticisms of F.C. Elliott regarding the veracity of Eben Mocke's serial, Kalahari Patrol. I only knew Mocke when he was taken off the "Roving Patrol" about 1916 though both Elliott and I, when patrolling down the railway line from Wankie (where we were stationed in 1914) to Ngamo and then across to the Gwaai and down it to the Zambesi, were aware of the fear of God he put into the railway gangers, pump men and permanent way inspectors – the possessors of "itchy trigger fingers" in so far as Royal Game was concerned. "Where's Mocke?" was the cry as they signed the Patrol Sheet. "Don't know," said we, and we were speaking the truth – we didn't know his movements as they were confidential between him and possibly Major Brundell of the CID and the DSP, Bulawayo. Kalahari Patrol is a damned good yarn and, like all good yarns, it has to have its excitement to sell to the public. Whether these could be supported in a court of law as evidence ... is beside the point. (I had a story returned to me from the USA because there was an anticlimax in my factual story of trying to capture the fugitive murderer of a policeman some twenty years before. The accused visited his old haunts in the Makoni Reserve and "Navy" Smith and I went after him – a lot of cloak and dagger stuff – and after finding his last camping spot in a cave, plus his gun, we arrived back at Rusape to find that he had given himself up at Headlands to Corporal Lofty Selwood saying "I'm tired of living like an animal in the veld in PEA and I have come home prepared to submit myself to the white man's justice." The agent in America offered me ten dollars for the story if I'd cut out the last anticlimax and put in something stirring such as: "galloping into camp with the prisoner tied over the front of my saddle, self bleeding from gun shot wounds received when making the capture and with a couple of poisoned arrows through my hat!" I replied that factual police experiences seldom ended that way and I would only write factual – alas non-selling – articles which could stand cross-examination in a court of law. I couldn't enter the fiction market, even for ten dollars!)

I tell you this as it may have motivated Mocke in romancing a bit. I cannot believe that he would be such a clot as to suffer those appalling legs when a machila would have got him to the railway line and a messenger would have resulted in the sending of a police buckboard (ambulance) together with a District Surgeon. They were available even in those days. I cannot believe that he would have been permitted by the Paymaster to keep his pay packet in abeyance for eight months. How did he buy his supplies? Pay his private servant? Pay the two African police he had with him? He must have bought his horse as for patrols of this type we usually rode mules. He did put in appearances to draw supplies and put in his patrol report at convenient stations such as Plumtree and Nyamandhlovu and the kaffir-hutted "one-man" camp on the Gwaai, run by Scotchburn. I like Mocke – everyone does: a grand horseman, veldtsman and linguist. He had the reputation of being one of the very few men who could speak the Bushman lingo with its multitude of clicks and vocal inflections.

His story conveys the impression of complete isolation and there is some repetition over encounters with dangerous game. For all that, it is a fine story, definitely has a reading public and I hope that it gets into print.

Best wishes to you all,
Monty Surgey.

Frank Elliott (1756) 1913–1917
The Editor, *The Outpost,*

Dear Mr Stock,

It was a very pleasant surprise to receive your letter of October 18 – many thanks indeed.
I am at a loss to understand how I have caused a storm by my comments on Kalahari Patrol. My recollection of the earlier publication in *Police Review* and of the name of the author may be all wrong, the actual occurrence was a little before my time but I was posted to Wankie at Christmas 1914 after returning from the Schuckmansburg affair and the Mocke patrol was still a frequent subject of conversation and discussion at that time. Some of the people one met had encountered Mocke while he was in the Ngamo Flats area. I was for a time on a border guard with our main camp at Pandamatenka and, while patrolling up and down the border, I frequently spent a night at Giese's farm at Deka (the

source of the Deka River). Giese is mentioned in Kalahari Patrol. He was a Pioneer who had, with considerable acumen, pegged out his farm on the Pandama- tenka Road, expected to be the eventual route for the railway to the north. Geise later discovered the coal at Wankie with the result that the railway went via Wankie and Giese's farm was left many miles away to the west...

Incidentally, for part of the time I was at Wankie, the Gwaai police post was closed down and from Wankie we took over an extra bit of the country as did the Nyamandhlovu people from the other direction. At that time living along the Gwaai north of the railway, I remember there was one Kennedy, a farmer, ex-B.S.A.P., reported to have shot the record Kudu head of all time; Chalmers, who made out in a very hush-hush manner that he knew where Lobengula's grave was (at that time a mystery); a man called Peter Briers who I believe was killed by a rhino in the Sebungwe; and a van Rooyen, a nondescript type but said to be a nephew of the real old van Rooyen.

Close to Malindi lived a farmer called Going (with a very pretty daughter) who was supposed to have extracted and made away with the tusks of an elephant killed by a train near Malindi siding. I remember that the elephant's skull, minus tusks, was set up as a sort of memorial at the siding. Giese I knew pretty well – first at his farm at the headwaters of the Deka and later when he was market gardening at Lukosi, growing vegetables which he sold in Wankie. Some months ago, I heard from Jack Merry who was in the same squad as myself. I recall with great pleasure the Sunday morning rides he and I used to have on "riding pass" when we were recruits together. It was pleasant the other evening at the Annual Dinner to sit next to and have a long "reminisce" with Noel Arnott. He, Jack Green, R.E. Lee, and Wiltshire were, I think, the only ones present that I ever knew in Rhodesia.

My only comment on *The Outpost* is to congratulate you on the continued excellence of the magazine and to wish it enduring and increasng success.

F.C. Elliott.

John Moray-Brown (3607) 1936–1961
The Editor, *The Outpost,*

Dear Sir,

Congratulations on your September issue and particularly on the completion of Kalahari Patrol. Could we please have more from Eben Mocke? He must have plenty of tales to tell. His series was of particular interest to me since I know that part of the country pretty well. I was in charge at Nyamandhlovu before Tjolotjo was built. (Actually, the latter was built partly from my own representations and was opened only a few days before I was transferred.)

Regarding the query as to whether there are any of the Bushmen who accompanied Trooper 1437 on his patrol left on the Gwaai, I think the answer must be in the negative. My own travels in 1952-55 covered the Western Gwaai from the Nata to the Sehume Valley, and I met no "true" Bushmen. There were many so-called Bushmen who even spoke the Bushman language but they were far too dark in complexion to be originals. They obviously had more than a sprinkling of Kalanga blood in them. Some were semi-settled along the banks of the Nata and even possessed a few cattle. Others were among hunting parties from Bechuanaland who raided into the Wankie Game Reserve and then hunted down east of the Pandamatenka Road. It was my sad duty at times to round up such parties for a spell in gaol for poaching – sad, because they were really doing no wrong, just living as their ancestors had always lived. Periodical court at Tjolotjo under Mr N.I. Boast often included a few cases against the Bushmen and for security reasons I used to transfer them from the Tjolotjo lock-up to Nyamandhlovu and many a fine job of braying skins they did for me there!

Much of the Western Gwaai, which in my time was completely unpopulated, has now been opened up and settled by Makalanga tribesmen, together with a few of the very few Matabele left. On the border there were a few "Bushmen". They were settled in communities but many had retained their amazing capacity as trackers and one in particular – and probably still – is the favourite of our present Chief Justice on his numerous forays after elephant.

Most of the names on 1437's map I know well – the Linkwasa (though I seem to remember this as "Nkwasa"), Sibanini and Tamasetsa, while I had excellent duck shooting at Ngwesha and at Dubi pans, and of course, on the giant pan at Ngamo.

The Mopani Forest is indeed a forest. The land is mostly dead flat Kalahari sand while the trees grow straight and tall with only a yard or two between the trunks, and the leaves form a complete canopy blocking out all but an occasional ray of sunshine. Towards the Nata the land is more undulating and the trees more widely spaced and interspersed with scrub, but the flat areas are remarkable and after heavy rain are completely flooded. The country around is truly a "thirst" land and it was a real achievement of 1437 to cover that route. What is peculiar is that he does not mention the two camps on the Nata, one of which lies between where he hit the Nata after the Thirst Trek and the Pandamatenka Road. Both lie beside dry pools of the Nata and ample water can be had for the digging.

The camps consist of groves of fever trees and their welcome shade covers a flat, grass-covered, green glade nearly all the year round. They are the favourite haunt of sable. Other phenomena unmentioned are the drinking holes of elephant along the Nata. Here they do not always dig in the dry sand of the riverbed but gouge out with their trunks great holes in the steep banks where the clay soil often holds pockets of clear water. Some of your readers may not realise that the Pandamatenka Road is no road at all – merely a route running roughly north-south, along which each traveller makes his own track. At one point I found that the distance between the extreme eastern and western tracks was over five miles. And this was the "border" between Rhodesia and Botswana – some border! I believe however that the Surveyor-General's Department has since put this right and erected proper markers.

Best of luck to you and to Trooper 1437 and to all readers,

J.P. Moray-Brown.

Gerard McClement (1661) 1913–1919

Gerard McClement reckons he is the only surviving member of the Gutu Patrol and relates an amusing incident of this adventure in 1913.

The patrol was made up of men from Salisbury (where I was a recruit), Gwelo and Bulawayo. Twenty-four mules pulled two wagons and there were 80 Europeans and 70 African police under the command of Sergeant-Major Schlacter (he was most experienced and was also with us on the 1914 Sesheke Column preparing the way for the Schuckmannsburg Column which crossed the Zambesi into German South West Africa.)

But to return to the wagons – the sergeant-major produced a drag rope for each wheel when the transport came to grief in the many dongas, and with the mules doubled up, most of the difficulties were overcome at the expense of 24 straining animals and 60 perspiring troopers, 15 to each wheel. The commissariat department was run by Corporal Breeder(?) and Trooper Johnny West. We had passed a broken-down wagon just before arriving at Fort Victoria from the railhead at Umvuma and when we reached the town Corporal Breeder went to the premises of the Bechuanaland Trading Company and demanded six cases of bully beef for the patrol. The manager replied that he was expecting the supplies at any minute, but we knew to the contrary having seen the wrecked wagon en route. Now the Government (the Chartered Company and a jolly good government too) had a contract to supply bully beef to the troops in times of emergency at a price of 9d. per tin. The poor manager, faced with the demand for meat from Corporal Breeder, had no alternative but to supply glass jars of Poneton and Noel's jellied brawn which retailed at 2/9d., at the contract price. The troops did no cooking for days and one saw nothing but men digging into the glass jars with their spoons. Our objective on this patrol was Ndanga where there was to be an indaba over hut tax. The NC was Mr Bazeley whose sister is now living in Umtali.

Commentary continues:

In the next (December) issue of the magazine, "The Chronicler" recorded the "reunion" of Eben Mocke and Frank Elliott:
Letters have also been flying between Eben Mocke and Mr F.C. Elliott following the publication of Kalahari Patrol and the controversy it aroused If anyone feels offended at the spirit in which the comments on Kalahari Patrol were published, they should have sight of the correspondence between these two. The snippets of real interest that emerge when this kind of argument arises are ample reward and justification for any "stirring" done by this office. Mr Mocke's covering letter, fowarded with the above, remarks how these names brought back many happy memories – so much for anyone being offended!

When Eben Mocke and some of his colleagues started setting down their memoirs and then widening their scope to write about a few of the heroes (or desperados) of their times, the storytellers were probably unaware that they themselves had or would become legendary figures in their own right. The letters above provided more than a hint of the esteem in which Mocke was held by his serving colleagues – let alone the fear and trembling he prompted among his adversaries – long before he started writing of his experiences. It was almost inevitable that by the late 1960s, when he was keeping young Bulawayo policemen out of their beds with his tales, he had become something of a legend.

Late in the last century, "tribal knowledge" crept into management parlance to define a company's unwritten wealth achieved by keeping eyes open or ears to the ground and quietly sharing the results. The term had a more obvious meaning to the successors to the British South Africa Company's Police but both old and new interpretations accurately described the valuable contributions downloaded to the magazine by Eben and his contemporaries.

An interesting letter to Eben from Bob Sutherland (1393) in Canada, who had served from 1911 to 1919, was recorded: "The Chronicler" reported that Bill Southgate (3426), the son-in-law of the late Sub Inspector George Cuff (786), had received a letter from Bob in which he recalled a host of reminders of incidents long ago – when he (Bob) was court-martialled at Goromonzi by Colonel Capell and Sergeant Cuff had pressed a £5 note into his hand and advised him to make for Salisbury to escape the NCO he had been charged with assaulting; the banjo duets which he had performed with Monty Surgey, the time at Mazoe when "H.H." tried to evict the scorpions from the brick pillars supporting the bug infested barrackroom, and the bizarre capers which he and

Eben Mocke got mixed up in when in Depot.

There are many more mentions of Eben Mocke by contemporaries, too many to mention here, but all go to enhance the reputation and legend of one who was one of the great story-tellers of the British South Africa Police, if not the greatest.

Alan Stock

www.ingramcontent.com/pod-product-compliance
Lightning Source LLC
Chambersburg PA
CBHW052051230426
43671CB00011B/1868